USHER
iBT TOEFL
FINAL TEST
SPEAKING

어셔 iBT 토플 파이널 테스트 스피킹

어셔 어학 연구소

USHER
iBT TOEFL FINAL TEST
SPEAKING
어셔 iBT 토플 파이널 테스트 스피킹

초   판 1쇄 발행 · 2012년 1월 1일
개정증보판 9쇄 발행 · 2023년 1월 1일

지은이 · 어셔 토플 연구소
펴낸곳 · (주) 어셔 어학 연구소
펴낸이 · 어셔 어학 연구소
주 소 · 서울시 서초구 잠원로3길 40 태남빌딩 2층 어셔 어학 연구소
전 화 · 02) 595-5679
홈페이지 · www.usher.co.kr
ISBN · 978-89-967161-9-8

정 가 · 25,000원

저작권자 · ⓒ2019, 어셔 어학연구소

이 책 및 mp3 내용의 저작권은 저자에게 있습니다.
서면에 의한 저자와 출판사의 허락없이 내용의 일부 혹은 전부를 인용하거나, 발췌하는 것을 금합니다.
COPYRIGHTⒸ 2019 by Usher Language Research Institute
All rights reserved including the rights of reproduction In whole or part in any form Printed in Korea

PREFACE

iBT TOEFL Speaking(iBT 토플 스피킹) 사상 최강의 실전교재 'USHER iBT TOEFL **FINAL TEST SPEAKING** (어셔 iBT 토플 파이널 테스트 스피킹)'을 선보이게 되어 매우 기쁩니다. 독자께서는 옳은 선택을 하셨고, 더 나은 미래로 가는 지름길을 찾으셨습니다. 그럼 이제 책장을 넘기기 전에 스스로에게 물어봅시다.

1. 아무리 늦게 영어를 시작해서 교육부가 만든 curriculum대로 시작했더라도, 중1부터 고3까지, 최소한 6년의 시간 동안은 가장 큰 비중을 두고 매일매일 공부해왔을 텐데도, 왜 우리는 대학생이 되어서도 영어에 미쳐 살아야 합니까?
2. 그렇게 근 10년 가까운 시간 동안 영어를 공부해왔는데도, 왜 우리는 영어로 말하는 것에 대한 complex를 갖고 있습니까?
3. TOEFL 공부를 아무리 열심히 해도, 왜 유독 speaking 점수는 오르지 않는 것입니까?

답은 간단합니다.
   (1) 당신은 지난 10년간 '읽고 abcd중에서 답 고르기'만 공부해왔기 때문입니다.
   (2) 당신은 지난 10년간 영어를 글로만 배워왔기 때문입니다.
   (3) 당신은 아직도 정신 못 차리고 1번만 반복하고 있기 때문입니다.

하루에 몇 분이나 영어를 들었습니까?
하루에 몇 분이나 영어로 말했습니까?
하루에 몇 시간이나 TOEFL Speaking에 할애했습니까?

이제껏 speaking에 투자한 시간을 고려하면, 당신이 받은 speaking 점수는 기적입니다. Speaking(스피킹) 점수가 오르길 원한다면, 지금껏 Reading에 투자한 만큼의 시간을 할애하시길 바랍니다. 방법은 본 교재에 담겨있습니다.

'USHER iBT TOEFL **FINAL TEST SPEAKING**(어셔 iBT 토플 파이널 테스트 스피킹)'은 많은 분들이 생각하는 영어말하기의 개념과 다릅니다. 일반 회화처럼 상대방의 반응을 신경 쓸 필요도, 주제의 변화를 걱정할 필요도 없습니다. 정해진 문제유형에 따라 해야 할 말만 녹음하시면 됩니다. 기초가 남들보다 약하더라도, 충분한 시간을 투자하고 꾸준히 노력하면, 누구나 원하는 점수를 얻을 수 있습니다. '열심히' 보다 '꾸준히' 가 중요합니다.

본 교재에 있는 문제들을 다 푸셨다고요? 그렇다면 처음부터 다시 푸세요.
문제의 내용을 이미 알아서 안 된다고요? 그렇다면 당신의 답은 완벽한가요?
답이 외워져서 더 이상 연습의 의미가 없다고요? 그렇다면 이제 당신은 준비가 되었습니다.

당신의 답이 완벽에 가까워지고, 원하는 점수를 얻을 때 쯤, 본 교재의 낱장 낱장이 흰색보다는 옅은 갈색에 가깝기를 바랍니다. 부디 원하는 토플 점수 꼭 받으시고, 그 점수를 갖고 원하는 학교 꼭 가시길 바랍니다. 아울러, 이 책이 나오기까지 수고해주신 많은 강사님들과 연구원들, 그리고 누구보다, speaking 고득점을 원하는 모든 학생들께 본 교재를 바칩니다.

마지막으로 여러분 공부하시는데 도움이 될까 싶어, 글 한편 인용하며 마칠까 합니다.

너는 말이다.
한번쯤 그 긴 혀를 뽑힐 날이 있을 것이다.
언제나 번지르르하게 늘어놓고 그 실천은 엉망이다.

오늘도 너는 열여섯 시간 분의 계획을 세워놓고
겨우 열 시간 분을 채우는데 그쳤다.

쓰잘 것 없는 호승심에 충동된 여섯 시간을 낭비하였다.

이제 너를 위해 주문을 건다.

남은 날 중에서 단 하루라도 그 계획량을 채우지 않거든
너는 이 시험에서 떨어져라.

하늘이 있다면 그 하늘이 도와 반드시 떨어져라.

그리하여 주정뱅이 떠돌이로 낯선 길바닥에서 죽든
일찌감치 독약을 마시든 하라.

-이문열 <젊은 날의 초상> 中

어셔 어학 연구소

TABLE OF CONTENTS

USHER
USHER iBT TOEFL FINAL TEST SPEAKING
어셔 iBT 토플 파이널 테스트 스피킹

Introduction

본 토플 교재의 구성	6
본 토플 교재만의 특징	8
홈페이지 이용 방법	10
iBT TOEFL(iBT 토플) 소개	12
iBT TOEFL Speaking 소개	14
교재 계획표	22
발음 연습	24

Strategies

Task 1 설명 및 Sample Question	33
Task 2 설명 및 Sample Question	34
Task 3 설명 및 Sample Question	36
Task 4 설명 및 Sample Question	38

Practice Tests 12회 / Script 해석

TOEFL TEST 01	40
TOEFL TEST 02	56
TOEFL TEST 03	72
TOEFL TEST 04	88
TOEFL TEST 05	104
TOEFL TEST 06	120
TOEFL TEST 07	136
TOEFL TEST 08	152
TOEFL TEST 09	168
TOEFL TEST 10	184
TOEFL TEST 11	200
TOEFL TEST 12	216
출제 예상 문제 리스트	232
부록 - 속담 120개	273

Practice Tests 12회

TOEFL TEST 01	279
TOEFL TEST 02	286
TOEFL TEST 03	293
TOEFL TEST 04	300
TOEFL TEST 05	307
TOEFL TEST 06	314
TOEFL TEST 07	321
TOEFL TEST 08	328
TOEFL TEST 09	335
TOEFL TEST 10	342
TOEFL TEST 11	349
TOEFL TEST 12	356

1 본 토플 교재의 구성
USHER iBT TOEFL **FINAL TEST** SPEAKING (어셔 iBT 토플 파이널 테스트 스피킹)

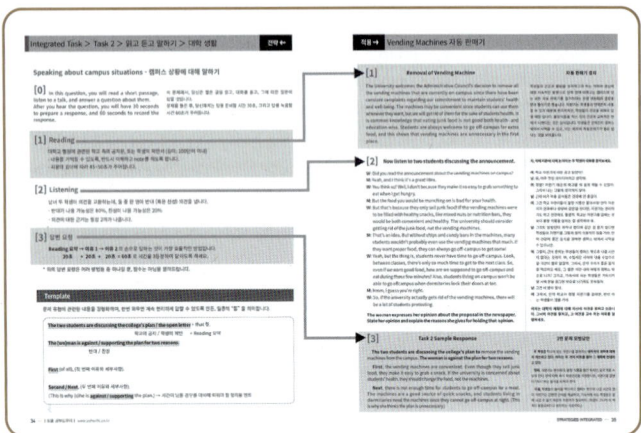

문제설명

iBT TOEFL(iBT 토플)을 처음 접하는 사람이라도 쉽게 이해할 수 있도록 각 문항을 상세히 설명하고, 좀 더 쉬운 이해를 위한 예제와 효율적인 답안 발표를 위한 답안 틀(template)도 준비했습니다.

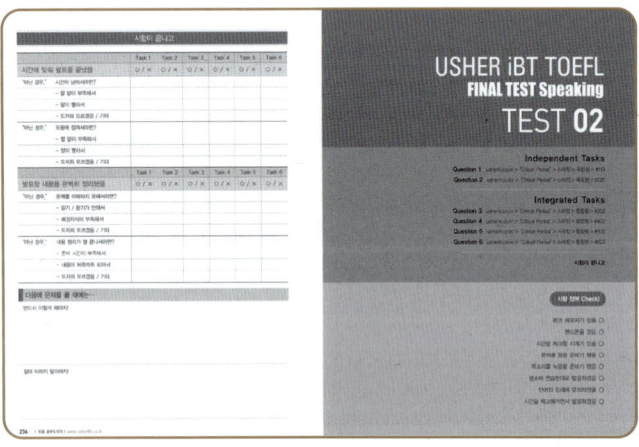

시험 전에 Check! & 시험이 끝나고

Test를 실행하기에 앞서 시험을 볼 준비가 되었는지 스스로 확인해볼 수 있도록 '시험 전에 Check!'를 마련했습니다. 또한 각 Test를 마친 후에는 '시험이 끝나고'를 활용하여 스스로가 시험에 임하는 태도와 그 과정을 돌아볼 수 있게끔 준비했습니다.

반드시 실행하시길 바랍니다.

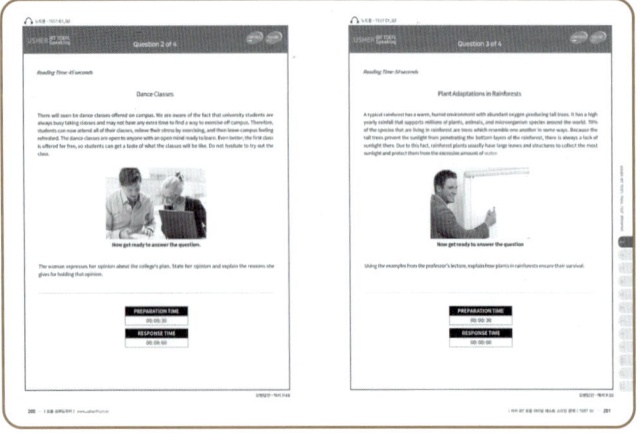

TEST

총 15회분(홈페이지 3회분 포함)을 준비하였고, 실제 시험에 빨리 적응할 수 있도록 실제 iBT TOEFL시험(iBT 토플시험) 모니터의 layout과 비슷하게 교재 내부를 디자인하였습니다. 각 test 목차에 usherin.usher.co.kr에서 풀어볼 수 있는 database 경로를 번호로 표기하였습니다.

| 토플 공부도우미 | usherin.usher.co.kr |

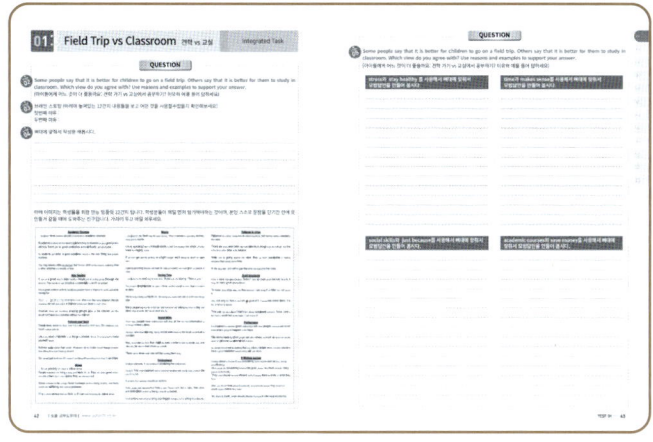

독립형 문제 (Independent Tasks)

만능 답안
가장 적게 외워서 가장 큰 효과를 볼 수 있도록 비슷한 주제끼리 묶어 겹치는 내용의 답안을 작성하였습니다. 반드시 외우시길 바랍니다.

출제 예상 주제 List
위의 만능 답안을 외우면 어떤 다른 문제들에 대비할 수 있는지를 List로 작성하였습니다. 지난 2년간 출제 되었던 모든 문제를 정리하여 학생들이 좀 더 쉽게 토플 시험에 대비할 수 있도록 하였습니다.

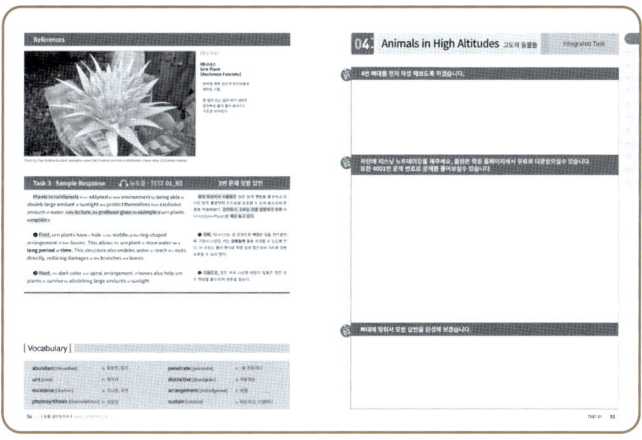

통합형 문제 (Integrated Tasks)

Script, 번역본, and 모범답안
(1) **Script** - 쉬운 내용 파악을 위해 중요한 포인트를 정리했습니다.
(2) **번역문** - 내용의 잘못된 이해를 막고 수월한 학습을 위해 본문 바로 옆에 번역본을 마련했습니다.
(3) **모범 답안** - 매번 반복되는 표현은 highlight로 표시하였습니다.
(4) **Vocabulary(토플 단어)** - 사전 찾는 시간을 아끼기 위해 페이지 우측 하단에 별도의 공간을 마련 하였습니다.

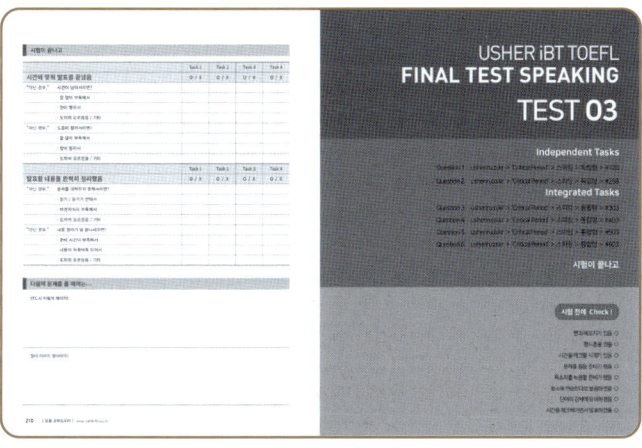

자기 평가표
자신의 답안을 스스로 평가할 수 있도록 평가표(rubric)를 준비하였습니다. 좀 더 쉽게 문제점을 찾아낼 수 있도록 ETS 스타일의 평가 항목을 세분화하였습니다. 또, 자신의 예상 점수를 가늠해볼 수 있도록 설계하였습니다.

USHER iBT TOEFL FINAL TEST SPEAKING

본 토플 교재의 구성

2 본 토플 교재만의 특징
USHER iBT TOEFL **FINAL TEST** SPEAKING (어서 iBT 토플 파이널 테스트 스피킹)

1 독립형 문제 (Task 1) 완벽 공략 - 만능 답안의 활용

독립형 문제의 난해한 점은 낮은 영어실력에서 비롯된 것만은 아닙니다. 대부분의 응시자들에 따르면, 문제는 갑자기 들이닥친 문제에 대한 해답이 머릿속에 없다는 점과 15초라는 짧은 준비시간이었습니다. 결국 관건은 15초 내에 말할 내용을 정리해야 한다는 것인데, 이는 상상보다 훨씬 어려운 일입니다. 한국말을 잘 한다고 면접시험의 돌발질문들을 다 멋지게 대답하지는 못하는 것과 같은 이치입니다.

이런 경우, 토플 문제를 미리 알고 그에 대한 답을 외우는 것이 최상의 선택이라 하겠으나, 출제될 토플 문제를 미리 알기란 보통 어려운 일이 아닙니다. 하지만, 그 범위를 좁히는 것은 가능하여, 지난 5년간 출제된 모든 토플 문제들을 빠뜨리지 않고 모두 분석하였습니다. 그 결과, 대부분의 문제들을 몇 개의 비슷한 내용 - 이를 앞으로 **만능 답안**이라 합시다 - 으로 답할 수 있다는 사실을 발견하였으며, 외워야 할 **만능 답안**의 수를 최소화하여, 학생들의 수고를 덜었습니다.

2 강의형 문제 (Task 3 & 4) 집중 공략 - Set 16회 추가 제공

수많은 응시자들을 접하면서 또 하나 알게 된 사실은, 강의형 문제(Task 3 & 4)를 어려워하더라는 것입니다. 특이한 점은, 이건 엄연히 '말하기'의 문제가 아니라 '내용이해'의 문제더라는 것입니다. 내용을 이해하지 못해 답을 얼버무리는 억울한 일이 없도록, 출제가능성이 가장 높은 분야와 그에 관한 문제들 위주로 정리하였습니다. 이 책을 공부한 학생이라면 누구나, 시험장에서 어려운 문제에 맞닥뜨려도, 그 내용이 친숙함을 쉽게 느낄 수 있을 것이라 확신합니다. 이외에도 총 16 Set의 강의형 문제가 추가로 홈페이지(http://usherin.usher.co.kr)에 준비되어 있으니 시험 전 반드시 활용하시길 바랍니다.

3 통합형 문제의 이해를 돕는 사진 첨부

백문(百聞)이 불여일견(不如一見)입니다. 강의형 문제의 경우, 자세한 설명에도 불구하고 완벽한 이해가 어려운 경우가 많습니다. 그런 경우를 대비해, 학생 여러분의 이해를 돕기 위하여 관련 내용의 사진을 실었습니다.

4 강세 학습을 위한 세심한 배려

원어민의 목소리가 담긴 모범답안 mp3를 제공하는 것 외에도, 학생들이 강세를 느낌으로 알 수 있도록, 모범답안의 글씨 크기를 단어마다 다르게 하였습니다. 큰 글씨는 크게, 작은 글씨는 작게 읽도록 하여, mp3 파일이 없어도 강세를 파악할 수 있도록 배려하였습니다.

5 발음에 대한 깊이 있는 설명

흔히들 발음과 강세, 억양 등의 문제들은 교재를 통해 극복할 수 없다고 생각합니다. 하지만, 이런 요소들은 연습을 통해 어느 정도는 충분히 극복 가능한 일이며, 그 방법론 또한 Speaking 교재가 갖춰야 할 필수덕목입니다. 시중의 다른 어떤 TOEFL (토플) 교재보다 발음에 대한 깊고 자세한 설명이 수록되어 있어, 혼자 공부하는 학생들도 충분히 원어민 발음에 가까운 말하기가 가능하도록 했습니다. 또한 학생들이 듣고 참고할 수 있도록, 본 토플 교재 안의 모든 모범답안에는 mp3 file이 usherin.usher.co.kr에 수록되었습니다.

6 자기주도학습을 이끄는 진행

TOEFL(토플)과 같은 시험은 토플 어학원을 다니지 않고 대비하는 것은 고사하고, 사실 문제집 한 권을 끝내기도 쉽지 않습니다. 하지만, **학습 계획표**를 이용하면 누구나 쉽게 정해진 시간 안에 목표를 달성할 수 있고, 해설지를 통해 별도의 설명 없이도 문제를 이해할 수 있으며, **자기 평가표**와 같은 체계를 통해서 자신의 실력을 직접 체크해볼 수 있게 했습니다.

7 실제 시험과 가장 가까운 대비책

문제 내용
TOEFL(토플) 주관사인 ETS의 자체제작교재인 Official Guide보다도 실제 시험에 훨씬 더 가깝다고 확신합니다. 무엇보다 자랑할 만한 점은 문제들의 출제예상 시점이 발행일 이후로 맞춰져 있다는 점입니다.

출제예상 주제 모음
토플 시험을 응시하기 직전에 어떤 문제가 출제될지 미리 예상하고 대비할 수 있도록 했습니다.

실전연습 프로그램
본 토플 교재의 답안을 http://usherin.usher.co.kr에서 언제든지 무료로 녹음하고 저장할 수 있어, 실제 토플 시험과 똑같은 환경에서 연습할 수 있게 준비했습니다. (각 test 목차에 http://usherin.usher.co.kr에서 풀어볼 수 있는 database경로를 번호로 표기하였습니다.)

3 홈페이지 이용 방법

USHER iBT TOEFL **FINAL TEST SPEAKING** (어셔 iBT 토플 파이널 테스트 스피킹)

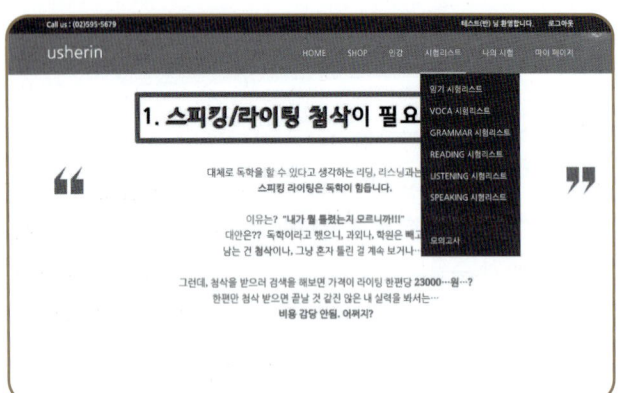

홈페이지 메인 화면

usherin.usher.co.kr에 가면 오른쪽 상단에 보다 시피 시험리스트에서 라이팅 시험보기를 누르면 아래와 같은 화면이 나타납니다.

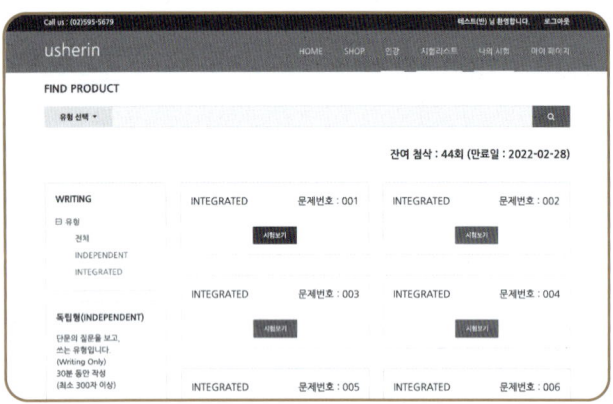

Writing 메뉴 화면

시험 시작 버튼을 누르면 실제 TOEFL 시험과 똑같은 설정의 시험이 자동으로 시작됩니다.

실전연습 프로그램

교재에 있는 문제의 답안을 여기서 녹음하여 실제 TOEFL (토플) 시험과 똑같이 연습할 수 있게 했습니다. 각 test 목차에 홈페이지 database 경로를 번호로 표기 하였습니다.

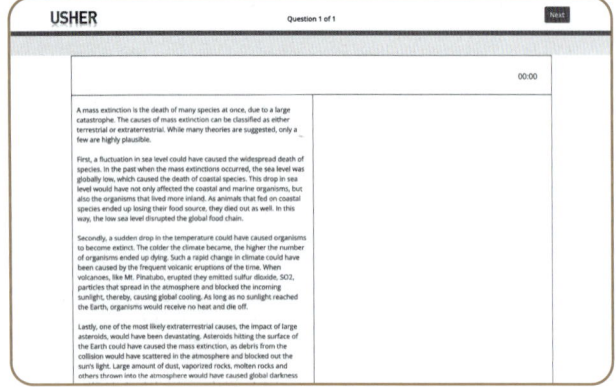

Test 진행 화면

실제 TOEFL (토플) 시험과 똑같은 설정의 시험이 진행되는 동안 자신이 작성한 답안은 컴퓨터에 자동으로 저장됩니다.

| 토플 공부도우미 | usherin.usher.co.kr

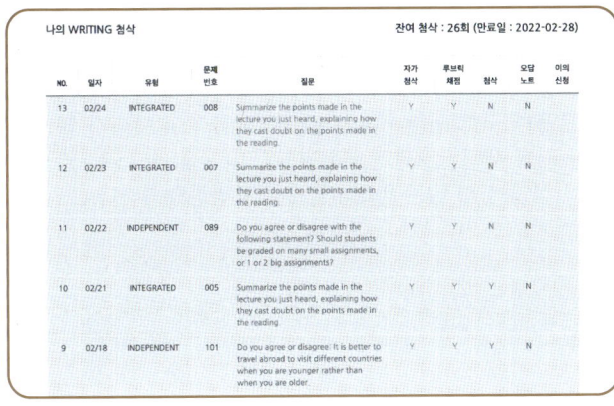

라이팅 성적 확인표

학생분들이 직접 글을 작성한후에 본인에 성적들을 확인할 수 있는 페이지 입니다.

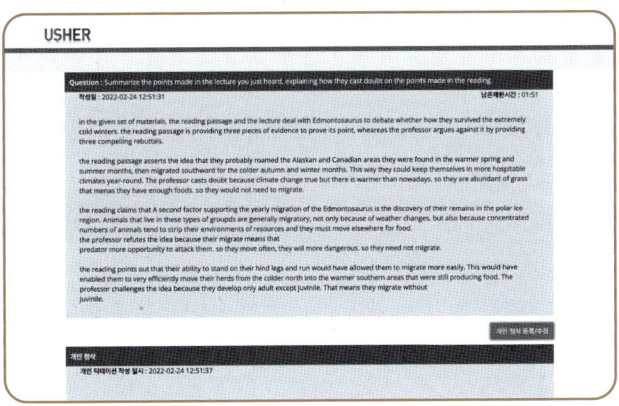

라이팅 첨삭 화면

첨삭 받은것들과 본인이 첨삭을 할 수 있는 공간 입니다. ETS가 제공한 채점표를 통해서 학생분들의 성적이 보다 객관적이게 채점됩니다.

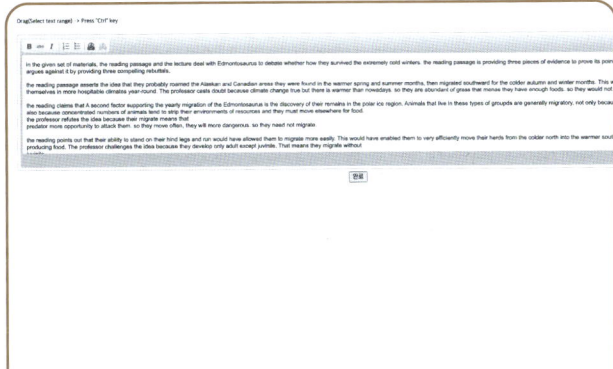

라이팅 자가 첨삭

본인이 스스로 펜 첨삭을 통해서 문법적인 오류를 찾아낼 수 있는 눈을 기를 수 있는 페이지 입니다.

 iBT TOEFL(iBT 토플) 소개

USHER iBT TOEFL **FINAL TEST SPEAKING** (어셔 iBT 토플 파이널 테스트 스피킹)

iBT TOEFL (iBT 토플)이란?

TOEFL(Test of English as a Foreign Language)이란 주로 영어권 국가의 대학교에 진학하는 외국인 학생의 영어실력을 평가하기 위하여 만들어진 시험입니다. 현재 TOEFL (토플)은 iBT(internet-Based Test) TOEFL이라 불리며, PBT(Paper-Based Test) 와 CBT(Computer-Based Test)를 거쳐 채택된 3세대 시험방식입니다. 읽기, 듣기, 말하기, 쓰기의 다양한 분야의 영어실력을 보기 때문에 현재 세계적으로 가장 공신력 있는 영어시험으로 자리잡았습니다.

iBT TOEFL (iBT 토플) 구성

시험순서	지문 개수	시간	세부사항	*더미 (Dummy)	만점
Reading (상대평가)	Passage 3개 (700단어 X 3개)	60~100분	**Passage 당** 18분 10문제	Passage 1개 더 출제 가능	30점
Listening (상대평가)	Conversation 2개	60~90분	**Conversation 당** 3분 5문제	Set 1개 (1Conversation + 2Lecture) 더 출제 가능	30점
	Lecture 3개		**Lecture 당** 5분 6문제		
Speaking (절대평가)	Independent 1개 Intergrated 3개	15분 내외	-	없음	30점
Writing (절대평가)	Intergrated 1개 Independent 1개	55분 (25 + 30분)	-	없음	30점
		총 약 4시간			총점 120점

*더미 (Dummy)란 원래 '꼭두각시, 연습용 인형'이란 뜻으로, TOEFL (토플)에서는 성적에 포함되지 않는 문제들을 일컫습니다. 원래의 출제 의도는 난이도 조절이었지만, iBT TOEFL (iBT 토플)에 와서 그 의미가 변하였으며, 외형상 실제 문제와 구분할 방법은 없습니다. (더 자세한 내용은 http://usherin.usher.co.kr 참조)

꼭 알아두세요!

접수	시험일정이 나오면 접수 가능 * Late fee(응시 7일 전 시험 신청 시) 40$추가
비용	시험 - 미화 $ 210 (원화결제 가능)
	취소한 성적 복원 - 미화 $ 20
	성적 전송 - 미화 $ 20 (1개 기관당)
	일자 변경 - 미화 $ 60
	재채점 - 미화 $ 80 (1개 section당: 성적 불신시 speaking, writing만 가능)

시험	한 달에 3회~5회 (토요일과 일요일에만 실시: http://ets.org/toefl에서 확인 가능)
시험장소	전국 27개 도시에 있는 Test Center 및 세계 각국의 ETS Test Center (안양, 아산, 부천, 부산, 천안, 청주, 춘천, 대구, 대전, 고성, 고양, 군포, 광주, 경기, 경주, 경산, 화성, 인천, 제주, 전주, 진주, 오산, 포천, 성남, 서울, 울산, 용인 등 27개 도시 - 토플 시험장에 대한 자세한 정보는 http://usherin.usher.co.kr 참조)
준비물	토플 web site에 등록되어 있는 신분증 지참
성적 발표일	토플 시험으로부터 최소 8일 ~ 최대 14일
성적 유효기간	2년
토플 시험 등록 취소	시험 등록 후 7일 까지 : 전액환불 시험 등록 후 8일 이후 : 금액의 50% 환불 시험보기 4일전 : 금액의 50% 환불 콜센터에 전화하거나 홈페이지에서 취소 (e-mail로는 불가능)

시험장에서!

1. 시험절차 시험장에 도착하면 여권 확인 후, 성적표에 나올 사진을 찍고 감독관의 안내에 따라 순서대로 시험을 시작한다.

2. 필기도구 연필과 종이는 감독관이 나누어주므로 따로 필요가 없고, 부족하면 얼마든지 더 달라고 할 수 있다. 다만, Section 시작 전에 종이에 필기할 경우, 부정행위로 간주될 수 있으므로 각별히 주의하자.

3. 헤드폰 음량 시험 도중 언제든지 조절할 수 있다.

4. 마이크 음량 시험 시작 직후와 Speaking Section 직전에 조절할 수 있다.

5. 휴식시간 Listening Section과 Speaking Section 사이에 10분의 휴식시간이 주어지고, 화장실에 가거나, 간식을 먹을 수 있다.
이 시간을 잘 활용해 Speaking에 대비하자!

6. 주의사항 각 응시자마다 시험 진행 시간이 다르기 때문에, 내가 Listening이나 Writing Section을 풀고 있을 때, 다른 사람의 목소리가 방해가 되는 경우가 많으니 염두해 두자.

5 iBT TOEFL Speaking 소개
USHER iBT TOEFL **FINAL TEST** SPEAKING (어셔 iBT 토플 파이널 테스트 스피킹)

iBT Speaking 문제 유형 분석 (총 30점 만점)

분류		준비기간 / 발표시간	Reading	Listening	기타
독립형	Task 1	15초 / 45초	×	×	선택 말하기 - 동의/반대 or 2중 택일
통합형	Task 2	30초 / 60초	100자 내외: 45~50초	O	대학 생활 (Conversation)
	Task 3	30초 / 60초	100자 내외: 45~50초	O	수업시간 교수의 강의 (Lecture)
	Task 4	20초 / 60초	×	O	수업시간 교수의 강의 (Lecture)

* 각 문제별 자세한 설명은 뒤의 Strategies Section을 참고하시기 바랍니다.

iBT Speaking 시험 진행 화면

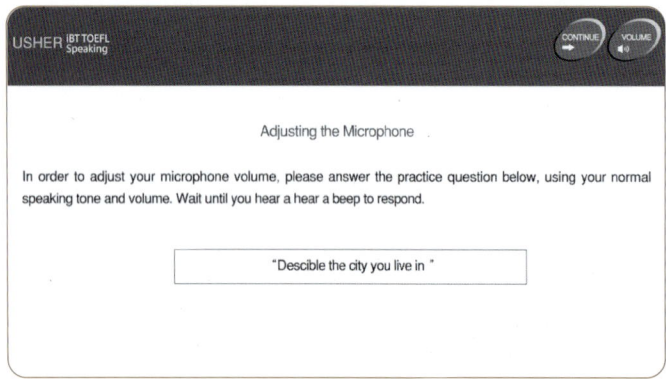

1. 마이크 소리 크기를 조절

"삐~"하고 소리가 나고, 화면의 문제에 답하고 나면, 녹음된 자신의 목소리를 체크할 수 있습니다. 마이크는 이 때만 조절이 가능합니다.

2. 헤드폰의 소리 크기를 조절

오른쪽 위의 volume 아이콘을 클릭하면 시험 보는 내내 언제든지 소리의 크기를 조절할 수 있습니다.

3. Speaking Section Directions

성우가 일일이 읽어주기 때문에 시간이 꽤 걸립니다. 지친 몸과 마음을 추스릴 수 있는 좋은 기회지만, 이 때 노트에 뭔가를 적게 되면 부정 행위로 간주되므로 주의합시다.

독립형 (Task 1)

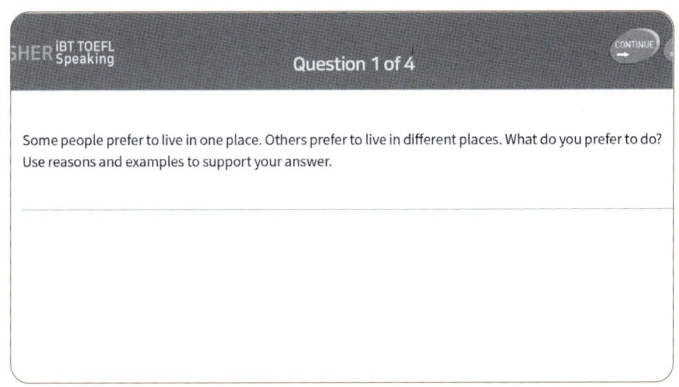

독립형 (Task 1)

1. 문제 화면
문제가 뜨면 성우가 직접 읽어줍니다.

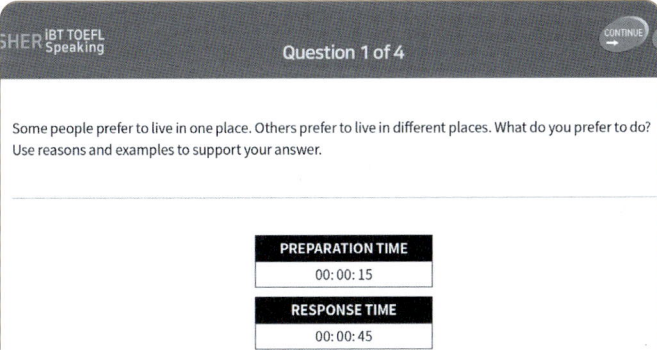

2. 답안 화면
남은 시간이 표시됩니다. (준비시간 15초, 발표시간 45초) "삐~"소리가 나야 녹음된다는 것을 잊지 마세요. 끝나면 자동으로 넘어갑니다.

5 iBT TOEFL Speaking 소개

통합형 (Task 2 ~ 4)

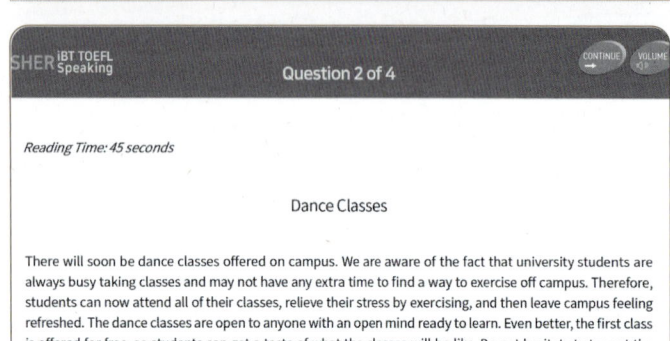

1. Reading Passage

100자 내외의 글이 나옵니다. Task 2는 공지문이나 제안서가, Task 3에서는 교과서의 일부가 나옵니다. 시간은 길이에 따라 45~50초가 주어지며, 남은 시간은 화면의 오른쪽 위에 나타납니다. (Task 4는 해당사항 없음.)

2. Listening Passage

Task 2는 대화가, Task 3 & 4는 강의가 나옵니다. 강의의 경우, 내용과 관련된 참고자료가 나오기도 합니다.

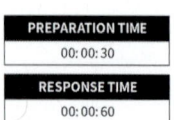

3. 답안 화면

남은 준비시간이 표시됩니다. (Task 2 & 3는 30초, Task 4은 20초) "삐~"소리가 나야 녹음 된다는 것을 잊지 마세요. (발표시간 60초) 끝나면 자동으로 넘어갑니다.

iBT TOEFL (iBT 토플) 성적표 (견본)

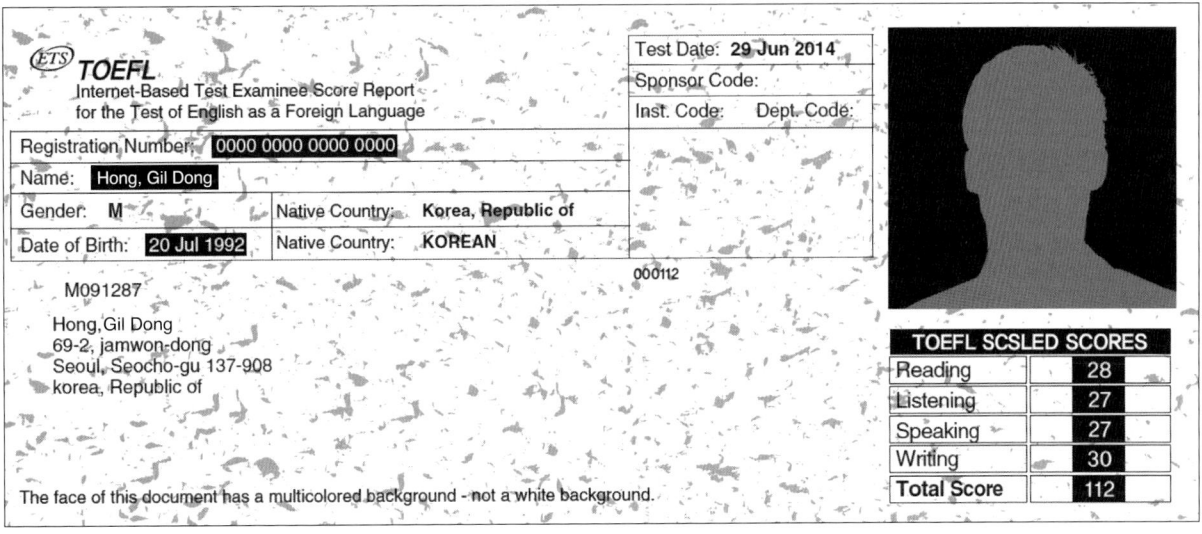

점수 계산법

총점	4문제 평균 점수
30	4.00
29	3.83
28	3.66
27	3.50
26	3.33
24	3.16
23	3.00
22	2.83
20	2.66
19	2.50
18	2.33
17	2.16
15	2.00
14	1.83
13	1.66
11	1.50
10	1.33
9	1.16
8	1.00
6	0.83
5	0.66
4	0.50
3	0.33
1	0.16
0	0.00

(출처: http://www.ets.org/toefl)

시험 응시자가 작성한 답안은 인터넷을 통해 ETS로 보내집니다. 성적의 신뢰도를 높이기 위해 세 명의 채점관을 거치게 되며, 0점과 4점 사이의 점수가 매겨집니다. 그리하여, 이 4문제의 평균점수는 0점에서 30점사이의 점수로 환산됩니다.
(왼쪽의 표 참조)

Independent Speaking Rubric

(출처: http://www.ets.org/toefl)

Score	General Description	Delivery	Language Use	Topic Development
4	The response fulfills the demands of the task, with at most minor lapses in completeness. It is highly intelligible and exhibits sustained, coherent discourse. A response at this level is characterized by all of the following:	Generally well-paced flow (fluid expression). Speech is clear. It may include minor lapses, or minor difficulties with pronunciation or intonation patterns, which do not affect overall intelligibility.	The response demonstrates effective use of grammar and vocabulary. It exhibits a fairly high degree of automaticity with good control of basic and complex structures (as appropriate). Some minor (or systematic) errors are noticeable but do not obscure meaning.	Response is sustained and sufficient to the task. It is generally well developed and coherent; relationships between ideas are clear (or clear progression of ideas).
3	The response addresses the task appropriately, but may fall short of being fully developed. It is generally intelligible and coherent, with some fluidity of expression though it exhibits some noticeable lapses in the expression of ideas. A response at this level is characterized by at least two of the following:	Speech is generally clear, with some fluidity of expression, though minor difficulties with pronunciation, intonation, or pacing are noticeable and may require listener effort at times (though overall intelligibility is not significantly affected).	The response demonstrates fairly automatic and effective use of grammar and vocabulary, and fairly coherent expression of relevant ideas. Response may exhibit some imprecise or inaccurate use of vocabulary or grammatical structures or be somewhat limited in the range of structures used. This may affect overall fluency, but it does not seriously interfere with the communication of the message.	Response is mostly coherent and sustained and conveys relevant ideas / information. Overall development is somewhat limited, usually lacks elaboration or specificity. Relationships between ideas may at times not be immediately clear.
2	The response addresses the task, but development of the topic is limited. It contains intelligible speech, although problems with delivery and/or overall coherence occur; meaning may be obscured in places. A response at this level is characterized by at least two of the following:	Speech is basically intelligible, though listener effort is needed because of unclear articulation, awkward intonation, or choppy rhythm/pace; meaning may be obscured in places.	The response demonstrates limited range and control of grammar and vocabulary. These limitations often prevent full expression of ideas. For the most part, only basic sentence structures are used successfully and spoken with fluidity. Structures and vocabulary may express mainly simple (short) and/or general propositions, with simple or unclear connections made among them (serial listing, conjunction, juxtaposition).	The response is connected to the task, though the number of ideas presented or the development of ideas is limited. Mostly basic ideas are expressed with limited elaboration (details and support). At times relevant substance may be vaguely expressed or repetitious. Connections of ideas may be unclear.
1	The response is very limited in content and/or coherence or is only minimally connected to the task, or speech is largely unintelligible. A response at this level is characterized by at least two of the following:	Consistent pronunciation, stress, and intonation difficulties cause considerable listener effort; delivery is choppy, fragmented, or telegraphic; frequent pauses and hesitations.	Range and control of grammar and vocabulary severely limit (or prevent) expression of ideas and connections among ideas. Some low-level responses may rely heavily on practiced or formulaic expressions.	Limited relevant content is expressed. The response generally lacks substance beyond expression of very basic ideas. Speaker may be unable to sustain speech to complete the task and may rely heavily on repetition of the prompt.

독립형 말하기 평가 기준

(출처: http://www.ets.org/toefl)

점수	일반적인 설명	전달력 (발음)	언어의 사용 (문법)	주제의 전개 (내용)
4	완성도에 지극히 미미한 결함이 있지만, 답안이 문제의 요구사항을 충족시킨다. 아주 명료하며, 일관성 있고 한결같은 화법을 보여준다. 이런 수준의 답은 다음의 특성을 모두 지닌다:	흐름이 대체로 만족스럽고 말투는 명확하다. 전체적인 명료함에 영향을 끼치지 않는 수준의, 발음이나 억양 상의 미미한 실수나 어려움이 있다.	답이 문법과 단어를 효과적으로 사용했다. 기본적 구조와 복합적 구조를 잘 조절하며, 꽤 높은 수준의 자동성을 보여준다. 몇몇 자잘한 실수가 눈에 띄지만, 의미를 애매하게 만드는 수준은 아니다.	답안은 과제를 충분히 뒷받침한다. 대체로 잘 전개되었고 논리정연하다; 의견 간의 관계가 분명하다. (또는 의견의 뚜렷한 전개)
3	답안은 문제에 답했지만, 주제의 전개가 부족하다. 비록 전달의 문제와 전반적인 논리적 결합에 문제가 있어도, 이해할 만한 수준의 답안을 포함한다. 곳곳에서 의미가 명료하지 않다. 이런 수준의 답은 다음 중 적어도 두 가지 특성을 지닌다:	비록 명확하지 않은 발음, 서투른 억양, 또는 고르지 못한 속도 때문에 듣는 이의 노력이 요구되지만, 답안은 기본적으로 이해가 가능하다. 곳곳에서 의미가 명료하지 않다.	답이 꽤 자동적이고 효과적인 문법과 어휘력, 그리고 관련된 의견과 일치하는 표현력을 보인다. 답이 부정확한 어휘의 사용이나 문법 구조를 보이고, 문장 구조의 활용 범위가 좁다. 이는 전체적 유창함에 영향을 미쳤을 수 있지만, 내용의 소통을 심각하게 방해하지는 않는다.	대답은 거의 논리정연하고 충분히 뒷받침되었으며 적절한 의견/정보를 전달한다. 전체적인 전개가 다소 부족하고, 섬세함과 자세함이 결여되어 있다. 때로는 의견 간의 관계가 바로 이해되지 않는다.
2	답안은 문제에 답했지만, 주제의 전개는 부족하다. 비록 전달이나 전반적인 일관성의 문제가 있음에도 이해하기 쉬운 말을 담고 있다; 뜻이 곳곳에서 애매할 수 있다. 이런 수준의 답안은 다음 중 적어도 두 가지 특성을 지닌다:	비록 불분명한 발음, 어색한 억양이나 고르지 못한 리듬/속도 때문에 듣는 이의 노력이 필요하지만 말투는 기본적으로 이해할 수 있다; 곳곳에서 뜻을 이해하기 힘들다.	답은 문법과 어휘를 다루는데 미숙한 능력을 보인다. 이런 능력의 부족은 종종 생각을 모두 표현하는 데에 장애가 된다. 기본적인 문장 구조 사용은 대체로 성공적이고, 말투는 유동적이다. (나열, 접속사, 병렬 배치 등) 이들 사이의 단순하고 불명확한 연결을 가지고, 구조와 어휘는 단순하게 표현된다.	비록, 제시된 의견의 수와 전개가 부족하지만, 답안은 과제와 관련이 있다. 기본적인 의견은 대체로 부족한 섬세함(디테일과 근거)으로 표현된다. 때때로 관련된 소재들은 모호하게 표현되거나 반복된다. 생각들의 연계가 불명확하다.
1	답안이 내용이나 일관성 면에서 매우 부족하거나, 과제와 거의 관계없거나, 대체로 이해할 수 없는 말이다. 이런 수준의 답안은 다음 중 적어도 두 가지 특성을 지닌다:	발음, 강세, 그리고 억양 상의 어려움은 듣는 이의 노력을 상당히 필요로 한다; 내용이 계속해서 끊어진다. 멈춤과 망설임이 잦다.	문법과 단어를 다루는 능력 부족 때문에 생각의 표현과 의견 간의 연결이 빈약하다. 일부 수준 낮은 답은 연습되었거나 정형화된 표현에 심하게 의지한다.	관련 내용의 표현이 부족하다. 아주 기본적인 의견 표현 이상의 내용이 없다. 발표자는 과제를 끝낼 때까지 발표를 잇지 못하고, 제시어의 반복에 심하게 의지한다.

Integrated Speaking Rubric

(출처: http://www.ets.org/toefl)

Score	General Description	Delivery	Language Use	Topic Development
4	The response fulfills the demands of the task, with at most minor lapses in completeness. It is highly intelligible and exhibits sustained, coherent discourse. A response at this level is characterized by all of the following:	Speech is generally clear, fluid, and sustained. It may include minor lapses or minor difficulties with pronunciation or intonation. Pace may vary at times as the speaker attempts to recall information. Overall intelligibility remains high.	The response demonstrates good control of basic and complex grammatical structures that allow for coherent, efficient (automatic) expression of relevant ideas. Contains generally effective word choice. Though some minor (or systematic) errors or imprecise use may be noticeable, they do not require listener effort (or obscure meaning).	The response presents a clear progression of ideas and conveys the relevant information required by the task. It includes appropriate detail, though it may have minor errors or minor omissions.
3	The response addresses the task appropriately, but may fall short of being fully developed. It is generally intelligible and coherent, with some fluidity of expression of ideas. A response at this level is characterized by at least two of the following:	Speech is generally clear, with some fluidity of expression, but it exhibits minor difficulties with pronunciation, intonation, or pacing and may require some listener effort at times. Overall intelligibility remains good, however.	The response demonstrates fairly automatic and effective use of grammar and vocabulary, and fairly coherent expression of relevant ideas. Response may exhibit some imprecise or inaccurate use of vocabulary or grammatical structures or be somewhat limited in the range of structures used. Such limitations do not seriously interfere with the communication of the message.	The response is sustained and conveys relevant information required by the task. However, it exhibits some incompleteness, inaccuracy, lack of specificity with respect to content, or choppiness in the progression of ideas.
2	The response is connected to the task, though it may be missing some relevant information or contain inaccuracies. It contains some intelligible speech, but at times problems with intelligibility and/or overall coherence may obscure meaning. A response at this level is characterized by at least two of the following:	Speech is clear at times, though it exhibits problems with pronunciation, intonation, or pacing and so may require significant listener effort. Speech may not be sustained at a consistent level throughout. Problems with intelligibility may obscure meaning in places (but not throughout).	The response is limited in the range and control of vocabulary and grammar demonstrated (some complex structures may be used, but typically contain errors). This results in limited or vague expression of relevant ideas and imprecise or inaccurate connections. Automaticity of expression may only be evident at the phrasal level.	The response conveys some relevant information but is clearly incomplete if it omits key ideas, makes vague reference to key ideas, or demonstrates limited development of important information. An inaccurate response demonstrates misunderstanding of key ideas from the stimulus. may not be well connected or cohesive so that familiarity with the stimulus is necessary to follow what is being discussed.
1	The response is very limited in content of coherence or is only minimally connected to the task. Speech may be largely unintelligible. A response at this level is characterized by at least two of the following:	Consistent pronunciation and intonation problems cause considerable listener effort and frequently obscure meaning. Delivery is choppy, fragmented, or telegraphic. Speech contains frequent pauses and hesitations.	Range and control of grammar and vocabulary severely limit (or prevent) expression of ideas and connections among ideas. Some very low-level responses may rely on isolated words or short utterances to communicate ideas.	The response fails to provide much relevant content. Ideas that are expressed are often inaccurate, limited to vague utterances, or repetitions (including repetition of prompt).

통합형 말하기 평가 기준

(출처: http://www.ets.org/toefl)

점수	일반적인 설명	전달력 (발음)	언어의 사용 (문법)	주제의 전개 (내용)
4	완성도에 지극히 미미한 결함이 있지만, 답안이 문제의 요구사항을 충족시킨다. 아주 명료하며, 일관성 있고 한결같은 화법을 보여준다. 이런 수준의 답은 다음의 특성을 모두 지닌다:	답안이 대체로 알아듣기 쉽고, 유동적이며 일관적이다. 발음이나 억양 상의 작은 실수나 어려움이 있을 수 있다. 말하는 이가 정보를 상기하려고 시도하기 때문에 속도는 변할 수 있다. 전체적으로 이해하기 쉽다.	답안은 관련된 의견을 일관되고 효과적으로 (자동적으로) 표현하도록 하는, 기본적 구조와 복합적 구조에 맞는 문장 사용 능력을 보여준다. 대체로 효과적인 어휘력을 보여준다. 몇몇 자잘한 실수가 있지만, 그것이 듣는 이의 노력(또는 애매한 뜻)을 야기시키지는 않는다.	답안은 사고의 명확한 진행을 보여주고 문제에 필요한 관련 정보를 전달하고 있다. 비록 사소한 오류나 누락이 있을 수 있지만, 적절한 세부사항을 포함한다
3	답안은 문제에 답했지만, 주제의 전개가 부족하다. 비록 전달의 문제와 전반적인 논리적 결합에 문제가 있어도, 이해할 만한 수준의 답안을 포함한다. 곳곳에서 의미가 명료하지 않다. 이런 수준의 답은 다음 중 적어도 두 가지 특성을 지닌다:	비록 명확하지 않은 발음, 서투른 억양, 또는 고르지 못한 속도 때문에 듣는 이의 노력이 요구되지만, 답안은 기본적으로 이해가 가능하다. (하지만 대체로 이해하기는 쉽다.)	답안이 꽤 자동적이고 효과적인 문법과 어휘력, 그리고 관련된 의견과 일치하는 표현력을 보인다. 답안이 부정확한 어휘의 사용이나 문법 구조를 보이고, 문장 구조의 활용 범위가 좁다. 그런 부족함이 내용의 소통을 심각하게 방해하지는 않는다.	답안은 한결같고 문제가 요구한 관련 정보를 전달한다. 하지만 약간의 불완전함, 부정확함, 특정 내용의 결여, 또는 사고의 진행의 고르지 못함을 보여준다.
2	비록 연관된 정보가 빠졌거나 틀린 것이 포함되어 있어도 답안은 문제에 답했다. 내용을 이해할 수는 있지만, 때때로 명료함 또는 전체적인 일관성의 문제가 의미의 전달을 막는다. 이런 수준의 답안은 다음 중 적어도 두 가지 특성을 지닌다:	비록 불분명한 발음, 어색한 억양이나 고르지 못한 속도 때문에 듣는 이의 노력이 필요하지만 때때로 알아듣기 쉽다. 발표하는 동안 일관된 수준을 유지하지 못한다. 명료함의 문제가 군데군데 의미를 모호하게 한다. (하지만 내내 그런 건 아니다.)	답안은 문법과 어휘를 다루는데 미숙한 능력을 보인다. (복잡한 문장이 좀 쓰였지만, 보통 실수가 있다) 이는 관련된 의견에 관한 부족하고 애매한 표현과 부정확한 연결을 야기시킨다. 자동적인 표현은 구절 수준에서만 눈에 띈다.	답안은 관련된 정보를 약간 전달하지만, 핵심 내용이 생략되었고, 주제에 대한 언급이 애매하며, 또는 중요한 정보의 전개가 부족하다는 면에서 확실히 미완성이다. 부정확한 답안은 문제의 핵심을 이해하지 못했음을 보여준다. 대체로, 표현된 의견이 잘 연결돼있지 않아, 논의 주제를 따라가려면 문제에 익숙해질 필요가 있다.
1	답안이 내용이나 일관성 면에서 매우 부족하거나, 과제와 거의 관계없거나, 대체로 이해할 수 없는 말이다. 이런 수준의 답안은 다음 중 적어도 두 가지 특성을 지닌다:	계속되는 발음과 억양상의 문제들이 듣는 이의 상당한 노력과 애매한 의미를 야기시킨다. 내용이 계속해서 끊어진다. 멈춤과 망설임이 잦다.	문법 실력과 어휘력이 의견의 표현과 연결을 심하게 방해한다. 아주 낮은 수준의 답안은 생각들을 전달하는 데 있어 끊어진 단어들과 짧은 말투에 의존한다.	답안이 관련 내용을 제공하는 데에 실패했다. 표현된 의견들은 대체로 부정확하고 애매한 말투와 반복(제시어의 반복 포함)에 국한된다.

 # 교재 계획표

USHER iBT TOEFL **FINAL TEST** SPEAKING (어셔 iBT 토플 파이널 테스트 스피킹)

2주 완성 계획표

	월	화	수	목	금	토	일
1주	Test 1 강의 Set 1 & 2	Test 2 강의 Set 3 & 4	Test 3 강의 Set 5 & 6	Test 4 강의 Set 7 & 8	Test 5 강의 Set 9 & 10	Test 6 강의 Set 11 & 12	Test 7 강의 Set 13 & 14
2주	Test 8 강의 Set 15 & 16	Test 9 강의 Set 복습	Test 10 홈피 Set 1	Test 11 홈피 Set 2	Test 12 홈피 Set 3	실제시험 (없으면 복습)	실제시험

* 강의 Set이란? http://usherin.usher.co.kr에 마련되어 있는 총 16회의 Task 3 & 4 문제 Set을 의미합니다.

4주 완성 계획표

	월	화	수	목	금	토	일
1주	Test 1	Test 2	Test 1&2 복습	Test 3	Test 4	Test 3&4 복습	강의 Set 1 ~ 3
2주	Test 5	Test 6	Test 5&6 복습	Test 7	Test 8	Test 7&8 복습	강의 Set 4 ~ 6
3주	Test 9	Test 10	Test 9&10 복습	Test 11	Test 12	Test 11&12 복습	강의 Set 7 ~ 9
4주	강의 Set 10 ~ 12	강의 Set 13 강의 1~13 복습	강의 Set 14 홈피 Set 1	강의 Set 15 홈피 Set 2	강의 Set 16 홈피 Set 3	실제시험 (없으면 복습)	실제시험

* 강의 Set이란? http://usherin.usher.co.kr에 마련되어 있는 총 16회의 Task 3 & 4 문제 Set을 의미합니다.

교재 계획표 활용법

"Test 1"이라고 쓰여있으면,

1. Test 1을 푼다.

    a. http://usherin.usher.co.kr > '시험리스트' > **Speaking 시험리스트**를 실행한다.

    b. **Speaking 시험리스트**를 쓸 수 없는 경우, 핸드폰이나 mp3플레이어 등을 이용하여 자신의 목소리를 반드시 녹음한다.

    또, 핸드폰이나 시계 등을 이용하여 시간을 정확히 잰다. (독립형: 45초 / 통합형: 60초)

    c. 가급적 홈페이지의 **Speaking 시험리스트**를 실행하도록 한다.

2. 해설집을 참고하여 문제를 확인한다.

3. 독립형 문제 (Task 1)의 **만능 답안** (예:Teach Children & Academics)은 무조건 외운다.

4. 통합형 문제 (Task 2 ~ 4)는 모범 답안을 참고하여 자신의 답안과 내용을 비교한다.

5. **자기 평가표**를 펼쳐놓고, **mp3 파일에 수록된 모범 답안을 들으며** 자신의 발음, 강세, 억양, 속도 등을 점검하고, 개선해야 할 점을 확인한다.

6. 통합형 (Task 2 ~ 4)의 경우, 해설집의 내용을 자신이 note-taking한 것과 비교해본다. 못 알아들은 부분이 있으면 script 를 확인해 보고, 완벽하게 들릴 때까지 **받아쓰기 연습(dictation)이나 따라읽기 연습(shadowing)**을 할 수도 있다.

7. **3번**에서 외운 **만능 답안** 과 해설집의 표현들을 제대로 외웠는지 **반드시** 확인한다.

"복습"이라고 쓰여있으면,

1. **Practice Set** 혹은 **강의 Set**을 다시 푼다.
2. **스스로가 만족할 때까지** 답안을 **다시 녹음**하고 처음 것과 비교한다.

 **7 발음 연습**
USHER iBT TOEFL **FINAL TEST SPEAKING** (어셔 iBT 토플 파이널 테스트 스피킹)

I. 강세(Stress)

강세 > 발음

자신있게 말씀드립니다 - 영어 말하기에서는 강세가 가장 중요합니다. 많은 학생들이 이 부분을 잘 모르는데, 발음이 완벽해도 강세가 엉망이라면, 오로지 한국사람만 알아들을 수 있습니다. 기억하세요 - 채점자는 미국인입니다.

A. 음절의 강세

두 번째 음절(syllable) 이후에 강세가 오는 단어들은 항상 조심해야 합니다. 강세 이전의 음절이 잘 들리지 않기 때문입니다. 이런 점들을 무시하고 첫 음절부터 강하게 발음한다면, 리듬이 깨지고 알아듣기 힘든 문장이 됩니다.

1. My advisor expected me to express my emotions before she interrogated me.
2. I had anticipated a specific question, so I was extremely surprised by his response.
3. I was incomparably surprised when the assumed Japanese man told me he was Canadian.
4. Throughout the campaign, we were attacked from behind by the opposing camp.
5. I awarded him for his success despite the amount of mistakes he had made before.

B. 문장 내에서 단어의 품사에 따른 강세

항상 그런 것은 아니지만, 일반적으로 단어의 강세는 품사에 따라 강·중·약으로 나뉩니다.
(특정 단어를 강조하는 경우는 예외)
강 - 명사, 동사, 형용사, 부사, 감탄사, 대명사 (주격, 소유대명사)
약 - 관사, 조동사, 전치사, 접속사, 대명사 (소유격, 목적격)

C. 부정문에서의 조동사의 강세

부정문에서 조동사 부분은 특별히 신경 쓰셔야 합니다. **isn't - doesn't - can't - shouldn't** 같은 부분에서 [트] 발음을 한다는 것은 있어서는 안될 일입니다. 이런 경우, 발음이 아닌 강세로 부정문임을 알려야 합니다.

　　I can do it. [아 큰 두 잇.] (강 - 약 - 강 - 중)

위와 같은 문장에서 '**can**'은 조동사이기 때문에 약하게 발음합니다. 강세가 없는 경우 [캔]이라고 발음하지 않고 [컨] 혹은 [큰]으로 발음합니다.

　　I can't do it. [아 캔 뚜 잇.] (강 - 초강 - 강 - 중)

어떤 경우라도 '**can't**' 를 [캔트]라고 발음하는 경우는 없습니다. 부정문에서는 조동사 부분에 강세가 들어가기 때문에 그때서야 비로소 [캔]이라고 발음합니다. 뒤의 동사가 '**D**'로 시작하는 경우엔 연음법칙에 의해 [두]가 [뚜]로 변합니다.

위와 같은 문장에서는 원어민들끼리도 헷갈려 하는 경우가 상당히 많습니다. 사실 가장 확실한 방법은 '**can't**' 가 아니라 '**cannot**' 을 쓰는 것이 가장 좋은 방법입니다. 강세가 뒤에 있기 때문에 '**not**' 이 아주 잘 들리기 때문입니다.

D. 억양

일반적으로 강세가 있는 부분은 높게, 없는 부분은 낮게 읽습니다.

II. 발음 (Pronunciation)

A. 모음 (Vowels)

모음 발음 > 자음 발음

발음에 자신이 없는 많은 분들은 자음 발음에만 신경쓰는 경우가 많습니다. 되려 발음에 자신있는 분들도 모음에 문제가 있는 경우가 다반사입니다. 하지만, 문장이 길어졌을 때, 정작 영향이 큰 것은 모음 발음입니다. 모음간의 차이를 이해하여 발음을 조율하고 원어민의 발음에 한 발짝 더 다가섭시다.

1. [æ] - [e]

간단히 말해, [애]와 [에]의 차이입니다. 한국어에서도 흔히 볼 수 있죠.

> **[애] 발음** - [에] 발음과의 가장 큰 차이는 입을 옆으로 크게 벌린다는 것입니다. 그러면서 [애]인지 [아]인지 구분이 안될 정도로 애매하게 발음합니다.
>
> **[에] 발음** - 절대 입을 크게 벌려선 안됩니다. 입술을 거의 움직이지 않은 상태에서 힘을 빼고 무성의하게 발음합니다.
>
> **요주의 단어 - man**: 음절 하나에 단수와 복수가 결정되는 만큼 매번 신경 씁시다. 사용빈도도 높습니다.

sat - set	bat - bet	land - lend	dad - dead	fad - fed
frat - fret	track - trek	rack - wreck	France - French	sand - send
rad - red	fast - fest	ham - hem	ban - Ben	man - men

2. [ee] - [i]

> **[ee] 발음** - 역시 입을 옆으로 크게 벌리셔야 합니다. 장음이니 만큼 발음도 길~게!
>
> **[i] 발음** - 역시 절대 입을 크게 벌려선 안됩니다. 역시 입술을 거의 움직이지 않은 상태에서 힘을 빼고 무성의하게 발음합니다. 정확한 [이] 발음이 아니라, 얼핏 들으면 [이]였는지 [어]였는지 [에]였는지 모를 정도로 애매하게 발음하는 것이 포인트입니다. 의외로 한국인들에게 어려운 발음입니다. 강세가 들어가지 않는 [i] 발음의 경우, 발음기호가 [어]로 표기되는 일도 있을 정도입니다.
>
> 예) infinity

7 발음 연습

> **요주의 단어 - is**: 발음이 'ease' 처럼 되지 않도록 주의합시다. 사용빈도도 높지만, 끊어 읽기 할 때 쉬어가는 부분이기 때문에 아주 잘 들립니다.
>
> **his**: 발음은 'is'와 마찬가지입니다. [hees]처럼 되지 않도록 주의합시다.

feet - fit	feel - fill	ease - is
fleet - flit	keen - kin	reap - rip
peel - pill	bean - bin	wheat - wit
gleam - grin	heat - hit	seat - sit
bream - brim	meet - mitt	beat - bit

3. [ou] - [ɔ]

> **[ou] 발음** - [오우]라고 읽읍시다. "Oh~!" 영어를 느끼하게 따라 할 때(?) 흔히 쓰는 표현인데요, 그래서인지 실전에서는 이 발음을 피하고 그냥 [오]라고 발음하는 경향이 있습니다. 느끼한 건 느끼한 거고, 따라할 건 따라해야지요.
>
> **[ɔ] 발음** - [오]와 [어]의 중간발음입니다. 발음이 어렵지 않지만, 많은 분들이 그냥 [오]라고 읽는 경향이 있습니다.
>
> **요주의 단어 - cost**: [코스트]와 [커스트]의 중간발음입니다.
>
> **don't**: [돈트]가 아니라 [도운트]입니다. 사용빈도가 높은 만큼 꼭 연습합시다.
>
> **won't**: 'want'와 확실히 구분할 필요가 있습니다. 실제 발음은 [원트]가 아니라 [우오운트] 혹은 [워운트]에 가깝습니다. 비음(콧소리)를 섞어주면 더욱 좋습니다.

coast - cost	both - boss	flow - flaw
goat - got	boat - bought	coat - cot
wrote - rot	sew - saw	bloat - blot
clone - clod	node - nod	rode - rod
vote - vault	row - raw	stroll - straw

4. [uː] - [u]

[uː]발음과 [u]발음은 단순히 장음과 단음의 차이가 아닙니다. 기본적으로 다른 발음이지만, 아쉽게도 발음기호로 표기하는 데는 한계가 있습니다.

> **단음으로써의 [u]** - [우]보다는 [으]에 가깝습니다.
>
> **요주의 단어 - good**: [굳]보다는 [긋]으로, **book**: [북]보다는 [븍]으로, **look**: [룩]보다는 [륵]으로, **took**: [툭]보다는 [특]으로 발음하면 실제 발음과 더 가깝습니다.

food - foot	touq - took	boot - book
cocoon - cook	crude - crook	balloon - blood
fruit - flood	brood - blood	hoot - hood
hoot - hook	hookah - hood	loo - look
snoop - nook	rude - rook	woo - wood

B. 자음 (Consonants)

1. [L] - [R]

시작음으로써의 [L] - 단어를 발음하기 전에 [을]을 아주 살짝 발음해 보세요. 익숙해지면 [을]발음을 뺍니다.

        leg - (을)레그   **lake** - (을)레이크
        loyal - (을)로열   **lift** - (을)리프트

마침음으로써의 [L] - 일단 [엘]이라고 읽기보다 [에으]라고 읽어보세요. 그 상태에서 혀를 곧게 뻗어 앞니 뒤에 댑니다.

[R] - 발음 시작 전에, [루]라고 발음을 시작합시다.
        reading - [뤼딩]   **writing** - [루와이팅]
        rift - [뤼프트]   **rid** - [뤼드]

요주의 단어 - lecture: 실제로 [**REC-ture**]로 발음하시는 분이 많습니다. 충분한 주의요망.

lag - rag	lead - reed	lift - rift
loyal - royal	loot - root	lid - rid
lake - rake	lot - rot	lest - rest

 # mp3 파일을 들으면서 다음 문장을 따라 읽어보세요.
1. Lilly likes to eat ripe lemons and limes for dessert while resting after lunch.
2. Tell Ron he was right about getting rid of the light leaking into the room.
3. He lied on the road to plead for a free ride to Louisiana.
4. The lamb rammed her head into the low wall made of brick.
5. Rick placed the lamp at the end of the ramp and tried to leap over it.

2. [B] - [V]

[V] 발음은 누구나 할 수 있지만, 방심하다가 많이 틀리는 부분입니다.

요주의 단어 - believe: '빌리브' 보다는 '블리브' 에 가깝습니다. 끝 부분의 'V' 발음을 조심합시다.
        very: '베리' 보다는 '베어리' 에 가깝습니다. 강세가 앞에 있음을 잊지 말 것!

boys - voice	robe - rove	bile - vial
bane - vain	bet - vet	bail - vale
dribble - drivel	bolt - volt	base - vase
Gabe - gave	bagel - vagal	ballad - valid
strobe - strove	berry - very	curb - curve

 # mp3 파일을 들으면서 다음 문장을 따라 읽어보세요.
1. There is a big crack at the base of the vase.
2. The bat was banished from this cave, which is why it vanished.
3. The women marveled over the marble of the new bathroom floor.
4. Vincent came up with a new ballad that was valid.
5. The black van was banned from this parking lot by the valet.

7 발음 연습

3. [P] - [F]

[F] 발음은 모두 할 줄 알지만, 습관이 되지 않아 문제가 되는 만큼 지속적인 연습이 필요합니다.

> **요주의 단어 - first**: speaking 시작할 때 계속 반복해서 쓰게 되므로, 반드시 익숙해질 때까지 연습하세요.
> **prefer**: 'P' 발음과 'F' 발음이 섞여 있어 어렵습니다. 보통 '**pre-PER**' 나 '**fre-FER**' 라고 발음하게 되는데요, 강세가 2번째 음절에 있는 만큼, 차라리 '**per-FER**' 라고 하는 것이 실제발음에 더 가깝습니다. Task 1에서는 매번 쓰게 되는 단어지요.

pat - fat	pill - fill	reap - reef	pun - fun
pain - feign	staple - stifle	leap - leaf	plunk - flunk
clip - cliff	plush - flush	pond - fond	drip - drift
plea - flea	lap - laugh	cap - calf	

mp3 파일을 들으면서 다음 문장을 따라 읽어보세요.

1. He tried to flush the plush doll down the toilet, but failed.
2. He pleaded for the fleas to flee his puppy.
3. The pig stepped over the fid and sniffed at a pan filled with pills.
4. The cheap chief peddled the products from a fan at a cheap price.
5. My father prefers using pans as fans over the air purifier.

4. [J] - [Z]

[Z] 발음 역시 누구나 할 수 있지만, 신경쓰지 않아 많이 틀리는 부분입니다.

Jen - zen	Jew - zoo	joy - zoy	legion - treason
jock - zonk	jing - zinc	jest - zest	jail - zale
jar - czar	jill - zeal	mojo - bozo	Joey - Zoe
Joan - zone	jig - zigzag	jab - zap	

mp3 파일을 들으면서 다음 문장을 따라 읽어보세요.

1. Jen is jinxed in that she cannot jog in a zigzag.
2. Zebras have zigzag stripes and live in their zone in zoos.
3. Jack and Zack cannot work their mojo on me, because of the zen in this room.
4. Jews don't worship Zeus for a zillion reasons.
5. Jennifer was zapped by her zipper made of zinc.

5. [D] - [TH]

[TH]의 두 발음 중 약한 발음인 '돼지꼬리' 발음은 누구나 할 수 있지만, 정신줄을 놓으면 문제가 되므로 꾸준한 연습이 필요합니다.

> **요주의 단어 - this, that, these, those, them**: 보시다시피 지시대명사 - 지시형용사에 많이 쓰이는 발음입니다. 자주 쓰이는 만큼 꼭 연습해 둡시다.
> **although**: 접속사라서 문장의 앞부분에 주로 쓰이기 때문에 실수할 경우 잘 들립니다.

though - dough	thy - die	thus - dust	this - diss
there - dare	lather - ladder	worthy - wordy	bathe - bad
breathe - breed	the - duh	thee - D	soothe - sued
than - Dan	then - den	neither - kneader	

mp3 파일을 들으면서 다음 문장을 따라 읽어보세요.

1. Though we're out of dough, continue to fill the thin dish.
2. The kneader needed neither thrifty Tim nor the thinking team.
3. My dad's essay about drone on the throne was wordy but still worthy.
4. Thus, the amount of dust on the ladder was rather thicker than I had thought.
5. He dared to go there with Dan rather than Thelma.

6. [S] - [SH]

영어의 'C' 와 'S' 는 한국어의 [씨]와 발음이 다릅니다.

[씨]를 발음할 때보다 혀끝을 둥글게 조여 더 작은 구멍을 통해서 바람이 새어나가도록 해야 합니다.
처음에는 [쓰이]라고 발음하며 연습하다가, 점점 [쓰이]에서 [씌]로, [씌]에서 [si]로 연습해 보면 쉽습니다.

> **요주의 단어 - since** : 'S' 로 시작한다고 방심하지 맙시다. 발음은 'Cince'
>
> **simple** : 'Cimple' 에 가깝게 발음해 봅시다.

sin - shin	sea - she	seat - sheathe
brassy - brash	classy - clash	seep - sheep
single - shingle	sissy - shish	seer - shear
sift - shift	seek - chic	sip - ship
sear - sheer	seat - sheet	since - shins

mp3 파일을 들으면서 다음 문장을 따라 읽어보세요.

1. The classy women clashed with Sydney on the ship by the seashore.
2. Since I hurt both shins, the pain shifts around from shin to shin.
3. The single shingle on the roof of the shack slid to the ground that had no sin.
4. The sick sheep's wool shield was sheared by the senior.
5. Cindy shrilled with sheer terror of her sister's single-minded sheep.

7. [W]

한국인이 가장 과소평가하는 발음입니다. 대부분의 경우 자신이 잘못 발음하는지조차 모르고 있습니다.
기본 발음은 [우]입니다.

> **요주의 단어 - wood & would** : 두 단어의 발음은 같습니다. 많은 분들이 단순히 '우드' 라고 발음합니다만, 실제 발음은 '우으드' 에 더 가깝습니다.
>
> **won't** : 'want'와 확실히 구분할 필요가 있습니다. 실제 발음은 [원트]가 아니라 [우오운트] 혹은 [워운트]에 가깝습니다. 비음(콧소리)를 섞어주면 더욱 좋습니다.

7. 발음 연습

> **woman** : '우먼'이 아니라 '워먼'임을 명심합시다. Task 2에서 매번 쓰게 되는 단어이니 주의합시다.
>
> **women** : 복수형은 예외적으로 '위민'이라고 발음합니다.

wood	would	wool
won't	want	wolf
woman	women	woven

\# mp3 파일을 들으면서 다음 문장을 따라 읽어보세요.

1. Would you ask the wolf what he wants?
2. Won't the woodchuck want to eat the wool of the wolf?
3. I would want to eat the wood if I were the wolf, but I know he won't.

C. 연음 (Liaison)

1. 기본 법칙 1

우리말과 마찬가지로 영어에도 자음동화와 같은 규칙이 존재합니다. 같은 종류의 자음이 붙어 이어진 경우, 두 번 발음하기 힘들기 때문에 뒤의 자음만 발음하게 됩니다.

1) **b - p**	subpoena	thumbprint	bombproof
2) **v - f**	sign of Virgo	citizen of Virginia	sights of Venice
3) **g - k**	hectic guys	frog king	thick gap
4) **th - s**	Months	paths	deaths
5) **d - t**	Don't do it.	midterm	good time

\# mp3 파일을 들으면서 다음 문장을 따라 읽어보세요.

1. The pet shop boys received a subpoena from the subpanel at court.
2. Citizens of Virginia arrived during the season of voting.
3. What does Stan suggest they do?

2. 기본 법칙 2

전 단어가 자음으로 끝나고 다음 단어가 모음으로 시작하는 상황에서는 다음과 같이 자음을 옮겨 읽는 것이 더 정확합니다.

| againsT all = agains Tall | hoPe everyone = ho Peveryone | asK others = as Kothers |

3. 언어의 경제성

미국영어에서는 water [워러]나 spaghetti [스파게리]처럼, [T] 발음을 제대로 하지 않고 넘기는 경우가 많습니다. 다음의 경우에는 'to' 를 [투]라고 발음하지 않습니다. (하지만, Writing에서는 옳지 않은 표현이니 주의합시다.)

want to (~하고 싶다) - [wanna]로 발음
going to (~할 예정이다) - [gonna]로 발음
have got to (~해야 한다) - [gotta]로 발음

 # mp3 파일을 들으면서 다음 문장을 따라 읽어보세요.
1. I want to know what you want.
2. Are you going to go to the party?
3. I have got to have that computer game.
4. Do you want to go catch a movie?
5. I am going to go get a bite to eat.

III. 기타 (Miscellaneous)

A. 띄어 읽기

문장을 어디서 끊을지는 읽는 사람의 호흡과 듣는 사람의 편의를 기준으로 결정됩니다. 띄어 읽기를 하는데 있어서 정해진 룰은 없지만, 일반적으로는 다음의 경우에 끊어 읽게 됩니다.
1. 쉼표
2. 접속사나 관계사 앞
3. 주어 앞의 부사구나 분사구문 뒤
4. 긴 부사구 앞

 # mp3 파일을 들으면서 다음 문장을 따라 읽어보세요.
1. I have decided to raise dust bunnies, thus, do not clean the dust and dirt under the drawers.
2. Delilah needs to get rid of the dirt on her computer disks for the disks to function in the drive.
3. There's nothing like waking up and walking through the water park with a dog wagging its tail.
4. Try not to get so defensive when being disciplined, because you probably brought it on yourself.
5. Let's leave him alone to review until he learns to accept himself, unless he directly asks for help.

B. 목소리

또박또박 높은 톤으로 천천히, 특히 남자분들은 목소리가 낮아서 더 신경 쓰셔야 합니다. 평소 목소리보다 훨씬 밝고 명랑하게 말해야 녹음본을 들을 때, 더 프로답게 들립니다. 동화 구연대회를 한다 생각하시면 되겠네요.

C. Q&A

Q: 60초 동안 말하라고 했는데 시간이 남았어요. (혹은 중간에 잘렸어요) 점수가 많이 깎일까요?
A: 일단 60초에 대해서는 걱정하지 않으셔도 됩니다. 시간보다 중요한 것은 내용입니다. 단, 내용을 다 전달하지 못했는데, 시간이 남았다거나 잘렸다면 감점요인입니다.

Q: Task 1에서 주어진 의견이 둘 다 좋다는 식으로 쓰면 안되나요?
A: 안됩니다! 주장은 언제나 확실하게 하세요. 아무리 두 의견이 다 좋아 보이고, 실제로 그렇게 생각하시더라도, 선택은 언제나 하나만 하셔야 합니다. 스스로가 특정회사의 영업사원이 됐다고 생각하세요. 영업하면서 우리회사 제품도 좋고, 경쟁회사 제품도 좋다고 하면, 판매실적을 올리기가 쉽지 않겠지요

USHER
iBT TOEFL
FINAL TEST SPEAKING
Strategies

반드시 유의하자!

1. 문제가 무엇을 원하는가?

발음이 좋아도 내용이 문제와 맞지 않으면 절대 고득점을 받을 수 없다.
아무리 익숙해져도 문제는 꼭 듣고 대답하자.

2. 평소에 연습한대로 발음하자.

열심히 발음 연습을 해놓고 실제 발표 때에는 원래의 엉터리 발음으로 돌아가는 경우가 허다하다. 수없이 반복하여 연습하고, 긴장하며 발표하자.

3. 단어와 강세에 유의하자.

발음보다 중요한게 강세이고, 강세를 지키지 않으면 억양도 엉망이 된다.
단어 끝에 굳이 "으" 발음을 해서 생기는 강세의 쏠림 현상에 유의하자.

4. 시간을 체크해가면서 발표하자.

말하는 데에 집중하다 보면 시계를 안 보게 되는 수가 있다.
마음 속으로 정한 시간에 맞춰 내용을 전개해야 체계적인 발표가 가능하다.

Independent Tasks

Task 1 - 설명 및 Sample 문제

Integrated Tasks

Task 2 - 설명 및 Sample 문제

Task 3 - 설명 및 Sample 문제

Task 4 - 설명 및 Sample 문제

Independent Task > Task 1 > 선택 말하기

Speaking about familiar topics - 익숙한 주제에 대해 말하기

- 주어진 문제에 동의 / 반대하거나, 2개의 선택 중 하나를 골라 그 이유를 서술하는 방식입니다.
- 답 → 이유 1 → 이유 2 의 순으로 답하는 것이 가장 이상적입니다.

Example Question

Do you prefer a friend who has the same thoughts or a friend who has different thoughts? Use reasons and examples to support your answer.

당신은 비슷한 생각을 가진 친구를 선호합니까, 아니면 다른 생각을 가진 친구를 선호합니까?
이유와 예를 들어 설명하세요.

A. You를 I로 바꾼다.
B. 의문문을 평서문으로 바꾼다.

Do **you** prefer a friend who has…?
→ **I** prefer a friend who has different thoughts because…

C. 근거를 2개정도 준비한다.
D. 근거에 대한 설명을 각각 준비한다.
E. **This is why + 주장**으로 마무리한다. (특히 시간이 남았을 경우)

Sample Response

(대 답)　**I prefer a friend who has different thoughts from mine.** I have two reasons.
(근거 1)　**First**, I love having healthy discussions with friends, over a cup of coffee or a pint of beer.
(설명 1)　Sometimes it can get pretty emotional, but it is part of the discussion I should take.
(근거 2)　**Next**, I can learn a lot from friends with different points of view while sharing ideas.
(설명 2)　It is quite surprising how much I can learn from friends with different knowledge and backgrounds.
(정 리)　(**This is why I prefer a friend who has different thoughts from mine.**)

모범 답안

(대 답)　**저는 제 생각과 다른 생각을 갖고 있는 친구를 선호합니다.** 이유는 두 가지 입니다.
(근거 1)　**첫째**, 저는 커피나 맥주를 한 잔 하면서 친구들과 토론하기를 아주 좋아합니다.
(설명 1)　가끔 꽤 감정적일 때도 있지만, 제가 감내해야 하는 토론의 일부지요.
(근거 2)　**다음**, 생각을 나누는 동안, 저는 다른 관점을 가진 친구들로부터 많은 것을 배울 수 있습니다.
(설명 2)　다른 지식과 배경을 가진 친구들로부터 얼마나 많이 배울 수 있는지 참으로 놀랍습니다.
(정 리)　(**이것이 제가 제 생각과 다른 생각을 갖고 있는 친구를 선호하는 이유입니다.**)

Integrated Task > Task 2 > 읽고 듣고 말하기 > 대학 생활   전략 ←

Speaking about campus situations - 캠퍼스 상황에 대해 말하기

[0] In this question, you will read a short passage, listen to a talk, and answer a question about them. After you hear the question, you will have 30 seconds to prepare a response, and 60 seconds to record the response.

이 문제에서, 당신은 짧은 글을 읽고, 대화를 듣고, 그에 대한 질문에 답할 것입니다.
문제를 들은 후, 당신에게는 답을 준비할 시간 30초, 그리고 답을 녹음할 시간 60초가 주어집니다.

[1] Reading

- 대학교 행정에 관련된 학교 측의 공지문, 또는 학생의 제안서 (길이: 100단어 이내)
- 내용을 기억할 수 있도록, 반드시 이해하고 note를 적도록 합니다.
- 지문의 길이에 따라 45~50초가 주어집니다.

[2] Listening

- 남녀 두 학생이 의견을 교환하는데, 둘 중 한 명이 반대 (혹은 찬성) 의견을 냅니다.
- 반대가 나올 가능성은 80%, 찬성이 나올 가능성은 20%
- 의견에 대한 근거는 항상 2개가 나옵니다.

[3] 답변 요령

Reading 요약 → 이유 1 → 이유 2 의 순으로 답하는 것이 가장 효율적인 방법입니다.
20초 + 20초 + 20초 = 60초 로 시간을 3등분하여 답하도록 하세요.

* 위의 답변 요령은 여러 방법들 중 하나일 뿐, 필수는 아님을 알려드립니다.

Template

문제 유형에 관련된 내용을 정형화하여, 한번 외우면 계속 편리하게 답할 수 있도록 만든, 일종의 "틀" 을 의미합니다.

The two students are discussing the college's plan / the open letter + that 절.
　　　　　　　　　　　학교의 공지 / 학생의 제안　　+ Reading 요약

The (wo)man is against / supporting the plan for two reasons.
　　　　　　반대 / 찬성

First (of all), (첫 번째 이유와 세부사항).

Second / Next, (두 번째 이유와 세부사항).
(This is why (s)he is **against / supporting** the plan.) → 시간이 남을 경우를 대비해 외워야 할 정리용 멘트

적용 → Vending Machines 자동 판매기

[1] Removal of Vending Machine

The University welcomes the Administrative Council's decision to remove all the vending machines that are currently on campus since there have been constant complaints regarding our commitment to maintain students' health and well-being. The machines may be convenient since students can use them whenever they want, but we will get rid of them for the sake of students' health. It is common knowledge that eating junk food is not good both health- and education-wise. Students are always welcome to go off-campus for extra food, and this shows that vending machines are unnecessary in the first place.

자동 판매기 설치

학생들의 건강과 웰빙을 유지하고자 하는 저희의 결심에 대한 지속적인 불평으로 인해 현재 대학교는 캠퍼스에 있는 모든 자동 판매기를 철거하자는 운영 위원회의 결정을 받아 들이기로 했습니다. 자판기는 학생들이 언제든지 사용할 수 있기 때문에 편리하지만, 학생들의 건강을 위해서 없앨 예정 입니다. 불량식품을 먹는 것이 건강과 교육적인 면에서 나쁘다는 것은 상식입니다. 학생들은 언제든지 캠퍼스 밖에서 사먹을 수 있고, 이는 애초에 자동판매기가 필요 없다는 것을 보여줍니다.

[2] Now listen to two students discussing the announcement.

W: Did you read the announcement about the vending machines on campus?
M: Yeah, and I think it's a great idea.
W: You think so? Well, I don't because they make it so easy to grab something to eat when I get hungry.
M: But the food you would be munching on is bad for your health.
W: But that's because they only sell junk food! If the vending machines were to be filled with healthy snacks, like mixed nuts or nutrition bars, they would be both convenient and healthy. The university should consider getting rid of the junk food, not the vending machines.
M: That's an idea. But without chips and candy bars in the machines, many students wouldn't probably even use the vending machines that much. If they want proper food, they can always go off-campus to get some!
W: Yeah, but the thing is, students never have time to go off-campus. Look, between classes, there's only so much time to get to the next class. So, even if we want good food, how are we supposed to go off-campus and eat during those few minutes? Also, students living on campus won't be able to go off-campus when dormitories lock their doors at ten.
M: Hmm, I guess you're right.
W: So, if the university actually gets rid of the vending machines, there will be a lot of students protesting.

The woman expresses her opinion about the college's plan. State her opinion and explain the reasons she gives for holding that opinion.

자, 이제 지문에 대해 논의하는 두 학생의 대화를 들어보세요.

여: 학교 자판기에 대한 공고 읽었어?
남: 응, 아주 멋진 아이디어라고 생각해.
여: 정말? 자판기 때문에 배고플 때 쉽게 먹을 수 있잖아. 그래서 나는 그렇게 생각하지 않아.
남: 근데 네가 먹을 음식들은 건강에 안 좋잖아.
여: 그건 학교 자판기들이 불량 식품만 팔아서야! 만약 자판기가 견과류나 영양바 같은걸 판다면, 자판기는 편리하기도 하고 건강에도 좋겠지. 학교는 자판기를 없애는 것보다 불량 식품을 없애는 걸 생각해야 돼.
남: 그것도 방법인데 과자나 캔디바 같은 걸 팔지 않으면 학생들이 자판기를 그렇게 많이 이용하지 않을 거야. 만약 건강에 좋은 음식을 원하면 캠퍼스 밖에서 사먹을 수 있으니까.
여: 그렇지, 근데 문제는 학생들이 캠퍼스 밖으로 나갈 시간이 없다는 것이지. 봐, 수업시간 사이에 다음 수업으로 갈 시간이 별로 없잖아. 그래서, 만약 우리가 좋은 음식을 먹으려고 해도, 그 짧은 시간 내에 어떻게 캠퍼스 밖으로 나가? 그리고, 기숙사에 사는 학생들은 기숙사가 열 시에 문을 잠그면 밖으로 나가지도 못하잖아.
남: 그건 네 말이 맞네.
여: 그래서, 만약 학교가 정말 자판기를 없애면, 반대 하는 학생들이 많을 거야.

여자는 대학의 계획에 대해 자신의 의견을 밝히고 있습니다. 그녀의 의견을 말하고, 그 의견을 고수 하는 이유를 설명하세요.

[3] Task 2 Sample Response

The two students are discussing the college's plan to remove the vending machines from the campus. **The woman is against the plan for two reasons**.

First, the vending machines are convenient. Even though they sell junk food, they make it easy to grab a snack. If the university is concerned about students' health, they should change the food, not the machines.

Next, there is not enough time for students to go off-campus for a meal. The machines are a good source of quick snacks, and students living in dormitories need the machines since they cannot go off-campus at night. (This is why she thinks the plan is unnecessary.)

2번 문제 모범답안

두 학생은 학교에 있는 자판기를 없애려는 **대학측의 계획에 대해서 의논하고 있다. 여자는 두 가지 이유를 들어 그 계획에 반대하고 있다.**

첫째, 자판기는 편리하다. 불량식품을 팔긴 하지만, 쉽게 먹을 수 있게 한다. 만약 대학 측이 학생건강을 걱정한다면, 자판기를 없앤다기보다 파는 음식을 바꿔야 한다.

다음, 학생들이 음식을 먹으려고 캠퍼스 밖으로 나갈 시간이 없다. 자판기는 간편한 간식을 제공하고, 기숙사에 사는 학생들은 밤에 나갈 수 없기 때문에 자판기가 필요하다. (이것이 그녀가 이 계획이 불필요하다고 생각하는 이유이다.)

USHER

Integrated Task > Task 3 > 읽고 듣고 말하기 > 대학 강의

← 전략

Speaking about academic course content - 학교 과목 내용에 대해 말하기

[0] In this question, you will read a short passage, listen to a talk, and answer a question about them. After you hear the question, you will have 30 seconds to prepare a response, and 60 seconds to record the response.

이 문제에서, 당신은 짧은 글을 읽고, 대화를 듣고, 그에 대한 질문에 답할 것입니다.
문제를 들은 후, 당신에게는 답을 준비할 시간 30초, 그리고 답을 녹음할 시간 60초가 주어집니다.

[1] Reading

사회, 경제, 심리, 생물 등의 분야 중 특정 이론에 대한 설명이 나온다. (길이: 100단어 이내)
- 문제가 시작되자 마자, 제목에 대한 정의(혹은 설명)를 찾아 종이에 옮겨 적습니다.
- 정해진 시간 동안 내용을 이해하지 못하더라도, 정의(혹은 설명)를 찾아 적는 것이 급선무입니다.

[2] Listening

Reading에서의 설명과 관련된 실제적인 예를 들어 이해를 돕습니다.
- 대체로 하나의 예가 나오지만, 두 개의 예가 나오기도 합니다.
- 하나의 예가 나오더라도, 대체로 중간 지점에 내용상의 전환점이 있습니다.

[3] 답변 요령

Reading 정의 → 예시 의 순으로 답하는 것이 가장 효율적인 방법입니다.
20초 + 40초 = 60초 로 시간을 나누어 답하도록 하세요.

* 위의 답변 요령은 여러 방법들 중 하나일 뿐, 필수는 아님을 알려드립니다.

Template

문제 유형에 관련된 내용을 정형화하여, 한번 외우면 계속 편리하게 답할 수 있도록 만든, 일종의 "틀" 을 의미합니다.

> **(주제) is** 주제에 대한 설명 또는 정의). **The professor gives an / two example(s) of** (예시 대상) **to explain it.**
>
> **First**, (첫 번째 예시).
>
> **Second / Next**, (두 번째 예시).

적용 → Self-Efficacy 자기 효험

[1] Self-Efficacy

Self-Efficacy refers to a person's belief in his/her abilities to produce information or perform tasks. The ability to develop self-efficacy is important for one's happiness and productivity, and it is related to the person's memories and his/her ability to utilize what he/she has learned and experienced. There are two methods to gain self-efficacy:

through master memory - to make use of the knowledge one has acquired. People may not consciously remember where they acquired this knowledge.

through social experiences - to make use of one's experiences interacting with others. People generally consciously remember where the experience came from.

자기 효험

자기 효험이란 사람이 자신의 능력을 믿고 정보를 만들어 내거나 업무를 해내는 것을 뜻한다. 자기효험을 개발하는 능력은 인간의 행복과 생산성에 중요한 역할을 하며, 인간의 기억과 배운 것을 이용하는 능력과 연관되어 있다. 자기 효험에는 두 가지 종류가 있다.

주요 기억을 통해 - 사람이 알고 있는 지식을 이용하는 것이다. 사람들은 지식을 배운 곳을 의식적으로 알지 못할 수도 있다.

사회 경험을 통해 - 다른 사람과 서로 교류하며 경험한 것을 이용하는 것이다. 사람들은 어떻게 그 경험을 하였는지 의식적으로 기억한다.

[2] Now listen to part of a lecture in a psychology class.

Well, I know these concepts are complicated, so let me clarify any confusion you may have. When you hear the word, Paris, if you were to use your master memory, you would recall the fact that it's the capital city of France, its population, history, main attractions, and all that. If you were to use your social experience, you would recall your trip to France, all the fun you had there with your family or friends. Still not enough?

Okay, let me give you some proper examples then. Hmm… let's say there's a teenage boy, talented in mathematics. He would try his best to take advantage of his knowledge and competence in math in order to get high scores on tests. He would be able to keep gaining self-efficacy and this in turn will drive his interest and make him study math harder. His knowledge of mathematics led him to gain greater self-efficacy.

In the case of social experiences, let's say, um, there's a girl who wants to be a pianist. But she is not sure whether she is good enough. If she has an older sister who already began learning how to play the piano, perhaps she can serve as her role model. Then, the girl can gain self-efficacy by watching her sister improving day by day and become confident enough to think that she could do just as well as her sister. In this case, her interaction with her sister led her to gain self-efficacy.

Using the example from the professor's lecture, explain what self-efficacy is and how it works.

심리학 강의의 일부를 들어보세요.

음, 이러한 개념이 복잡하단 걸 알아요, 그렇기에 여러분이 가질만한 궁금한 점들에 대해 설명해 주겠어요. '파리'라는 단어를 듣고 능숙하게 기억해 낸다면, 여러분은 파리가 프랑스의 수도이며, 그곳의 인구, 역사, 명소들을 떠올릴 거예요. 만약 사회 경험을 사용하려 한다면, 프랑스 여행과 여러분이 친구나 가족들과 가졌던 행복한 순간들을 떠올리겠죠. 충분하지 않나요?

좋아요, 제대로 된 예를 들지요. 음… 수학을 잘하는 소년이 있다고 가정합시다. 그는 최선을 다해 수학에 대한 지식과 능숙함을 이용하여 시험에서 좋은 결과를 내려 할 거예요. 그는 계속해서 자기 효험을 얻을 수 있을 것이고, 그것은 그가 더 흥미를 느끼고 공부를 더 열심히 할 수 있게 해줄 거예요. 수학에 대한 지식이 더 큰 자기 효험을 가질 수 있도록 한 거죠.

사회 경험의 경우, 음, 피아니스트가 되고픈 소녀가 있다 가정해 봅시다. 그녀는 그녀의 실력이 충분한지에 대한 확신이 없었어요. 만약 그녀에게 피아노를 먼저 배운 언니가 있다면, 그녀는 소녀의 롤 모델이 될 수 있겠지요. 그러면, 소녀는 그녀의 언니가 매일 실력이 느는 것을 보고 자신도 언니처럼 될 수 있다고 느끼며 자기 효험을 얻을 수 있게 돼요. 이런 상황에서는, 언니와의 관계가 자기효험을 얻을 수 있도록 도와주게 된 것이지요.

강의에서의 예를 들어, 자기 효험이 무엇이고 어떻게 작용하는지 설명하세요.

[3] Task 3 Sample Response

Self-efficacy is a person's belief in his or her own competence to produce information or perform tasks. The professor gives examples on two different ways to gain self-efficacy.

The first way is to use master memory, or one's own knowledge. If a student is good at math, he can use his knowledge and competence to get high scores on tests and become more confident in the subject.

Another way is to use social experiences, or one's interaction with others. If a girl wants to be a pianist, she can gain confidence by seeing her older sister getting better at playing the piano.

3번 문제 모범답안

자기 효험이란 인간이 정보를 만들어 내거나 업무를 처리할 때 가지는 자신에 대한 믿음이다. 교수는 두 가지의 다른 자기효험을 얻는 방법을 예로 들고 있다.

첫 번째 방법은 능숙한 기억 혹은 지식을 사용하는 것이다. 학생이 수학을 잘한다면, 그는 자신이 가진 지식과 능숙함으로 시험을 잘 보고 그 과목에 더 큰 자신감을 가질 수 있게 될 것이다.

다른 방법은 사회 경험, 또는 다른 사람과의 관계를 이용하는 것이다. 만약 한 소녀가 피아니스트가 되고 싶어 한다면, 그녀의 언니의 피아노 실력이 느는 것을 보면서 자신감을 얻을 수 있다.

Integrated Task > Task 4 > 듣고 말하기 > 대학 강의

전략 ←

[0] In this question, you will listen to part of a lecture and answer a question about it.
After you hear the question, you will have 20 seconds to prepare a response, and 60 seconds to record the response.

이 문제에서, 당신은 강의의 일부를 듣고, 그에 대한 질문에 답할 것입니다. 문제를 들은 후, 당신에게는 답을 준비할 시간 20초, 그리고 답을 녹음할 시간 60초가 주어집니다.

[1] Listening

교수가 특정 주제에 대해 두 가지 예를 들어 설명한다.
- 문제유형은 아주 간단합니다. 들은 내용을 그대로 요약하면 됩니다.

[2] 답변 요령

주제 → 예시 1 → 예시 2 의 순으로 답하는 것이 가장 효율적인 방법입니다.
20초 + 20초 + 20초 = 60초로 시간을 3등분하여 답하도록 하세요.

* 위의 답변요령은 여러 방법들 중 하나일 뿐, 필수는 아님을 알려드립니다.

Template

문제 유형에 관련된 내용을 정형화하여, 한번 외우면 계속 편리하게 답할 수 있도록 만든, 일종의 "틀"을 의미합니다.

> **In the lecture, the professor gives two examples of** (주제).
>
> **First**, (첫 번째 예시).
>
> **Second / Next**, (두 번째 예시).

적용 → **Roman Empire** 로마제국

[1] Listen to part of a lecture in a history class.

I'm pretty sure you all know the greatness of the Roman Empire already. The Romans created one of the biggest empires in the historic world. You all know the saying, "All roads lead to Rome." right? Well, that's how huge the Roman Empire was. In fact, most of Europe was under their rule and the Romans even reached lands as far as Asia and Africa. But how did one lone city-state, Rome, develop into one of the greatest empires in the world? I mean, no other ancient city-state was able to do it, right? So there must have been a reason why this was possible. Let's take a look at a few reasons.

The biggest reason for the Roman's success was technology. Roman technology was the most advanced of its time. It may surprise you that the Romans were one of the first people to develop and use concrete. This brought about the 'Roman Architectural Revolution' and is why the construction of the renowned Roman arches, vaults and domes was possible. Concrete was used to build most of the Roman architectural structures. Amongst these structures, bridges were the most noticeable. The Roman bridges were the first large and lasting bridges because they were built using stone and concrete and had a stable arch as their basic structure. These bridges connected the vast lands of Rome into one.

The second reason for their success was the supply of drinking water. This was possible because of the aqueducts. I'm sure you've all heard about these aqueducts already, but you must keep one thing in mind. You shouldn't confuse them with arches because most of the aqueducts were built underground. By doing so, the water was free from diseases because human waste was not able to get into the aqueducts, and they could be protected from enemy attacks. Large amounts of fresh water were brought from the mountains, so the Romans always had plenty of water to drink and keep healthy. In fact, they had enough water to provide public baths and fountains.

Using the examples from the professor's lecture, explain why the Roman Empire was so successful.

역사학 강의의 일부를 들어보세요.

저는 여러분 모두 로마 제국의 위대함에 대해서 이미 알고 있으리라 확신합니다. 로마인들은 세계 역사상 가장 큰 제국 중 하나를 이뤘냈습니다. 여러분 모두 "모든 길은 로마로 통한다" 라는 말 아시죠? 음, 그것이 로마 제국이 얼마나 컸는지 알려줍니다. 사실상, 대부분의 유럽은 그들의 지배하에 있었고, 로마인들은 심지어 아시아와 아프리카 같이 먼 나라들에도 도달했습니다. 하지만 어떻게 로마, 이 하나의 도시국가가 세계에서 가장 큰 제국 중 하나로 발전할 수 있었을까요? 다시 말하자면, 그 어느 고대의 도시국가도 할 수 없었죠, 그렇죠? 그래서 이것이 가능하게 된 이유가 반드시 있을 것입니다. 몇 가지 예를 들어봅시다.

로마의 성공의 가장 큰 이유는 기술입니다. 로마 기술은 당대에 가장 앞선 것이었습니다. 로마인들이 처음으로 콘크리트를 개발하고 사용한 사람들 중 하나라는 것이 여러분들에게 놀라울 수 있습니다. 이것은 '로마 건축 혁명'을 불러왔고, 이것이 로마의 유명한 아치 구조물, 반구형 천장과 반구형 돔의 건축이 가능한 이유였습니다. 콘크리트는 대부분의 로마 건축학의 구조물들을 건축하는데 쓰여졌습니다. 이 구조물들 중에는, 다리가 가장 돋보였습니다. 로마의 다리는 돌과 콘크리트를 사용해서 지어졌고, 기초 구조로써 안정적인 아치를 사용했기 때문에 처음으로 크고 견고한 다리였습니다. 이 다리들은 로마의 넓은 땅들을 하나로 연결시켜 주었습니다.

그들의 성공의 두 번째 이유는 식수의 공급이었습니다. 이것은 송수로 덕분에 가능한 일이었습니다. 저는 여러분 모두 이 송수로에 대해 이미 들어봤으리라 확신하지만 여러분이 염두에 두어야 할 것이 하나 있습니다. 대부분의 송수로는 지하에 건설되었기 때문에 여러분은 이를 아치형 구조와 혼동하면 안됩니다. 그렇게 함으로써, 사람의 폐수가 송수로에 들어가지 못해 그 안의 물은 질병으로부터 자유로웠고, 적의 공격으로부터 보호 받을 수 있었습니다. 많은 양의 신선한 물이 산으로부터 운송되어서 로마인들은 항상 마실 물이 많았고 건강을 유지했습니다. 사실, 그들은 공중 목욕탕과 분수를 만들 정도로 물이 넉넉하게 있었습니다.

강의에서의 예를 들어, 로마 제국이 왜 성공할 수 있었는지 그 이유를 설명하세요.

[2] Task 4 Sample Response

In the lecture, the professor gives two reasons why the Roman Empire was so successful.

First, the Romans' technology was far more advanced than that of others. They were the first people to make and use concrete and the use of concrete made construction of arches possible. The use of arches made construction of large structures such as bridges possible, and the bridges connected all the roads to Rome.

Second, the Romans could get clean water through underground aqueducts. Since waste matter couldn't reach them, they stayed clean. Also, they were protected from enemies, so the Romans had enough water to stay healthy.

4번 문제 모범답안

강의에서 교수는 로마 제국이 왜 성공적 이었는지에 대한 **두 예**를 들고 있습니다.

첫 번째로, 로마인들의 기술력은 다른 이들에 비해 훨씬 앞서 있었습니다. 그들은 처음으로 콘크리트를 만들고 사용한 사람들이었고, 콘크리트의 사용은 아치 구조물의 건축을 가능하게 만들었습니다. 아치의 사용은 다리와 같은 큰 건축물들의 건축을 가능하게 만들었고, 다리들은 모든 길들을 로마로 연결되었습니다.

두 번째로, 로마인들은 지하 송수로를 통해서 깨끗한 물을 얻을 수 있었습니다. 노폐물들이 닿을 수 없었기 때문에, 그것은 깨끗하게 유지되었습니다. 또한, 적들로부터 보호되었기 때문에 로마인은 건강을 유지할 만큼 풍족한 물이 있었습니다.

USHER
iBT TOEFL
FINAL TEST SPEAKING
TEST 01

Independent Tasks

Task 1 - 모범 답안
Question 1　usherin.usher.co.kr > 시험리스트 > Speaking 시험리스트 > Task 1 > #1027

Integrated Tasks

Task 2 - Script / 해석 / 모범 답안
Question 2　usherin.usher.co.kr > 시험리스트 > Speaking 시험리스트 > Task 2 > #2001

Task 3 - Script / 해석 / 모범 답안
Question 3　usherin.usher.co.kr > 시험리스트 > Speaking 시험리스트 > Task 3 > #3001

Task 4 - Script / 해석 / 모범 답안
Question 4　usherin.usher.co.kr > 시험리스트 > Speaking 시험리스트 > Task 4 > #4001

자기평가표

1번 문제 유형은 학생들이 본인에 생각을 주제에 맞춰서 말 해야하는 시험입니다.
본인이 처음부터 끝까지 45초 동안 말해야하다 보니 학생들이 제일 어려워 하는 시험입니다.
하지만, 먼저 외우고 익힌후에 말하는것이 가능할수 있게 하겠습니다.
가장 기본이 되는 뼈대 입니다. 먼저 외우도록 합시다.

> if i were to answer the question, i would say
> there are many reasons why, but here is a couple
> first
> for example,
> second
> for instance
> that's why

다음은 2번 문제 유형입니다.
2번 문제는 리딩에 학교에 계획이 적혀있거나 학교가 변해야하는 방향에 대해서 학생들에 주장이 적혀있습니다.
리딩에서 빠르게 파악해야하는 것은 도대체 누가 무엇을 주장하는가 입니다.
45~50초에 리딩 지문이 나오고 난 다음에 리스닝으로 학생들에 대화가 나오는 문제입니다.
리스닝에서는 학생이 리딩 지문에 대한 본인에 좋고 나쁜지에 대한 의견을 얘기해줄겁니다.
이유 2가지와 예시 2가지를 꼭 말할 수 있어야 합니다.

이에 따라서 2번 스피킹 문제에 뼈대는

> The reading states that university (plans to) / (should)
> the (woman / man) in the conversation thinks it is a good / bad idea.
> He/she provides two reasons to support his / her opinion.
> first,
> Second,
> the woman / man thinks it's a great / horrible idea.

다음은 3번 문제 유형입니다.
3번 문제는 2번 문제 유형과 같이 리딩과 리스닝이 나오는 문제 입니다. 하지만, 이번에는 이전 문제와는 달리 매우 학술적인 내용이 들어 있습니다. 리딩에서는 교과서에 나올만한 주제 한개를 자세하게 다룹니다. 여기서 학생분들은 제목과 이에 대한 정의를 잘 받아적으셔야 합니다. 리스닝에서는 교수님이 리딩에 나온 내용으로 예시를 들어 줍니다.

> The article is about
> which the passage defines as
> The professor provides an example of
> first,
> Second,
> The example clearly illustrates

다음은 4번 문제 유형입니다.
4번 문제는 이전 문제와 달리 리스닝만 나오는 문제 유형입니다. 3번 문제에 나온 리딩 지문이 리스닝으로 변환되었다 라고 생각 하시면 됩니다. 그렇기에 3번 문제에 리스닝 내용보다 리딩 길이 만큼 깁니다.

> In the lecture, professor explains
> first,
> second,
> That's how the professor explain it.

USHER

01. Field Trip vs Classroom 견학 vs 교실 — Independent Task

QUESTION

 Some people say that It is better for children to go on a field trip. Others say that It is better for them to study in classroom. Which view do you agree with? Use reasons and examples to support your answer.
(아이들에게 어느 것이 더 좋을까요: 견학 가기 vs 교실에서 공부하기? 이유와 예를 들어 답하세요)

 브레인 스토밍 (아래에 놓여있는 12간지 내용들을 보고 어떤 것을 사용할 수 있을지 확인해보세요)
첫번째 이유 :
두번째 이유 :

 뼈대에 맞춰서 작성을 해봅시다.

_____
_____
_____
_____
_____
_____
_____

아래 이미지는 학생들을 위한 만능 템플릿 12간지 입니다. 학생분들이 제일 먼저 암기해야하는 것이며, 본인 스스로 문장을 단기간 안에 못 만들거 같을 때에 도와주는 친구입니다. 가까이 두고 매일 외우세요.

Academic Courses
...because I think students should concentrate on academic courses.

Academic courses are the most important thing for students because good grades will help them get into good universities and, eventually, get great jobs.

As students get older, a good academic record is the only thing that actually matters.

This may sound a little far-fetched, but it's true, and for this reason, investing time in other activities is a waste of time.

Stay Healthy
It can be a great way to stay healthy. People join a cycling group through the internet. The members use bicycles to commute to work or school.

It is a great outdoor activity because people have a chance to work out while having fun.

Also, it is a great way to meet new people with similar interests. People nowadays do not have much chance to become close to each other.

However, there are numerous unique groups active on the internet, and this would not have been possible without the internet.

Follows your heart
Carpe diem, seize the days, and YOLO all stand for one thing. Do whatever your heart makes you do.

Life is too short to hesitate or do things to please others. It is essential to make yourself happy.

Actions speak louder than words. Whatever I do to make myself happy is better than sitting in a room thinking about it.

So I would just do it even if it means I am biting off something more than I can chew.

Stress
...if it can possibly be a way to relieve stress.

People nowadays are living a busy and hectic life, so they are under great stress, but a lot of them don't even realize they are stressed out.

Stress is known to be a major factor that keeps us from being healthy, and many people are suffering from various problems.

This is more serious than we think, so if it can ever be a way to relieve stress...

Money
...because it's the best way to save money. When it comes to spending money, every penny counts.

A thrifty spending habit is indispensable in our lives because little drops of water make the mighty ocean.

If we don't get used to working on a tight budget, we'll always be short on cash later.

A penny-pinching lifestyle will lead to financial stability, and it will give us peace of mind.

Saving Time
...because it's the best way to save time. There's an old saying, "Time is gold."

This proverb emphasizes the value of time, and this cannot be more true in modern society.

We're living a busy and hectic life, so saving time means we can do a lot more things later.

Many say that life is not fair, but everyone has twenty-four hours a day and seven days a week, so I would save time by...

Social Skills
Nowadays, people have smartphones with them all the time, and that information is no longer limited to elites.

Therefore, rather than learning, having social skills became the be-all and end-all to succeed rather than education.

Also, social skills are more than meet the eyes. To have social skills, one must also be able to read others like a book.

There will be times when one will truly need them.

Environment
because eventually, it can contribute to protecting the environment.

I think it's THE most important task for humanity because we cannot bring it back to life once it's too late.

Saving Earth all starts from seemingly insignificant actions.

Small actions from everyone bring about bigger changes, so I'm willing to participate.

Patience is virtue
Patience is a virtue. Saving time is indeed important, but waiting calmly is needed in this case.

There are times when one must wait patiently for things to go accordingly, and this is when time is the solution.

When going against the clock, they are more susceptible to making mistakes than taking some time.

In the long run, one will be glad that one has waited in this case.

Just because
I love it more than the given choices. Since I have so many great memory about it, It brings so many great reminiscences.

time flies whenever I am doing it, so how can I not choose it?

Also, not only do I love it, but I am also good at it. Everyone has talent, and it is like "a dime a dozen."

This was the inborn talent I had that I always surpassed everyone. Since a bird in the hand is worth two in the bush, I will choose it.

Politeness
It is important to maintain good relationships with other people because we never know what will happen in the future.

Decisions made by other people can affect others, and such decisions are usually based on personal and sentimental reasons.

So, people should not do anything that may offend or disturb others. It is also crucial to have a good reputation and get along well with others.

It Makes sense
It makes sense to choose it when considering many aspects such as time, money, and efficiency.

When people are considering between the given choices, they must consider many aspects economically.

They must choose the most efficient method because there are limits on what they have.

Also, one should think about it realistically and practically because they should not count chickens before they hatch.

So, down to Earth, people should choose it because it is the most economical

QUESTION

Some people say that It is better for children to go on a field trip. Others say that It is better for them to study in classroom. Which view do you agree with? Use reasons and examples to support your answer.
(아이들에게 어느 것이 더 좋을까요: 견학 가기 vs 교실에서 공부하기? 이유와 예를 들어 답하세요)

stress와 stay healthy 를 사용해서 뼈대에 맞춰서 모범답안을 만들어 봅시다.

time과 makes sense를 사용해서 뼈대에 맞춰서 모범답안을 만들어 봅시다.

social skills와 just because를 사용해서 뼈대에 맞춰서 모범답안을 만들어 봅시다.

academic courses와 save money를 사용해서 뼈대에 맞춰서 모범답안을 만들어 봅시다.

QUESTION

Some people say that It is better for children to go on a field trip. Others say that It is better for them to study in classroom. Which view do you agree with? Use reasons and examples to support your answer.
(아이들에게 어느 것이 더 좋을까요: 견학 가기 vs 교실에서 공부하기? 이유와 예를 들어 답하세요)

stress와 stay healthy 를 사용해서 뼈대에 맞춰서 모범답안을 만들어 봅시다.

If I were to answer the question, I would say they should go on a field trip. There are many reasons why, but here is a couple.

stress

First, it can be a way to relieve stress. For example, children nowadays are living a busy and hectic life, so they are under great stress. It is more dangerous than we think, so if it can be a way to relieve the stress they should go.

stay healthy

Second, it can be a great way to work out for children. For instance, it is a great outdoor activity because children have a chance to work out while having fun. That's why I think they should be able to go on a field trip.

time과 makes sense를 사용해서 뼈대에 맞춰서 모범답안을 만들어 봅시다.

If I were to answer the question, I would say children should not go on a field trip. There are many reasons why, but here is a couple.

time

First, it can be a way to save time. For example, students are living a busy and hectic life, so saving time means they can do a lot more studying.

makes sense

Second, it makes sense to not go when considering many aspects such as time, money, and efficiency. For instance, when people are considering between given choices, they must consider many aspects economically. This makes perfect sense.
That's why I think children should just stay in the classroom and study.

social skills와 just because를 사용해서 뼈대에 맞춰서 모범답안을 만들어 봅시다.

If I were to answer the question, children should go on a field trip. There are many reasons why, but here is a couple.

social skills

First, children can develop social skills by going on a field trip. For example, information is no longer limited because of smartphones. Therefore, rather than learning in the classroom, having social skills become a be-all and end-all to succeed.

just because

Second, it can be a great memory for children. For instance, going on field trips will bring so many great reminiscences when they grow up.
That's why I think they should go on a field trip.

academic courses와 save money를 사용해서 뼈대에 맞춰서 모범답안을 만들어 봅시다.

If I were to answer the question, I would say they should study in a classroom. there are many reasons why, but here is a couple.

academic courses

first, I think students should concentrate on academic courses instead of going on a field trip. for example, academic courses are the most important thing for students because good grades will help them get into good universities and eventually get great jobs.

save money

second, it can be a way to save money. for instance, when it comes to spending money on children, every penny counts. a penny-pinching lifestyle will lead to financial stability when parents are old.
that's why I think children should just stay in the classroom.

02. Dance Classes 댄스 수업 — Integrated Task

읽기 지문

Dance Classes

There will soon be dance classes offered on campus. We are aware of the fact that university students are always busy taking classes and may not have any extra time to find a way to exercise off campus. Therefore, students can now attend all of their classes, and **relieve** their **stress** by exercising, and then leave campus feeling refreshed. The dance classes are open to anyone with an open mind ready to learn. Even better, the first class is offered for free so students can **get a taste of** what the classes will be like. **Do not hesitate to** try out the class.

대화 스크립트

 STEP 01 뼈대를 먼저 작성해 보도록 하겠습니다.

 STEP 02 작성하신 뼈대 빈칸에 맞춰서 리딩 지문을 읽고 주요 포인트를 넣어주세요.

 STEP 03 하단에 리스닝 노트테이킹을 해주세요. 음원은 학원 홈페이지에서 무료로 다운받으실 수 있습니다. 또한 2001번 문제 번호로 문제를 풀어보실 수 있습니다.

STEP 04
아래 하단에 리스닝 스크립트를 보고 베꼈어야 하는 부분을 찾아서 적어 보도록 하겠습니다.

대화 스크립트

🎧 뉴토플 - TEST 01_Q2

Now listen to two students discussing the announcement.

M: Hey, did you read the school's announcement about open dance classes?
W: Yeah, I think it's a fantastic idea.

여자의 의견 — 찬성

M: Really? Why?
W: Well, right now, I try to go jogging **by myself on a daily basis**. I really like exercising, but it's hard to keep exercising when I'm doing it alone. It gets really boring, so I **end up skipping it**. This is really bad since exercise is so good for you. By attending a dance class, I would be exercising **on a regular basis** with other students. It'll not only be fun, but also be a good way to make friends.

이유 ❶ — 정기적으로 운동할 수 있다

M: Yeah, you're right. Since it's held on campus, it'll probably be really convenient, too.
W: Yeah, and do you know what the best part is?
M: What?
W: The first class is free!
M: Really? I don't think I read that part…
W: Yeah, the first class is apparently completely free of charge. That means I can try out the class and decide for myself whether it'll be worth the money or not. I mean, if they're offering to make the first class free, they've got to be confident about it, right? If I try the class out and end up not liking it, I won't be losing anything, right? It's **a win-win situation**. Hey, you should come with me! Try it out.

이유 ❷ — 첫 수업이 무료라 잃을 게 없음

M: Yeah… I'll think about it.

문제 — The woman expresses her opinion about the college's plan. State her opinion and explain the reasons she gives for holding that opinion.

자, 이제 지문에 대해 논의하는 두 학생의 대화를 들어보세요.

남: 야, 개설된 댄스 수업에 대해 읽어봤어?

여: 응, 아주 멋진 아이디어라 생각해.

남: 진짜? 왜?

여: 지금 난 **매일 혼자서** 조깅을 하려고 해. 운동하는 것은 좋아하지만, 혼자서 하게 되면 계속하기 힘들어. 지루해서 **건너뛰어버리고 말지**. 운동은 좋은 거니까 이러면 안 되는데. 댄스 수업을 들으면, 다른 학생들과 **정기적으로** 운동하게 될 거야. 재미있기도 하겠지만, 친구들도 많이 생길 거야.

남: 그래, 네가 맞아. 캠퍼스에서 하니까, 편리하기도 할거야.

여: 맞아, 그리고 뭐가 짱인줄 알아?

남: 뭔데?

여: 첫 수업은 공짜라는 것!

남: 진짜? 그 부분은 안 읽은 것 같은데.

여: 응, 첫 수업은 완전히 공짜인가 봐. 수업료가 그 값어치를 할지 안 할지를 결정하기 위해서 첫 수업을 들어볼 수 있다는 말이지. 첫 수업이 무료라면, 그만큼 자신 있다는 얘기 아니겠어? 수업 들어봐서 맘에 안 들어도, 잃을게 없잖아, 그렇지? **밑져야 본전**이지. 나랑 같이 가자!

남: 그렇네. 생각해보고.

여자는 대학의 계획에 대해 자신의 의견을 밝히고 있습니다. 그녀의 의견을 말하고, 그 의견을 고수하는 이유를 설명하세요.

STEP 05 Note-taking

STEP 06 다시한번 모범 답안을 작성해 보도록 하겠습니다

Dance Classes

There will soon be dance classes offered on campus. We are aware of the fact that university students are always busy taking classes and may not have any extra time to find a way to exercise off campus. Therefore, students can now attend all of their classes, and **relieve** their **stress** by exercising, and then leave campus feeling refreshed. The dance classes are open to anyone with an open mind ready to learn. Even better, the first class is offered for free so students can **get a taste of** what the classes will be like. **Do not hesitate to** try out the class.

Note-taking	노트테이킹
Reading - dance classes will be available - help students exercise - the first class is free **Woman** - supporting **Reason ❶** - will help to exercise regularly - can meet with other students **Reason ❷** - the first class is free of charge - the college must be confident with the class	**지문** - 댄스 수업이 열릴 것 - 학생들이 운동하는데 도움 - 첫 수업은 무료 **여자** - 찬성 **이유 ❶** - 정기적으로 운동하는데 도움 - 다른 학생들을 만날 수 있음 **이유 ❷** - 첫 수업은 무료 - 학교 측은 자신 있는 것이 분명함

Task 2 Sample Response 🎧 뉴토플 - TEST 01_R2 | 2번 문제 모범 답안

The two students are discússing the college's plan to open dance classes to help students exercise and reláx. The woman is suppórting the plan for two reasons.

❶ First, dance classes would be good for students since it would help them **work out** regularly. Plus, it would be fun since other students could **take part**.

❷ Next, the first class is **free of charge**, so she has nothing to lose. Since the first class is free, it can be seen that the univérsity has confidence in the class. If she is not happy with the class, she can simply **drop** the class and lose nothing. (This is why she thinks the plan is necessary.)

두 학생은 학생들이 운동하고 긴장을 풀 수 있도록 댄스 반을 열려는 대학 측의 계획에 대해서 의논하고 있다. 여자는 두 가지 이유를 들어 그 계획에 찬성하고 있다.

❶ 첫째, 댄스 반은 정기적으로 **운동하도록** 도와주기 때문에 학생들에게 좋을 것이다. 게다가 다른 학생들도 **참여하기** 때문에 재미있을 것이다.

❷ 다음, 첫 수업이 **무료**이기 때문에, 잃을게 없다. 첫 수업이 무료이기 때문에, 대학 측이 자신 있어 한다고 볼 수 있다. 수업이 마음에 안들면, **수업을 취소**해도 잃을 것이 없다. (이것이 그녀가 이 계획이 필요하다고 생각하는 이유이다.)

Vocabulary

relieve stress	phr. 스트레스를 풀다	get a taste of	phr. ~을 맛보다
do not hesitate to	phr. ~하기를 망설이지 말라	on a daily basis	phr. 매일 (= daily, everyday)
end up ~ing	phr. ~해버리고 말다	on a regular basis	phr. 정기적으로 (= regularly)
free of charge	phr. 가격이 무료	a win-win situation	phr. 서로 좋은 상황

03. Plants in Rainforests 열대 우림의 식물들

Integrated Task

읽기 지문

Plant Adaptations in Rainforests

A typical rainforest has a warm, humid environment with abundant oxygen-producing tall trees. It has a high yearly rainfall that supports millions of plants, animals, and microorganism species around the world. 70% of the species that are living in rainforest are trees which resemble one another in some ways. Because the tall trees prevent the sunlight from **penetrating** the bottom layers of the rainforest, there is always a lack of sunlight there. Due to this fact, rainforest plants usually have large leaves and structures to collect the most sunlight and protect them from the **excessive** amount of water.

대화 스크립트

 STEP 01 뼈대를 먼저 작성해 보도록 하겠습니다.

 STEP 02 작성하신 뼈대 빈칸에 맞춰서 리딩 지문을 읽고 주요 포인트를 넣어주세요.

 STEP 03 하단에 리스닝 노트테이킹을 해주세요. 음원은 학원 홈페이지에서 무료로 다운받으실 수 있습니다. 또한 3001번 문제 번호로 문제를 풀어보실 수 있습니다.

 아래 하단에 리스닝 스크립트를 보고 베꼈어야 하는 부분을 찾아서 적어 보도록 하겠습니다.

대화 스크립트

🎧 뉴토플 - TEST 01_Q3

Now listen to part of a lecture in an ecology class.

이제 생태학 수업의 일부를 들어보세요.

As I mentioned in the earlier class, the rainforests support millions of species, especially plant species. Rainforests, unlike what everyone believes, have, conditions that are somewhat not very favorable to plants. Therefore, many plants, such as urn plants, have adapted to their particular rainforest climate.

전 시간에 말했듯이, 열대 우림은 수백만 종의 생물들, 특히 식물들을 지탱합니다. 모두가 믿는 바와 달리, 열대 우림은 식물들에게 그렇게 좋지만은 않는 조건을 갖추고 있습니다. 그래서 urn plant(아나나스)와 같은 많은 식물들은, 열대의 기후에 적응했습니다.

예시 ❶
잎의 배열

세부사항
잎의 배열이 물 저장하는데 도움이 됨

Urn plants are about 60cm tall with stiff green-grey spiny leaves. The most **distinctive** characteristic of urn plants is the presence of a hole in the middle of the ring-shaped **arrangement** of their leaves. Deriving their name from this arrangement, which looks like an urn, urn plants can store rainwater in the wild for a long time. Although rainforests have **abundant** sources of water, this unique shape directs the water directly to the root, making the branches and leaves less likely to break.

Urn plant(아나나스)는 높이가 60cm정도 이고, 가시가 있는 두꺼운 회녹색 잎들을 가지고 있습니다. Urn plant(아나나스)의 가장 **두드러진** 점은, 링 모양으로 **배열**되어 있는 잎들 한 가운데에 있는 구멍입니다. **항아리**처럼 보이는 이 배열에서 이름을 딴 이 식물은, 야생에서 긴 시간 동안 물을 저장할 수 있습니다. 열대 우림에는 물이 **많지만**, 이 특이한 모양은 물을 곧장 뿌리로 모이게 해서 가지나 잎이 부러지는 것을 막습니다.

예시 ❷
짙은 색깔

세부사항
짙은 색깔이 많은 양의 햇빛을 흡수

Not only that, their dark coloration and the spiral arrangement of their leaves allow the plants to absorb as much sunlight as possible from their environment. This in turn allows the urn plants to undergo **photosynthesis**, allowing them to survive and **sustain** the overall rainforest ecosystem.

그 뿐만 아니라, 짙은 색깔과 잎들의 나사형 배열은 환경으로부터 가능한 한 많은 햇빛을 흡수할 수 있도록 합니다. 이는 urn plant(아나나스)가 **광합성**을 하도록 돕고, 열대 우림에서 살아남고 열대 우림 생태계를 **유지시켜** 줍니다.

문제

Using the examples from the professor's lecture, explain how plants in rainforests ensure their survival.

교수의 강의를 예로들어, 열대 우림에서 식물들이 어떻게 살아남는지 설명하세요.

STEP 05 다시한번 음원듣고 노트테이킹 해보도록 하겠습니다.
Note-taking

STEP 06 다시 한번 뼈대와 함께 모범 답안을 작성해 보도록 하겠습니다.

Plant Adaptations in Rainforests

A typical rainforest has a warm, humid environment with abundant oxygen-producing tall trees. It has a high yearly rainfall that supports millions of plants, animals, and microorganism species around the world. 70% of the species that are living in rainforest are trees which resemble one another in some ways. Because the tall trees prevent the sunlight from **penetrating** the bottom layers of the rainforest, there is always a lack of sunlight there. Due to this fact, rainforest plants usually have large leaves and structures to collect the most sunlight and protect them from the **excessive** amount of water.

References

Photo by Paul & Aline Burland, available under the Creative Commons Attribution-Share Alike 2.0 Generic license.

[참고자료]

아나나스
Urn Plant
(Aechmea Fasciata)

- 브라질 북부 원산의 파인애플과 외떡잎 식물.

꽃 밑에 있는 잎에 비가 내리면 중앙부로 물이 흘러 들어가는 구조로 되어있다.

Task 3 Sample Response 뉴토플 - TEST 01_R3   3번 문제 모범 답안

Plants in rainforests have adápted to their envíronment by being able to absórb large amóunt of sunlight and protéct themsélves from excéssive amóunt of water. In the lecture, the proféssor gives the exámple of urn plants to expláin it.

❶ First, urn plants have a hole in the middle of the ring-shaped arrángement of their leaves. This allows the urn plant to store water for a long period of time. This structure also enábles water to reach the roots directly, redúcing damages to the branches and leaves.

❷ Next, the dark color and spiral arrángement of leaves also help urn plants to survíve by absórbing large amóunts of sunlight.

열대 우림에서 식물들은 많은 양의 햇빛을 흡수하고 지나친 양의 물로부터 스스로를 보호할 수 있게 됨으로써 환경에 적응해왔다. 강의에서, 교수는 이를 설명하기 위해 아나나스(Urn Plant)를 예로 들고 있다.

❶ 첫째, 아나나스는 링 모양으로 배열된 잎들 한가운데에 구멍이 나있다. 이는 **오랫동안** 물을 저장할 수 있도록 한다. 이 구조는 물이 뿌리로 직접 닿게 함으로써 가지와 잎을 보호할 수 있게 한다.

❷ 다음으로, 짙은 색과 나선형 배열의 잎들은 많은 양의 햇빛을 흡수하여 생존을 돕는다.

Vocabulary

abundant [əbʌ́ndənt]	a. 충분한, 많은	penetrate [pénətrèit]	v. ~을 관통하다
urn [əːrn]	n. 항아리	distinctive [distíŋktiv]	a. 구분되는
excessive [iksésiv]	a. 지나친, 과한	arrangement [əréindʒmənt]	n. 배열
photosynthesis [fòutəsínθəsis]	n. 광합성	sustain [səstéin]	v. 떠받치다, 지탱하다

04. Animals in High Altitudes 고도의 동물들 — Integrated Task

STEP 01 4번 뼈대를 먼저 작성해 보도록 하겠습니다.

STEP 02 하단에 리스닝 노트테이킹을 해주세요. 음원은 학원 홈페이지에서 무료로 다운받으실 수 있습니다. 또한 4001번 문제 번호로 문제를 풀어보실 수 있습니다.

STEP 03 뼈대에 맞춰서 모범 답안을 완성해 보겠습니다.

대화 스크립트

 뉴토플 - TEST 01_Q4

Listen to part of a lecture in a zoology class.

동물학 강의의 일부를 들어보세요.

주제
동물들이 높은 고도에서 살아남는 법

Although the mountain ranges of North America are **well known for** their majestic beauty, they are also pretty hazardous places to live for wild animals. The mountain range peaks at over 4,000 meters, and at that height the ground is constantly covered with snow and ice. The mountains are quite steep and prone to unpredictable weather patterns with a lot of **precipitation**. But some animals have evolved some interesting features to help them survive in such extreme conditions.

북미의 산악지대는 웅장한 아름다움으로 널리 **알려져 있지만**, 야생동물에게는 살기에 꽤 위험한 곳이기도 하다. 산맥의 정상은 4000미터가 넘고, 그 높이면 땅은 내내 눈과 얼음으로 덮여있다. 산맥은 꽤 가파르고 **강수량이** 높은 예측 불가능한 날씨에 노출되어 있다. 하지만 어떤 동물들은 그런 가혹한 조건에서도 살아남을 수 있도록 흥미로운 특징을 진화시켜왔다.

예시 ❶
야생염소는 두꺼운 모피로 추위를 견딤

One of the biggest animals that lives there is the mountain goat. They are protected from the harsh weather by woolly white double-layered coat. In springtime when the weather gets warmer, the goat rubs itself against tree bark to **pull off** its outer layer. But when winter approaches, the goat grows back its outer layer to help it **withstand** the harsh temperatures of -46 degrees Celsius and 160km/h wind currents. Additionally, these goats have much more muscle mass in their chests, which increases the strengths of their **forelimbs**. The goat's feet can **hold firm** at angles of up to 60 degrees allowing it to climb near-vertical slopes.

그곳에 사는 가장 큰 동물 중 하나는 야생염소이다. 이중으로 된 하얀 모피 덕에 가혹한 날씨를 견딘다. 봄에 날씨가 따뜻해지면, 야생염소는 나무껍질에 몸을 비벼 모피의 겉 겹을 **벗겨낸다**. 하지만 겨울이 다가오면, 영하 46도의 추위와 160km에 이르는 바람을 **견디기** 위해 겉 겹이 다시 자란다. 게다가, 이 염소들은 가슴부위에 더 많은 근육을 갖고 있어 더욱 튼튼한 **앞다리를** 갖고 있다. 야생염소의 발은 60도까지 **버틸** 수 있어서, 직각에 가까운 경사면도 오를 수 있다.

예시 ❷
록키 양은 굽 모양이 경사면에 적합

Bighorn sheep are another species that live in the same habitat, but are limited in the elevation they can climb to, compared to the thick-coated mountain goat. They also live in very angular **ranges**, and need to be able to hide from predators by fleeing to hard-to-reach cliffs. This is **made possible by its cloven hoof**, or… say, its split foot. The hoof splits into two and can move separately for ideal gripping on different angles. Not only that, the inner pad of the hoof is soft and spongy, so it **conforms** to each variable surface. It maximizes **friction** so that the foot does not slip, even on smooth rocks.

록키 양은 같은 서식지에 살고 있지만, 모피가 두꺼운 야생 염소만큼 높은 곳에서 살 수는 없다. 록키 양 역시 경사진 **지대에** 살며, 다가가기 힘든 절벽으로 도망가 천적으로부터 숨을 수 있어야 한다. 이는 **갈라진 굽** - 갈라진 발이랄까 - **덕분에 가능하다**. 굽은 둘로 갈라져있고, 다양한 각(도)들을 이상적으로 잡을 수 있도록 따로 움직일 수 있게 되어있다. 그뿐 아니라, 굽의 안쪽 면은 부드럽고 푹신해서, 표면의 모양에 따라 **변화한다**. 이는 매끄러운 바위에서도 **마찰을** 극대화하여 발이 미끄러지지 않게 한다.

문제

Using the examples from the professor's lecture, explain how some animals can survive in high altitudes.

교수의 강의를 예를 들어, 동물들이 어떻게 높은 고도에서 살아남는지 설명하세요.

References

Photo by Darklich14, available under the Creative Commons Attribution 3.0 Unported license.

Photo by Glenlarson

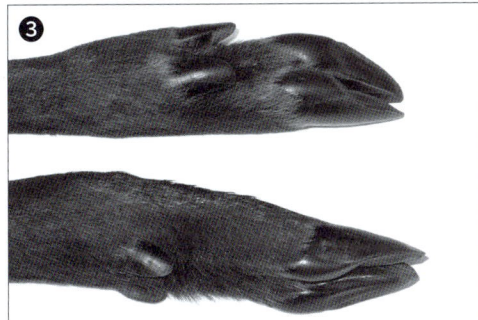
Photo by Joachim Backer

[참고자료]

❶ 좌측 위: Mountain Goat (야생 염소)

❷ Bighorn Sheep (록키 양)

❸ Cloven Hoof (갈라진 발굽)
굽 양쪽이 따로 움직여 고르지 못한 표면에서도 마찰을 최대화 할 수 있다. 또 푹신한 가죽 재질이어서 어떤 노면에서도 미끄러지지 않고 몸을 지탱할 수 있다.

Task 4   Sample Response   🎧 TEST 01_R4   4번 문제 모범 답안

In the lecture, the professor is explaining how some animals can survive in high altitudes. She is using the mountain goat and the bighorn sheep as examples.

❶ The mountain goat has double-layered fur to keep warm in extreme temperatures and strong winds; they shed their outer layer to keep cooler in summer. They also have strong front legs that help them stand even on steep ranges.

❷ The bighorn sheep has special feet structures that help them escape from predators easily even on steep mountain ranges. Their feet are split into two parts and have soft layers that help them maximize friction on slippery surfaces.

강의에서 교수는 동물들이 어떻게 높은 고도에서 살아남을 수 있는지를 설명하고 있다. 그는 야생염소와 록키 양을 예로 들고 있다.

❶ 야생염소는 극한의 온도와 강한 바람에도 따뜻할 수 있게 두 겹으로 된 모피를 갖고 있다. 여름에는 시원하게 지내기 위해 겉 겹을 벗는다. 경사진 지대에서도 서기 위해 튼튼한 앞다리를 갖고 있다.

❷ 록키 양은 가파른 산악지대에서도 천적으로부터 도망치기 위해 특이한 발 구조를 갖고 있다. 그들은 미끄러운 면에서도 마찰을 극대화하기 위해 둘로 갈라진 발과 부드러운 표면을 갖고 있다.

Vocabulary

withstand [wiðstǽnd, wiθ-]	v. ~에 견디다	
forelimbs [fɔ́ːrlìm]	n. 앞다리, 앞날개	
hoof [huf, huːf]	n. 발굽	
friction [fríkʃən]	n. 마찰	
precipitation [prisìpətéiʃən]	n. 낙하, 강수량	
cloven [klóuvən]	a. 갈라진	
conform [kənfɔ́ːrm]	v. 따르다, 순응하다	
range [reindʒ]	n. 산맥, 산줄기	

USHER
iBT TOEFL
FINAL TEST SPEAKING
TEST 02

Independent Tasks

Task 1 - 모범 답안
Question 1   usherin.usher.co.kr > 시험리스트 > Speaking 시험리스트 > Task 1 > #1026

Integrated Tasks

Task 2 - Script / 해석 / 모범 답안
Question 2   usherin.usher.co.kr > 시험리스트 > Speaking 시험리스트 > Task 2 > #2002

Task 3 - Script / 해석 / 모범 답안
Question 3   usherin.usher.co.kr > 시험리스트 > Speaking 시험리스트 > Task 3 > #3002

Task 4 - Script / 해석 / 모범 답안
Question 4   usherin.usher.co.kr > 시험리스트 > Speaking 시험리스트 > Task 4 > #4002

자기평가표

USHER 어셔어학원

1번 문제 유형은 학생들이 본인에 생각을 주제에 맞춰서 말 해야하는 시험입니다.
본인이 처음부터 끝까지 45초 동안 말해야하다 보니 학생들이 제일 어려워 하는 시험입니다.
하지만, 먼저 외우고 익힌후에 말하는것이 가능할수 있게 하겠습니다.
가장 기본이 되는 뼈대 입니다. 먼저 외우도록 합시다.

> if i were to answer the question, i would say
> there are many reasons why, but here is a couple
> first
> for example,
> second
> for instance
> that's why

다음은 2번 문제 유형입니다.
2번 문제는 리딩에 학교에 계획이 적혀있거나 학교가 변해야하는 방향에 대해서 학생들에 주장이 적혀있습니다.
리딩에서 빠르게 파악해야하는 것은 도대체 누가 무엇을 주장하는가 입니다.
45~50초에 리딩 지문이 나오고 난 다음에 리스닝으로 학생들에 대화가 나오는 문제입니다.
리스닝에서는 학생이 리딩 지문에 대한 본인에 좋고 나쁜지에 대한 의견을 얘기해줄겁니다.
이유 2가지와 예시 2가지를 꼭 말할 수 있어야 합니다.

이에 따라서 2번 스피킹 문제에 뼈대는

> The reading states that university (plans to) / (should)
> the (woman / man) in the conversation thinks it is a good / bad idea.
> He/she provides two reasons to support his / her opinion.
> first,
> Second,
> the woman / man thinks it's a great / horrible idea.

다음은 3번 문제 유형입니다.
3번 문제는 2번 문제 유형과 같이 리딩과 리스닝이 나오는 문제 입니다. 하지만, 이번에는 이전 문제와는 달리 매우 학술적인 내용이 들어 있습니다. 리딩에서는 교과서에 나올만한 주제 한개를 자세하게 다룹니다. 여기서 학생분들은 제목과 이에 대한 정의를 잘 받아적으셔야 합니다. 리스닝에서는 교수님이 리딩에 나온 내용으로 예시를 들어 줍니다.

> The article is about
> which the passage defines as
> The professor provides an example of
> first,
> Second,
> The example clearly illustrates

다음은 4번 문제 유형입니다.
4번 문제는 이전 문제와 달리 리스닝만 나오는 문제 유형입니다. 3번 문제에 나온 리딩 지문이 리스닝으로 변환되었다 라고 생각 하시면 됩니다. 그렇기에 3번 문제에 리스닝 내용보다 리딩 길이 만큼 깁니다.

> In the lecture, professor explains
> first,
> second,
> That's how the professor explain it.

USHER

01. Alone vs Homestay 혼자 vs 홈스테이 — Independent Task

QUESTION

 When students study abroad, should they stay alone or stay with a family already living there? Use reasons and examples to support your answer.
(학생들이 해외에서 공부하면, 혼자 지내야 할까요, 아니면 이미 그 곳에 살고 있는 가족과 지내야 할까요? 이유와 예를 들어 답하세요.)

 브레인 스토밍 (아래에 놓여있는 12간지 내용들을 보고 어떤 것을 사용할 수 있을지 확인해보세요)
첫번째 이유 :
두번째 이유 :

 뼈대에 맞춰서 작성을 해봅시다.

_____
_____
_____
_____
_____
_____
_____

아래 이미지는 학생들을 위한 만능 템플릿 12간지 입니다. 학생분들이 제일 먼저 암기해야하는 것이며, 본인 스스로 문장을 단기간 안에 못 만들거 같을 때에 도와주는 친구입니다. 가까이 두고 매일 외우세요.

Academic Courses

…because I think students should concentrate on academic courses.

Academic courses are the most important thing for students because good grades will help them get into good universities and, eventually, get great jobs.

As students get older, a good academic record is the only thing that actually matters.

This may sound a little far-fetched, but it's true, and for this reason, investing time in other activities is a waste of time.

Stay Healthy

It can be a great way to stay healthy. People join a cycling group through the internet. The members use bicycles to commute to work or school.

It is a great outdoor activity because people have a chance to work out while having fun.

Also, it is a great way to meet new people with similar interests. People nowadays do not have much chance to become close to each other.

However, there are numerous unique groups active on the internet, and this would not have been possible without the internet.

Follows your heart

Carpe diem, seize the days, and YOLO all stand for one thing. Do whatever your heart makes you do.

Life is too short to hesitate or do things to please others. It is essential to make yourself happy.

Actions speak louder than words. Whatever I do to make myself happy is better than sitting in a room thinking about it.

So I would just do it even if it means I am biting off something more than I can chew.

Stress

…if it can possibly be a way to relieve stress.

People nowadays are living a busy and hectic life, so they are under great stress, but a lot of them don't even realize they are stressed out.

Stress is known to be a major factor that keeps us from being healthy, and many people are suffering from various problems.

This is more serious than we think, so if it can ever be a way to relieve stress…

Money

…because it's the best way to save money. When it comes to spending money, every penny counts.

A thrifty spending habit is indispensable in our lives because little drops of water make the mighty ocean.

If we don't get used to working on a tight budget, we'll always be short on cash later.

A penny-pinching lifestyle will lead to financial stability, and it will give us peace of mind.

Saving Time

…because it's the best way to save time. There's an old saying, "Time is gold."

This proverb emphasizes the value of time, and this cannot be more true in modern society.

We're living a busy and hectic life, so saving time means we can do a lot more things later.

Many say that life is not fair, but everyone has twenty-four hours a day and seven days a week, so I would save time by…

Social Skills

Nowadays, people have smartphones with them all the time, and that information is no longer limited to elites.

Therefore, rather than learning, having social skills became the be-all and end-all to succeed rather than education.

Also, social skills are more than meet the eyes. To have social skills, one must also be able to read others like a book.

There will be times when one will truly need them.

Environment

because eventually, it can contribute to protecting the environment.

I think it's THE most important task for humanity because we cannot bring it back to life once it's too late.

Saving Earth all starts from seemingly insignificant actions.

Small actions from everyone bring about bigger changes, so I'm willing to participate.

Patience is virtue

Patience is a virtue. Saving time is indeed important, but waiting calmly is needed in this case.

There are times when one must wait patiently for things to go accordingly, and this is when time is the solution.

When going against the clock, they are more susceptible to making mistakes than taking some time.

In the long run, one will be glad that one has waited in this case.

Just because

I love it more than the given choices. Since I have so many great memory about it, It brings so many great reminiscences.

time flies whenever I am doing it, so how can I not choose it?

Also, not only do I love it, but I am also good at it. Everyone has talent, and it is like "a dime a dozen."

This was the inborn talent I had that I always surpassed everyone. Since a bird in the hand is worth two in the bush, I will choose it.

Politeness

It is important to maintain good relationships with other people because we never know what will happen in the future.

Decisions made by other people can affect others, and such decisions are usually based on personal and sentimental reasons.

So, people should not do anything that may offend or disturb others. It is also crucial to have a good reputation and get along well with others.

It Makes sense

It makes sense to choose it when considering many aspects such as time, money, and efficiency.

When people are considering between the given choices, they must consider many aspects economically.

They must choose the most efficient method because there are limits on what they have.

Also, one should think about it realistically and practically because they should not count chickens before they hatch.

So, down to Earth, people should choose it because it is the most economical

QUESTION

When students study abroad, should they stay alone or stay with a family already living there? Use reasons and examples to support your answer.
(학생들이 해외에서 공부하면, 혼자 지내야 할까요, 아니면 이미 그 곳에 살고 있는 가족과 지내야 할까요? 이유와 예를 들어 답하세요.)

academic과 stress를 사용해서 뼈대에 맞춰서 모범답안을 만들어 봅시다.

---

academic과 stress를 사용해서 뼈대에 맞춰서 모범답안을 만들어 봅시다.

---

makes sense와 stay healthy를 사용해서 뼈대에 맞춰서 모범답안을 만들어 봅시다.

---

social skills와 patience를 사용해서 뼈대에 맞춰서 모범답안을 만들어 봅시다.

QUESTION

When students study abroad, should they stay alone or stay with a family already living there? Use reasons and examples to support your answer.
(학생들이 해외에서 공부하면, 혼자 지내야 할까요, 아니면 이미 그 곳에 살고 있는 가족과 지내야 할까요? 이유와 예를 들어 답하세요.)

academic과 stress를 사용해서 뼈대에 맞춰서 모범답안을 만들어 봅시다.

If I were to answer the question, I would say they should stay alone. There are many reasons why, but here is a couple.

academic

First, staying alone can be a great way to study. For example, academic courses are the most important thing for students because good grades will help them get into a good university and eventually, get great jobs. Staying with their family will only bother them.

stress

Second, staying with family can be stressful. For instance, students abroad are already living a busy and hectic life, so they are under great stress. They do not need another stress from their family by nagging.

That's why I think they should stay alone.

academic과 stress를 사용해서 뼈대에 맞춰서 모범답안을 만들어 봅시다.

If I were to answer the question, I would say they should stay with their family. There are many reasons why, but here is a couple.

academic

First, they can concentrate on academic courses better by family doing chores for them. For example, academic courses are the most important things for students because good grades will them get into a good university and eventually get great jobs.

stress

Second, living alone abroad is stressful. For instance, students living abroad are under great stress by living alone, but they do not realize they are stressed out.

That's why I think they should stay with their family.

makes sense와 stay healthy를 사용해서 뼈대에 맞춰서 모범답안을 만들어 봅시다.

If I were to answer the question, I would say staying with family is better. There are many reasons why, but here is a couple.

makes sense

First, it makes sense to choose it when considering many aspects such as time, money, and efficiency. For example, when people are considering between the given choices, they must consider many aspects economically. They must choose the most efficient method because there are limits on what they have.

stay healthy

Second, it is a great way to stay healthy by eating healthy food. For instance, eating with family is great because they can eat healthy food while having a great time.

that's why I think they should stay with their family.

social skills와 patience를 사용해서 뼈대에 맞춰서 모범답안을 만들어 봅시다.

If I were to answer the question, I would say children should stay alone. There are many reasons why, but here is a couple.

social skills

First, they can develop social skills by attending and meeting other people. For example, they will not have a curfew, so it will be the time when they will be needing to stay alone truly.

patience

Second, they can learn how to live alone. For instance, there are times when one must wait patiently for things to go accordingly, and this is the time when staying alone can teach them how to live independently.

That's why I think they should stay alone.

02 Food Carts 식품노점 — Integrated Task

읽기 지문

Removal of Food Carts

The university plans to ban food carts already on campus. It is hoped that by removing these carts, the vast amount of trash on campus will decrease as well. There has been way too much trash around campus, all of which are assumed to be the remaining wrappers and such of the products on food carts. By banning food carts, the amount of trash has to be reduced since the areas in which foods are sold will be reduced, and thus, people will not be eating all over campus, trashing the place. Furthermore, the foods sold on these carts are not good **in regards to** the students' health.

대화 스크립트

 STEP 01 뼈대를 먼저 작성해 보도록 하겠습니다.

 STEP 02 작성하신 뼈대 빈칸에 맞춰서 리딩 지문을 읽고 주요 포인트를 넣어주세요.

 STEP 03 하단에 리스닝 노트테이킹을 해주세요. 음원은 학원 홈페이지에서 무료로 다운받으실 수 있습니다. 또한 2002번 문제 번호로 문제를 풀어보실 수 있습니다.

 아래 하단에 리스닝 스크립트를 보고 베꼈어야 하는 부분을 찾아서 적어 보도록 하겠습니다.

대화 스크립트

뉴토플 - TEST 02_Q2

Now listen to two students discussing the announcement.

M: So what do you think of the college's plan regarding the food carts?

W: I don't think it's a good idea. Those food carts were a good way to get something to eat before class.

M: Yeah... but it is true that the amount of trash increased after they were introduced to the university.

W: Mm... can't disagree with you there. But, that's because they don't have enough garbage cans on campus. I don't understand why the school is considering getting rid of the food carts instead of increasing the number of garbage cans to deal with the growing amount of trash. Isn't that more logical?

M: You're right.

W: Yep, and their statement regarding the students' health doesn't make sense either.

M: What do you mean? The food sold from the food carts aren't exactly veggies.

W: That's not true. I mean, they sell junk food, yeah. But, **aside from** the candy and the chocolates, they also sell lots of other food too, including fresh fruits and juice. Those aren't bad for my health, are they? They're just focusing on the fact that they sell junk food **to make an excuse** to ban the food carts.

M: I guess not.

W: Yeah... since the food carts were all around campus, it was really easy to buy a snack and go to class. They can't just get rid of the food carts.

여자의 의견 — 반대

이유 ❶ — 수업 전에 쉽게 간식을 먹게 하고 대신 쓰레기통을 설치해야 함

이유 ❷ — 불량 식품 외 좋은 음식도 팜

문제 — The woman expresses her opinion about the college's plan. State her opinion and explain the reasons she gives for holding that opinion.

이제 지문에 대해 논의하는 두 학생의 대화를 들어보세요.

남: 식품노점에 대한 학교의 계획에 대해서 어떻게 생각해?

여: 별로 좋은 아이디어는 아닌 것 같아. 식품노점 때문에 수업 들어가기 전에 먹을 수 있었는데.

남: 맞아... 근데 학교에 식품노점이 생긴 뒤에 쓰레기가 많아지긴 했잖아.

여: 그것에 대해선 할 말이 없는데, 그건 캠퍼스에 쓰레기통이 충분히 있지 않아서야. 왜 학교는 쓰레기 양에 대처하기 위해서 쓰레기통의 양을 늘리는 것 대신에 식품노점을 없애는 걸 생각하는지 모르겠어. 그게 더 논리적이지 않아?

남: 그건 그러네.

여: 응, 그리고 우리 건강에 대한 주장도 말이 되지 않아.

남: 무슨 말이야? 학교 식품노점에서 파는 음식이 채소 같은 건 아니잖아.

여: 아니지. 군것질 거리를 팔긴 팔지. 그런데, 캔디나 초콜릿 **말고도**, 신선한 과일이나 주스처럼 다른 음식들도 팔아. 그것들이 건강에 나쁘진 않잖아? 학교는 식품노점을 없앨 **핑계를 만들려고** 군것질 거리 파는 것에만 집중 하는 거야.

남: 그렇네.

여: 응, 캠퍼스 전체에 식품노점이 있어서 수업에 들어 가기 전에, 간식 사는 게 얼마나 쉬웠는데. 그냥 없앨 수는 없지.

여자는 대학의 계획에 대해 자신의 의견을 밝히고 있습니다. 그녀의 의견을 말하고, 그 의견을 고수하는 이유를 설명하세요.

Note-taking

STEP 06 다시한번 모범 답안을 작성해 보도록 하겠습니다

Removal of Food Carts

The university plans to ban food carts already on campus. It is hoped that by removing these carts, the vast amount of trash on campus will decrease as well. There has been way too much trash around campus, all of which are assumed to be the remaining wrappers and such of the products on food carts. By banning food carts, the amount of trash has to be reduced since the areas in which foods are sold will be reduced, and thus, people will not be eating all over campus, trashing the place. Furthermore, the foods sold on these carts are not good **in regards to** the students' health.

Note-taking	노트테이킹
Reading - ban food carts on campus - the amount of trash increased - foods sold on these are bad for students' health **Woman** - against **Reason ❶** - they allow the students to have easy foods before class - they should put more garbage cans instead **Reason ❷** - they also sell fresh fruits and juice - they're focusing on junk food just to make an excuse	**지문** - 식품 노점 금지 - 쓰레기가 많아졌음 - 파는 음식이 학생 건강에 안 좋음 **여자** - 반대 **이유 ❶** - 수업 전에 음식을 쉽게 먹게 함 - 대신 쓰레기통을 더 놓아야 함 **이유 ❷** - 신선한 과일 주스도 판다 - 핑계를 대려고 junk food에만 집중

Task 2 Sample Response 🎧 뉴토플 - TEST 02_R2   2번 문제 모범 답안

The two students are discussing the college's plan to ban food carts on campus because of too much garbage and concerns for student health. The woman is against the plan for two reasons.

❶ First, the carts allow the students to have easy snacks before class. If the amount of trash increased because of the carts, then the university should have more garbage cans around the campus to cope with the problem.

❷ Second, the carts sell junk food, but they also sell fresh fruits and juice which are good for students' health. The university is only focusing on junk food to make an excuse for banning the carts, which is illogical. (This is why she thinks the plan is unnecessary.)

두 학생은 많은 양의 쓰레기와 학생들의 건강 때문에 식품 노점을 금지하려는 대학 측의 계획에 대해서 의논하고 있다. 여자는 두 가지 이유를 들어 그 계획에 반대하고 있다.

❶ 첫째, 식품노점은 학생들이 수업 전에 간단한 간식을 먹게 한다. 만약 식품노점 때문에 쓰레기의 양이 증가했다면, 학교 측은 이 문제를 해결 하기 위해서 더 많은 쓰레기통을 설치해야 한다.

❷ 둘째, 식품노점에서 군것질거리를 팔긴 하지만, 학생들의 건강에 좋은 신선한 과일과 주스도 판다. 학교 측이 식품노점을 없애는 것에 대한 변명을 하기 위해서 불량 식품에만 초점을 맞추는 것은 억지다. (이것이 그녀가 이 제안이 필요 없다고 생각하는 이유이다)

Vocabulary

in regards to	phr. ~에 관해서	aside from	phr. ~을 제하고
to make an excuse	phr. 변명하다	to cope with	phr. 잘 대처하다

03. Exaptation 굴절적응

Integrated Task

읽기 지문

Exaptation

Animals **undergo** various changes in their characteristics over time. The idea of **adaptation** is widely known to people as a process of natural selection that serves to keep or **discard** a particular trait. Different from adaptation, however, animals undergo exaptation, which refers to a feature of an animal that has evolved to serve a particular function, but subsequently provides another unintended function. This idea was originated in mid-19th century when interest in evolution of animals was **immense**. It was firstly known as "preadaptation" among the scientists.

대화 스크립트

STEP 01 뼈대를 먼저 작성해 보도록 하겠습니다.

STEP 02 작성하신 뼈대 빈칸에 맞춰서 리딩 지문을 읽고 주요 포인트를 넣어주세요.

STEP 03 하단에 리스닝 노트테이킹을 해주세요. 음원은 학원 홈페이지에서 무료로 다운받으실 수 있습니다. 또한 3002번 문제 번호로 문제를 풀어보실 수 있습니다.

STEP 04
아래 하단에 리스닝 스크립트를 보고 베꼈어야 하는 부분을 찾아서 적어 보도록 하겠습니다.

대화 스크립트

뉴토플 - TEST 02_Q3

Now listen to part of a lecture in a zoology class.

이제 동물학 수업의 일부를 들어보세요.

Well, exaptation is an unfamiliar concept for many people. Let's start with a concept that we all know, in order to have a better understanding of exaptation. We all know what adaptation is right? Just to clarify, adaptation refers to a specific change of an animal's features, or behavior, to suit the environment and may serve as an important factor for animal's survival. This process embeds the concept of natural selection which results in adaptation of animals'. On the other hand, exaptation **disregards** direct involvement of natural selection in its change.

음, 굴절적응은 많은 사람들에게 생소합니다. 굴절적응을 더 쉽게 이해하기 위해 우리 모두가 아는 개념으로 시작합시다. 우리 모두 환경적응은 무엇인지 알죠? 명확하게 하기 위해 환경적응은 특정한 행위나 성질을 주변환경에 더 맞게 바꾸고 동물의 생존에 도움을 주는 것을 뜻합니다. 이 과정은 자연도태의 개념을 내포하고 있습니다. 반면에 굴절적응은 자연도태와의 직접적인 관계를 **무시합니다**.

예시 ❶
날개의 용도

세부사항
비행능력을 갖게 해줌

Take an example of herons that utilize their wings when preying on fish in the water. Through the natural selection, birds developed the ability to fly with their wings, having better **mobility**.

날개를 이용하여 물 안에 있는 물고기를 잡는 왜가리를 예로 듭시다. 새는 자연도태를 통해 날개를 이용해 날 수 있고 더 나은 **기동성**을 가질 수 있습니다.

예시 ❷
다른 용도

세부사항
그림자를 만들어 사냥을 도움

However, the presence of wings also aids when **foraging** for prey by blocking the sunlight on the surface of water. During a bright day, it's hard for herons to see fish in the water due to the reflection of the sun. By using their wide and long wings as an umbrella, herons block the sunshine which in turn provides a better view inside the water. Thereby, herons can more easily detect fish which they can prey on. This ability of wings to provide a function other than their intended **utility** can be called exaptation.

하지만 날개가 있어 수면에 비치는 햇빛을 가려 **먹이를 잡을 때도** 도움을 주기도 합니다. 맑은 날에는 해가 비치는 수면 때문에 왜가리는 물고기를 보기가 어렵습니다. 마치 우산같이 넓고 긴 날개를 이용하여 햇빛을 막으면 수면 아래는 더 잘 보이게 됩니다. 그리하여 왜가리는 더 쉽게 먹이를 찾을 수 있습니다. 날개의 이 **용도**는 원래 의도했던 것과 다르게 쓰이니 굴절적응이라 말할 수 있습니다.

문제

Using the example from the professor's lecture, explain what exaptation is and how it works.

교수의 강의를 예로들어, 굴절적응이 무엇이며, 어떻게 작용하는지 설명하세요.

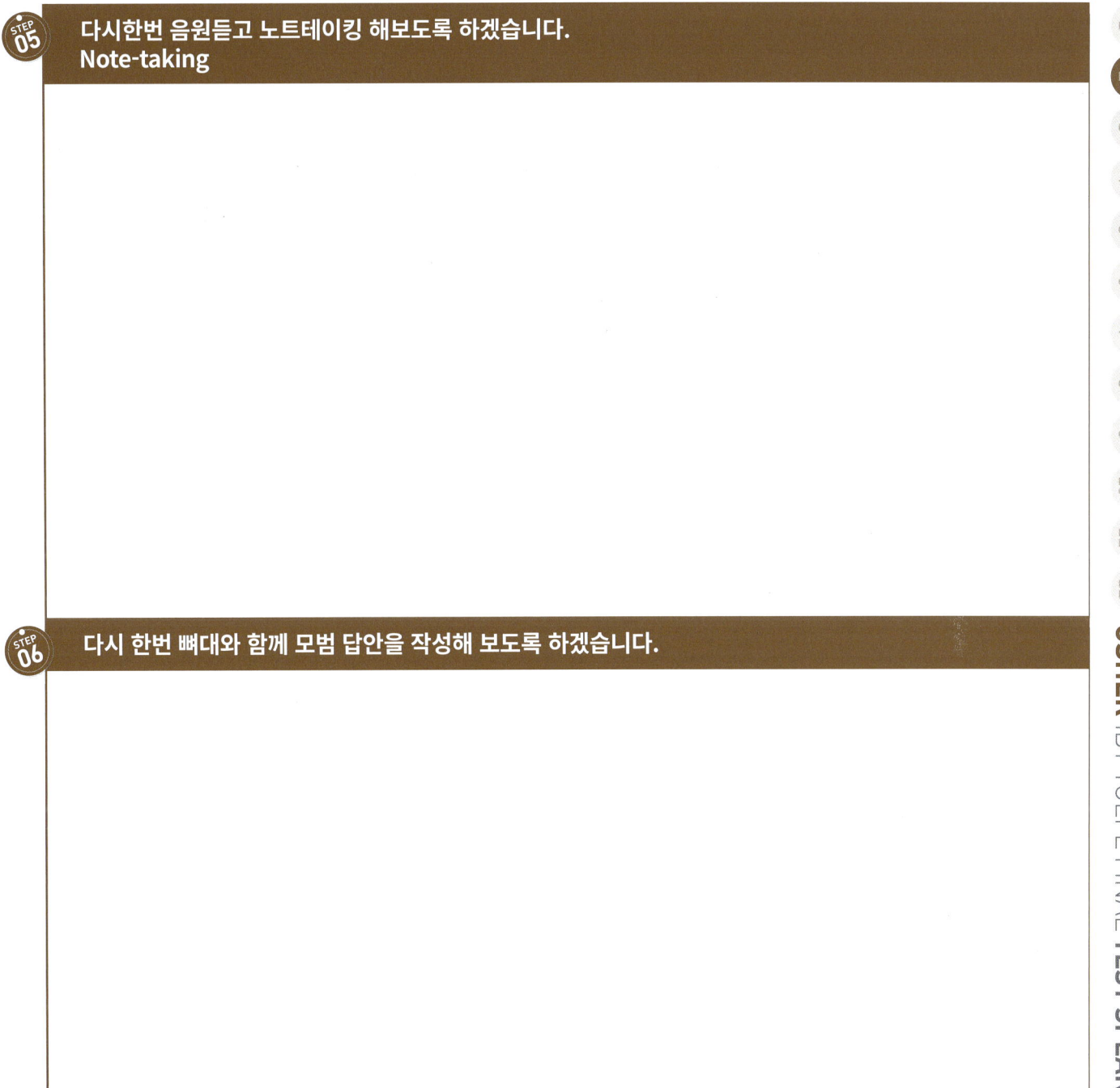

Exaptation

Animals **undergo** various changes in their characteristics over time. The idea of **adaptation** is widely known to people as a process of natural selection that serves to keep or **discard** a particular trait. Different from adaptation, however, animals undergo exaptation, which refers to a feature of an animal that has evolved to serve a particular function, but subsequently provides another unintended function. This idea was originated in mid-19th century when interest in evolution of animals was **immense**. It was firstly known as "preadaptation" among the scientists.

References

[참고자료]

왜가리가 물 위에 비치는 날개의 그림자를 이용해 먹이를 찾는 모습.

Photo by Chris Harshaw, available under the Creative Commons Attribution-Share Alike 3.0 Unported license.

Task 3   Sample Response   뉴토플 - TEST 02_R3   3번 문제 모범 답안

Exaptátion is a characterístic of an animal that evólved to serve uninténded functions. In the lecture, the proféssor gives the exámple of the heron to expláin it.

❶ Wings of herons, like those of most birds, have evólved to enáble them to fly and move freely. But herons also use these wings to catch fish in the water.

❷ On sunny days, the large wings block the sunlight so that no refléction on the surface of the water interféres with the heron's view. This way, herons can see better underwáter to catch fish. The use of wings in this uninténded manner is a good exámple of exaptátion.

굴절적응은 의도치 않은 용도로 쓰이는 동물의 특성입니다. 강의에서 교수는 왜가리를 예로 들어 설명했습니다.

❶ 왜가리의 날개는 다른 새들과 같이 날 수 있고 움직이기 편하게 진화되었습니다. 하지만 왜가리의 날개를 물 속에 있는 물고기를 잡는데 쓰기도 합니다.

❷ 화창한 날에 큰 날개는 햇빛을 가려 수면에 반사되는 빛을 차단하고 왜가리의 시야를 방해하지 않게 합니다. 이 방법을 통해 왜가리는 수중에 있는 물고기를 잡을 수 있습니다. 의도치 않은 날개의 사용법은 굴절적응에 좋은 예입니다.

Vocabulary

undergo [ʌ̀ndərgóu]	v. 겪다, 경험하다, 견디다		adaptation [æ̀dəptéiʃən]	n. 적응, 개조
discard [diskáːrd]	v. 버리다, 처분하다		immense [iméns]	a. 거대한, 막대한
disregard [dìsrigáːrd]	v. 무시하다, 경시하다		mobility [moubíləti]	n. 이동성, 기동력
forage [fɔ́ːridʒ, fǽr- / fɔr-]	n. 먹이 / v. 먹이를 찾다		utility [juːtíləti]	n. 유용, 효용

04. Animals' Play 동물의 놀이 — Integrated Task

STEP 01 4번 뼈대를 먼저 작성해 보도록 하겠습니다.

STEP 02 하단에 리스닝 노트테이킹을 해주세요. 음원은 학원 홈페이지에서 무료로 다운받으실 수 있습니다. 또한 4002번 문제 번호로 문제를 풀어보실 수 있습니다.

STEP 03 뼈대에 맞춰서 모범 답안을 완성해 보겠습니다.

Listen to part of a lecture in a zoology class.

Most animal behaviors are intuitive with a specific purpose. Mating occurs for **reproduction**, while **imprinting**, which is a term for describing when offspring blindly chase after their parents, is for keeping the young close to the protection of an adult. So how about play? Play itself is an extremely loosely-defined term, and experts still disagree on its definition. We can't say that we know the exact answer, but one feature that has been agreed upon by most theories is that playful behavior is not merely for enjoyment, but is an essential tool for survival in the individual's adult life.

It probably isn't clear how playing can help you to survive, so let me try to explain. Many playful behaviors are **repetitive**: look at the **nestlings** of almost any bird species. Within two weeks after **hatching**, many nestlings begin to show playful behavior in their nests. Using their beaks, they pick up feathers, and drop them back on the ground. The nestling repeats this process over and over again. How does this help the bird? Well, this type of repetitive behavior is believed to be a sort of practice for adulthood when the birds will have to use their beaks to pick up food they have **scavenged**.

Like the bird example, many playful behaviors mimic actions performed by adults. Let's take a look at another example. Baby monkeys swing from one tree to another using their arms. This motion **inconspicuously** increases the muscle mass of the monkeys' arms, and at the same time accustoms the monkey to such motion. When the monkey grows into an adult and leaves the protection of its parents, it will have had enough training to escape from predators by swinging on trees. Through repetition, they acquire the speed and **agility** that they need, while familiarizing themselves with the movements.

Using the examples from the professor's lecture, explain what young animals can learn from play.

References

[참고자료]

줄과 꼬리를 이용해 이동하고 있는 중남미 원산의 거미원숭이.

Photo by Lea Maimone, available under the Creative Commons Attribution 2.5 Generic license.

Task 4 Sample Response  TEST 02_R4   4번 문제 모범 답안

In the lecture, the professor is explaining how playful behaviors help young animals survive in the wild. He is giving examples of young birds and monkeys.

❶ Most bird species use their beaks to pick up feathers and drop them back on the ground. Although this movement may look rather pointless, this helps them practice scavenging food for when they become adults. So they repeat this process.

❷ In the case of baby monkeys, they swing from one tree to another only using their arms. They also repeat this process, and by the time they become adults, they will have enough strength to escape from danger without difficulty.

강의에서 교수는 동물들의 장난기 있는 행동이 어떻게 생존에 도움을 주는지 설명해 주고 있습니다. 그는 새와 원숭이, 두 가지를 예로 들고 있습니다.

❶ 대부분의 새들은 부리를 이용하여 깃털을 들었다 놨다 합니다. 이런 움직임은 의미없어 보이지만 어른이 되었을 때 먹이 줍는 연습이 됩니다. 그렇기에 아기 새들은 이 동작을 반복합니다.

❷ 어린 원숭이의 경우, 팔을 이용하여 나무를 옮겨 다닙니다. 원숭이들도 이 움직임을 반복하여 다 컸을 때에 위험이 닥치면 쉽게 벗어날 수 있는 힘을 기를 수 있습니다.

Vocabulary

reproduction [riˌprədəˈkʃən]	n. 번식, 재생, 복제	imprinting [imprɪ́ntiŋ]	n. 각인
repetitive [ripétətiv]	a. 되풀이하는	nestling [néstliŋ]	n. 햇병아리
hatch [hætʃ]	v. (알을) 까다, (알이) 깨다	scavenge [skǽvindʒ]	v. (썩은 고기 등을) 찾아 다니다
inconspicuously [ìnkənspíkjuəsli]	ad. 눈에 띄지 않게	agility [ədʒíləti]	n. 민첩성

USHER
iBT TOEFL
FINAL TEST SPEAKING
TEST 03

Independent Tasks

Task 1 - 모범 답안
Question 1   usherin.usher.co.kr > 시험리스트 > Speaking 시험리스트 > Task 1 > #1058

Integrated Tasks

Task 2 - Script / 해석 / 모범 답안
Question 2   usherin.usher.co.kr > 시험리스트 > Speaking 시험리스트 > Task 2 > #2003

Task 3 - Script / 해석 / 모범 답안
Question 3   usherin.usher.co.kr > 시험리스트 > Speaking 시험리스트 > Task 3 > #3003

Task 4 - Script / 해석 / 모범 답안
Question 4   usherin.usher.co.kr > 시험리스트 > Speaking 시험리스트 > Task 4 > #4003

자기평가표

1번 문제 유형은 학생들이 본인에 생각을 주제에 맞춰서 말 해야하는 시험입니다.
본인이 처음부터 끝까지 45초 동안 말해야하다 보니 학생들이 제일 어려워 하는 시험입니다.
하지만, 먼저 외우고 익힌후에 말하는것이 가능할수 있게 하겠습니다.
가장 기본이 되는 뼈대 입니다. 먼저 외우도록 합시다.

> if i were to answer the question, i would say
> there are many reasons why, but here is a couple
> first
> for example,
> second
> for instance
> that's why

다음은 2번 문제 유형입니다.
2번 문제는 리딩에 학교에 계획이 적혀있거나 학교가 변해야하는 방향에 대해서 학생들에 주장이 적혀있습니다.
리딩에서 빠르게 파악해야하는 것은 도대체 누가 무엇을 주장하는가 입니다.
45~50초에 리딩 지문이 나오고 난 다음에 리스닝으로 학생들에 대화가 나오는 문제입니다.
리스닝에서는 학생이 리딩 지문에 대한 본인에 좋고 나쁜지에 대한 의견을 얘기해줄겁니다.
이유 2가지와 예시 2가지를 꼭 말할 수 있어야 합니다.

이에 따라서 2번 스피킹 문제에 뼈대는

> The reading states that university (plans to) / (should)
> the (woman / man) in the conversation thinks it is a good / bad idea.
> He/she provides two reasons to support his / her opinion.
> first,
> Second,
> the woman / man thinks it's a great / horrible idea.

다음은 3번 문제 유형입니다.
3번 문제는 2번 문제 유형과 같이 리딩과 리스닝이 나오는 문제 입니다. 하지만, 이번에는 이전 문제와는 달리 매우 학술적인 내용이 들어 있습니다. 리딩에서는 교과서에 나올만한 주제 한개를 자세하게 다룹니다. 여기서 학생분들은 제목과 이에 대한 정의를 잘 받아적으셔야 합니다. 리스닝에서는 교수님이 리딩에 나온 내용으로 예시를 들어 줍니다.

> The article is about
> which the passage defines as
> The professor provides an example of
> first,
> Second,
> The example clearly illustrates

다음은 4번 문제 유형입니다.
4번 문제는 이전 문제와 달리 리스닝만 나오는 문제 유형입니다. 3번 문제에 나온 리딩 지문이 리스닝으로 변환되었다 라고 생각 하시면 됩니다. 그렇기에 3번 문제에 리스닝 내용보다 리딩 길이 만큼 깁니다.

> In the lecture, professor explains
> first,
> second,
> That's how the professor explain it.

USHER

01 Class Discussion 수업시간의 토론 — Independent Task

QUESTION

 Do you agree or disagree with the following statement? Students learn more by participating in class discussions. Use reasons and examples to support your answer. (당신은 다음 주장에 동의하십니까, 아니면 반대하십니까? 학생들은 수업시간의 토론을 통해서 더 많이 배운다. 이유와 예를 들어 답하세요)

 브레인 스토밍 (아래에 놓여있는 12간지 내용들을 보고 어떤 것을 사용할 수 있을지 확인해보세요)
첫번째 이유 :
두번째 이유 :

 뼈대에 맞춰서 작성을 해봅시다.

___

아래 이미지는 학생들을 위한 만능 템플릿 12간지 입니다. 학생분들이 제일 먼저 암기해야하는 것이며, 본인 스스로 문장을 단기간 안에 못 만들거 같을 때에 도와주는 친구입니다. 가까이 두고 매일 외우세요.

Academic Courses
…because I think students should concentrate on academic courses.

Academic courses are the most important thing for students because good grades will help them get into good universities and, eventually, get great jobs.

As students get older, a good academic record is the only thing that actually matters.

This may sound a little far-fetched, but it's true, and for this reason, investing time in other activities is a waste of time.

Stay Healthy
It can be a great way to stay healthy. People join a cycling group through the internet. The members use bicycles to commute to work or school.

It is a great outdoor activity because people have a chance to work out while having fun.

Also, it is a great way to meet new people with similar interests. People nowadays do not have much chance to become close to each other.

However, there are numerous unique groups active on the internet, and this would not have been possible without the internet.

Follows your heart
Carpe diem, seize the days, and YOLO all stand for one thing. Do whatever your heart makes you do.

Life is too short to hesitate or do things to please others. It is essential to make yourself happy.

Actions speak louder than words. Whatever I do to make myself happy is better than sitting in a room thinking about it.

So I would just do it even if it means I am biting off something more than I can chew.

Stress
…if it can possibly be a way to relieve stress.

People nowadays are living a busy and hectic life, so they are under great stress, but a lot of them don't even realize they are stressed out.

Stress is known to be a major factor that keeps us from being healthy, and many people are suffering from various problems.

This is more serious than we think, so if it can ever be a way to relieve stress…

Money
…because it's the best way to save money. When it comes to spending money, every penny counts.

A thrifty spending habit is indispensable in our lives because little drops of water make the mighty ocean.

If we don't get used to working on a tight budget, we'll always be short on cash later.

A penny-pinching lifestyle will lead to financial stability, and it will give us peace of mind.

Saving Time
…because it's the best way to save time. There's an old saying, "Time is gold."

This proverb emphasizes the value of time, and this cannot be more true in modern society.

We're living a busy and hectic life, so saving time means we can do a lot more things later.

Many say that life is not fair, but everyone has twenty-four hours a day and seven days a week, so I would save time by…

Social Skills
Nowadays, people have smartphones with them all the time, and that information is no longer limited to elites.

Therefore, rather than learning, having social skills became the be-all and end-all to succeed rather than education.

Also, social skills are more than meet the eyes. To have social skills, one must also be able to read others like a book.

There will be times when one will truly need them.

Environment
because eventually, it can contribute to protecting the environment.

I think it's THE most important task for humanity because we cannot bring it back to life once it's too late.

Saving Earth all starts from seemingly insignificant actions.

Small actions from everyone bring about bigger changes, so I'm willing to participate.

Patience is virtue
Patience is a virtue. Saving time is indeed important, but waiting calmly is needed in this case.

There are times when one must wait patiently for things to go accordingly, and this is when time is the solution.

When going against the clock, they are more susceptible to making mistakes than taking some time.

In the long run, one will be glad that one has waited in this case.

Just because
I love it more than the given choices. Since I have so many great memory about it, It brings so many great reminiscences.

time flies whenever I am doing it, so how can I not choose it?

Also, not only do I love it, but I am also good at it. Everyone has talent, and it is like "a dime a dozen."

This was the inborn talent I had that I always surpassed everyone. Since a bird in the hand is worth two in the bush, I will choose it.

Politeness
It is important to maintain good relationships with other people because we never know what will happen in the future.

Decisions made by other people can affect others, and such decisions are usually based on personal and sentimental reasons.

So, people should not do anything that may offend or disturb others. It is also crucial to have a good reputation and get along well with others.

It Makes sense
It makes sense to choose it when considering many aspects such as time, money, and efficiency.

When people are considering between the given choices, they must consider many aspects economically.

They must choose the most efficient method because there are limits on what they have.

Also, one should think about it realistically and practically because they should not count chickens before they hatch.

So, down to Earth, people should choose it because it is the most economical

QUESTION

Do you agree or disagree with the following statement? Students learn more by participating in class discussions. Use reasons and examples to support your answer. (당신은 다음 주장에 동의하십니까, 아니면 반대하십니까? 학생들은 수업 시간의 토론을 통해서 더 많이 배운다. 이유와 예를 들어 답하세요)

Social skills와 follow your heart를 사용해서 뼈대에 맞춰서 모범답안을 만들어 봅시다.

academic과 waste of time을 사용해서 뼈대에 맞춰서 모범답안을 만들어 봅시다.

stress와 just because를 사용해서 뼈대에 맞춰서 모범답안을 만들어 봅시다.

patience is virtue와 it makes sense를 사용해서 뼈대에 맞춰서 모범답안을 만들어 봅시다.

QUESTION

Do you agree or disagree with the following statement? Students learn more by participating in class discussions. Use reasons and examples to support your answer. (당신은 다음 주장에 동의하십니까, 아니면 반대하십니까? 학생들은 수업 시간의 토론을 통해서 더 많이 배운다. 이유와 예를 들어 답하세요)

Social skills와 follow your heart를 사용해서 뼈대에 맞춰서 모범답안을 만들어 봅시다.

If I were to answer the question, I would say children can learn better by participating in class discussions. There are many reasons why, but here is a couple.

Social skills

First, they can develop social skills. For example, learning is overrated. People have smartphones with them all the time. Information can be found without learning, but social skills became the be-all and end-all to students to succeed.

follow your heart

Second, it can help children speak for themselves. For instance, actions speak louder than words. Whatever students to in-class participation are sitting in a room doing nothing.

That's why i think it is important for them to participate in classroom.

stress와 just because를 사용해서 뼈대에 맞춰서 모범답안을 만들어 봅시다.

If I were to answer the question, I would say I agree with the topic. There are many reasons why, but here is a couple.

stress

First, sitting in a classroom and doing nothing is stressful. For example, students nowadays are living a boring and hectic life, so they are under great stress. However, class participating can be a great way to relieve stress.

just because

Second, it can make a great memory to children about being in a classroom. For instance, students can have so much great memory about participating in the classroom because they can speak for themselves.

That's why I think children should be able to participate in the classroom.

academic과 waste of time을 사용해서 뼈대에 맞춰서 모범답안을 만들어 봅시다.

If I were to answer the question I would say I disagree with this topic. There are many reasons why, but here is a couple.

academic

First, learning academically is the most important thing for students, instead of discussing.

For example, good academically learning will help them get into good universities and eventually, get great jobs. As students get older, a good academic record is the only thing that actually matters.

waste of time

Second, participating in class discussions is a waste of time for students.

For instance, there's an old saying, "Time is gold." This proverb emphasizes the value of time, and this cannot be more true in students. That's why I disagree with this topic.

patience is virtue와 it makes sense를 사용해서 뼈대에 맞춰서 모범답안을 만들어 봅시다.

If I were to answer the question, they should listen to teachers instead of participating in the classroom. There are many reasons why, but here is a couple.

patience is virtue

First, they can learn how to be patient. For example, patience and focusing is a virtue. There will be times when one must wait patiently for things to go accordingly, and school is the place to learn it.

it makes sense

Second, it is an efficient method to learn, instead of wasting time discussing. For instance, people should think about it realistically on what is the most efficient method to learn. Down to earth, they should choose it.

That's why I think they should not participate in the classroom.

02 Computer Lab 컴퓨터실

Integrated Task

읽기 지문

Computer Installations in Dormitories

We are living in the age of computers, and it is hard to imagine living without one. It is a great pleasure to announce that the university has decided to create computer labs in all the dormitories, with help and support from Orange Computers, Inc. As the computer labs will be built in the lobby, it should be easy to access for all students as well. The computers may be used for various purposes, either for academics or for personal entertainment. For those students who do not have personal computers, it would only be fair to install computer labs, which would prove to be helpful and useful.

대화 스크립트

 뼈대를 먼저 작성해 보도록 하겠습니다.

 작성하신 뼈대 빈칸에 맞춰서 리딩 지문을 읽고 주요 포인트를 넣어주세요.

 하단에 리스닝 노트테이킹을 해주세요. 음원은 학원 홈페이지에서 무료로 다운받으실 수 있습니다. 또한 2003번 문제 번호로 문제를 풀어보실 수 있습니다.

아래 하단에 리스닝 스크립트를 보고 베꼈어야 하는 부분을 찾아서 적어 보도록 하겠습니다.

대화 스크립트

🎧 뉴토플 - TEST 03_Q2

Now listen to two students discussing the announcement.

M: So, what do you think of the university's new plan?

W: I think it's a great idea.

M: Oh, yeah? How so?

W: Well, it is going to be a lot easier to check e-mail. Before, I had to go to the library to check my mail. It was a big waste of time going **back and forth** for something so simple.

M: That's true, but most students now check e-mail with their own computers, don't they?

W: They do, but even for them, it is a lot easier and faster. They had to run up to their rooms, wait for the computer **to boot**, and then come **all the way** back down just to check their mail. But now, they can just go to the lobby to use the computers!

M: Sure, it will be more convenient, but does that mean those were really necessary?

W: What are you talking about! For those of us who don't have a computer, the computer lab is **a life saver**. You know, during midterms and finals, there weren't enough computers available, so I sometimes had **to write my papers by hand** and **boy**, did that take a long time. The new computers will make it so much easier to write term papers as well.

M: Now I see what you mean. It really must be great news.

이제 지문에 대해 논의하는 두 학생의 대화를 들어보세요.

남: 학교의 새로운 계획에 대해서 어떻게 생각해?

여: 아주 멋진 아이디어라 생각해.

남: 정말? 어떤 점이?

여: 이메일 체크하는데 훨씬 쉬울 것 아니야. 예전엔 메일 체크하는데 도서관까지 갔어야 했어. 그렇게 단순한 일 가지고 **왔다 갔다** 하는 건 큰 낭비였지.

남: 그건 그렇지만 대부분 학생들은 개인 컴퓨터로 이메일을 체크 하잖아?

여: 그건 그런데, 그 학생들한테도 훨씬 쉽고 빠르겠지. 이메일 체크 하나 하려고 방까지 올라가서, **컴퓨터 켜지길** 기다리고, 다시 내려와야 하잖아. 근데 이젠, 그냥 로비에 가서 컴퓨터를 사용할 수 있잖아!

남: 그렇지, 훨씬 편리하긴 할거야. 근데, 그게 정말 필요하다는 의미일까?

여: 대체 무슨 소리하는 거야! 개인 컴퓨터가 없는 학생들한테는 컴퓨터실은 **생명의 은인** 같은 존재지! 중간이나 기말고사 기간에, 컴퓨터가 부족해서 매일 **손으로 써서 레포트** 써야 됐는데, **와**, 어찌나 오래 걸리던지! 이제 새로운 컴퓨터가 있으니까 레포트 쓰는데도 훨씬 수월해 질 거야.

남: 무슨 말인지 알겠다. 진짜 좋은 소식이네.

여자의 의견 — 찬성

이유 ❶ — 이메일을 체크하는 데 훨씬 편리할 것임

이유 ❷ — 개인 컴퓨터가 없는 학생들은 레포트 쓰는데 이용할 수 있음

문제 — The woman expresses her opinion about the college's plan. State her opinion and explain the reasons she gives for holding that opinion.

여자는 대학의 계획에 대해 자신의 의견을 밝히고 있습니다. 그녀의 의견을 말하고, 그 의견을 고수하는 이유를 설명하세요.

Note-taking

다시한번 모범 답안을 작성해 보도록 하겠습니다

Computer Installations in Dormitories

We are living in the age of computers, and it is hard to imagine living without one. It is a great pleasure to announce that the university has decided to create computer labs in all the dormitories, with help and support from Orange Computers, Inc. As the computer labs will be built in the lobby, it should be easy to access for all students as well. The computers may be used for various purposes, either for academics or for personal entertainment. For those students who do not have personal computers, it would only be fair to install computer labs, which would prove to be helpful and useful.

Note-taking	노트테이킹
Reading - computer labs will be installed - it will be built in the lobby - not all students have personal computers **Woman** - supporting **Reason ❶** - checking e-mails will be much easier - save time and energy used to check e-mails **Reason ❷** - students can use it to write term papers - students no longer have to write by hand	**지문** - 컴퓨터실이 설치될 것 - 로비에 지어질 것 - 모든 학생이 컴퓨터가 있는 것은 아님 **여자** - 찬성 **이유 ❶** - 이메일 체크가 훨씬 쉬워짐 - 이메일 체크에 시간과 에너지 절약 **이유 ❷** - 과제물 작성하는데 쓸 수 있음 - 더 이상 손으로 쓰지 않아도 됨

Task 2 Sample Response 뉴토플 - TEST 03_R2 — 2번 문제 모범 답안

The two students are discussing the college's plan to build computer labs in the dormitories. The woman is supporting the plan for two reasons.

❶ First, checking e-mails will be much easier and more convenient for all students. They don't have to waste time and energy going all the way to their rooms or to the library just to check e-mail anymore.

❷ Next, students can use the computer labs to write term papers as well. Not all students have a personal computer, so the computer lab will enable students to type and print their assignments. Students don't have to write reports by hand anymore. (This is why she is supporting the plan.)

두 학생은 기숙사에 컴퓨터실을 설치하려는 대학 측의 계획에 대해서 의논하고 있다. 여자는 두 가지 이유를 들어 그 계획에 찬성하고 있다.

❶ 첫째, 이메일을 체크하는데 훨씬 쉽고 편리할 것이다. 시간뿐만 아니라, 단지 이메일을 체크하려고 각자 방이나 도서관에 갈 힘을 낭비하지 않아도 된다.

❷ 다음, 학생들은 레포트를 쓰는데 컴퓨터실을 이용할 수 있다. 모든 학생들이 개인 컴퓨터를 갖고 있지 않기 때문에, 컴퓨터실은 학생들이 숙제를 하고 출력할 수 있게 할 것이다. 학생들은 이제 더 이상 손으로 레포트를 쓰지 않아도 된다. (이것이 그녀가 이 계획이 필요하다고 생각하는 이유이다)

Vocabulary

back and forth	phr. 왕복으로	to boot	phr. 컴퓨터를 시동하다
all the way	phr. 끝까지	boy [bɔi]	n. 소년/ int. (놀람) 이런
a life saver	phr. 생명의 은인	to write by hand	phr. 손으로 쓰다

03. Optimal Foraging 최적 섭이

Integrated Task

읽기 지문

Optimal Foraging

In ecology, all animals must consume a source of energy which in turn is used for all the bodily functions. Therefore, it is essential that animals not waste energy on unnecessary activities. The ecologists developed a theory called **optimal** foraging which is the idea whereby organisms forage **in a fashion** that minimizes the amount of energy and time and maximizes the net energy intake. In other words, all animals attempt to take the most calories by using the least amount of energy. It is believed that the animals developed their methods of foraging through a long process of adaptation to the environment.

대화 스크립트

STEP 01 뼈대를 먼저 작성해 보도록 하겠습니다.

STEP 02 작성하신 뼈대 빈칸에 맞춰서 리딩 지문을 읽고 주요 포인트를 넣어주세요.

STEP 03 하단에 리스닝 노트테이킹을 해주세요. 음원은 학원 홈페이지에서 무료로 다운받으실 수 있습니다. 또한 3003번 문제 번호로 문제를 풀어보실 수 있습니다.

 아래 하단에 리스닝 스크립트를 보고 베꼈어야 하는 부분을 찾아서 적어 보도록 하겠습니다.

대화 스크립트

🎧 뉴토플 - TEST 03_Q3

Now listen to part of a lecture in a biology class.

이제 생물학 수업의 일부를 들어보세요.

예시 ❶
까마귀의 섭이

세부사항
날아서 고둥을 떨어뜨림

All right, let's consider Northwestern crows and how they forage for whelks, a kind of sea snail, to clearly see the idea of optimal foraging. Just like other animals, crows **put** optimal foraging **into practice** when foraging for and consuming whelks. Whelks are marine mollusks, which have a hard shell for protection from predators. It's usually hard for animals to depend on whelks as a stable food source. Crows, however, can easily break the shell of whelks by employing a simple trick. Using their ability to fly, they fly high into the sky and drop the whelks on the ground to crack the shells.

좋아요, 노스웨스턴 까마귀와 그들이 고둥류의 하나인 쇠고둥을 어떻게 잡는가를 예로 들어 최적 섭이에 대해 명확하게 알아봅시다. 다른 동물들처럼 까마귀도 먹이를 잡을 때와 쇠고둥을 먹을 때 최적 섭이를 **실행에 옮깁니다**. 쇠고둥은 딱딱한 껍데기가 있어 포식 동물로부터 보호받는 해양 연체동물입니다. 동물들로 하여금 쇠고둥을 안정된 주식으로 삼기에는 어렵습니다. 하지만 까마귀는 간단한 방법을 이용해 쉽게 껍데기를 깰 수 있습니다. 그들은 날 수 있는 능력을 이용하여 높게 비상한 다음 쇠고둥을 바닥에 떨어트려 껍데기를 깹니다.

예시 ❷
최적 섭이 방법

세부사항
높으면 에너지 낭비고, 낮으면 재시도 가능성이 높으므로 적당히

The process of dropping the whelks also **incorporates** the various decisions that the crows have to make in order to achieve optimal foraging. For example, the height of flight must be decided. The bigger and heavier the whelk is, the lower the crow has to fly to break the shell. So, if the crow flies too high, it becomes inefficient **in terms of** energy consumption. But then, if it's too low, the crow would have to repeat the process. Crows are intelligent birds so they can calculate the optimal height to break the shell.

쇠고둥을 떨어뜨리는 과정에서 까마귀가 최적 섭이를 하기 위해선 여러 가지 결정을 **포함해야** 합니다. 예를 들어, 비행의 높이를 정해야 합니다. 쇠고둥이 더 크고 더 무거울수록 까마귀는 더 높게 날아야 껍데기를 깰 수 있습니다. 그리하여 만약 까마귀가 너무 높이 날면 그것은 효율성 **면에서** 낮은 에너지 소비가 됩니다. 하지만 너무 낮게 날았다면 까마귀는 같은 과정을 반복해야 합니다. 까마귀는 영리한 새이기 때문에 껍데기를 깨기 위한 최적의 높이를 계산할 수 있습니다.

문제

Using the example from the professor's lecture, explain what optimal foraging is and how it works.

교수의 강의를 예로 들어, 최적 섭이가 무엇이고 어떻게 작용하는지 설명하세요.

STEP 05
다시한번 음원듣고 노트테이킹 해보도록 하겠습니다.
Note-taking

STEP 06
다시 한번 뼈대와 함께 모범 답안을 작성해 보도록 하겠습니다.

Optimal Foraging

In ecology, all animals must consume a source of energy which in turn is used for all the bodily functions. Therefore, it is essential that animals not waste energy on unnecessary activities. The ecologists developed a theory called **optimal** foraging which is the idea whereby organisms forage **in a fashion** that minimizes the amount of energy and time and maximizes the net energy intake. In other words, all animals attempt to take the most calories by using the least amount of energy. It is believed that the animals developed their methods of foraging through a long process of adaptation to the environment.

USHER

References

Photo by Ianare Sevi, available under the Creative Commons Attribution-Share Alike 3.0 Unported license.

Photo by Graham Bould

[참고자료]

❶ 까마귀 (Northwestern Crow)
❷ 쇠고둥 (Whelk)

Task 3 Sample Response 🎧 뉴토플 - TEST 03_R3   3번 문제 모범 답안

Optimal foraging is animals' way of minimizing the loss of time and energy when hunting. In the lecture, the professor gives an example of Northwestern crows to explain it.

❶ Northwestern crows prey on whelks, a type of sea snails. Crows drop them from the sky and make cracks in the shells, which they can then open.

❷ These crows have to decide the right height when dropping the whelks. If they fly too high, they would consume a lot of energy. If they fly too low, the whelks might not crack, so they would have to fly again. So crows have learned to measure the weight of the whelks and calculate the best height for each.

최적 섭이는 동물들이 사냥을 할 때 시간과 에너지 손실을 최소화하는 방법을 말합니다. 강의에서 교수는 노스웨스턴 까마귀를 예로 들며 설명하였습니다.

❶ 노스웨스턴 까마귀는 고둥류의 하나인 쇠고둥을 잡아 먹습니다. 까마귀는 하늘에서 떨어뜨려 껍데기에 금이 가게 하여 열 수 있게 합니다.

❷ 이 까마귀들은 쇠고둥을 떨어뜨릴 적당한 높이를 결정해야 합니다. 만약에 너무 높게 난다면 너무 많은 에너지를 사용합니다. 만약에 너무 낮게 난다면 쇠고둥이 **안 깨질** 수 있고 그러면 또 다시 날아야 합니다. 그리하여 까마귀들은 높이를 계산하는 법을 익혔고 최적의 높이를 계산할 수 있습니다.

Vocabulary

optimal [áptəməl]	a. 최선의, 최적의	in a fashion	phr. ~의 방법으로
put into practice	phr. 실행하다	incorporate [inkɔ́ːrpərèit]	v. 통합시키다
in terms of	phr. ~의 측면에서	crack [kræk]	n. 갈라진, 금 / ad. 탁 / v. 깨다

04. Loon's Plumage 아비새의 깃털　　Integrated Task

STEP 01
4번 뼈대를 먼저 작성해 보도록 하겠습니다.

STEP 02
하단에 리스닝 노트테이킹을 해주세요. 음원은 학원 홈페이지에서 무료로 다운받으실 수 있습니다. 또한 4003번 문제 번호로 문제를 풀어보실 수 있습니다.

STEP 03
뼈대에 맞춰서 모범 답안을 완성해 보겠습니다.

Listen to part of a lecture in a zoology class.

Have you ever tried swimming in the winter? If you have, you must know that the temperature of the water is extremely low. Yet, a species of birds called loons spends the majority of their time on water, because their legs are positioned at the back, near the tail, and they cannot balance their weight well. They therefore need to be able to stay warm in winter, and their special **plumage** provides exactly that ability.

Okay, so when you look at a loon, their feathers don't look very special compared to other birds. That is because the features that we see, the feathers on the outside called **contour** feathers, aren't unique. They are mainly composed of these, um, hair-like **veins**, tightly packed and **intertwined**, preventing water from **seeping** through. But that's not all. The feather is coated with an oily substance, and as we all know, oil and water **repel** each other. This means that the feathers cannot get wet, which is fortunate as water steals body heat when evaporating.

What makes loons unique, however, is what's underneath the contour feathers. Between the skin and the contour feathers, there is a different type of feather called down feathers. Of all the different types of feathers, down feathers have the simplest structure: they are basically like cotton. But the structure doesn't **do justice to** its significant benefits. These feathers are able to trap a fairly large volume of air, inducing an **insulating** effect. People already appreciate the effectiveness of heat insulation in down feathers and use them in jackets and in bedding. Also, you would have never guessed it, but down feathers help loons float! Remember when I said down feathers trap air? Well, that air remains trapped even when the loon is swimming, and is able to **contribute** to the **buoyancy** of the bird.

Using the examples from the professor's lecture, explain the functions of the two types of feathers.

References

Photo by Rita Ballantyne

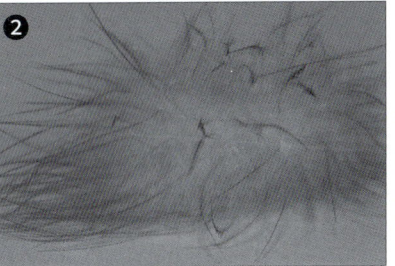
Photo by Yoky, available under the Creative Commons Attribution-Share Alike 3.0 Unported, 2.5 Generic, 2.0 Generic and 1.0 Generic license.

Photo by Tim Bowman, USFWS

[참고자료]

❶ 겉 깃털(Contour Feather)
❷ 솜 깃털(Down Feather)
❸ 아비새(Loon)

Task 4 Sample Response 🎧 TEST 03_R4

4번 문제 모범 답안

In the lecture, the professor explains the functions of the two types of feathers loons have. Loons are a type of bird that spends most of their time swimming in cold water.

❶ First, contour feathers are placed on the outside. They are packed and intertwined to keep water away and this function is reinforced by the oily coating on the outside.

❷ Second, down feathers are placed in between contour feathers and the skin. It has a simple structure like cotton and can trap a lot of air. The trapped air insulates heat and helps loons to float in the water.

강의에서 교수는 아비새가 가지고 있는 두 가지 깃털의 역할을 설명하고 있습니다. 아비새는 차가운 물위에서 수영을 하며 대부분의 시간을 보내는 조류입니다.

❶ 첫째, 겉 깃털은 밖에 위치해 있습니다. 촘촘하게 꼬여 있는 겉 깃털은 기름막까지 있어 물이 스미는 것을 막는 역할을 합니다.

❷ 둘째, 솜깃털은 겉 깃털과 피부 사이에 있습니다. 솜 같은 단순한 구조를 가지고 있으며 공기를 많이 가두어 둘 수 있습니다. 공기를 가두어 열을 유지하고 물에 뜨는 데에 도움을 줍니다.

Vocabulary

plumage [plúːmidʒ]	n. 깃털	contour [kántuər]	n. 윤곽, 외형
vein [vein]	n. 정맥, 결	intertwine [intərtwaiˈn]	v. 서로 엮다
seep [siːp]	v. 스며 나오다, 침투하다	repel [ripél]	v. 쫓아버리다, 반발하다
do justice to	phr. 정당하게 평가하다	contribute to	phr. ~에 기여하다
insulate [ínsəlèit]	v. 단열하다, 반응하다	buoyancy [bɔ́iənsi]	n. 부력

USHER
iBT TOEFL
FINAL TEST SPEAKING
TEST 04

Independent Tasks

Task 1 - 모범 답안
Question 1   usherin.usher.co.kr > 시험리스트 > Speaking 시험리스트 > Task 1 > #1023

Integrated Tasks

Task 2 - Script / 해석 / 모범 답안
Question 2   usherin.usher.co.kr > 시험리스트 > Speaking 시험리스트 > Task 2 > #2004

Task 3 - Script / 해석 / 모범 답안
Question 3   usherin.usher.co.kr > 시험리스트 > Speaking 시험리스트 > Task 3 > #3004

Task 4 - Script / 해석 / 모범 답안
Question 4   usherin.usher.co.kr > 시험리스트 > Speaking 시험리스트 > Task 4 > #4004

자기평가표

1번 문제 유형은 학생들이 본인에 생각을 주제에 맞춰서 말 해야하는 시험입니다.
본인이 처음부터 끝까지 45초 동안 말해야하다 보니 학생들이 제일 어려워 하는 시험입니다.
하지만, 먼저 외우고 익힌후에 말하는것이 가능할수 있게 하겠습니다.
가장 기본이 되는 뼈대 입니다. 먼저 외우도록 합시다.

> if i were to answer the question, i would say
> there are many reasons why, but here is a couple
> first
> for example,
> second
> for instance
> that's why

다음은 2번 문제 유형입니다.
2번 문제는 리딩에 학교에 계획이 적혀있거나 학교가 변해야하는 방향에 대해서 학생들에 주장이 적혀있습니다.
리딩에서 빠르게 파악해야하는 것은 도대체 누가 무엇을 주장하는가 입니다.
45~50초에 리딩 지문이 나오고 난 다음에 리스닝으로 학생들에 대화가 나오는 문제입니다.
리스닝에서는 학생이 리딩 지문에 대한 본인에 좋고 나쁜지에 대한 의견을 얘기해줄겁니다.
이유 2가지와 예시 2가지를 꼭 말할 수 있어야 합니다.

이에 따라서 2번 스피킹 문제에 뼈대는

> The reading states that university (plans to) / (should)
> the (woman / man) in the conversation thinks it is a good / bad idea.
> He/she provides two reasons to support his / her opinion.
> first,
> Second,
> the woman / man thinks it's a great / horrible idea.

다음은 3번 문제 유형입니다.
3번 문제는 2번 문제 유형과 같이 리딩과 리스닝이 나오는 문제 입니다. 하지만, 이번에는 이전 문제와는 달리 매우 학술적인 내용이 들어 있습니다. 리딩에서는 교과서에 나올만한 주제 한개를 자세하게 다룹니다. 여기서 학생분들은 제목과 이에 대한 정의를 잘 받아적으셔야 합니다. 리스닝에서는 교수님이 리딩에 나온 내용으로 예시를 들어 줍니다.

> The article is about
> which the passage defines as
> The professor provides an example of
> first,
> Second,
> The example clearly illustrates

다음은 4번 문제 유형입니다.
4번 문제는 이전 문제와 달리 리스닝만 나오는 문제 유형입니다. 3번 문제에 나온 리딩 지문이 리스닝으로 변환되었다 라고 생각하시면 됩니다. 그렇기에 3번 문제에 리스닝 내용보다 리딩 길이 만큼 깁니다.

> In the lecture, professor explains
> first,
> second,
> That's how the professor explain it.

01. Junk Food Advertisement
인스턴트 식품 광고

Independent Task

QUESTION

Do you agree or disagree with the following statement? Advertising junk food or candy bars should be prohibited for children. Use reasons and examples to support your answer. (다음 주장에 동의하십니까, 반대하십니까? 인스턴트 식품과 캔디바를 광고하는 것은 아이들을 위해서 금지되어야 한다. 이유와 예를 들어 답하세요.)

브레인 스토밍 (아래에 놓여있는 12간지 내용들을 보고 어떤 것을 사용할 수 있을지 확인해보세요)

첫번째 이유 :
두번째 이유 :

뼈대에 맞춰서 작성을 해봅시다.

_____
_____
_____
_____
_____
_____

아래 이미지는 학생들을 위한 만능 템플릿 12간지 입니다. 학생분들이 제일 먼저 암기해야하는 것이며, 본인 스스로 문장을 단기간 안에 못 만들거 같을 때에 도와주는 친구입니다. 가까이 두고 매일 외우세요.

Academic Courses
…because I think students should concentrate on academic courses.

Academic courses are the most important thing for students because good grades will help them get into good universities and, eventually, get great jobs.

As students get older, a good academic record is the only thing that actually matters.

This may sound a little far-fetched, but it's true, and for this reason, investing time in other activities is a waste of time.

Stay Healthy
It can be a great way to stay healthy. People join a cycling group through the internet. The members use bicycles to commute to work or school.

It is a great outdoor activity because people have a chance to work out while having fun.

Also, it is a great way to meet new people with similar interests. People nowadays do not have much chance to become close to each other.

However, there are numerous unique groups active on the internet, and this would not have been possible without the internet.

Follows your heart
Carpe diem, seize the days, and YOLO all stand for one thing. Do whatever your heart makes you do.

Life is too short to hesitate or do things to please others. It is essential to make yourself happy.

Actions speak louder than words. Whatever I do to make myself happy is better than sitting in a room thinking about it.

So I would just do it even if it means I am biting off something more than I can chew.

Stress
…if it can possibly be a way to relieve stress.

People nowadays are living a busy and hectic life, so they are under great stress, but a lot of them don't even realize they are stressed out.

Stress is known to be a major factor that keeps us from being healthy, and many people are suffering from various problems.

This is more serious than we think, so if it can ever be a way to relieve stress…

Money
…because it's the best way to save money. When it comes to spending money, every penny counts.

A thrifty spending habit is indispensable in our lives because little drops of water make the mighty ocean.

If we don't get used to working on a tight budget, we'll always be short on cash later.

A penny-pinching lifestyle will lead to financial stability, and it will give us peace of mind.

Saving Time
…because it's the best way to save time. There's an old saying, "Time is gold."

This proverb emphasizes the value of time, and this cannot be more true in modern society.

We're living a busy and hectic life, so saving time means we can do a lot more things later.

Many say that life is not fair, but everyone has twenty-four hours a day and seven days a week, so I would save time by…

Social Skills
Nowadays, people have smartphones with them all the time, and that information is no longer limited to elites.

Therefore, rather than learning, having social skills became the be-all and end-all to succeed rather than education.

Also, social skills are more than meet the eyes. To have social skills, one must also be able to read others like a book.

There will be times when one will truly need them.

Environment
because eventually, it can contribute to protecting the environment.

I think it's THE most important task for humanity because we cannot bring it back to life once it's too late.

Saving Earth all starts from seemingly insignificant actions.

Small actions from everyone bring about bigger changes, so I'm willing to participate.

Patience is virtue
Patience is a virtue. Saving time is indeed important, but waiting calmly is needed in this case.

There are times when one must wait patiently for things to go accordingly, and this is when time is the solution.

When going against the clock, they are more susceptible to making mistakes than taking some time.

In the long run, one will be glad that one has waited in this case.

Just because
I love it more than the given choices. Since I have so many great memory about it, It brings so many great reminiscences.

time flies whenever I am doing it, so how can I not choose it?

Also, not only do I love it, but I am also good at it. Everyone has talent, and it is like "a dime a dozen."

This was the inborn talent I had that I always surpassed everyone. Since a bird in the hand is worth two in the bush, I will choose it.

Politeness
It is important to maintain good relationships with other people because we never know what will happen in the future.

Decisions made by other people can affect others, and such decisions are usually based on personal and sentimental reasons.

So, people should not do anything that may offend or disturb others. It is also crucial to have a good reputation and get along well with others.

It Makes sense
It makes sense to choose it when considering many aspects such as time, money, and efficiency.

When people are considering between the given choices, they must consider many aspects economically.

They must choose the most efficient method because there are limits on what they have.

Also, one should think about it realistically and practically because they should not count chickens before they hatch.

So, down to Earth, people should choose it because it is the most economical

QUESTION

Do you agree or disagree with the following statement? Advertising junk food or candy bars should be prohibited for children. Use reasons and examples to support your answer. (다음 주장에 동의하십니까, 반대하십니까? 인스턴트 식품과 캔디바를 광고하는 것은 아이들을 위해서 금지되어야 한다. 이유와 예를 들어 답하세요.)

save money와 stay healthy를 사용해서 뼈대에 맞춰서 모범답안을 만들어 봅시다.

stress와 follow your heart를 사용해서 뼈대에 맞춰서 모범답안을 만들어 봅시다.

it makes sense와 academic courses를 사용해서 뼈대에 맞춰서 모범답안을 만들어 봅시다.

just because와 social skills를 사용해서 뼈대에 맞춰서 모범답안을 만들어 봅시다.

QUESTION

Do you agree or disagree with the following statement? Advertising junk food or candy bars should be prohibited for children. Use reasons and examples to support your answer. (다음 주장에 동의하십니까, 반대하십니까? 인스턴트 식품과 캔디바를 광고하는 것은 아이들을 위해서 금지되어야 한다. 이유와 예를 들어 답하세요.)

save money와 stay healthy를 사용해서 뼈대에 맞춰서 모범답안을 만들어 봅시다.

If I were to answer the question, I would say I agree. There are many reasons why, but here is a couple.

save money

First, children spend their money compulsively on junk food. For example, it can be a way to save money. A thrifty spending habit is indispensable in our lives because little drops of water make the mighty ocean.

stay healthy

Second, children should work out instead of eating junk food. For instance, students can join a cycling group through the advertisement when there is one. They can commute to school together. It is a great outdoor activity because they will have a chance to work out.

That's why I think advertising junk food should be prohibited.

stress와 follow your heart를 사용해서 뼈대에 맞춰서 모범답안을 만들어 봅시다.

If I were to answer the question, I would say I disagree. There are many reasons why, but here is a couple.

stress

First, eating junk food can be a way to relieve stress. For example, stress is known to be a major factor that keeps us from being healthy. Stress is more dangerous than junk foods.

follow your heart

Second, they should be able to eat whatever they want. For instance, carpe diem, seize the days, and YOLO all stand for one thing. Do whatever your heart makes you do. They should be able to do whatever they want.

That's why I think they should be able to eat junk food.

it makes sense와 academic courses를 사용해서 뼈대에 맞춰서 모범답안을 만들어 봅시다.

If I were to answer the question I would say advertising junk food or candy bars should be prohibited for children. There are many reasons why, but here is a couple.

it makes sense

First, it makes sense to prohibit advertising junk food or candy bars. For example, when a government thinks about the money, time, and health of the students, they must choose to ban advertising junk food.

academic courses

Second, they should study instead of watching television. For instance, academic courses are the most important thing for students because good grades will help them get into a good university and eventually get great jobs. They should study instead of watching television and eating junk food.

That's why I agree with the statement.

just because와 social skills를 사용해서 뼈대에 맞춰서 모범답안을 만들어 봅시다.

If I were to answer the question, I would say advertising junk food or candy bars should not be prohibited for children. There are many reasons why, but here is a couple.

just because

First, I love junk food. For example, I have so much great memory about eating junk food and watching funny junk food advertisements. To make a long story short, it should not be banned.

social skills.

Second, even without advertisements, students can look for junk foods. For instance, these days, children have smartphones with them all the time. advertisement is not the only source to gather information anymore.

That's why I disagree.

02. Check-Out Policy 대여 정책

Integrated Task

읽기 지문

Changes to the Check-Out Policy

Currently, the library allows students to keep books for a period of a month when they **check** them **out**. However, it has been determined that one month is too long of a period. By reducing the lending period to two weeks, it will allow the books to be read by a large number of people, who might be waiting for the book. Since the library is limited by the number of books they have, by allowing one person to keep a book for a whole month is unfair, as there might be a lot of students **in need of** it.

대화 스크립트

 뼈대를 먼저 작성해 보도록 하겠습니다.

 작성하신 뼈대 빈칸에 맞춰서 리딩 지문을 읽고 주요 포인트를 넣어주세요.

 하단에 리스닝 노트테이킹을 해주세요. 음원은 학원 홈페이지에서 무료로 다운받으실 수 있습니다. 또한 2004번 문제 번호로 문제를 풀어보실 수 있습니다.

아래 하단에 리스닝 스크립트를 보고 베꼈어야 하는 부분을 찾아서 적어 보도록 하겠습니다.

대화 스크립트

뉴토플 - TEST 04_Q2

Now listen to two students discussing the announcement.

M: Hey, did you hear about the library's plans to reduce the lending period for books?

W: Yeah… I don't think it's a good idea.

M: Why not?

W: Well, two weeks is just too short! I mean, sure, we can read the book in two weeks, but most of the books that we borrow from the library aren't just for reading purposes. We often borrow the **reference books** to **look back on** when we need to write research papers. We don't keep the books for a month to read, but rather, **to refer to** them.

M: Yeah, you're right. But, what about the other students who may need the book? It's not exactly fair for one student to **hold onto** a book that may be needed by multiple students.

W: Well… I don't want to sound cold or anything, but that's their problem. It's unfair to take the book away from students who borrowed the book **ahead of time** to give it to students who are late.

M: Right.

W: If the late students REALLY need the book, they can check out the Library Link program. The university links our library to other libraries, so students can look for more reference materials outside the library.

M: Well, maybe I should **check that out**.

여자의 의견
반대

이유 ❶
참고하려고 책을
빌리기 때문에
2주는 너무 짧음

이유 ❷
책을 늦게
빌리게 된 건
그들 사정임

문제
The woman expresses her opinion about the college's plan. State her opinion and explain the reasons she gives for holding that opinion.

이제 지문에 대해 논의하는 두 학생의 대화를 들어보세요.

남: 야, 대출 기간을 2주로 줄이려는 도서관 계획에 대해서 들어봤어?

여: 응, 별로 좋은 생각 같지는 않아.

남: 왜??

여: 글쎄, 2주는 너무 짧아! 내 말은, 우리가 책을 2주안에 읽을 수는 있는데, 우리가 도서관에서 빌리는 책들은 단지 읽으려고 빌리는 게 아니란 거야. 논문 쓸 때 필요한 걸 **다시 보려고 참고서적**을 빌리는 거잖아. 읽으려고 한달 동안 갖고 있는 게 아니라, **참고하려고 하는** 거지.

남: 그래, 맞아. 근데, 그 책을 필요로 하는 다른 학생들은? 여러 명이 필요로 하는 책들을 한 사람이 **갖고 있는** 게 그다지 공평하진 않잖아.

여: 글쎄… 쌀쌀맞게 굴려는 것은 아닌데, 그건 걔네 문제지. **미리** 책을 빌린 사람한테서 늦은 다른 학생들에게 주려고 책을 뺏는 건 불공평하다고 봐.

남: 맞아.

여: 만약에 그 늦은 학생이 정말로 책이 필요하다면, 도서관 연결 프로그램을 사용할 수 있지. 우리 도서관을 다른 데랑 연결해서, 학생들은 우리 도서관 밖의 참고서를 찾아 볼 수 있어.

남: 그래, 그럼 그걸 알아봐야겠다.

여자는 대학의 계획에 대해 자신의 의견을 밝히고 있습니다. 그녀의 의견을 말하고, 그 의견을 고수하는 이유를 설명하세요.

Note-taking
STEP 05

STEP 06 다시한번 모범 답안을 작성해 보도록 하겠습니다

Changes to the Check-Out Policy

Currently, the library allows students to keep books for a period of a month when they **check** them **out**. However, it has been determined that one month is too long of a period. By reducing the lending period to two weeks, it will allow the books to be read by a large number of people, who might be waiting for the book. Since the library is limited by the number of books they have, by allowing one person to keep a book for a whole month is unfair, as there might be a lot of students **in need of** it.

Note-taking	노트테이킹
Reading - reduce the lending time from a month to two weeks - one month is too long - it is unfair for other students in need of the book **Woman** - against **Reason ❶** - period of two weeks is too short - students borrow books as a reference as well **Reason ❷** - library should not worry about the late students - they can use the Library Link program	**지문** - 대여기간을 한달에서 2주로 줄임 - 한달이 너무 김 - 책이 필요한 학생들은 억울함 **여자** - 반대 **이유 ❶** - 2주는 너무 짧음 - 학생들은 참고자료용으로도 책을 빌림 **이유 ❷** - 도서관이 늦은 학생을 걱정할 필요 없음 - 도서관 연결 정책을 이용하면 됨

Task 2 Sample Response 🎧 뉴토플 - TEST 04_R2 | 2번 문제 모범 답안

The two students are discussing the college's plan to reduce the lending time of borrowed books from a month to two weeks. The woman is against the plan for two reasons. ❶ First, the suggested time limit of two weeks is rather too short. Students borrow books not only for reading purposes but also to refer to them when writing research papers. ❷ Second, the library doesn't need to worry about the late students. If they can't get the book, they can always use the Library Link service and get books from other libraries. (This is why she thinks the plan is unnecessary.)	두 학생은 책의 대출 기간을 한 달에서 2주로 줄이려는 대학 측의 계획에 대해 의논하고 있다. 여자는 두 가지 이유를 들어 그 계획에 반대하고 있다. ❶ 첫째, 제안 된 2주의 시간 제한은 너무 짧다. 학생들은 읽기 목적으로 책들을 빌리는 것뿐만 아니라 논문을 쓸 때 참고하려고 빌린다. ❷ 다음, 도서관은 늦은 학생들을 걱정할 필요가 없다. 만약 그들이 책을 못 빌린다면, 그들은 도서관 연결 서비스를 사용해서 다른 도서관으로부터 책을 빌릴 수 있다. (이것이 그녀가 이 계획이 불필요하다고 생각하는 이유이다.)

Vocabulary

to check out	phr. (책 등을) 대여하다, 알아보다	in need of	phr. ~이 필요한
look back on	phr. 떠올리다	refer to	phr. ~에 대해 언급하다, 참고하다
hold onto	phr. 꼭 잡고 있다, 의지하다	ahead of time	phr. 미리

03. Mental Accounting 심적 회계 — Integrated Task

읽기 지문

Mental Accounting

Mental accounting refers to the process by which people **encode, categorize** and evaluate economic outcomes. One example of mental accounting is the so-called **behavioral** life cycle **hypothesis**. It assumes that people have a tendency to classify assets into different accounts such as current income, current wealth and future income. In people's minds, the accounts are not **interchangeable** and their habits of consumption from each account tend to be different. Mental accounting is considered a major psychological problem that people have to overcome, especially when suffering from financial issues.

대화 스크립트

STEP 01 뼈대를 먼저 작성해 보도록 하겠습니다.

STEP 02 작성하신 뼈대 빈칸에 맞춰서 리딩 지문을 읽고 주요 포인트를 넣어주세요.

STEP 03 하단에 리스닝 노트테이킹을 해주세요. 음원은 학원 홈페이지에서 무료로 다운받으실 수 있습니다. 또한 3004번 문제 번호로 문제를 풀어보실 수 있습니다.

USHER

STEP 04 — 아래 하단에 리스닝 스크립트를 보고 베꼈어야 하는 부분을 찾아서 적어 보도록 하겠습니다.

대화 스크립트

🎧 뉴토플 - TEST 04_Q3

Now listen to part of a lecture in a business class.

So let me tell you about my own experience with this when I was an office worker in the first few years of my career. I was quite young back then, so I had some spare time and energy. I decided to work part-time as a waitress at a restaurant on weekends. I have to admit that it was physically challenging, but I kept working because I was more than happy to earn extra cash.

이제 경영학 수업의 일부를 들어보세요.

자, 제가 사무실 직원으로 일했던 첫 몇 해간의 경험에 대해 얘기해 드리겠습니다. 당시 저는 꽤 어려서 여유시간도 있었고 에너지도 있었습니다. 저는 주말에 음식점에서 웨이트리스로 아르바이트 하기로 결정했습니다. 육체적으로 힘들었지만, 돈을 더 벌 수 있는 것이 너무 기뻐서 저는 계속 일했습니다.

예시 ❶ — 사무실 월급
세부사항 — 은행에 예금하고 건드리지 않음

Having these two different sources of income, I decided to use those differently. Whenever I got paid from my office job, I decided to deposit the money into my bank account and forget about it. I was saving money to buy a house, so I didn't use it at all; I didn't even touch it. The plan was successful and I could later buy a nice, decent house. This was possible because I thought of the savings account as untouchable.

두 개의 수입원을 갖게 된 저는 둘을 다르게 쓰기로 결정했습니다. 사무실 월급은 은행에 넣어놓기로 했습니다. 저는 집을 사려고 돈을 모으고 있었기 때문에 그 돈을 절대 쓰지도, 건드리지도 않았습니다. 이 계획은 성공적이어서 저는 후에 좋은 집을 살 수 있었습니다. 이것은 제가 저축 예금을 건드릴 수 없는 돈으로 생각했기 때문에 가능했습니다.

예시 ❷ — 음식점 월급
세부사항 — 제약없이 사고 싶은 것을 삼

The salary from the restaurant, however, was different. With the money from this job, I bought anything I wanted, even things I didn't need. I used the money without **constraints**, but it was, okay because I thought of it as extra money, like a bonus. **Come to think of it**, if I hadn't labeled the part-time salary as extra, but had saved the money, then I could have bought the house earlier much earlier actually.

그러나, 음식점 월급은 달랐습니다. 이 일에서 번 돈으로 저는 원하는 것, 심지어 필요없는 것까지 샀습니다. 저는 아무런 **제약**없이 이 돈을 썼지만, 보너스와 같은 여분의 돈으로 생각했기에 괜찮았습니다. **지금 생각해보면**, 아르바이트로 번 돈을 여분으로 분류하지 않고 모았다면 집을 더 빨리 살 수 있었을 것입니다. 훨씬 더 빨리.

문제 — Using the example from the professor's lecture, explain what mental accounting is and how it works.

교수의 강의를 예로 들어, 심적 회계가 무엇이고 어떻게 작용하는지 설명하세요.

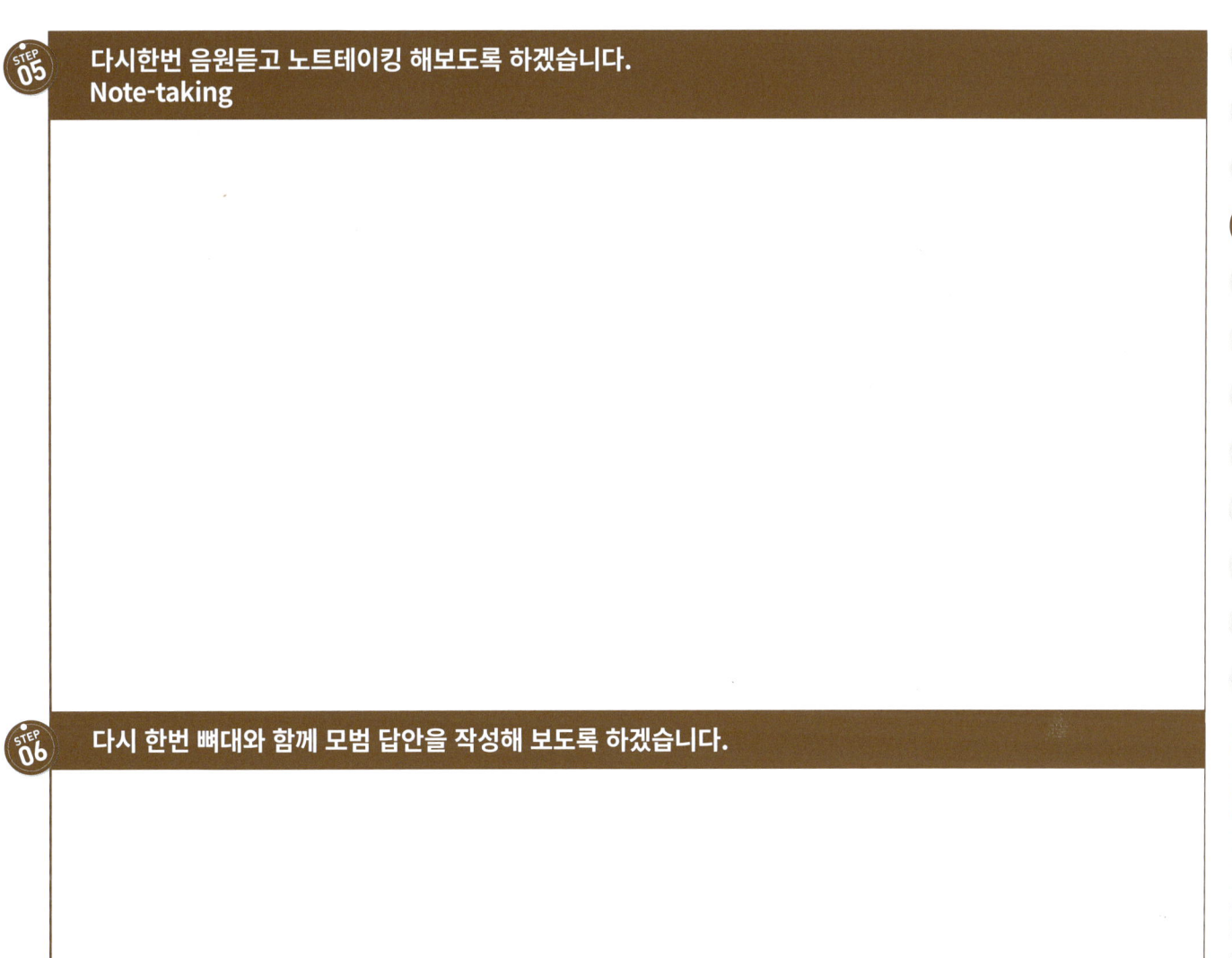

Mental Accounting

Mental accounting refers to the process by which people **encode, categorize** and evaluate economic outcomes. One example of mental accounting is the so-called **behavioral** life cycle **hypothesis**. It assumes that people have a tendency to classify assets into different accounts such as current income, current wealth and future income. In people's minds, the accounts are not **interchangeable** and their habits of consumption from each account tend to be different. Mental accounting is considered a major psychological problem that people have to overcome, especially when suffering from financial issues.

References

심적 회계

1980년 독일계 미국인 경제학자 리차드 H. 탈러 (Richard H. Thaler b. 1945~)에 의해 처음 고안된 개념이다.

예를 들어, 사람들이 땀 흘려 일해서 번 돈 백만 원과 도박으로 번 돈 백만 원을 다르게 생각하는 것이 대표적인 케이스이다. 이처럼 사람들은 각자 '마음 속의 회계장부'를 가지고 돈의 출처에 따라 다른 의미를 부여하고 용도를 차별한다.

이는 곧 낭비로 이어지기 쉬운데, 이를 막기 위해서는 출처와 관계없이 모든 돈은 그 절대 금액이 같다고 생각해야 한다.

Task 3 Sample Response 🎧 뉴토플 - TEST 04_R3   3번 문제 모범 답안

Mental accóunting is how people encode, categorize and eváluate económic resúlts. In the lecture, the proféssor gives an exámple of hersélf to expláin it.

❶ The proféssor had two jobs when she was younger. She worked in an office on weekdays, and worked part-time at a restaurant on weekends. She saved the money from the office job, so she could buy a house later.

❷ She could have bought the house much earlier if she could have saved the money from the weekend job as well. She should not have thought of the two sources as separate accóunts.

심적 회계는 사람들이 경제적 결과를 어떻게 암호화하고, 분류하고 평가하느냐 입니다. 강의에서, 교수는 그녀 자신의 예를 들어 설명합니다.

❶ 교수는 젊었을 적 두 개의 직업을 가지고 있었습니다. 주중에는 사무실에서 일하고 주말에는 레스토랑에서 아르바이트를 했습니다. 사무실에서 일한 돈을 저축해서 후에 집을 살 수 있었습니다.

❷ 주말에 일한 돈을 모았다면 집을 훨씬 더 일찍 살 수 있었을 것입니다. 그녀는 두 원천을 다른 계좌로 생각하지 말았어야 했습니다.

Vocabulary

encode [inkóud]	v. 암호로 바꾸다	categorize [kǽtəgəràiz]	v. 분류하다
behavioral [bihéivjərəl]	a. 행동에 관한	hypothesis [haipáθəsis]	n. 가설
asset [ǽset]	n. 자산, 재산	interchangeable [intərtipe'ndənt]	n. 호환성 있는
constraint [kənstréint]	n. 압박, 제약	come to think of it	phr. 생각해보니

04. Antipredator Adaptation 천적 퇴치법

Integrated Task

STEP 01
4번 뼈대를 먼저 작성해 보도록 하겠습니다.

STEP 02
하단에 리스닝 노트테이킹을 해주세요. 음원은 학원 홈페이지에서 무료로 다운받으실 수 있습니다. 또한 4004번 문제 번호로 문제를 풀어보실 수 있습니다.

STEP 03
뼈대에 맞춰서 모범 답안을 완성해 보겠습니다.

대화 스크립트

 뉴토플 - TEST 04_Q4

Listen to part of a lecture in a zoology class.

동물학 강의의 일부를 들어보세요.

주제
동물들이 천적을 막기 위해 서로 돕는 법

Today, we'll talk about cooperative anti-predator adaptation. In a purely evolutionary concept, the most successful species is the one that can increase and maintain its population best. There are many factors to consider in order to keep a population growing steadily, and one of the most important ones is dealing with predators. That's why most species have developed cooperative adaptations rather than individual behaviors to increase the likelihood of survival for the entire species. Let's look at some examples.

우리는 오늘 협동적인 천적 퇴치법에 대하여 얘기해 보려 합니다. 진화적 측면에서 가장 성공한 동물은 그 개체 수를 늘리고 유지할 수 있어야 합니다. 개체 수를 지속적으로 늘리기 위해 많은 요인을 고려해야 하며 그 중 천적에 대응하는 것이 가장 중요합니다. 그렇기 때문에 대부분의 동물들은 종족의 생존을 위하여 혼자서 행동을 하기보다는 협동을 통한 천적 퇴치법을 발전시켜 왔습니다. 몇 가지 예를 들어봅시다.

예시 ❶
사향소는 일렬로 서거나 원을 만들어 천적에 맞섬

Muskoxen **are native to** Canada, Greenland, and the Arctic region. Their physical characteristics are very **intimidating**, standing taller than most other **bovines**. But their long horns and thick fur make them appear even bigger. They are still herbivores, though, and are prey to some **menacing** carnivores such as Arctic wolves and grizzly bears. To increase survivability and the chances of **warding off** predators, the muskoxen developed a few distinctive formations. When attacked by a single predator, the bulls form a line facing the predator. This gives the impression of being larger in number to the predator. When attacked by a pack, the males form a tight circle facing outward around the **calves** and cows.

사향소는 캐나다, 그린랜드, 북극에 **분포되어** 있습니다. 사향소는 대부분의 **소**들보다 몸집이 커 **위협적인** 외형적 특징을 가지고 있습니다. 심지어 길쭉한 뿔과 두꺼운 털 때문에 더 거대하게 보이기도 합니다. 그렇다고 해도 사향소는 초식 동물이기 때문에 북극 늑대나 회색곰과 같은 **무시무시한** 포식자의 먹이가 되곤 합니다. 천적을 **쫓아내고**, 생존율을 높이기 위하여, 사향소는 몇 가지 특이한 대형을 발달시켰습니다. 한 마리의 천적이 공격할 경우 소들은 일렬로 줄을 섭니다. 이는 포식자에게 사향소의 수가 더욱 많다는 인상을 줍니다. 다수의 포식자에게 공격 받을 경우, 숫소들은 암소와 **송아지**를 동그랗게 둘러싸 무리를 보호합니다.

예시 ❷
흉내지빠귀도 둥지를 지키기 위해 집단공격을 함

Mockingbirds have also developed a distinct behavior to protect their nests and the young, called mobbing. In mobbing, the birds assemble around a predator and attack together. But once again, the goal of mobbing is to fend off the predator, rather than to injure it. The behavior is merely a survival instinct. So, when a fox intrudes upon the nesting area of the mockingbirds, the first bird to spot it will call nearby individuals and will stand in front, distracting it. While the fox is **preoccupied**, other birds will attack the fox from behind with their beaks. Other ways to scare off the predator include flying around the **intruder**, loud **squawking**, and **defecating** on it.

흉내지빠귀도 새끼와 둥지를 보호하기 위하여 모빙이라는 독특한 행동을 발전시켜 왔습니다. 모빙은 새들이 무리를 지어 천적 주변을 날아다니면서 공격하는 것입니다. 다시 말하지만, 모빙의 목적은 천적에게 상처를 주는 것보단, 둥지를 지키기 위함에 있습니다. 이런 행동은 생존 본능에 의한 것입니다. 그렇기에, 여우가 둥지를 침략한다면, 이를 가장 먼저 본 흉내지빠귀는 가까이 있는 새들을 부르고 앞에 서서 여우의 주위를 산만케 할 것입니다. 여우가 **혼란에 빠진** 동안 다른 새들은 부리를 이용하여 뒤에서 공격합니다. **천적을** 겁주는 다른 방법으로는 주변을 날아다니거나, 큰소리로 **지저귀기**, 배설하기 등이 있습니다.

문제

Using the examples from the professor's lecture, explain how some animals protect themselves from predators.

교수의 강의를 예로 들어, 동물들이 어떻게 천적으로 부터 스스로를 보호하는지 설명하세요.

References

Photo by Dixi, available under the Creative Commons Attribution-Share Alike 3.0 Unported license.

Photo by USFWS

[참고자료]

❶ 사향소 (Muskox)
❷ 사향소들이 한 마리의 천적을 맞닥뜨렸을 때 갖추는 일자대형

Task 4   Sample Response   TEST 04_R4

In the lecture, the professor is explaining how animals coóperate in order to ward off predators. He is giving an exámple of muskóxen and mockingbirds to expláin it.

❶ Muskóxen protéct themsélves from wolves and bears by making formátions. When there is one predator, they face the predator in a single line; when there are many predators, adult males surróund the young and females and face outward.

❷ Mockingbirds gather aróund predators, such as foxes, to attáck them. The first bird will alarm others and distráct the predator. In the meantime, the other members will attáck from behínd. They have many other ways to scare off predators as well.

4번 문제 모범 답안

강의에서 교수는 동물들이 포식자를 쫓아내기 위하여 어떻게 협동하는지 설명하고 있습니다. 그는 사향소와 흉내지빠귀를 예로 들어 설명합니다.

❶ 사향소는 대형을 구축하여 늑대와 곰들부터 자신들을 보호합니다. 한 마리의 포식자를 대할 때는 한 줄로 나란히 줄을 서고, 여러 마리 포식자가 있다면, 숫소가 암소와 송아지를 둘러싸 보호합니다.

❷ 흉내지빠귀는 여우와 같은 천적을 공격하기 위해 둘러쌉니다. 처음 포식자를 발견한 새는 다른 새들에게 위급함을 알리고 천적을 산만하게 만듭니다. 그 동안 다른 새들은 뒤에서 천적을 공격합니다. 흉내지빠귀는 이외에 여러 가지 다른 방법으로 천적들을 쫓아냅니다.

Vocabulary

be native to	phr. ~의 원산인	intimidating [intímədèitiŋ]	a. 위협적인, 겁을 주는
bovine [bóuvain]	n. 소과의 동물	menacing [ménisiŋ]	a. 위협적인
ward off (fend off)	v. 내쫓다	calf [kæf, ka:f]	n. 송아지
defecate [défikèit]	v. 배변하다	preoccupied [pri:ákjəpàid]	a. 몰두한, 여념이 없는
intruder [intrú:dər]	n. 침입자	squawk [skwɔ:k]	v. 꽥꽥 울다

USHER
iBT TOEFL
FINAL TEST SPEAKING
TEST 05

Independent Tasks

Task 1 - 모범 답안
Question 1   usherin.usher.co.kr > 시험리스트 > Speaking 시험리스트 > Task 1 > #1009

Integrated Tasks

Task 2 - Script / 해석 / 모범 답안
Question 2   usherin.usher.co.kr > 시험리스트 > Speaking 시험리스트 > Task 2 > #2005

Task 3 - Script / 해석 / 모범 답안
Question 3   usherin.usher.co.kr > 시험리스트 > Speaking 시험리스트 > Task 3 > #3005

Task 4 - Script / 해석 / 모범 답안
Question 4   usherin.usher.co.kr > 시험리스트 > Speaking 시험리스트 > Task 4 > #4005

자기평가표

STEP 01 1번 문제 유형은 학생들이 본인에 생각을 주제에 맞춰서 말 해야하는 시험입니다.
본인이 처음부터 끝까지 45초 동안 말해야하다 보니 학생들이 제일 어려워 하는 시험입니다.
하지만, 먼저 외우고 익힌후에 말하는것이 가능할수 있게 하겠습니다.
가장 기본이 되는 뼈대 입니다. 먼저 외우도록 합시다.

> if i were to answer the question, i would say
> there are many reasons why, but here is a couple
> first
> for example,
> second
> for instance
> that's why

다음은 2번 문제 유형입니다.
2번 문제는 리딩에 학교에 계획이 적혀있거나 학교가 변해야하는 방향에 대해서 학생들에 주장이 적혀있습니다.
리딩에서 빠르게 파악해야하는 것은 도대체 누가 무엇을 주장하는가 입니다.
45~50초에 리딩 지문이 나오고 난 다음에 리스닝으로 학생들에 대화가 나오는 문제입니다.
리스닝에서는 학생이 리딩 지문에 대한 본인에 좋고 나쁜지에 대한 의견을 얘기해줄겁니다.
이유 2가지와 예시 2가지를 꼭 말할 수 있어야 합니다.

이에 따라서 2번 스피킹 문제에 뼈대는

> The reading states that university (plans to) / (should)
> the (woman / man) in the conversation thinks it is a good / bad idea.
> He/she provides two reasons to support his / her opinion.
> first,
> Second,
> the woman / man thinks it's a great / horrible idea.

다음은 3번 문제 유형입니다.
3번 문제는 2번 문제 유형과 같이 리딩과 리스닝이 나오는 문제 입니다. 하지만, 이번에는 이전 문제와는 달리 매우 학술적인 내용이 들어 있습니다. 리딩에서는 교과서에 나올만한 주제 한개를 자세하게 다룹니다. 여기서 학생분들은 제목과 이에 대한 정의를 잘 받아적으셔야 합니다. 리스닝에서는 교수님이 리딩에 나온 내용으로 예시를 들어 줍니다.

> The article is about
> which the passage defines as
> The professor provides an example of
> first,
> Second,
> The example clearly illustrates

다음은 4번 문제 유형입니다.
4번 문제는 이전 문제와 달리 리스닝만 나오는 문제 유형입니다. 3번 문제에 나온 리딩 지문이 리스닝으로 변환되었다 라고 생각 하시면 됩니다. 그렇기에 3번 문제에 리스닝 내용보다 리딩 길이 만큼 깁니다.

> In the lecture, professor explains
> first,
> second,
> That's how the professor explain it.

105

USHER

01. Talent vs Hard Work 재능 vs 노력 — Independent Task

QUESTION

 Some people say in-born talent is the most important to become an artist. Others say hard work is more important. Which view do you agree with? Use reasons and examples to support your answer.
(어떤 사람들은 타고난 재능이 예술가가 되기 위해 가장 중요하다고 합니다. 다른 사람들은 노력이 더 중요하다 말합니다. 어느 관점에 동의하십니까? 이유와 예를 들어 답하세요.)

 브레인 스토밍 (아래에 놓여있는 12간지 내용들을 보고 어떤 것을 사용할 수 있을지 확인해보세요)
첫번째 이유 :
두번째 이유 :

 뼈대에 맞춰서 작성을 해봅시다.

아래 이미지는 학생들을 위한 만능 템플릿 12간지 입니다. 학생분들이 제일 먼저 암기해야하는 것이며, 본인 스스로 문장을 단기간 안에 못 만들거 같을 때에 도와주는 친구입니다. 가까이 두고 매일 외우세요.

Academic Courses
…because I think students should concentrate on academic courses.

Academic courses are the most important thing for students because good grades will help them get into good universities and, eventually, get great jobs.

As students get older, a good academic record is the only thing that actually matters.

This may sound a little far-fetched, but it's true, and for this reason, investing time in other activities is a waste of time.

Stay Healthy
It can be a great way to stay healthy. People join a cycling group through the internet. The members use bicycles to commute to work or school.

It is a great outdoor activity because people have a chance to work out while having fun.

Also, it is a great way to meet new people with similar interests. People nowadays do not have much chance to become close to each other.

However, there are numerous unique groups active on the internet, and this would not have been possible without the internet.

Follows your heart
Carpe diem, seize the days, and YOLO all stand for one thing. Do whatever your heart makes you do.

Life is too short to hesitate or do things to please others. It is essential to make yourself happy.

Actions speak louder than words. Whatever I do to make myself happy is better than sitting in a room thinking about it.

So I would just do it even if it means I am biting off something more than I can chew.

Stress
…if it can possibly be a way to relieve stress.

People nowadays are living a busy and hectic life, so they are under great stress, but a lot of them don't even realize they are stressed out.

Stress is known to be a major factor that keeps us from being healthy, and many people are suffering from various problems.

This is more serious than we think, so if it can ever be a way to relieve stress…

Money
…because it's the best way to save money. When it comes to spending money, every penny counts.

A thrifty spending habit is indispensable in our lives because little drops of water make the mighty ocean.

If we don't get used to working on a tight budget, we'll always be short on cash later.

A penny-pinching lifestyle will lead to financial stability, and it will give us peace of mind.

Saving Time
…because it's the best way to save time. There's an old saying, "Time is gold."

This proverb emphasizes the value of time, and this cannot be more true in modern society.

We're living a busy and hectic life, so saving time means we can do a lot more things later.

Many say that life is not fair, but everyone has twenty-four hours a day and seven days a week, so I would save time by…

Social Skills
Nowadays, people have smartphones with them all the time, and that information is no longer limited to elites.

Therefore, rather than learning, having social skills became the be-all and end-all to succeed rather than education.

Also, social skills are more than meet the eyes. To have social skills, one must also be able to read others like a book.

There will be times when one will truly need them.

Environment
because eventually, it can contribute to protecting the environment.

I think it's THE most important task for humanity because we cannot bring it back to life once it's too late.

Saving Earth all starts from seemingly insignificant actions.

Small actions from everyone bring about bigger changes, so I'm willing to participate.

Patience is virtue
Patience is a virtue. Saving time is indeed important, but waiting calmly is needed in this case.

There are times when one must wait patiently for things to go accordingly, and this is when time is the solution.

When going against the clock, they are more susceptible to making mistakes than taking some time.

In the long run, one will be glad that one has waited in this case.

Just because
I love it more than the given choices. Since I have so many great memory about it, It brings so many great reminiscences.

time flies whenever I am doing it, so how can I not choose it?

Also, not only do I love it, but I am also good at it. Everyone has talent, and it is like "a dime a dozen."

This was the inborn talent I had that I always surpassed everyone. Since a bird in the hand is worth two in the bush, I will choose it.

Politeness
It is important to maintain good relationships with other people because we never know what will happen in the future.

Decisions made by other people can affect others, and such decisions are usually based on personal and sentimental reasons.

So, people should not do anything that may offend or disturb others. It is also crucial to have a good reputation and get along well with others.

It Makes sense
It makes sense to choose it when considering many aspects such as time, money, and efficiency.

When people are considering between the given choices, they must consider many aspects economically.

They must choose the most efficient method because there are limits on what they have.

Also, one should think about it realistically and practically because they should not count chickens before they hatch.

So, down to Earth, people should choose it because it is the most economical

QUESTION

Some people say in-born talent is the most important to become an artist. Others say hard work is more important. Which view do you agree with? Use reasons and examples to support your answer.
(어떤 사람들은 타고난 재능이 예술가가 되기 위해 가장 중요하다고 합니다. 다른 사람들은 노력이 더 중요하다 말합니다. 어느 관점에 동의하십니까? 이유와 예를 들어 답하세요.)

academic courses와 stay healthy를 사용해서 뼈대에 맞춰서 모범답안을 만들어 봅시다.

patience와 just because를 사용해서 뼈대에 맞춰서 모범답안을 만들어 봅시다.

stress와 saving time을 사용해서 뼈대에 맞춰서 모범답안을 만들어 봅시다.

follow your heart와 politeness를 사용해서 뼈대에 맞춰서 모범답안을 만들어 봅시다.

QUESTION

Some people say in-born talent is the most important to become an artist. Others say hard work is more important. Which view do you agree with? Use reasons and examples to support your answer.
(어떤 사람들은 타고난 재능이 예술가가 되기 위해 가장 중요하다고 합니다. 다른 사람들은 노력이 더 중요하다 말합니다. 어느 관점에 동의 하십니까? 이유와 예를 들어 답하세요.)

academic courses와 stay healthy를 사용해서 뼈대에 맞춰서 모범답안을 만들어 봅시다.

If I were to answer the question, I would say it is important to have in-born talent. There are many reasons why, but here is a couple.

academic courses

First, anyone can work hard. For example, inborn talents are the most important thing for artists because good talents will help them. As students get older, everyone can work hard.

stay healthy

Second, there are a lot of people who have talents and work hard. For instance, there are countless amazing people in the world. They are all working hard, so they cannot succeed without talents.

That's why I think it is important to have in-born talent.

patience와 just because를 사용해서 뼈대에 맞춰서 모범답안을 만들어 봅시다.

If I were to answer the question, I would say hard work is more important than inborn talents. There are many reasons why, but here is a couple.

patience

First, working hard is a virtue. For example, inborn talents are important, but trying hard to improve is needed in this case. There are times when one must try hard for things to go accordingly, and this is the time when working hard is the solution.

just because

Second, I love people who try hard. For instance, I love artists who try hard more than artists with inborn talents. Therefore, how can I not choose it?

That's why I think hard work is more important than inborn talents.

stress와 saving time을 사용해서 뼈대에 맞춰서 모범답안을 만들어 봅시다.

If I were to answer the question, I would agree with the former. There are many reasons why, but here is a couple.

stress

First, working hard is too stressful. For example, artists nowadays are under great stress, and stress is known to be a major factor that keeps that from being healthy. Artists are suffering from various mental problems. Therefore, it is important to have in-born talents instead of being stressed out.

saving time

Second, inborn talents can save time. For instance, there is an old saying "time is gold." This proverb emphasizes the value of time, and this cannot be more true for artists. They must succeed when they are young. Being successful and making money when they are old or dead mean nothing.

This is why I think I agree with the former.

follow your heart와 politeness를 사용해서 뼈대에 맞춰서 모범답안을 만들어 봅시다.

If I were to answer the question, I would agree with the latter. There are many reasons why, but here is a couple.

follow your heart

First, one must be able to enjoy drawing by working hard. For example, carpe diem, seize the days, and YOLO all stand for one thing: Live the day to the fullest. Therefore, they must try with all they have.

politeness

Second, others will think greatly about you. For instance, decisions made by others can affect people's lives. Such decisions are usually based on what people have actually done before. So, people should try hard.

That's why I think I agree with the latter.

02. Mandatory Dormitory 의무적 기숙사　　Integrated Task

읽기 지문

Dormitories to Become Mandatory for freshmen

A university official has stated that there are plans to make living in the dormitories mandatory for incoming **freshmen**. Lately, since **juniors and seniors are leaning towards the trend of** not living in dormitories, for economic reasons, living in the dorms may become a mandatory process that freshmen need to go under. There are some advantages that come with living on campus, including being able to participate in various activities. By living in the dorms, it will become more convenient to take part in school events. Since one's house is nearby, time spent going back and forth from home to school will also be able to be saved.

대화 스크립트

STEP 01 뼈대를 먼저 작성해 보도록 하겠습니다.

STEP 02 작성하신 뼈대 빈칸에 맞춰서 리딩 지문을 읽고 주요 포인트를 넣어주세요.

STEP 03 하단에 리스닝 노트테이킹을 해주세요. 음원은 학원 홈페이지에서 무료로 다운받으실 수 있습니다. 또한 2005번 문제 번호로 문제를 풀어보실 수 있습니다.

 아래 하단에 리스닝 스크립트를 보고 베꼈어야 하는 부분을 찾아서 적어 보도록 하겠습니다.

대화 스크립트

🎧 뉴토플 - TEST 05_Q2

Now listen to two students discussing the announcement.

자, 이제 지문에 대해 논의하는 두 학생의 대화를 들어보세요.

M: Hey, did you read the article in the newspaper about the dormitories?

남: 야, 너 기숙사에 대한 신문기사 읽어봤어?

W: Yeah... I don't really think it's a great idea.

여: 응, 별로 좋은 아이디어는 아닌것 같아.

M: Really? Why not?

남: 정말? 왜?

여자의 의견
반대

W: Well, they make it sound really great, but I can think of a few disadvantages.

여: 되게 좋은 쪽으로 말하기는 하는데, 몇 가지 불이익도 있는 것 같아.

M: Like what?

남: 어떤 점이?

이유 ❶
입학률이 줄어들 것임

W: Well, first of all, I think the admission rate will fall for sure. Making it absolutely mandatory to live in the dorms for freshmen will definitely affect the rate. Since dorms aren't really popular places to live in, if it's made mandatory, a lot of students will not **look into** our university for their school of choice.

여: 일단, 분명히 입학률은 줄어들 거야. 신입생의 기숙사 생활을 의무화하는 것은 당연히 입학률에게 영향을 주겠지. 기숙사는 살기에 인기 있는 곳이 아니니깐, 만약 의무화 하면, 많은 학생들이 우리 학교를 **주의 깊게** 보지 않을 거야.

M: That's true. Not a lot of freshmen want to live in the dorms for their first year, right?

남: 그렇네. 대부분의 신입생들은 처음부터 기숙사에 살고 싶어하진 않을 거야. 그렇지?

이유 ❷
경제적 악화로 기숙사비나 학비가 오를 것임

W: Right! Even more, if this is to be true, then there will probably be more financial difficulties, since this is supposed to be a way to help relieve the financial crisis.

여: 그렇지! 그리고, 만약 이게 사실이라면, 이건 재정 위기에서 벗어나려는 의도인데, 사실상 더 경제적으로 위험에 빠질 거야.

M: Yeah... but, that doesn't really affect us directly does it?

남: 응. 근데, 그게 우리에게 직접적으로 영향을 주진 않잖아?

W: Wrong! It does affect us directly. If the school falls into a financial crisis, that means the cost of dorms and tuition will probably increase as a result. This is terrible news for the current students, especially those living in the dorms.

여: 땡! 영향을 주지. 만약 학교가 재정 위기에 빠지면, 그 말은 기숙사나 학비가 결과적으로 오를 거란 소리지. 지금 기숙사에 살고 있는 재학생들에게는 특히나 안 좋은 소식이지!

M: You're right. They should really re-think this plan.

남: 맞다. 이 계획에 대해서 다시 생각해야 해.

W: It doesn't make sense to make living in the dorms mandatory. It'll just lead to more disaster.

여: 기숙사에 사는 것을 의무화하는 건 말도 안돼. 상황만 더 악화 될 거야.

문제
The woman expresses her opinion about the proposal in the newspaper. State the woman's opinion and explain the reasons she gives for holding that opinion.

여자는 대학의 계획에 대해 자신의 의견을 밝히고 있습니다. 그녀의 의견을 말하고, 그 의견을 고수하는 이유를 설명하세요.

Note-taking

다시한번 모범 답안을 작성해 보도록 하겠습니다

Dormitories to Become Mandatory for freshmen

A university official has stated that there are plans to make living in the dormitories mandatory for incoming **freshmen**. Lately, since **juniors and seniors are leaning towards the trend of** not living in dormitories, for economic reasons, living in the dorms may become a mandatory process that freshmen need to go under. There are some advantages that come with living on campus, including being able to participate in various activities. By living in the dorms, it will become more convenient to take part in school events. Since one's house is nearby, time spent going back and forth from home to school will also be able to be saved.

Note-taking	노트테이킹
Reading - living in dorms will be mandatory for freshmen - the occupancy rate went down - it is good to live in dorms **Woman** - against **Reason ❶** - the admission rate will fall - the applicants may look into other schools **Reason ❷** - the school will be financially unstable - housing and tuition will rise	**지문** - 신입생 기숙사 생활 의무화 - 점거율이 내려갔음 - 기숙사에 살면 좋음 **여자** - 반대 **이유 ❶** - 입학률이 떨어질 것임 - 지원자들이 다른 학교 알아볼 것임 **이유 ❷** - 학교 재정이 불안해짐 - 기숙사비와 학비가 오름

Task 2   Sample Response   뉴토플 - TEST 05_R2   2번 문제 모범 답안

The two students are discussing the college's plan to make living in the school dormitories a requirement for freshmen because the occupancy rate has been going down. The woman is against the plan for two reasons.

❶ First, the admission rate of the university would fall if it becomes mandatory to live in dormitories. Since living in dormitories is not popular among students, university applicants may look for other universities.

❷ Second, if the suggested plan becomes effective, the university would become financially unstable, causing housing fees and tuition to rise. This news would be a disaster for students living on campus. (This is why she thinks the plan is unnecessary.)

두 학생은 기숙사의 점거율이 낮아져서 신입생의 기숙사 생활을 의무화하려는 대학의 계획에 대해서 의논하고 있다. 여자는 두 가지 이유를 들어 그 계획에 반대하고 있다.

❶ 첫째, 기숙사 생활을 의무화하면 입학률이 낮아질 것이다. 학생들 사이에서 기숙사에 사는 것은 인기가 없기 때문에, 대학 지원자들은 다른 대학을 찾아 볼 것이다.

❷ 다음, 만약 제안된 이 계획이 시행된다면, 기숙사비와 학비의 인상을 야기해서 학교는 경제적으로 불안정해 질 것이다. 이 소식은 기숙사에 사는 학생들에게 큰 불행일 것이다. (이것이 그녀가 이 계획이 필요없다고 생각하는 이유이다)

Vocabulary

freshman [fréʃmən]	n. (대학의) 1학년생, 신참	sophomore [sáfəmɔ̀:r]	n. (대학의) 2학년생
junior [dʒú:njər]	n. 3학년생, 후배 / a. 손아래의	senior [sí:njər]	n. 졸업반 학생, 선배 / a. 손위의
lean towards	phr. ~로 편향되다	look into	phr. 들여다 보다

03. Selling Technique 판매 기술

Integrated Task

읽기 지문

Selling Technique

Selling techniques are the ways in which consumers are motivated to purchase products. These techniques take on many forms, from the modern consultative selling in which salesmen act as expert consultants helping consumers understand a product to the pressurized hard sales approach. While these approaches are based on the sales force, producers' decisions on which products to manufacture also **play an important part** in the process of selling. By **specializing** in a certain type of product, producers have the ability to increase their sales through brand recognition and diversification. Both of these make the jobs of their sales people easier.

대화 스크립트

 STEP 01 뼈대를 먼저 작성해 보도록 하겠습니다.

 STEP 02 작성하신 뼈대 빈칸에 맞춰서 리딩 지문을 읽고 주요 포인트를 넣어주세요.

 STEP 03 하단에 리스닝 노트테이킹을 해주세요. 음원은 학원 홈페이지에서 무료로 다운받으실 수 있습니다. 또한 3005번 문제 번호로 문제를 풀어보실 수 있습니다.

 아래 하단에 리스닝 스크립트를 보고 베꼈어야 하는 부분을 찾아서 적어 보도록 하겠습니다.

대화 스크립트

🎧 뉴토플 - TEST 05_Q3

Now listen to part of a lecture in a business class.

Movies such as Death of a Salesman have **reinforced** the image of the salesman as a hard-selling machine, but few show the decisions made by the producer as part of this process. These decisions are also selling techniques and assist the sales people in making the products more desirable to the buying public.

예시 ❶
기존 기술력의 사용

세부사항
텔레비전 만들던 회사는 모니터도 잘 만들 것임

An initial selling technique that producers' decisions aid is in utilizing the technology they have already mastered. The number of companies that begin to sell products that are based on something they already manufacture evidences this. A good example of this would be a consumer electronics manufacturer. As they have a long history of producing electronic devices, such as the television, when more advanced products were invented, they focused on similar products, such as computer monitors. Having the base technology in place means that they can simply adapt them to make new products, without having to start over in the design process. Further, because their brand image is strong **in regards to** televisions, consumers will **be more apt to** choose them for a similar product.

예시 ❷
관련제품 생산

세부사항
스노보드 만들던 회사는 이미지를 이용해 관련 용품을 만듦

A secondary way in which manufacturers' decisions act as selling techniques is through their ability to create **complementary** products. For instance, companies which create snowboards can **leverage** their brand loyalty by creating products such as jackets, gloves, and goggles. Since consumers who buy snowboards also need these products, they can be easily convinced that a manufacturer of quality snowboards will produce accessories of an equal quality as well.

문제

Using the example from the professor's lecture, explain what selling technique is and how it works.

이제 경영학 수업의 일부를 들어보세요.

'세일즈맨의 죽음'같은 영화는 세일즈맨의 모습을 마치 물건 파는 기계처럼 **강조했지만** 이런 과정에서 정작 생산자의 결정력을 보여주는 경우는 거의 없습니다. 이러한 결정들 역시 판매 기술이며, 소비자로 하여금 사고 싶은 욕망을 더 가질 수 있도록 세일즈맨을 도와 줍니다.

첫 번째로 생산자들의 결정이 도움이 되는 경우는 그들이 이미 가진 기술을 이용하는 것입니다. 몇몇 회사들이 이미 만든 제품을 기반으로 생산한 제품을 판매하기 시작하는 것이 이를 증명합니다. 좋은 예는 가전제품 제조사들입니다. 그들은 텔레비전 같은 전자 제품 생산에 오랜 역사를 가지고 있기 때문에, 컴퓨터 모니터 같이 더 앞선 제품이 발명되었을 때, 비슷한 제품에 집중했습니다. 기초 기술력을 가졌다는 것은 이를 이용해 새로운 제품을 만들 수 있다는 의미입니다. 처음의 모든 디자인 작업을 거치지 않고 말입니다. 또한, 그들의 텔레비전**에 관해서**는 인지도가 높기 때문에, 소비자들은 비슷한 제품을 구매**하려고** 합니다.

제조회사의 결정이 판매 기술로 작용하는 두 번째 경우는 **관련**제품을 생산하는 능력을 이용하는 것입니다. 예를 들어, 스노보드를 판매 하는 회사는 재킷, 장갑, 안경 등을 만듦으로써 브랜드 충성도를 **옮겨**올 수 있습니다. 스노보드를 구매하는 소비자들은 그 제품들도 필요하기 때문에, 그 제조회사가 스노보드와 동일한 품질의 제품을 생산 할 거라 쉽게 믿게 됩니다.

교수의 강의를 예로 들어, 판매 기술이 무엇이고 어떻게 작용하는지 설명하세요.

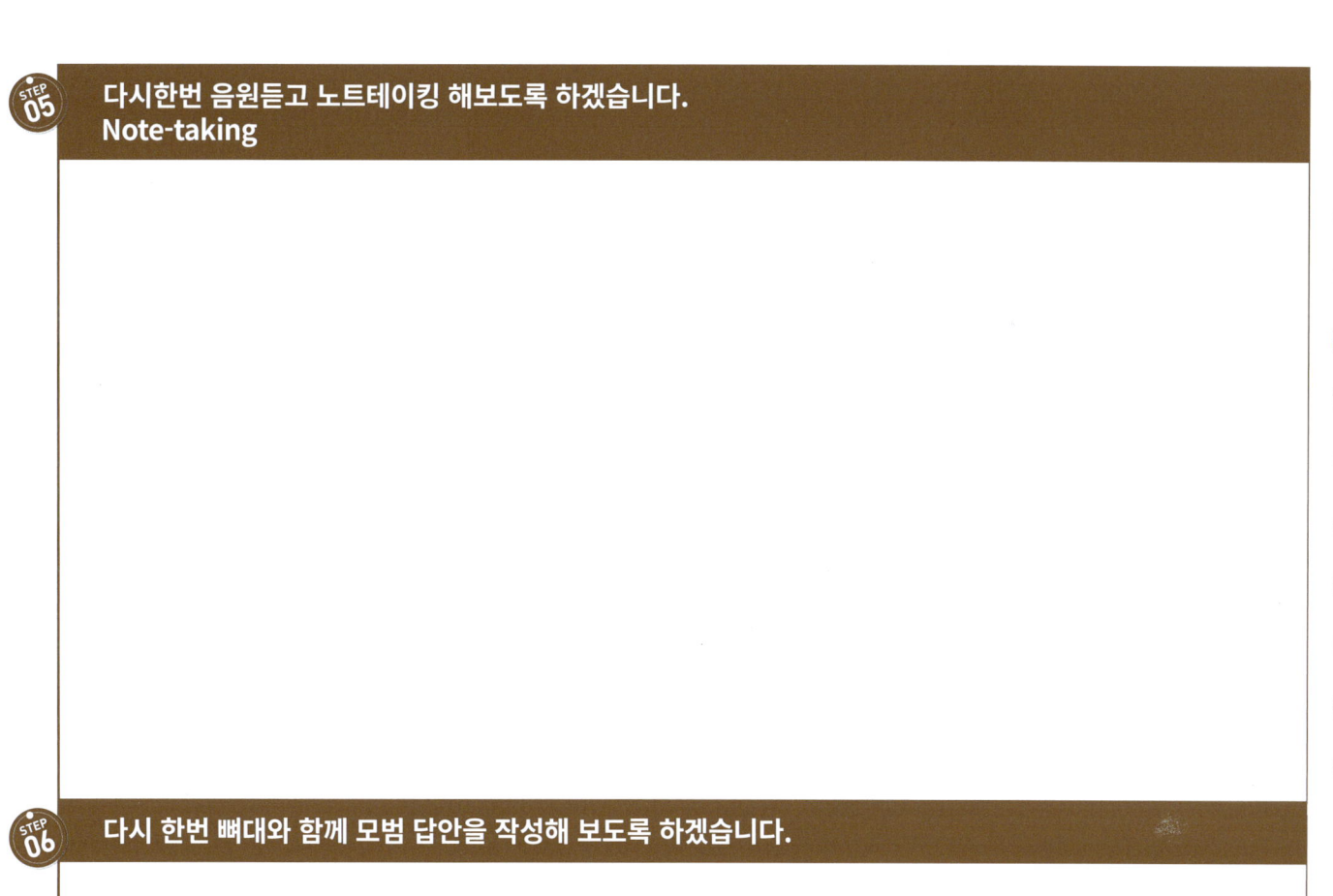

Selling Technique

Selling techniques are the ways in which consumers are motivated to purchase products. These techniques take on many forms, from the modern consultative selling in which salesmen act as expert consultants helping consumers understand a product to the pressurized hard sales approach. While these approaches are based on the sales force, producers' decisions on which products to manufacture also **play an important part** in the process of selling. By **specializing** in a certain type of product, producers have the ability to increase their sales through brand recognition and diversification. Both of these make the jobs of their sales people easier.

References

세일즈맨의 죽음

미국의 극작가 아서 밀러(Arthur Miller)가 1949년에 초연한 작품이다. 주인공 윌리 로만(Willy Loman)은 30년간 세일즈맨으로 살아오면서 성실하게 일하면 반드시 성공한다는 신념을 그의 두 아들 비프(Biff)와 해피(Happy)에게도 불어넣으며 그들의 성공을 기대했지만, 두 아들은 타락해 버렸고 그 자신도 회사에서 몰인정하게 해고당한다.

궁지에 몰린 그는 장남에게 보험금을 남겨 주려고 자동차를 과속으로 달려 자살한다. 그의 장례식날 아내 린다(Linda)는 집의 할부금 납입도 끝나고 모든 것이 해결되자 정작 아무도 살 사람이 없다고 울부짖으며 연극은 끝난다.

Task 3 Sample Response — 뉴토플 - TEST 05_R3 — 3번 문제 모범 답안

Selling techniques are the ways to attract and motivate consumers to purchase products. The professor gives an example of two companies to explain them.

❶ One way is to take advantage of the technology they already possess. For example, a producer of television sets will find it relatively easy to produce computer monitors because those two are similar in terms of manufacturing process.

❷ Another way is to introduce related products to the existing ones. If an established snowboard manufacturer introduces related items such as snowboard jackets, consumers will be attracted to them because of the reputation of the brand.

판매 기술은 소비자들의 구매를 유도하는 기술들이다. 교수는 이것을 설명하기 위해 두 개의 회사를 예로 든다.

❶ 첫 번째 방법은 그들이 이미 가진 기술을 이용하는 것이다. 예를 들어 텔레비전 생산자는 생산 과정이 비슷한 컴퓨터 모니터를 생산하는 게 비교적 쉬울 것이다.

❷ 또 다른 방법은 기존 제품과 연관된 제품을 출시하는 것이다. 인지도를 갖춘 스노보드 생산자가 스노보드 재킷과 비슷한 제품을 출시하게 되면, 소비자들은 그 브랜드의 명성 때문에 제품에 끌릴것이다.

Vocabulary

play a part	phr. 역할을 하다	specialize in	phr. ~을 전공하다
diversification [divə̀ːrsəfikéiʃən]	n. 다양화	reinforce [rìːinfɔ́ːrs]	v. 강화하다
in regards to	phr. ~에 관해서는	be apt to	phr. ~하기 쉽다
complementary [kɑ̀mpləméntəri]	a. 보완적인	leverage [lévəridʒ]	v. ~에 지레를 사용하다 / n. 지레작용

04 Group Hunting 단체 사냥 — Integrated Task

STEP 01 4번 뼈대를 먼저 작성해 보도록 하겠습니다.

STEP 02 하단에 리스닝 노트테이킹을 해주세요. 음원은 학원 홈페이지에서 무료로 다운받으실 수 있습니다. 또한 4005번 문제 번호로 문제를 풀어보실 수 있습니다.

STEP 03 뼈대에 맞춰서 모범 답안을 완성해 보겠습니다.

Listen to part of a lecture in a biology class.

Every animal species uses its own unique hunting skills in order to obtain food. There are various ways in which animals do this. Overall, hunting is essential for the survival of animals. While some species of animals may hunt alone, there are others that **cooperate** with one another in order to get their food. This way of getting food is called group hunting, and there are several different ways of this.

Some species of animals work amongst themselves in order to hunt. This is known as cooperative hunting, and animals who hunt this way are known as **pack** hunters. One type of animal that hunts cooperatively is the lion. Lions typically hunt large animals like zebras but since they don't have very high stamina, it's much more effective and easier for them to hunt in groups. Several lionesses work together and **encircle** a **herd** of zebras from different angles. Once they have encircled them, they usually target the closest zebra. The attack is short and powerful as they attempt to catch the victim quickly with one **fatal** attack.

Some animals work with other types of animals in order to hunt food, this is a type of **mutualism**. I'm pretty sure you've heard of it before. Well, mutualism is a **symbiotic** relationship between individuals of different species in which both individuals benefit. The cooperation between honey guide birds and badgers is an example of this. Since the honey guide bird is too small to break open a **beehive** and the badger's eyesight is too weak to find them, they work together. First, a honey guide bird leads a badger to a beehive. Then, the badger breaks apart the hive with its powerful paws. After the beehive is open, the badger gets the honeycomb and eats it while the honey guide bird gets anything that remains. Thus, these two species need each other in order to survive.

Using the examples from the professor's lecture, explain how animals use cooperation to feed themselves more effectively.

References

Photo by BadgerHero, available under the Creative Commons Attribution-Share Alike 3.0 Unported license.

Photo by Alan Manson, available under the Creative Commons Attribution-Share Alike 2.0 Generic license.

[참고자료]

❶ 오소리 (Badger)
❷ 꿀잡이새 (Honeyguide)

Task 4   Sample Response   🎧 TEST 05_R4   4번 문제 모범 답안

In the lecture, the professor gives two examples of group hunting. Group hunting is a type of hunting where animals cooperate with each other to hunt.

❶ First, cooperative hunting is when the same species of animals hunt together. When lions hunt zebras, lionesses surround a herd, and attack the closest animal. They try to finish the attack quickly, which makes them powerful.

❷ Second, mutualism is when different species of animals both benefit from the hunt. Badgers can't see well and birds are too small to break a hive, so birds lead badgers to a hive and badgers break open the hive and eat the honeycomb. The bird then gets the leftovers.

강의에서 교수는 그룹 사냥의 두 가지 예를 들고 있습니다. 그룹 사냥은 동물들이 사냥하기 위해서 서로로 협력하는 사냥의 종류를 말합니다.

❶ 첫 번째로, 협력하는 사냥은 같은 종의 동물이 같이 사냥하는 것을 말합니다. 사자가 얼룩말을 사냥할 때, 암사자들은 한 떼를 둘러싸고, 가장 가까이 있는 동물을 공격합니다. 빠르게 해치우려고 하기 때문에, 그들의 공격은 강력할 수 밖에 없습니다.

❷ 두 번째로, 상리 공생은 다른 종의 동물들이 사냥에서 모두 이득을 보는 것을 말합니다. 오소리들은 앞을 잘 보지 못하고, 새들은 벌집을 깨기에는 너무 작기 때문에, 오소리를 벌집으로 인도해 벌집을 깨고 꿀을 먹게 합니다. 그리고 새들은 남는 것을 먹습니다.

Vocabulary

cooperate [kouápərèit]	v. 협력하다, 합동하다	pack [pæk]	n. 동물의 한 떼
encircle [insə́:rk]	v. ~을 둘러싸다, 에워싸다	herd [hə:rd]	n. 짐승의 떼, 가축의 무리
fatal [féitl]	a. 치명적인, 생명에 관계되는	mutualism [mjú:tʃuəlìzm]	n. 상리 공생
symbiotic [sìmbiátik, -bai-]	a. 공생의, 공생하는	hive [haiv]	n. 꿀벌통 (= beehive)

USHER
iBT TOEFL
FINAL TEST SPEAKING
TEST 06

Independent Tasks

Task 1 - 모범 답안
Question 1   usherin.usher.co.kr > 시험리스트 > Speaking 시험리스트 > Task 1 > #1024

Integrated Tasks

Task 2 - Script / 해석 / 모범 답안
Question 2   usherin.usher.co.kr > 시험리스트 > Speaking 시험리스트 > Task 2 > #2006

Task 3 - Script / 해석 / 모범 답안
Question 3   usherin.usher.co.kr > 시험리스트 > Speaking 시험리스트 > Task 3 > #3006

Task 4 - Script / 해석 / 모범 답안
Question 4   usherin.usher.co.kr > 시험리스트 > Speaking 시험리스트 > Task 4 > #4006

자기평가표

1번 문제 유형은 학생들이 본인에 생각을 주제에 맞춰서 말 해야하는 시험입니다.
본인이 처음부터 끝까지 45초 동안 말해야하다 보니 학생들이 제일 어려워 하는 시험입니다.
하지만, 먼저 외우고 익힌후에 말하는것이 가능할수 있게 하겠습니다.
가장 기본이 되는 뼈대 입니다. 먼저 외우도록 합시다.

> if i were to answer the question, i would say
> there are many reasons why, but here is a couple
> first
> for example,
> second
> for instance
> that's why

다음은 2번 문제 유형입니다.
2번 문제는 리딩에 학교에 계획이 적혀있거나 학교가 변해야하는 방향에 대해서 학생들에 주장이 적혀있습니다.
리딩에서 빠르게 파악해야하는 것은 도대체 누가 무엇을 주장하는가 입니다.
45~50초에 리딩 지문이 나오고 난 다음에 리스닝으로 학생들에 대화가 나오는 문제입니다.
리스닝에서는 학생이 리딩 지문에 대한 본인에 좋고 나쁜지에 대한 의견을 얘기해줄겁니다.
이유 2가지와 예시 2가지를 꼭 말할 수 있어야 합니다.

이에 따라서 2번 스피킹 문제에 뼈대는

> The reading states that university (plans to) / (should)
> the (woman / man) in the conversation thinks it is a good / bad idea.
> He/she provides two reasons to support his / her opinion.
> first,
> Second,
> the woman / man thinks it's a great / horrible idea.

다음은 3번 문제 유형입니다.
3번 문제는 2번 문제 유형과 같이 리딩과 리스닝이 나오는 문제 입니다. 하지만, 이번에는 이전 문제와는 달리 매우 학술적인 내용이 들어 있습니다. 리딩에서는 교과서에 나올만한 주제 한개를 자세하게 다룹니다. 여기서 학생분들은 제목과 이에 대한 정의를 잘 받아적으셔야 합니다. 리스닝에서는 교수님이 리딩에 나온 내용으로 예시를 들어 줍니다.

> The article is about
> which the passage defines as
> The professor provides an example of
> first,
> Second,
> The example clearly illustrates

다음은 4번 문제 유형입니다.
4번 문제는 이전 문제와 달리 리스닝만 나오는 문제 유형입니다. 3번 문제에 나온 리딩 지문이 리스닝으로 변환되었다 라고 생각 하시면 됩니다. 그렇기에 3번 문제에 리스닝 내용보다 리딩 길이 만큼 깁니다.

> In the lecture, professor explains
> first,
> second,
> That's how the professor explain it.

01. Long vs Short Course 긴 vs 짧은 과목 — Independent Task

QUESTION

Some people say it is better to take long but relaxed courses in college. Others say it is better to take short but intensive courses. Which view do you agree with? Use reasons and examples to support your answer.
(어떤 이들은 대학에서 길어도 평이한 수업을 듣는게 낫다고 합니다. 다른 이들은 짧지만 집중적인 수업을 듣는 게 낫다고 합니다. 당신은 어느 관점에 동의하십니까? 이유와 예를 들어 답하세요.)

브레인 스토밍 (아래에 놓여있는 12간지 내용들을 보고 어떤 것을 사용할 수 있을지 확인해보세요)
첫번째 이유 :
두번째 이유 :

뼈대에 맞춰서 작성을 해봅시다.

_____
_____
_____
_____
_____
_____

아래 이미지는 학생들을 위한 만능 템플릿 12간지 입니다. 학생분들이 제일 먼저 암기해야하는 것이며, 본인 스스로 문장을 단기간 안에 못 만들거 같을 때에 도와주는 친구입니다. 가까이 두고 매일 외우세요.

Academic Courses
…because I think students should concentrate on academic courses.

Academic courses are the most important thing for students because good grades will help them get into good universities and, eventually, get great jobs.

As students get older, a good academic record is the only thing that actually matters.

This may sound a little far-fetched, but it's true, and for this reason, investing time in other activities is a waste of time.

Stay Healthy
It can be a great way to stay healthy. People join a cycling group through the internet. The members use bicycles to commute to work or school.

It is a great outdoor activity because people have a chance to work out while having fun.

Also, it is a great way to meet new people with similar interests. People nowadays do not have much chance to become close to each other.

However, there are numerous unique groups active on the internet, and this would not have been possible without the internet.

Follows your heart
Carpe diem, seize the days, and YOLO all stand for one thing. Do whatever your heart makes you do.

Life is too short to hesitate or do things to please others. It is essential to make yourself happy.

Actions speak louder than words. Whatever I do to make myself happy is better than sitting in a room thinking about it.

So I would just do it even if it means I am biting off something more than I can chew.

Stress
…if it can possibly be a way to relieve stress.
People nowadays are living a busy and hectic life, so they are under great stress, but a lot of them don't even realize they are stressed out.

Stress is known to be a major factor that keeps us from being healthy, and many people are suffering from various problems.

This is more serious than we think, so if it can ever be a way to relieve stress…

Money
…because it's the best way to save money. When it comes to spending money, every penny counts.

A thrifty spending habit is indispensable in our lives because little drops of water make the mighty ocean.

If we don't get used to working on a tight budget, we'll always be short on cash later.

A penny-pinching lifestyle will lead to financial stability, and it will give us peace of mind.

Saving Time
…because it's the best way to save time. There's an old saying, "Time is gold."

This proverb emphasizes the value of time, and this cannot be more true in modern society.

We're living a busy and hectic life, so saving time means we can do a lot more things later.

Many say that life is not fair, but everyone has twenty-four hours a day and seven days a week, so I would save time by…

Social Skills
Nowadays, people have smartphones with them all the time, and that information is no longer limited to elites.

Therefore, rather than learning, having social skills became the be-all and end-all to succeed rather than education.

Also, social skills are more than meet the eyes. To have social skills, one must also be able to read others like a book.

There will be times when one will truly need them.

Environment
because eventually, it can contribute to protecting the environment.

I think it's THE most important task for humanity because we cannot bring it back to life once it's too late.

Saving Earth all starts from seemingly insignificant actions.

Small actions from everyone bring about bigger changes, so I'm willing to participate.

Patience is virtue
Patience is a virtue. Saving time is indeed important, but waiting calmly is needed in this case.

There are times when one must wait patiently for things to go accordingly, and this is when time is the solution.

When going against the clock, they are more susceptible to making mistakes than taking some time.

In the long run, one will be glad that one has waited in this case.

Just because
I love it more than the given choices. Since I have so many great memory about it, It brings so many great reminiscences.

time flies whenever I am doing it, so how can I not choose it?

Also, not only do I love it, but I am also good at it. Everyone has talent, and it is like "a dime a dozen."

This was the inborn talent I had that I always surpassed everyone. Since a bird in the hand is worth two in the bush, I will choose it.

Politeness
It is important to maintain good relationships with other people because we never know what will happen in the future.

Decisions made by other people can affect others, and such decisions are usually based on personal and sentimental reasons.

So, people should not do anything that may offend or disturb others. It is also crucial to have a good reputation and get along well with others.

It Makes sense
It makes sense to choose it when considering many aspects such as time, money, and efficiency.

When people are considering between the given choices, they must consider many aspects economically.

They must choose the most efficient method because there are limits on what they have.

Also, one should think about it realistically and practically because they should not count chickens before they hatch.

So, down to Earth, people should choose it because it is the most economical

QUESTION

Some people say it is better to take long but relaxed courses in college. Others say it is better to take short but intensive courses. Which view do you agree with? Use reasons and examples to support your answer.
(어떤 이들은 대학에서 길어도 평이한 수업을 듣는게 낫다고 합니다. 다른 이들은 짧지만 집중적인 수업을 듣는 게 낫다고 합니다. 당신은 어느 관점에 동의하십니까? 이유와 예를 들어 답하세요.)

academic courses와 save time을 사용해서 뼈대에 맞춰서 모범답안을 만들어 봅시다.

stress와 just because를 사용해서 뼈대에 맞춰서 모범답안을 만들어 봅시다.

money와 social skills을 사용해서 뼈대에 맞춰서 모범답안을 만들어 봅시다.

follow your heart와 patience를 사용해서 뼈대에 맞춰서 모범답안을 만들어 봅시다.

QUESTION

Some people say it is better to take long but relaxed courses in college. Others say it is better to take short but intensive courses. Which view do you agree with? Use reasons and examples to support your answer.
(어떤 이들은 대학에서 길어도 평이한 수업을 듣는게 낫다고 합니다. 다른 이들은 짧지만 집중적인 수업을 듣는 게 낫다고 합니다. 당신은 어느 관점에 동의하십니까? 이유와 예를 들어 답하세요.)

academic courses와 save time을 사용해서 뼈대에 맞춰서 모범답안을 만들어 봅시다.

If I were to answer the question, I would say it is important to take intensive courses. There are many reasons why, but here is a couple.

academic courses

First, I can study better when I am in intensive courses. For example, academic courses are the most important thing for students. Therefore, it is important for me to take intensive courses so that I can have good grades.

save time

Second, taking short classes can be a way to save time. For instance, there is an old saying "time is gold." This proverb emphasizes the value of time, this cannot be more true for college students who have a lot of works to do.

That's why I think I prefer to take short and intensive courses.

stress와 just because를 사용해서 뼈대에 맞춰서 모범답안을 만들어 봅시다.

If I were to answer the question, I would say I prefer to take long and relaxed courses. There are many reasons why, but here is a couple.

stress

First, I hate being in a stressful situation. For example, students nowadays are living a busy and hectic life, so they are under great stress. I do not want to add more stress to it.

just because

Second, I like long and relaxed courses. For instance, I love it more than the other given choice. I have a great memory of long and relaxed courses with good grades and a great professor. That's why I prefer to take long and relaxed courses.

money와 social skills을 사용해서 뼈대에 맞춰서 모범답안을 만들어 봅시다.

If I were to answer the question, I would say short and intensive courses. There are many reasons why, but here is a couple.

money

First, with time left, I can work after short classes. For example, when it comes to money, every penny counts. Little drops of water can make the mighty ocean. It is important for students to make money when they are young.

social skills

Second, I can develop social skills after class while working. For instance, these days, people have smartphones with them all the time that knowledge is no longer limited to elites. Rather than spend their time learning, students should spend their time developing social skills.

That's why I think it is important for them to take short and intensive courses.

follow your heart와 patience를 사용해서 뼈대에 맞춰서 모범답안을 만들어 봅시다.

If I were to answer the question, I would say long and relaxed courses are better than short and intensive courses. There are many reasons why, but here is a couple.

follow your heart

First, students should enjoy life. For example, carpe diem, seize the days, and YOLO all stand for one thing: enjoy your life. Life is too short to hurry. Students should be able to relax and enjoy the journey.

patience

Second, they can easily make mistakes when it is intensive. For instance, learning is important. Saving time is needed, but digesting what they have learned is needed in this case. There are times when one must relax for things to go accordingly, and this is the time.

That's why I think students should take long and relaxed courses.

02. Advisory Meetings 상담 회의   Integrated Task

읽기 지문

Advisory Meetings Should Be Optional

Advisory meetings should not be required by the university, as they are right now. All of the information that the advisors provide to us students can be easily found on the web. Just going to related websites, or even the school website, will give us an organized version of what the advisors will tell us. Thus, meetings are not exactly needed because they don't give us any new information. Also, as it is a meeting between two people, it is difficult to schedule. Students and advisors are both busy, but in order to have an advisory meeting, both the student and the advisor have to be free.

대화 스크립트

 뼈대를 먼저 작성해 보도록 하겠습니다.

 작성하신 뼈대 빈칸에 맞춰서 리딩 지문을 읽고 주요 포인트를 넣어주세요.

 하단에 리스닝 노트테이킹을 해주세요. 음원은 학원 홈페이지에서 무료로 다운받으실 수 있습니다. 또한 2006번 문제 번호로 문제를 풀어보실 수 있습니다.

 아래 하단에 리스닝 스크립트를 보고 베꼈어야 하는 부분을 찾아서 적어 보도록 하겠습니다.

대화 스크립트

🎧 뉴토플 - TEST 06_Q2

Now listen to two students discussing the letter.

W: Did you see John's letter in the newspaper?

M: Yeah, but I don't think he's right about what he's saying.

W: Really? Why not? Did you get anything from the advisory meetings?

M: Yeah. Even though John said that all of the information can be found on the web, I don't think so. The advisors actually have a lot of information that isn't available on the web. If you know how to ask the advisors for more specific information, they will always **be willing to** help. I mean, that's what they're there for, right?

W: Yeah, I guess you're right.

M: Information on the web is limited since you can't ask questions and get responses right away like you can with an advisor.

W: Hmm… yeah. I see your point. But as helpful as they are, it's hard to meet with them because of the need to schedule a meeting.

M: Well, maybe it could be spontaneous, but don't you usually make a schedule **ahead of time**?

W: Yeah… but you would still have to find a time when both aren't busy.

M: That's not too hard if we plan ahead. If we schedule a meeting time maybe a week before the appointment, then we can **leave the day empty** for the meeting and not **make any other plans**. It isn't that hard to make appointments, well, **under the condition that** it isn't scheduled, like, on the day or the day before the advisory meeting.

남자의 의견
반대

이유 ❶
선생님들은
웹사이트 보다
더 많은
정보를 제공

이유 ❷
미리 약속을
잡는다면
어렵지 않음

문제
The man expresses his opinion about the proposal in the newspaper. State his opinion and explain the reasons he gives for holding that opinion.

이제 지문에 대해 논의하는 두 학생의 대화를 들어보세요.

여: 신문에 John이 쓴 거 봤어?

남: 응, 근데 걔가 말하는 건 옳다고 생각 안 해.

여: 정말? 왜? 상담에서 도움 받은 거라도 있어?

남: 응. John이 모든 정보를 홈페이지에서 볼 수 있다고 하지만, 그렇지 않아. 카운슬러들은 웹사이트에 없는 많은 정보를 갖고 있거든. 만약 더 구체적인 정보를 물어 볼 줄 안다면, 카운슬러들이 **기꺼이** 도와 줄 거야. 내 말은, 그게 카운슬러들이 하는 일이잖아. 안 그래?

여: 응, 맞는 것 같아.

남: 홈페이지에 있는 정보는 한계가 있어. 왜냐면 네가 카운슬러들이랑 있을 때처럼 질문하고 바로 답을 들을 수 없으니까.

여: 그래, 무슨 말인지 알겠다. 근데 도움이 되긴 하지만 약속을 잡아야 하니까 카운슬러들이랑 만나기 힘들어.

남: 글쎄, 즉석으로 만날 수도 있지만, 보통 약속을 **미리** 잡지 않아?

여: 응, 근데 그래도 둘 다 바쁘지 않는 날을 찾아야 하잖아.

남: 미리 계획하면 그다지 어렵지 않아. 만약 일주일 전에 약속을 잡는다면, **그 날은 비우고** 다른 약속을 안 잡으면 되지. 상담 당일이나 그 전날에 **약속을 잡지 않**는**다면** 그렇게 어렵진 않아.

남자는 대학의 계획에 대해 자신의 의견을 밝히고 있습니다. 그의 의견을 말하고, 그 의견을 고수하는 이유를 설명하세요.

Note-taking

다시한번 모범 답안을 작성해 보도록 하겠습니다

Advisory Meetings Should Be Optional

Advisory meetings should not be required by the university, as they are right now. All of the information that the advisors provide to us students can be easily found on the web. Just going to related websites, or even the school website, will give us an organized version of what the advisors will tell us. Thus, meetings are not exactly needed because they don't give us any new information. Also, as it is a meeting between two people, it is difficult to schedule. Students and advisors are both busy, but in order to have an advisory meeting, both the student and the advisor have to be free.

Note-taking	노트테이킹
Reading - advisory meetings should not be mandatory - the websites offers the same information - it's hard to make an appointment **Man** - against **Reason ❶** - advisors have much more information - they can offer answers more specifically **Reason ❷** - it is not that hard to schedule a meeting - if students can make an appointment beforehand	**지문** - 상담은 필수여서는 안 된다 - 같은 정보가 홈페이지에 있음 - 약속을 잡기가 어려움 **남자** - 반대 **이유 ❶** - 카운슬러들이 정보가 훨씬 많음 - 더 자세히 답해줄 수 있음 **이유 ❷** - 약속 잡기가 그리 어렵지 않음 - 학생들이 미리 약속을 잡으면

Task 2 Sample Response 🎧 뉴토플 - TEST 06_R2   2번 문제 모범 답안

The two students are discussing the suggestion that the university should not make advisory meetings mandatory because the website offers the same information and it's difficult to make an appointment. The man is against the plan for two reasons.

❶ First, the advisors have much more information than the university website, and they can offer answers when students ask questions.

❷ Second, unlike what the suggestion says, it is not that difficult to schedule a meeting. If students make an appointment beforehand, it would be much more convenient for both students and advisors. (This is why he thinks the plan is unnecessary.)

두 학생은 웹사이트가 같은 정보를 제공하고 약속을 잡기 힘들기 때문에 학교에서 상담을 의무화 하면 안 된다는 제안에 대해서 얘기하고 있다. 남자는 두 가지 이유를 들어 그 계획에 반대하고 있다.

❶ 첫째, 카운슬러들은 웹사이트 보다 더 많은 정보를 가지고 있고 그들은 학생들이 물어보면 답변을 줄 수 있다.

❷ 다음, 제안이 주장하는 바와 다르게, 약속 잡기가 그리 어렵지 않다. 만약 학생들이 미리 약속을 잡는다면, 학생과 선생님 모두에게 더 편리할 것이다. (이것이 그가 이 제한이 필요하지 않다고 생각하는 이유이다.)

Vocabulary

advisory meeting	phr. 상담 (회의)	be willing to	phr. 흔쾌히 ~하다
ahead of time	phr. 미리	leave the day empty	phr. 하루 종일 약속을 비우다
make an appointment	phr. 약속을 잡다, 예약하다	under the condition	phr. ~이라는 조건 하에

03 Environmental Disturbance 환경 교란 — Integrated Task

읽기 지문

Environmental Disturbance

There are many events which occur in nature that cause harm to not only the environment, but also to the organisms living there. Environmental change can be both natural or **anthropogenic**, meaning caused by human action. No matter the type however, environment disturbances cause changes that have effects on the plants living there and their ways of growing. Since nature is mostly made up of plants, it is obvious that environmental disturbances would impact them the most. Some of these changes even affect the plants **permanently** over **successive** generations and are usually **irreversible**.

대화 스크립트

STEP 01 뼈대를 먼저 작성해 보도록 하겠습니다.

STEP 02 작성하신 뼈대 빈칸에 맞춰서 리딩 지문을 읽고 주요 포인트를 넣어주세요.

STEP 03 하단에 리스닝 노트테이킹을 해주세요. 음원은 학원 홈페이지에서 무료로 다운받으실 수 있습니다. 또한 3006번 문제 번호로 문제를 풀어보실 수 있습니다.

USHER

STEP 04 아래 하단에 리스닝 스크립트를 보고 베꼈어야 하는 부분을 찾아서 적어 보도록 하겠습니다.

대화 스크립트

뉴토플 - TEST 06_Q3

Now listen to part of a lecture in a biology class.

So, I'm sure you all have participated in trying to save the environment or something, right? With all the campaigns going on lately to save the environment, it would have been hard not to participate, whether it's something as trivial as separating paper from plastic or as active as picking up trash on the beach. Although you may think humans are the main causes of environmental disturbances, there are also natural environmental disturbances as well.

예시 ❶
블루그래스

세부사항
파란 꼬투리에서 이름을 따옴

Well, let me give you an example of a natural disturbance. Bluegrass is a common name for a **genus** of plants that consists of about 500 species of grasses found in **temperate** regions around the world, but we usually use the term to refer to the ones in North America. It's called bluegrass not because it has blue leaves - duh - but because of the blue seed heads when its height reaches two to three feet. Pretty tall for grass, huh?

예시 ❷
블루그래스의 높이가 문제

세부사항
소들이 먹어 치우게 해서 해결

Well, it's this height that becomes a problem for other plants in the field. In places where there is little sunlight, bluegrass grows at a relatively slow rate, but in sunny areas, it blocks sunlight and prevents other plants from growing. As a result, in order to get rid of this environmental disturbance, cows are put out to **pasture** in these areas. The cows clear the places of bluegrass, eating everything without hesitation. Thanks to these hungry cows, the amount of blue grass decreased dramatically and this created room for other plants to **photosynthesize**.

이제 생물학 수업의 일부를 들어보세요.

자, 저는 여러분 모두가 환경 보호에 참여하려고 노력한 적이 있다고 확신합니다. 최근 환경을 살리기 위한 캠페인들 속에서, 종이를 비닐에 분리하는 것처럼 사소하거나 해변에서 쓰레기를 줍는 것처럼 적극적이든 간에, 그 어떤 것이라도 참여하지 않기는 힘들 것입니다. 여러분은 인간이 환경 교란의 주된 원인이라고 생각할 수도 있지만, 자연적인 환경 교란 또한 존재합니다.

자, 제가 자연적인 환경 교란의 예를 들겠습니다. 블루그래스는 전 세계의 **온대** 지역에서 찾을 수 있는 약 500여종의 풀로 이루어져 있는 식물 속의 흔한 이름이지만 우리는 대게 북미에 있는 것들에 대하여 이야기 할 때 이 용어를 사용합니다. 이것은 파란 잎을 가지고 있어서 블루그래스라고 불리는 것이 아니라 - 설마 - 이것이 2에서 3피트만큼 컸을 때의 파란 꼬투리 때문입니다. 풀치곤 꽤 크죠, 그렇죠?

음, 들판에 있는 다른 식물들에게 이 높이는 문제가 됩니다. 햇빛이 잘 들지 않는 곳에서는 블루그래스는 상대적으로 느리게 자라지만 햇빛이 잘 드는 지역에서는 이것이 햇빛을 막고 다른 식물들을 못 자라게 합니다. 결과적으로, 이러한 환경 교란을 없애기 위하여, 이러한 지역에는 소를 **목장**에 풉니다. 소들은 주저하지 않고 모든 것을 먹어버려 블루그래스를 없앱니다. 이 고마운 굶주린 소들 덕분에, 블루그래스의 수는 급격히 줄었고, 다른 식물들이 **광합성** 할 여지가 생겼습니다.

문제 — **Using the example from the professor's lecture, explain what environmental disturbance is and how it works.**

교수의 강의를 예로 들어, 환경 교란이 무엇이고 어떻게 작용하는지 설명하세요.

STEP 05 다시한번 음원듣고 노트테이킹 해보도록 하겠습니다.
Note-taking

STEP 06 다시 한번 뼈대와 함께 모범 답안을 작성해 보도록 하겠습니다.

Environmental Disturbance

There are many events which occur in nature that cause harm to not only the environment, but also to the organisms living there. Environmental change can be both natural or **anthropogenic**, meaning caused by human action. No matter the type however, environment disturbances cause changes that have effects on the plants living there and their ways of growing. Since nature is mostly made up of plants, it is obvious that environmental disturbances would impact them the most. Some of these changes even affect the plants **permanently** over **successive** generations and are usually **irreversible**.

USHER

References

Photo by Rasbak, available under the Creative Commons Attribution-Share Alike 3.0 Unported license.

Uploaded by Americasroof at en.wikipedia, available under the Creative Commons Attribution-Share Alike 3.0 Unported license.

[참고자료]

❶ 포아풀
벼목에 속하는 500여종의 잔디를 아우르는 속(genus)으로 블루그래스(bluegrass)는 북미 지역에서 불리는 이름이다.

❷ 포아풀의 꼬투리
익을수록 녹색-보라빛 파랑-갈색으로 변한다. 블루그래스 (bluegrass)라는 이름은 이 꼬투리의 색깔에서 비롯됐다.

Task 3 Sample Response 뉴토플 - TEST 06_R3   3번 문제 모범 답안

Environméntal distúrbances cause changes that have efféects on the plants living there and their ways of growing. In the lecture, the proféssor gives an exámple of bluegrass to expláin it.

❶ Bluegrass got its name from its blue seed heads when it's fully grown. When it reaches its full height, it becómes tall enóugh to block sunlight for other plants on the field.

❷ The rapid growth becáme a natural environméntal distúrbance for other plants in the field. In order to take care of this problem, cows were reléased into the field. The cows ate up the bluegrass and enóugh sunlight becáme available for other flowers.

환경교란은 자라고 있는 식물과 그들의 성장에 영향을 주는 변화를 일으킵니다. 강의에서, 교수는 이를 설명하기 위해 블루그래스의 예를 듭니다.

❶ 블루그래스는 다 자랐을 때의 파란 꼬투리에서 그 이름을 얻었습니다. 다 자라고 나면, 들판에 있는 다른 식물들을 햇빛으로부터 가릴 정도로 커집니다.

❷ 빠른 성장은 들판의 다른 식물들에게 자연적 환경 교란이 됩니다. 이 문제를 해결하기 위해 들에 소들이 방목되었습니다. 소들은 블루그래스를 먹었고, 꽃들은 충분한 햇빛을 받을 수 있었습니다.

Vocabulary

anthropogenic [ænθrəpoudʒénik]	a. 사람이 일으키는	
successive [səksésiv]	a. 연속되는	
genus [dʒíːnəs]	n. (분류학에서) 속	
pasture [pǽstʃə]	n. 목장	
permanently [pə́ːrmənəntli]	ad. 영구히	
irreversible [ìrivə́ːrsəbl]	a. 되돌릴 수 없는	
temperate [témpərət]	a. 절제할 줄 아는, 온대의	
photosynthesize [fòutousínθəsàiz]	v. 광합성하다	

04. Sculpting 조각법 — Integrated Task

STEP 01 4번 뼈대를 먼저 작성해 보도록 하겠습니다.

STEP 02 하단에 리스닝 노트테이킹을 해주세요. 음원은 학원 홈페이지에서 무료로 다운받으실 수 있습니다. 또한 4006번 문제 번호로 문제를 풀어보실 수 있습니다.

STEP 03 뼈대에 맞춰서 모범 답안을 완성해 보겠습니다.

대화 스크립트

뉴토플 - TEST 06_Q4

Listen to part of a lecture in an art class.

미술 강의의 일부를 들어보세요.

주제
조각을 하는
두 가지 방법

Sculptures have been made for thousands of years and are a major component of public art. These pieces of **figurative** artwork come in a variety of forms, but one aspect of them that people may overlook is the process used to create them. This process can be categorized in two ways based on the method of manufacture, and the two are called either subtractive or additive sculpting.

조각상은 수천 년 전부터 만들어져 왔으며 대중미술의 중요한 부분을 차지합니다. 이런 **조형** 미술들은 다양한 형태로 이루어져 있지만, 정작 조각이 만들어지는 과정은 간과하기 일쑤입니다. 이 과정은 만드는 방법에 따라 두 가지로 나누어지는데 깎아내는 조각술과 덧붙이는 조각술이 있습니다.

예시 ❶
조각
(깎는 조각 법)

세부사항
미켈란젤로의
피에타는 대리석
으로 만들었음

실수는 되돌릴 수
없는 단점

Subtractive sculpting is creating a sculpture by removing pieces from a solid piece of material, such as stone, wood, or ivory. This is the oldest form of sculpting and is **exemplified** by Ancient Greek, Roman, and Renaissance **statuary**. The Pieta by Michelangelo is a great example. The word Pieta means pity in Italian, and it depicts Mary holding her dying son Jesus on her lap after **crucifixion**. In this marble masterpiece, marble was carved or chipped away at until the desired form came into shape. Due to this method of manufacture, mistakes can cause great problems, as it is a finite process and can't be corrected by putting the piece back together.

조각법(깎는 조각법)은 돌, 나무, 또는 상아 같이 단단한 것을 깎아내면서 조각을 만드는 방법입니다. 이는 가장 오래된 조각법이며 그 **예로는** 고대 그리스, 로마, 르네상스 **조각상**이 있습니다. 미켈란젤로의 '피에타'는 아주 좋은 예입니다. 이태리어로 '피에타'는 '연민'이라는 뜻을 가진 단어로, **십자가에서 처형된** 예수를 무릎 위에 눕히고 슬퍼하는 마리아의 모습을 담고 있습니다. 대리석으로 만들어진 이 걸작은 원하는 모양이 나올 때까지 깎고 쪼아낸 것입니다. 이 방법은 한번 조각하면 고칠 수 없기 때문에 실수는 큰 문제를 가져올 수 있습니다.

예시 ❷
소조
(더하는 조각법)

세부사항
로버트 인디애나의
'사랑'은 철로
만들었음

더욱 다양한
모양이 가능

Additive sculpting, on the other hand, is accomplished by using softer, moldable materials, such as cement, clay or plastic, which can be **cast**, reshaped or otherwise altered. This type of sculpture allows the artist more freedom, as more of the medium can be added or changed as needed. One of the most famous examples is the modern art installation Love by Robert Indiana. It's basically the letters LO on the top and VE at the bottom. This design has been used in many other forms. It must have been relatively easy to create as it is made of steel. With this freedom, the sculptor had been able to create a more **abstract**, stylized piece.

소조(더하는 조각법)는 시멘트, 진흙, 플라스틱과 같이 **모양을 뜨거나** 변화를 줘서 만듭니다. 이 조각법은 필요에 따라 모양을 바꾸거나, 더할 수 있기 때문에 조각가가 좀 더 자유롭습니다. 가장 유명한 설치미술품 중 하나는 로버트 인디애나의 '사랑'입니다. 이 작품은 단순히 글자 'LO'는 위에 'VE'는 아래에 위치한 모양입니다. 이 디자인은 다른 여러 유형으로 사용되어 왔습니다. 철로 만들어졌기 때문에 작품을 상대적으로 만들기가 쉬웠을 것입니다. 이런 자유로움 덕분에, 조각가는 더 **추상적**이고, 개성있는 작품을 만들 수 있게 되었습니다.

문제

Using the examples from the professor's lecture, explain the two methods of sculpting.

교수의 강의를 예로 들어, 조각법의 두 방식을 설명하세요.

References

Photo by Stanislav Traykov, available under the Creative Commons Attribution-Share Alike 3.0 Unported license.

Photo by Hu Totya

[참고자료]

❶ 미켈란젤로의 피에타
미켈란젤로가 24세에 조각한 작품으로, 자신의 이름을 새긴 유일한 조각이다. 바티칸의 성 베드로 성당에 소장되어 있다.

❷ 로버트 인디애나의 '사랑'
Subtractive sculpting은 카빙 (carving)이라고도 하며, additive sculpting은 모델링 (modeling)이라고도 한다.

Task 4   Sample Response   🎧 TEST 06_R4   4번 문제 모범 답안

In the lecture, the professor is explaining the two ways of creating sculptures, subtractive sculpting and additive sculpting. The professor gives examples of two famous sculptures to explain it.

❶ Subtractive sculptures are made from solid materials such as stone and wood. They are more difficult to work with because mistakes cannot be easily corrected. 'The Pieta' by Michelángelo is a good example of subtractive sculpting.

❷ Additive sculptures are made from softer materials such as cement, clay or plastic. They are easier to work with because they can be cast and even reshaped if necessary. 'Love' by Robert Indiána is a good example of additive sculpting.

강의에서 교수는 깎는 조각법과, 더하는 조각법에 대하여 설명하고 있습니다. 교수는 유명한 두 조각을 예로 들어 이를 설명합니다.

❶ 조각상은 돌이나, 나무 같은 단단한 재료로 만들어 집니다. 실수를 하면 쉽게 고칠 수 없기 때문에 이 방법으로 조각하는 것은 어렵습니다. 미켈란젤로의 '피에타'는 깎는 조각법으로 만들어진 조각의 좋은 예입니다.

❷ 소조(더하는) 조각은 시멘트, 플라스틱, 진흙과 같은 부드러운 재질로 만들어 집니다. 필요하면 언제든지 벗겨 내거나 고칠 수 있기 때문에 만들기가 쉽습니다. 로버트 인디애나의 '사랑'은 대표적인 소조(더하는) 조각이라고 할 수 있습니다.

Vocabulary

figurative [fígjurətiv]	a. 비유적인, 모양의	exemplify [igzémpləfài]	v. 예시하다
statuary [stǽtʃuèri]	n. 조각	crucifixion [krùːsəfíkʃən]	n. 십자가에 못 박음
cast [kæst]	v. 모양을 뜨다	abstract [ǽbstrækt]	a. 추상적인

USHER
iBT TOEFL
FINAL TEST SPEAKING
TEST 07

Independent Tasks

Task 1 - 모범 답안
Question 1   usherin.usher.co.kr > 시험리스트 > Speaking 시험리스트 > Task 1 > #1020

Integrated Tasks

Task 2 - Script / 해석 / 모범 답안
Question 2   usherin.usher.co.kr > 시험리스트 > Speaking 시험리스트 > Task 2 > #2007

Task 3 - Script / 해석 / 모범 답안
Question 3   usherin.usher.co.kr > 시험리스트 > Speaking 시험리스트 > Task 3 > #3007

Task 4 - Script / 해석 / 모범 답안
Question 4   usherin.usher.co.kr > 시험리스트 > Speaking 시험리스트 > Task 4 > #4007

자기평가표

1번 문제 유형은 학생들이 본인에 생각을 주제에 맞춰서 말 해야하는 시험입니다.
본인이 처음부터 끝까지 45초 동안 말해야하다 보니 학생들이 제일 어려워 하는 시험입니다.
하지만, 먼저 외우고 익힌후에 말하는것이 가능할수 있게 하겠습니다.
가장 기본이 되는 뼈대 입니다. 먼저 외우도록 합시다.

> if i were to answer the question, i would say
> there are many reasons why, but here is a couple
> first
> for example,
> second
> for instance
> that's why

다음은 2번 문제 유형입니다.
2번 문제는 리딩에 학교에 계획이 적혀있거나 학교가 변해야하는 방향에 대해서 학생들에 주장이 적혀있습니다.
리딩에서 빠르게 파악해야하는 것은 도대체 누가 무엇을 주장하는가 입니다.
45~50초에 리딩 지문이 나오고 난 다음에 리스닝으로 학생들에 대화가 나오는 문제입니다.
리스닝에서는 학생이 리딩 지문에 대한 본인에 좋고 나쁜지에 대한 의견을 얘기해줄겁니다.
이유 2가지와 예시 2가지를 꼭 말할 수 있어야 합니다.

이에 따라서 2번 스피킹 문제에 뼈대는

> The reading states that university (plans to) / (should)
> the (woman / man) in the conversation thinks it is a good / bad idea.
> He/she provides two reasons to support his / her opinion.
> first,
> Second,
> the woman / man thinks it's a great / horrible idea.

다음은 3번 문제 유형입니다.
3번 문제는 2번 문제 유형과 같이 리딩과 리스닝이 나오는 문제 입니다. 하지만, 이번에는 이전 문제와는 달리 매우 학술적인 내용이 들어 있습니다. 리딩에서는 교과서에 나올만한 주제 한개를 자세하게 다룹니다. 여기서 학생분들은 제목과 이에 대한 정의를 잘 받아적으셔야 합니다. 리스닝에서는 교수님이 리딩에 나온 내용으로 예시를 들어 줍니다.

> The article is about
> which the passage defines as
> The professor provides an example of
> first,
> Second,
> The example clearly illustrates

다음은 4번 문제 유형입니다.
4번 문제는 이전 문제와 달리 리스닝만 나오는 문제 유형입니다. 3번 문제에 나온 리딩 지문이 리스닝으로 변환되었다 라고 생각 하시면 됩니다. 그렇기에 3번 문제에 리스닝 내용보다 리딩 길이 만큼 깁니다.

> In the lecture, professor explains
> first,
> second,
> That's how the professor explain it.

USHER

01. Getting Dressed Up 옷 차려 입기 — Independent Task

QUESTION

 Do you agree or disagree with the following statement? It is important to get dressed up and stay fashionable. Use reasons and examples to support your answer.
(당신은 다음 주장에 동의하십니까, 아니면 반대하십니까? 옷을 차려 입고 멋을 유지하는 것은 중요하다. 이유와 예를 들어 답하세요.)

 브레인 스토밍 (아래에 놓여있는 12간지 내용들을 보고 어떤 것을 사용할 수 있을지 확인해보세요)
첫번째 이유 :
두번째 이유 :

 뼈대에 맞춰서 작성을 해봅시다.

_____
_____
_____
_____
_____
_____
_____
_____

아래 이미지는 학생들을 위한 만능 템플릿 12간지 입니다. 학생분들이 제일 먼저 암기해야하는 것이며, 본인 스스로 문장을 단기간 안에 못 만들거 같을 때에 도와주는 친구입니다. 가까이 두고 매일 외우세요.

Academic Courses
…because I think students should concentrate on academic courses.

Academic courses are the most important thing for students because good grades will help them get into good universities and, eventually, get great jobs.

As students get older, a good academic record is the only thing that actually matters.

This may sound a little far-fetched, but it's true, and for this reason, investing time in other activities is a waste of time.

Stay Healthy
It can be a great way to stay healthy. People join a cycling group through the internet. The members use bicycles to commute to work or school.

It is a great outdoor activity because people have a chance to work out while having fun.

Also, it is a great way to meet new people with similar interests. People nowadays do not have much chance to become close to each other.

However, there are numerous unique groups active on the internet, and this would not have been possible without the internet.

Follows your heart
Carpe diem, seize the days, and YOLO all stand for one thing. Do whatever your heart makes you do.

Life is too short to hesitate or do things to please others. It is essential to make yourself happy.

Actions speak louder than words. Whatever I do to make myself happy is better than sitting in a room thinking about it.

So I would just do it even if it means I am biting off something more than I can chew.

Stress
…if it can possibly be a way to relieve stress.

People nowadays are living a busy and hectic life, so they are under great stress, but a lot of them don't even realize they are stressed out.

Stress is known to be a major factor that keeps us from being healthy, and many people are suffering from various problems.

This is more serious than we think, so if it can ever be a way to relieve stress…

Money
…because it's the best way to save money. When it comes to spending money, every penny counts.

A thrifty spending habit is indispensable in our lives because little drops of water make the mighty ocean.

If we don't get used to working on a tight budget, we'll always be short on cash later.

A penny-pinching lifestyle will lead to financial stability, and it will give us peace of mind.

Saving Time
…because it's the best way to save time. There's an old saying, "Time is gold."

This proverb emphasizes the value of time, and this cannot be more true in modern society.

We're living a busy and hectic life, so saving time means we can do a lot more things later.

Many say that life is not fair, but everyone has twenty-four hours a day and seven days a week, so I would save time by…

Social Skills
Nowadays, people have smartphones with them all the time, and that information is no longer limited to elites.

Therefore, rather than learning, having social skills became the be-all and end-all to succeed rather than education.

Also, social skills are more than meet the eyes. To have social skills, one must also be able to read others like a book.

There will be times when one will truly need them.

Environment
because eventually, it can contribute to protecting the environment.

I think it's THE most important task for humanity because we cannot bring it back to life once it's too late.

Saving Earth all starts from seemingly insignificant actions.

Small actions from everyone bring about bigger changes, so I'm willing to participate.

Patience is virtue
Patience is a virtue. Saving time is indeed important, but waiting calmly is needed in this case.

There are times when one must wait patiently for things to go accordingly, and this is when time is the solution.

When going against the clock, they are more susceptible to making mistakes than taking some time.

In the long run, one will be glad that one has waited in this case.

Just because
I love it more than the given choices. Since I have so many great memory about it, it brings so many great reminiscences.

time flies whenever I am doing it, so how can I not choose it?

Also, not only do I love it, but I am also good at it. Everyone has talent, and it is like "a dime a dozen."

This was the inborn talent I had that I always surpassed everyone. Since a bird in the hand is worth two in the bush, I will choose it.

Politeness
It is important to maintain good relationships with other people because we never know what will happen in the future.

Decisions made by other people can affect others, and such decisions are usually based on personal and sentimental reasons.

So, people should not do anything that may offend or disturb others. It is also crucial to have a good reputation and get along well with others.

It Makes sense
It makes sense to choose it when considering many aspects such as time, money, and efficiency.

When people are considering between the given choices, they must consider many aspects economically.

They must choose the most efficient method because there are limits on what they have.

Also, one should think about it realistically and practically because they should not count chickens before they hatch.

So, down to Earth, people should choose it because it is the most economical

QUESTION

Do you agree or disagree with the following statement? It is important to get dressed up and stay fashionable. Use reasons and examples to support your answer.
(당신은 다음 주장에 동의하십니까, 아니면 반대하십니까? 옷을 차려 입고 멋을 유지하는 것은 중요하다. 이유와 예를 들어 답하세요.)

---

academic courses와 stay healthy를 사용해서 뼈대에 맞춰서 모범답안을 만들어 봅시다.

---

follow your heart와 stress를 사용해서 뼈대에 맞춰서 모범답안을 만들어 봅시다.

---

money와 saving time을 사용해서 뼈대에 맞춰서 모범답안을 만들어 봅시다.

---

social skills와 politeness를 사용해서 뼈대에 맞춰서 모범답안을 만들어 봅시다.

QUESTION

Do you agree or disagree with the following statement? It is important to get dressed up and stay fashionable. Use reasons and examples to support your answer.
(당신은 다음 주장에 동의하십니까, 아니면 반대하십니까? 옷을 차려 입고 멋을 유지하는 것은 중요하다. 이유와 예를 들어 답하세요.)

academic courses와 stay healthy를 사용해서 뼈대에 맞춰서 모범답안을 만들어 봅시다.

If I were to answer the question, I would say it is not important to get dressed up. There are many reasons why, but here is a couple.

academic courses

First, I am a student. I need to study instead of being fashionable. For example, academic courses are the most important thing for me, because good grades will help me get into a good university and eventually get great jobs.

stay healthy

Second, I rather care about my health. For instance, outdoor activity is important because people will have a chance to work out while having fun. Also, it is a great way to meet new people who have the same interest.

That's why I think it's not important to dress up.

follow your heart와 stress를 사용해서 뼈대에 맞춰서 모범답안을 만들어 봅시다.

If I were to answer the question, I would say people should dress up. There are many reasons why, but here is a couple.

follow your heart

First, life is too short to hesitate. For example, there are old sayings "carpe diem, seize the days, and YOLO." They all stand for one thing: try your best on everything which means people need to do their best in dressing up.

stress

Second, dressing up can relieve their stress by looking good. For instance, people nowadays are living a busy and hectic life, so they are under great stress. Dressing up can be a great way to relieve stress by looking good.

That's why I think people should dress up.

money와 saving time을 사용해서 뼈대에 맞춰서 모범답안을 만들어 봅시다.

If I were to answer the question, I would say people should not dress up. There are many reasons why, but here is a couple.

money

First, dressing up costs a lot. For example, not dressing up can be a good way to save money. When it comes to spending money, every penny counts. A thrifty spending habit is indispensable in people's lives.

saving time

Second, dressing up takes too much time to do. For instance, there is an old saying "time is gold." This proverb emphasizes the value of time, and this cannot be more true in modern society. People are living busy and hectic life, so saving time means they can do a lot more things later.

That's why I think they should not dress up.

social skills와 politeness를 사용해서 뼈대에 맞춰서 모범답안을 만들어 봅시다.

If I were to answer the question, I would say people should dress up. There are many reasons why, but here is a couple.

social skills

First, dressing up helps people socialize. For example, having social skills became the be-all and end-all to succeed. Also, dressing up is more than meets the eye. Therefore, people should dress up.

politeness

Second, it can look great to others. For instance, it is important to look good to others, because we never know what is going to happen in the future. Decisions made by other people can affect them.

That's why I think people should dress up.

02. More Parkinglot 주차장 하나 더 — Integrated Task

읽기 지문

University Should Build a New Parking Lot

The university has a vast area covered with trees near the school library. I think this place would the perfect spot for another parking lot. Since the area is covered by many trees, we would not be affecting the environment too much by using a little space for parking. There are not enough parking spaces on campus **in relation to** the number of students' cars. There is especially not enough space for cars, by the library, which is frequently used by students. By building a new parking space, students with cars will be able to use the library more conveniently.

대화 스크립트

STEP 01 뼈대를 먼저 작성해 보도록 하겠습니다.

STEP 02 작성하신 뼈대 빈칸에 맞춰서 리딩 지문을 읽고 주요 포인트를 넣어주세요.

STEP 03 하단에 리스닝 노트테이킹을 해주세요. 음원은 학원 홈페이지에서 무료로 다운받으실 수 있습니다. 또한 2007번 문제 번호로 문제를 풀어보실 수 있습니다.

 아래 하단에 리스닝 스크립트를 보고 베꼈어야 하는 부분을 찾아서 적어 보도록 하겠습니다.

대화 스크립트

뉴토플 - TEST 07_Q2

Now listen to two students discussing the letter.

M: Hey, Jen. Did you see the letter in the school paper?

W: Yeah, I did, and I don't think it's a great idea.

M: **How come?**

W: Well, it may be true that there are limited parking spaces near the library, but does that mean we really need to build a whole new parking lot?

M: What do you mean?

W: I mean, there are empty parking spaces by nearby buildings. Students with cars can park in those spaces and walk to the library, can't they? I mean, it's not even that far of a walk when compared to students without cars.

M: Hmm… I guess you're right. I always see empty parking spaces near other buildings when I walk around campus.

W: Yeah, and even worse is that that place is a place of rest for students. We use that place to relax and hang out with friends outside of the school environment. The trees make it feel like we're outside in nature and it really helps students relax when they're **stressed out**, especially after a long day at the library.

M: Yeah, I always go there **to cool my head** when I feel overloaded with schoolwork and stuff.

W: Right! And, that place is the only spot on campus with so many trees. They can't just cut down all the trees and decide to build a parking lot.

여자의 의견 — 반대

이유 ❶ — 근처 건물들 옆에 주차 공간이 많음

이유 ❷ — 나무로 덮인 공간은 학생들에게 휴식 장소임

문제 — The woman expresses her opinion about the proposal in the newspaper. State the woman's opinion and explain the reasons she gives for holding that opinion.

이제 지문에 대해 논의하는 두 학생의 대화를 들어보세요.

남: 안녕, Jen. 학교 신문에 실린 편지 읽어봤어?

여: 응, 읽었어. 근데 좋은 생각이 아닌 것 같아.

남: 왜?

여: 도서관 근처에 주차 공간이 한정돼있긴 하지만, 그게 새 주차공간을 만들어야 한단 뜻일까?

남: 무슨 말이야?

여: 내 말은, 근처 건물들 옆에 빈 주차 공간들이 있어. 차를 가지고 있는 학생들은 거기에 주차를 하고 도서관으로 걸어가면 되잖아? 차가 없는 학생들에 비해서 그다지 걷기에 먼 거리도 아닌데 말이야.

남: 음, 맞는 말 같은데. 캠퍼스를 걸으면서 다른 건물들 근처에 빈 주차 공간을 보곤 하거든.

여: 그렇지, 그리고 더 안 좋은 점은, 그 공간은 학생들이 쉬는 공간이야. 학교에서 벗어나서 쉬거나 친구들과 **어울려 놀** 수 있는 공간이지. 나무들은 마치 우리가 자연에 있는 것처럼 느끼게 해주고 특히 하루 종일 도서관에서 있어서 **지친** 학생들에겐 스트레스를 해소시켜주지.

남: 맞아, 학교 일 때문에 머리가 무거울 때마다 **머리 좀 식히려고** 항상 그 곳에 가는데.

여: 그렇지? 그리고, 그 곳은 유일하게 학교에서 나무가 많은 공간이야. 그 나무들을 그냥 잘라내고 주차장을 만들 순 없지.

여자는 대학의 계획에 대해 자신의 의견을 밝히고 있습니다. 그녀의 의견을 말하고, 그 의견을 고수하는 이유를 설명하세요.

Note-taking

다시한번 모범 답안을 작성해 보도록 하겠습니다

University Should Build a New Parking Lot

The university has a vast area covered with trees near the school library. I think this place would the perfect spot for another parking lot. Since the area is covered by many trees, we would not be affecting the environment too much by using a little space for parking. There are not enough parking spaces on campus **in relation to** the number of students' cars. There is especially not enough space for cars, by the library, which is frequently used by students. By building a new parking space, students with cars will be able to use the library more conveniently.

Note-taking	노트테이킹
Reading - build a new parking lot near the library - there is a space with trees near the library - not enough parking space near the library **Woman** - against **Reason ❶** - there're many spaces by the buildings nearby - students can park there and walk to the library **Reason ❷** - the trees are important for students' well-being - the campus doesn't have other places with trees	**지문** - 도서관 옆에 새 주차장을 만들 것 - 도서관 옆에 나무로 된 공간이 있음 - 도서관 옆에 주차공간이 부족 **여자** - 반대 **이유 ❶** - 주변 건물에 공간이 많음 - 그곳에 차를 대고 걸어오면 됨 **이유 ❷** - 나무는 학생의 웰빙을 위해 중요 - 캠퍼스에 나무 있는 곳이 없음

Task 2 Sample Response 🎧 뉴토플 - TEST 07_R2 | 2번 문제 모범 답안

The two students are discussing the suggestion that the university should build a new parking lot near the library, where there are many trees. The woman is against the plan for two reasons.

❶ First, the library parking lot may be small, but there are plenty of parking spaces by the buildings nearby. They aren't far from the library, so students could walk there.

❷ Second, the trees are important for students' well-being. The green space provides a great place for students to relax and relieve stress. Also, the campus doesn't have other places with many trees, so the university shouldn't cut them down to make a parking lot. (This is why she thinks the plan is unnecessary.)

두 학생은 많은 나무들이 있는, 도서관 주변에 새로운 주차장을 세워야 한다는 제안에 대해서 의논하고 있다. 여자는 두 가지 이유를 들어 그 제안에 반대하고 있다.

❶ 첫째, 도서관 주차장이 작을 진 몰라도, 주변 건물들 옆에 많은 주차 공간이 있다. 도서관에서 별로 멀지 않기 때문에, 학생들은 걸어 갈 수 있다.

❷ 다음, 나무들은 학생들의 복지에 있어서 중요하다. 녹지 구역은 학생들이 쉬거나 **스트레스를 해소할** 수 있는 좋은 공간이다. 그리고, 학교에 나무가 많은 또 다른 공간이 없기 때문에, 주차장을 만들려고 나무를 잘라서는 안 된다. (이것이 그녀가 이 제안이 필요 없다고 생각하는 이유이다)

Vocabulary

how come	phr. 왜, 어쩌다	in relation to	phr. ~에 비해서
hang out	phr. 어울려 놀다	be stressed out	phr. 스트레스를 많이 받다
cool one's head	phr. ~의 머리를 식히다	relieve stress	phr. 스트레스를 풀다

03 Bait Pricing 미끼 가격정책 — Integrated Task

읽기 지문

Bait Pricing

Marketing experts use a variety of methods to **entice** consumers **to take note of** and purchase specific products or brands. In addition, they often attempt to draw customers into a specific store. One way this can be accomplished is through **bait pricing**, or a **bait-and-switch**. This is a tactic through which the consumer **is lured to** a store through the use of a specific **bait product**. These products are usually advertised at unrealistically low prices when compared to others in a similar category, thereby attracting more consumers to come in to the store looking for the bait product.

대화 스크립트

 STEP 01 뼈대를 먼저 작성해 보도록 하겠습니다.

 STEP 02 작성하신 뼈대 빈칸에 맞춰서 리딩 지문을 읽고 주요 포인트를 넣어주세요.

 STEP 03 하단에 리스닝 노트테이킹을 해주세요. 음원은 학원 홈페이지에서 무료로 다운받으실 수 있습니다. 또한 3007번 문제 번호로 문제를 풀어보실 수 있습니다.

USHER

아래 하단에 리스닝 스크립트를 보고 베꼈어야 하는 부분을 찾아서 적어 보도록 하겠습니다.

대화 스크립트

Now listen to part of a lecture in a marketing class.

Bait pricing is one method that marketing experts use to entice consumers to buy their products, or to visit their brands. This is done in many ways, with the most common being advertising a specific product at a very low rate. This may even take the form of '**loss leaders**' which are sold below their actual cost to get consumers to try a new product and build a loyal base early on in the product cycle. This may sound like a classic 'bait-and-switch' **scam**, but it is a useful tool. Let's look at some examples of this.

예시 ❶
특매품

세부사항
수량이 한정된 저가 제품으로 유인

Perhaps the example of pre-Christmas sales can illustrate one aspect of it. About a month before Christmas, I received a **flyer** advertising DVD players for $20 at a local store. Since I was looking to buy my son one, I went into the store, but found that the cheapest DVD player was actually $50. This may seem like illegal false advertising, but the store actually had the cheaper players, but they were 'loss leaders' and in limited supply. By the time I'd gotten there, they were **sold out** and I was stuck buying a more expensive player.

예시 ❷
신제품 특가

세부사항
낮은 특가에 사보고, 맘에 들면 더 높은 가격에 또 구입

Another aspect of price baiting is introducing customers to products that are new on the market. In the case of **disposable products**, like razors or pens, the marketers may decide to offer '**introductory pricing**' which is often near, or below, production cost of the product. This is done so people become familiar with the product and repurchase it after satisfactorily using it up.

문제

Using the example from the professor's lecture, explain what bait pricing is and how it works.

뉴토플 - TEST 07_Q3

이제 마케팅 수업의 일부를 들어보세요.

미끼 가격정책은 소비자들이 제품을 사거나 상점에 방문하도록 마케팅 전문가들이 사용하는 방법입니다. 이것은 여러 가지 방법으로 이루어지지만, 가장 흔한 방법은 특정 제품을 아주 싼 가격으로 광고하는 것입니다. 이것은 소비자들에게 실제 가격보다 낮은 가격에 판매하여 새로운 제품을 시도해보고 발매초기에 신뢰도를 쌓는 **특매품**의 형태를 띠기도 합니다. 이것은 일반적인 유인 상술같은 **사기행위**로 보이지만, 유용한 방법인데요. 몇 가지 예를 들어봅시다.

성탄절 전 세일의 예가 이것을 일부 설명할 수 있습니다. 성탄절 되기 한 달쯤 전, DVD 플레이어가 20불이란 **전단지**를 봤습니다. 아들에게 선물을 사주려고 하던 차에, 저는 매장에 갔지만 가장 싼 DVD 플레이어가 50불이라는걸 발견했죠. 이는 불법 허위 광고 같지만 상점에는 더 싼 기기들이 있었습니다. 하지만 그것들은 특매품이었고 수가 한정되어 있었죠. 제가 갔을 때, 그것은 이미 **품절되어** 있었고 저는 어쩔 수 없이 더 비싼 플레이어를 사야 했습니다.

미끼 가격정책의 또 다른 예는 고객에게 새로 출시된 제품을 소개하는 것입니다. 면도기나 펜 같은 **일회용품**의 경우, 마케터들은 생산가와 비슷하거나 더 낮은 '**신제품 특가**'를 제공하기로 결정합니다. 이렇게 사람들은 제품에 익숙해지고 만족스럽게 사용한 후에 다시 사게 되죠.

교수의 강의를 예로 들어, 미끼 가격정책이 무엇이고 어떻게 작용하는지 설명하세요.

STEP 05 다시한번 음원듣고 노트테이킹 해보도록 하겠습니다.
Note-taking

STEP 06 다시 한번 뼈대와 함께 모범 답안을 작성해 보도록 하겠습니다.

Bait Pricing

Marketing experts use a variety of methods to **entice** consumers **to take note of** and purchase specific products or brands. In addition, they often attempt to draw customers into a specific store. One way this can be accomplished is through **bait pricing**, or a **bait-and-switch**. This is a tactic through which the consumer **is lured to** a store through the use of a specific **bait product**. These products are usually advertised at unrealistically low prices when compared to others in a similar category, thereby attracting more consumers to come in to the store looking for the bait product.

References

Bait pricing policy - 미끼 가격정책. 특매품을 이용해 소비자를 매장으로 끌어들이는 모든 전략을 통칭하는 말.

Bait products - 미끼 상품. 소비자를 매장으로 끌어들이는 목적으로 마련된 상품.

Bait-and-switch - 유인상술. 미끼 가격정책(bait pricing)과 같이 쓰임.

Loss leaders - 특매품. 특별히 싼값으로 파는 상품으로 보통 수량이 지극히 한정되어 있다.

Introductory pricing - 신제품 특가. 신제품이 처음 시장에 나왔을 때, 홍보를 목적으로 원가에 가깝게 가격을 낮추는 정책. 제품이 자리를 잡으면 철수한다.

Task 3 Sample Response 뉴토플 - TEST 07_R3 3번 문제 모범 답안

Bait pricing is attracting customers through the use of a specific bait product with an unrealistically low price. The professor is giving examples of pre-Christmas sales and new products to explain it.

❶ The professor went to a store to purchase a $20 DVD player, but they were in limited supply. The DVD players were sold out, so he ended up buying a more expensive one.

❷ Another example is introducing a new product. In the case of disposable products, people can buy at a cheap price to get familiar with the products. Then, customers can keep using them at a higher price.

미끼 가격정책은 미끼 제품을 비상식적으로 싸게 판매함으로써 소비자를 유혹하는 것이다. 교수는 성탄절 세일과 새 제품을 예로 들며 설명하고 있다.

❶ 교수는 20달러짜리 dvd플레이어를 사려고 상점에 갔지만 그 제품은 수량이 적었다. 그 dvd 플레이어는 품절됐고, 그는 결국 더 비싼 제품을 샀다.

❷ 또 다른 예는 새로운 제품을 출시하는 것이다. 일회용품의 경우, 사람들은 그 제품에 익숙해지기 위해 싼 값에 살 수 있다. 그 후 소비자는 더 비싼 가격에 계속 쓸 수 있다.

Vocabulary

take note of	phr. ~에 주목하다	bait-and-switch [beitnswitʃ]	n. 유인상술
be lured to	phr. ~에 유혹당하다	entice [entáis]	v. 꾀다, 유인하다
scam [skæm]	n. 사기	flyer [fláiər]	n. 전단지
sold out	phr. 매진된	disposable product	phr. 일회용품

04. Hair Color Change 털 색깔의 변화 — Integrated Task

STEP 01
4번 뼈대를 먼저 작성해 보도록 하겠습니다.

STEP 02
하단에 리스닝 노트테이킹을 해주세요. 음원은 학원 홈페이지에서 무료로 다운받으실 수 있습니다. 또한 4007번 문제 번호로 문제를 풀어보실 수 있습니다.

STEP 03
뼈대에 맞춰서 모범 답안을 완성해 보겠습니다.

대화 스크립트

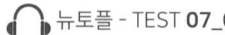

Listen to part of a lecture in a zoology class.

주제
계절에 따라 털의 색을 바꾸는 이유

We love furry animals. Fur has a way of making **menacing** animals appear **adorable**. But animal fur has much more important functions than **beautifying**. It acts as a water **repellent**, thermal **insulator**, shock absorber, and **camouflage**. So what do you think are the reasons why some animals change the color of their fur with the seasons?

예시 ❶
사냥할 때 성공률을 높임

세부사항
북극여우는 갈색에서 흰색으로 변함

Well, some predators change color to hide, so they can approach their prey more easily, hence improving their chances of hunting. The Arctic Fox, for example, lives in the northern hemisphere, where the environment changes drastically as summer approaches. In winter, the fields are completely covered in snow. During this time, the fox has a white coat. In the summer months, however, between May to July, the ice and snow melt, and the fields get covered in dry leaves and wood, so the fox grows brown fur. You see, the changing amounts of daylight, or shifts in temperature, trigger a **hormonal** reaction that causes it to produce different **biochromes**.

예시 ❷
사냥감들도 색을 바꿈

세부사항
멧토끼도 갈색에서 흰색으로 변함

Similarly, the prey of the fox has the same color change scheme. The snowshoe hare, which is a major source of food for the arctic fox, changes its color in much the same way. The difference between them is that while the fox produces a new coat from the same hair **follicles**, the hare has separate follicles for white fur. You see, the white fur of the hare is very different from normal fur; it is composed of hollow tubes filled with air. The round surface of the **translucent** fur bends and reflects light, making the fur appear white. Not only does this help the hare stay hidden, it also insulates because the heat from sunlight is captured inside the air of the fur.

문제
Using the examples from the professor's lecture, explain why some animals change the color of their fur.

References

Photo by Richard Lydekker   Photo by USDA

Photo by Walter Siegmund, available under the Creative Commons Attribution-Share Alike 3.0 Unported, 2.5 Generic, 2.0 Generic and 1.0 Generic license.

[참고자료]
❶ 북극 여우가 털갈이하는 과정
❷ 여름 동안의 멧토끼
❸ 겨울 동안의 멧토끼

Task 4   Sample Response   TEST 07_R4   4번 문제 모범 답안

In the lecture, the professor is explaining why animals need to change the color of their fur as seasons change. The professor gives two examples.

❶ The arctic fox changes its fur color to get closer to their prey without being detected. In winter when the field is covered in snow, the color turns white; when the snow melts, the fur turns brown.

❷ The snowshoe hare changes its fur color to hide from the arctic fox. They also turn white in winter, but unlike the fox, the white hair grows from different places on the skin. The hair is hollow, which is also good for heat preservation.

강의에서 교수는 왜 동물들이 계절에 따라 털갈이를 해야 하는지 설명하고 있습니다. 교수는 두가지 예를 듭니다.

❶ 북극 여우는 털 갈이를 통해 사냥감에게 들키지 않고 더욱 가까이 접근할 수 있습니다. 눈 덮인 겨울에는 털이 흰 색을 띠고, 눈이 녹은 후에는 갈색을 띱니다.

❷ 멧토끼는 북극 여우로부터 숨기 위해 털 색깔을 바꿉니다. 토끼도 겨울이 되면 하얀 털을 갖게 되지만, 여우와 다르게 흰털이 다른 모양에서 자랍니다. 이 털은 속이 비어 있어 열을 보존하는 역할도 합니다.

Vocabulary

menacing [ménisiŋ]	a. 위협적인	adorable [ədɔ́:rəbl]	a. 귀여운
beautify [bjú:təfài]	v. 아름다워지다	repellent [ripélənt]	n. 방수 가공제, 방충제
insulator [ínsəlèitər, -sju-]	n. 절연체, 방열재	camouflage [kǽməflà:ʒ]	n. 위장수단
hormonal [hɔ:rmóunl]	a. 호르몬에 의한	biochrome [báikròum]	n. 색물색소
follicle [fálikl]	n. 모낭	translucent [trænslú:snt, trænz-]	a. 반투명의

USHER
iBT TOEFL
FINAL TEST SPEAKING
TEST 08

Independent Tasks

Task 1 - 모범 답안

Question 1 usherin.usher.co.kr > 시험리스트 > Speaking 시험리스트 > Task 1 > #1059

Integrated Tasks

Task 2 - Script / 해석 / 모범 답안

Question 2 usherin.usher.co.kr > 시험리스트 > Speaking 시험리스트 > Task 2 > #2008

Task 3 - Script / 해석 / 모범 답안

Question 3 usherin.usher.co.kr > 시험리스트 > Speaking 시험리스트 > Task 3 > #3008

Task 4 - Script / 해석 / 모범 답안

Question 4 usherin.usher.co.kr > 시험리스트 > Speaking 시험리스트 > Task 4 > #4008

자기평가표

1번 문제 유형은 학생들이 본인에 생각을 주제에 맞춰서 말 해야하는 시험입니다.
본인이 처음부터 끝까지 45초 동안 말해야하다 보니 학생들이 제일 어려워 하는 시험입니다.
하지만, 먼저 외우고 익힌후에 말하는것이 가능할수 있게 하겠습니다.
가장 기본이 되는 뼈대 입니다. 먼저 외우도록 합시다.

> if i were to answer the question, i would say
> there are many reasons why, but here is a couple
> first
> for example,
> second
> for instance
> that's why

다음은 2번 문제 유형입니다.
2번 문제는 리딩에 학교에 계획이 적혀있거나 학교가 변해야하는 방향에 대해서 학생들에 주장이 적혀있습니다.
리딩에서 빠르게 파악해야하는 것은 도대체 누가 무엇을 주장하는가 입니다.
45~50초에 리딩 지문이 나오고 난 다음에 리스닝으로 학생들에 대화가 나오는 문제입니다.
리스닝에서는 학생이 리딩 지문에 대한 본인에 좋고 나쁜지에 대한 의견을 얘기해줄겁니다.
이유 2가지와 예시 2가지를 꼭 말할 수 있어야 합니다.

이에 따라서 2번 스피킹 문제에 뼈대는

> The reading states that university (plans to) / (should)
> the (woman / man) in the conversation thinks it is a good / bad idea.
> He/she provides two reasons to support his / her opinion.
> first,
> Second,
> the woman / man thinks it's a great / horrible idea.

다음은 3번 문제 유형입니다.
3번 문제는 2번 문제 유형과 같이 리딩과 리스닝이 나오는 문제 입니다. 하지만, 이번에는 이전 문제와는 달리 매우 학술적인 내용이 들어 있습니다. 리딩에서는 교과서에 나올만한 주제 한개를 자세하게 다룹니다. 여기서 학생분들은 제목과 이에 대한 정의를 잘 받아적으셔야 합니다. 리스닝에서는 교수님이 리딩에 나온 내용으로 예시를 들어 줍니다.

> The article is about
> which the passage defines as
> The professor provides an example of
> first,
> Second,
> The example clearly illustrates

다음은 4번 문제 유형입니다.
4번 문제는 이전 문제와 달리 리스닝만 나오는 문제 유형입니다. 3번 문제에 나온 리딩 지문이 리스닝으로 변환되었다 라고 생각 하시면 됩니다. 그렇기에 3번 문제에 리스닝 내용보다 리딩 길이 만큼 깁니다.

> In the lecture, professor explains
> first,
> second,
> That's how the professor explain it.

USHER

01 | Video Games 비디오 게임 — Independent Task

QUESTION

 Do you agree or disagree with the following statement? Video and computer games have a bad influence on children. Use reasons and examples to support your answer.
(당신은 다음 주장에 동의하십니까, 아니면 반대하십니까? 비디오 게임과 컴퓨터 게임은 아이들에게 나쁜 영향을 끼친다. 이유와 예를 들어 답하세요.)

 브레인 스토밍 (아래에 놓여있는 12간지 내용들을 보고 어떤 것을 사용할 수 있을지 확인해보세요)
첫번째 이유 :
두번째 이유 :

 뼈대에 맞춰서 작성을 해봅시다.

___
___
___
___
___

아래 이미지는 학생들을 위한 만능 템플릿 12간지 입니다. 학생분들이 제일 먼저 암기해야하는 것이며, 본인 스스로 문장을 단기간 안에 못 만들거 같을 때에 도와주는 친구입니다. 가까이 두고 매일 외우세요.

Academic Courses
…because I think students should concentrate on academic courses.

Academic courses are the most important thing for students because good grades will help them get into good universities and, eventually, get great jobs.

As students get older, a good academic record is the only thing that actually matters.

This may sound a little far-fetched, but it's true, and for this reason, investing time in other activities is a waste of time.

Stay Healthy
It can be a great way to stay healthy. People join a cycling group through the internet. The members use bicycles to commute to work or school.

It is a great outdoor activity because people have a chance to work out while having fun.

Also, it is a great way to meet new people with similar interests. People nowadays do not have much chance to become close to each other.

However, there are numerous unique groups active on the internet, and this would not have been possible without the internet.

Follows your heart
Carpe diem, seize the days, and YOLO all stand for one thing. Do whatever your heart makes you do.

Life is too short to hesitate or do things to please others. It is essential to make yourself happy.

Actions speak louder than words. Whatever I do to make myself happy is better than sitting in a room thinking about it.

So I would just do it even if it means I am biting off something more than I can chew.

Stress
…if it can possibly be a way to relieve stress.

People nowadays are living a busy and hectic life, so they are under great stress, but a lot of them don't even realize they are stressed out.

Stress is known to be a major factor that keeps us from being healthy, and many people are suffering from various problems.

This is more serious than we think, so if it can ever be a way to relieve stress…

Money
…because it's the best way to save money. When it comes to spending money, every penny counts.

A thrifty spending habit is indispensable in our lives because little drops of water make the mighty ocean.

If we don't get used to working on a tight budget, we'll always be short on cash later.

A penny-pinching lifestyle will lead to financial stability, and it will give us peace of mind.

Saving Time
…because it's the best way to save time. There's an old saying, "Time is gold."

This proverb emphasizes the value of time, and this cannot be more true in modern society.

We're living a busy and hectic life, so saving time means we can do a lot more things later.

Many say that life is not fair, but everyone has twenty-four hours a day and seven days a week, so I would save time by…

Social Skills
Nowadays, people have smartphones with them all the time, and that information is no longer limited to elites.

Therefore, rather than learning, having social skills became the be-all and end-all to succeed rather than education.

Also, social skills are more than meet the eyes. To have social skills, one must also be able to read others like a book.

There will be times when one will truly need them.

Environment
because eventually, it can contribute to protecting the environment.

I think it's THE most important task for humanity because we cannot bring it back to life once it's too late.

Saving Earth all starts from seemingly insignificant actions.

Small actions from everyone bring about bigger changes, so I'm willing to participate.

Patience is virtue
Patience is a virtue. Saving time is indeed important, but waiting calmly is needed in this case.

There are times when one must wait patiently for things to go accordingly, and this is when time is the solution.

When going against the clock, they are more susceptible to making mistakes than taking some time.

In the long run, one will be glad that one has waited in this case.

Just because
I love it more than the given choices. Since I have so many great memory about it, It brings so many great reminiscences.

time flies whenever I am doing it, so how can I not choose it?

Also, not only do I love it, but I am also good at it. Everyone has talent, and it is like "a dime a dozen."

This was the inborn talent I had that I always surpassed everyone. Since a bird in the hand is worth two in the bush, I will choose it.

Politeness
It is important to maintain good relationships with other people because we never know what will happen in the future.

Decisions made by other people can affect others, and such decisions are usually based on personal and sentimental reasons.

So, people should not do anything that may offend or disturb others. It is also crucial to have a good reputation and get along well with others.

It Makes sense
It makes sense to choose it when considering many aspects such as time, money, and efficiency.

When people are considering between the given choices, they must consider many aspects economically.

They must choose the most efficient method because there are limits on what they have.

Also, one should think about it realistically and practically because they should not count chickens before they hatch.

So, down to Earth, people should choose it because it is the most economical

QUESTION

Do you agree or disagree with the following statement? Video and computer games have a bad influence on children. Use reasons and examples to support your answer.
(당신은 다음 주장에 동의하십니까, 아니면 반대하십니까? 비디오 게임과 컴퓨터 게임은 아이들에게 나쁜 영향을 끼친다. 이유와 예를 들어 답하세요.)

academic courses와 stay healthy를 사용해서 뼈대에 맞춰서 모범답안을 만들어 봅시다.

follows your heart와 stress를 사용해서 뼈대에 맞춰서 모범답안을 만들어 봅시다.

money와 saving time을 사용해서 뼈대에 맞춰서 모범답안을 만들어 봅시다.

social skills와 just because를 사용해서 뼈대에 맞춰서 모범답안을 만들어 봅시다.

QUESTION

Do you agree or disagree with the following statement? Video and computer games have a bad influence on children. Use reasons and examples to support your answer.
(당신은 다음 주장에 동의하십니까, 아니면 반대하십니까? 비디오 게임과 컴퓨터 게임은 아이들에게 나쁜 영향을 끼친다. 이유와 예를 들어 답하세요.)

academic courses와 stay healthy를 사용해서 뼈대에 맞춰서 모범답안을 만들어 봅시다.

If I were to answer the question, I would say video and computer games have a bad influence on children. There are many reasons why, but here is a couple.

academic courses

First, video games take time away from studying. For example, I think children should concentrate on academic courses. Academic courses are the most important thing for students because good grades will help them get into a good university and eventually get great jobs.

stay healthy

Second, children should go outside and play. For instance, children should go out and play in order to stay healthy. Cycling is a great outdoor activity because children have a chance to work out while having fun.

That's why I think games have a bad influence on children.

money와 saving time을 사용해서 뼈대에 맞춰서 모범답안을 만들어 봅시다.

If I were to answer the question, I would say games have a bad influence on children. There are many reasons why, but here is a couple.

money

First, buying games is a waste of money. For example, when it comes to spending money, every penny counts. A thrifty spending habit is indispensable in our lives because little drops of water make the mighty ocean.

saving time

Second, playing games is a waste of time. For instance, there is an old saying "time is gold." This proverb emphasizes the value of time, and this cannot be more true in modern society.

That's why I think games have a bad influence on children.

follows your heart와 stress를 사용해서 뼈대에 맞춰서 모범답안을 만들어 봅시다.

If I were to answer the question, I would say video games and computer games do not have a bad influence on children. There are many reasons why, but here is a couple.

follows your heart

First, children should do anything they want to do. For example, carpe diem, seize the days, and YOLO all stand for one thing: do whatever your heart makes you do. life is too short to hesitate or do things to please others. They should just do whatever they want.

stress

Second, playing sports can be a great way to relieve stress. For instance, students nowadays are living a busy and hectic life, so they are under great stress. Stress is known to be a major factor that keeps students from being healthy. So in order to relieve their stress, they should play video games.

That's why I think students should play video games.

social skills와 just because를 사용해서 뼈대에 맞춰서 모범답안을 만들어 봅시다.

If I were to answer the question, I would say games do not have a bad influence on children. There are many reasons why, but here is a couple.

social skills

First, students meet friends through playing games. For example, having social skills became the be-all and end-all to succeed rather than learning. So if playing games help students to socialize, I think it is beneficial.

just because

Second, I love playing video games. For instance, I have so much great memory about it, and it brings so many great reminiscences. To make a long story short, time flies whenever I am doing it so how can I not choose it.

That's why I think it's not a bad thing.

Internship Program 인턴 프로그램 — Integrated Task

읽기 지문

Internship Programs for Students

The university will be starting an international culture internship as of this year. This idea was thought of a couple years ago, but is finally being **put into action** this year for the first time. A certain number of students will be picked, **after careful consideration**, to take part in an internship at businesses in other countries. Furthermore, all **expenses will be covered** by the international department of our university, so the students picked will not be financially burdened by taking part. We anticipate many students will apply for the positions because this internship will offer lots of hands-on experience, which will look good on their college records.

대화 스크립트

 뼈대를 먼저 작성해 보도록 하겠습니다.

 작성하신 뼈대 빈칸에 맞춰서 리딩 지문을 읽고 주요 포인트를 넣어주세요.

 하단에 리스닝 노트테이킹을 해주세요. 음원은 학원 홈페이지에서 무료로 다운받으실 수 있습니다. 또한 2008번 문제 번호로 문제를 풀어보실 수 있습니다.

아래 하단에 리스닝 스크립트를 보고 베꼈어야 하는 부분을 찾아서 적어 보도록 하겠습니다.

대화 스크립트

🎧 뉴토플 - TEST 08_Q2

Now listen to two students discussing the announcement.

M: Hey, did you read the school's announcement about the internship?

여자의 의견
반대

W: Yeah, I don't really think it's necessary though.

M: Yeah?

W: Mm-hmm. The school's making a mistake.

M: Why?

이유 ❶
지역에서도 외국 문화를 경험 할 수 있음

W: Well, students don't necessarily have to go to foreign countries to gain experience with foreign businesses. Our city might be small, but there are still lots of businesses that host business meetings with foreign companies.

M: Really?

W: Yeah, my friend's sister interned at one of the companies around here and was able to get plenty of experience with foreign companies.

M: Hmm… I guess you're right. Well, what about the all-expenses-paid part? We wouldn't be losing anything, so it would be good to get experience of other cultures though, right?

W: Mm… yeah. It's a good deal for those who get the internship positions, but other students of the university aren't so lucky.

M: What do you mean?

이유 ❷
다른 학부의 학생들이 악영향을 받을 것임

W: Well, the international department isn't exactly **loaded with money**, which means it'll probably borrow from the school's general funds, right?

M: Right, maybe. But, how would that affect other students?

W: If the international department uses funds from the school that means other departments will be given less funding…

M: Oh… I think I see where you're coming from.

W: Yeah! Students will be affected by this internship even if they don't intend to try out for it.

이제 발표에 대해 논의하는 두 학생의 대화를 들어보세요.

남: 야, 인턴직에 대한 학교 안내문 읽었어?

여: 응, 근데 별로 필요한 것 같진 않은데.

남: 그래?

여: 으응. 학교는 지금 실수하고 있는 거야.

남: 왜?

여: 음, 학생들이 외국 기업에서 경험을 얻으려고 외국에 갈 필요가 없어. 우리 도시가 작을진 몰라도, 외국 회사들과 사업 회의를 주최하는 많은 회사들이 있잖아.

남: 정말?

여: 응, 내 친구의 누나가 근처에 있는 회사에서 인턴을 했는데 외국 회사들과의 많은 경험을 얻을 수 있었어.

남: 네가 맞는 것 같다. 근데 '비용 전액 부담' 부분은? 밑져야 본전인데 다른 문화를 경험하는 것이 좋겠지?

여: 음, 그래. 인턴 학생들 관점에서는 좋게 보여도, 다른 학생들한텐 그렇지 않지.

남: 무슨 말이야?

여: 국제학부가 그렇게 **돈이 많진** 않잖아. 그래서 학교 자금에서 돈을 빌리겠지?

남: 아마. 근데, 그게 다른 학생에게 무슨 영향을 끼쳐?

여: 만약 국제학부가 학교 자금을 쓴다면, 다른 학부한테 더 적은 자금을 준다는 얘기지.

남: 아, 뭔지 알겠다.

여: 그래! 인턴직을 원하지도 않는 학생들도 이 영향을 받을 거야.

문제	**The woman expresses her opinion about the college's plan. State her opinion and explain the reasons she gives for holding that opinion.**	여자는 대학의 계획에 대해 자신의 의견을 밝히고 있습니다. 그녀의 의견을 말하고, 그 의견을 고수하는 이유를 설명하세요.

Note-taking

다시한번 모범 답안을 작성해 보도록 하겠습니다

Internship Programs for Students

The university will be starting an international culture internship as of this year. This idea was thought of a couple years ago, but is finally being **put into action** this year for the first time. A certain number of students will be picked, **after careful consideration**, to take part in an internship at businesses in other countries. Furthermore, all **expenses will be covered** by the international department of our university, so the students picked will not be financially burdened by taking part. We anticipate many students will apply for the positions because this internship will offer lots of hands-on experience, which will look good on their college records.

Note-taking	노트테이킹
Reading - international culture internship program - take part in an internship in other countries - all expenses will be covered **Woman** - against **Reason ❶** - local businesses have international meetings - they can still experience foreign cultures **Reason ❷** - students not in the program will be affected - international department will use school funds	**지문** - 국제 문화 인턴 프로그램 - 외국의 인턴직에 참여 - 모든 비용이 충당됨 **여자** - 반대 **이유 ❶** - 지역 회사들도 국제 회의를 함 - 외국 문화를 경험할 수 있음 **이유 ❷** - 프로그램을 택하지 않는 학생들도 영향 받을 것 - 국제학부가 학교의 돈을 쓸 것이다.

Task 2 Sample Response 🎧 뉴토플 - TEST 08_R2   2번 문제 모범 답안

The two students are discussing the college's plan to introduce an international internship program in order to help students gain experience. The woman is against the plan for two reasons.

❶ First, it is unnecessary to send students abroad since local businesses have frequent interactions with foreign businesses. Students can experience foreign cultures without having to go overseas.

❷ Second, students not participating in the program will be negatively affected. The university will pay all the expenses, which would eventually come from school funds. The international department is not financially independent, so students in other departments would be affected. (This is why the woman is against the plan.)

두 학생은 학생들이 경험 얻게 도와주려고 국제 인턴 프로그램을 시작하려는 대학 측의 계획에 대해 의논하고 있다. 여자는 두 가지 이유를 들어 그 계획에 반대하고 있다.

❶ 첫째, 지역 회사들도 외국 회사들과 자주 거래하기 때문에 학생들을 해외로 보낼 필요가 없다. 학생들은 외국에 나가지 않아도 국제 문화를 경험 할 수 있다.

❷ 다음, 인턴직에 참여하지 않는 학생들은 악영향을 받을 것이다. 학교에서 모든 비용을 충당할 것이고, 이것은 결과적으로 학교 자금에서 올 것이다. 국제 학부는 경제적으로 독립적이지 않아서, 다른 학부의 학생들에게 영향을 끼칠 것이다. (이것이 그녀가 이 계획이 불필요하다고 생각하는 이유이다.)

Vocabulary

put into action	phr. 실행에 옮기다	cover the expense of	phr. ~의 비용을 충당하다
after careful consideration	phr. 충분히 검토한 후	be loaded with	phr. ~로 가득하다

03. Evolution in Action 작동되고 있는 진화 — Integrated Task

읽기 지문

Evolution in Action

Evolution can be defined as a very slow process where life forms go through various changes, and environments, over many generations. It consists of changes that are passed from generation to generation and cannot occur in an individual organism. A narrower form of evolution would be "evolution in action," which is rapid evolution due to human **intervention**. The term evolution in action is applied when an organism continuously changes its structure or functions to adjust to the environment in order to find a suitable way to survive.

대화 스크립트

STEP 01 뼈대를 먼저 작성해 보도록 하겠습니다.

STEP 02 작성하신 뼈대 빈칸에 맞춰서 리딩 지문을 읽고 주요 포인트를 넣어주세요.

STEP 03 하단에 리스닝 노트테이킹을 해주세요. 음원은 학원 홈페이지에서 무료로 다운받으실 수 있습니다. 또한 3008번 문제 번호로 문제를 풀어보실 수 있습니다.

 아래 하단에 리스닝 스크립트를 보고 베꼈어야 하는 부분을 찾아서 적어 보도록 하겠습니다.

대화 스크립트

🎧 뉴토플 - TEST 08_Q3

Now listen to part of a lecture in a biology class.

Evolution... we are all familiar with evolution. But **what on earth** is 'evolution in action'? Briefly, it is evolution caused by humans. What I mean is, if humans intervene in the process of evolution to make it faster, acting as a sort of **catalyst**, it's called evolution in action.

예시 ❶
박하의 번창

세부사항
나무와 함께 자라던 풀이 혼자 번창하기 시작

Let me give you an example. Mint was a wild grass growing in the forests or plains of America about 200 years ago. In the plains and forests, it used to grow with other trees, but as humans started to cut down trees and build houses on the plains, the areas around the houses were made into suitable environments for the mint plant, and that's where they started to grow rapidly. This change made by humans, is a **prime** example of evolution in action.

예시 ❷
박하의 생존

세부사항
잔디깎이의 등장으로 옆으로도 자라기 시작함

Another change took place, however, about 100 years ago, when the **lawn mower** was invented to make it easier to cut grass. As a result of this sudden change, the mint plant underwent a sudden change as well. Though the mint plant was originally a vertically growing plant, after the appearance of the lawn mower, it adapted to grow horizontally. Thus, its original characteristic of **vertical** growth changed to **horizontal**, and it became harder for the lawn mower to cut the mint plant. The mint plant has used this new characteristic in order to survive in a tougher environment, which is an example of evolution in action.

이제 생물학 강의의 일부를 들어보세요.

진화…우리는 진화에 익숙합니다. 그러나 **도대체** '작동되고 있는 진화'**는 무엇**일까요? 간단히 말해, 이는 인간에 의해 야기된 진화입니다. 다시 말하면, **촉매** 역할을 하는 인간이 진화를 더 빠르게 하는 과정에 개입했다면, 그것을 작동되고 있는 진화라고 합니다.

예를 하나 들지요. 약 200년 전 박하는 숲이나 평야에서 자라던 야생 풀이었습니다. 평야와 숲에서 박하는 다른 나무들과 함께 자랐었지만, 사람들이 나무를 베어 평야에 집을 짓기 시작하자 집 주변이 박하가 자라기에 적합한 환경이 되었고, 그 곳에서 박하는 빠르게 자라기 시작했습니다. 인간에 의한 이 변화가 작동되고 있는 진화의 **좋은** 예입니다.

그러나, 약 100년 전에 잔디를 더 쉽게 깎기 위해 **잔디깎이**가 발명되면서 또 다른 변화가 생겼습니다. 이 갑작스런 변화의 결과로, 박하도 갑작스런 변화를 겪었습니다. 원래 박하는 수직으로 자라는 식물임에도 불구하고, 잔디깎이가 나오고 나서부터 수평으로 자라도록 적응했습니다. 그러므로, 본 특성이었던 **수직** 성장은 **수평**으로 변하였고, 잔디 깎이로 박하를 자르는 것은 더 어려워 졌습니다. 박하는 더 험난한 환경에서 살아남기 위해 이 새로운 특성을 사용했고, 이는 작동되고 있는 진화의 예입니다.

문제

Using the example from the professor's lecture, explain what evolution in action is and how it works.

교수의 강의를 예로 들어, 작동되고 있는 진화가 무엇이고 어떻게 작용하는지 설명하세요.

STEP 05
다시한번 음원듣고 노트테이킹 해보도록 하겠습니다.
Note-taking

STEP 06
다시 한번 뼈대와 함께 모범 답안을 작성해 보도록 하겠습니다.

Evolution in Action

Evolution can be defined as a very slow process where life forms go through various changes, and environments, over many generations. It consists of changes that are passed from generation to generation and cannot occur in an individual organism. A narrower form of evolution would be "evolution in action," which is rapid evolution due to human **intervention**. The term evolution in action is applied when an organism continuously changes its structure or functions to adjust to the environment in order to find a suitable way to survive.

References

[참고자료]

박하의 일종인 스페어민트 (spearmint)

Photo by Simon Eugster, available under the Creative Commons Attribution-Share Alike 3.0 Unported, 2.5 Generic, 2.0 Generic and 1.0 Generic license.

Task 3 Sample Response 🎧 뉴토플 - TEST 08_R3   3번 문제 모범 답안

Evolution in action is a rapid evolution caused by human interference. In the lecture, the professor gives an example of the mint plant to explain evolution in action.

❶ The mint plant used to be a wild plant that grew alongside trees in forests. When people began to cut down trees and build houses, it adapted to grow in the areas around houses and flourished.

❷ When the lawn mower was invented, it had to adapt to the change again. It was originally a vertically growing plant, but in order to survive, it adapted to grow horizontally. It, therefore, became harder for lawn mowers to cut the mint plant.

작동되고 있는 진화는 인간의 개입으로 인해 빨라진 진화입니다. 강의에서 교수는 작동되고 있는 진화를 설명하기 위해 박하를 예로 듭니다.

❶ 박하는 숲에서 나무와 함께 자라던 야생 식물이었습니다. 사람들이 나무를 베어 집을 짓기 시작하자, 박하는 집 주변의 지역에 적응하여 잘 자랐습니다.

❷ 잔디깎이가 발명되자, 박하는 또 변화에 적응해야 했습니다. 박하는 원래 수직으로 자라는 식물이지만 살아남기 위해서 수평으로 자라는 것에 적응했습니다. 그리하여, 잔디깎이로 박하를 자르는 것은 더 어려워졌습니다.

Vocabulary

intervention [ìntərvénʃən]	n. 개입, 간섭	what on earth	phr. 도대체 무엇이
catalyst [kǽtəlist]	n. 촉매	prime [praim]	a. 제1의, 주된 / n. 전성기
lawn [lɔːn]	n. 잔디밭	mower [móuər]	n. 풀 베는 기계
vertical [vɔ́ːrtikəl]	a. 수직의	horizontal [hɔ̀ːrəzántl, hàrəzántl]	a. 수평의

04. Subsurface Locomotion 지표 밑 이동능력   Integrated Task

 4번 뼈대를 먼저 작성해 보도록 하겠습니다.

 하단에 리스닝 노트테이킹을 해주세요. 음원은 학원 홈페이지에서 무료로 다운받으실 수 있습니다. 또한 4008번 문제 번호로 문제를 풀어보실 수 있습니다.

 뼈대에 맞춰서 모범 답안을 완성해 보겠습니다.

대화 스크립트

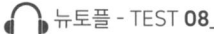

Listen to part of a lecture in a zoology class.

주제
어떤 동물들은 모래 속을 헤엄치듯 움직임

As we discover more species of animals, we realize the diverse methods of adaptations animals have developed to their surroundings. One of the most interesting types of adaptive **locomotion** is called **subsurface** locomotion, in which the so-called 'sand swimmers' dig in and swim through soft sand as if it was water. There are several species that do this, but my favorite 'sand swimmer' is a lizard called the sandfish.

예시 ❶
온도조절

세부사항
땅 속으로 들어가 사막의 열기를 피함

The advantages of subsurface locomotion are diverse. First of all, the sandfish is a cold-blooded animal, so it needs to control the temperature of its surroundings in order to survive. But its habitat is the desert where temperature can get extremely high. Considering the fact that a body temperature of over 39 degrees Celsius can cause death, the temperature of 45 degrees is very threatening. So, the sandfish hides under a bed of sand to avoid the heat. You will be surprised at the temperature difference between the surface of the sand and just 5 centimeters below. In order to control the temperature of its surroundings, the sandfish digs deeper or shallower into the sand.

예시 ❷
사냥에 도움

세부사항
먹잇감의 움직임을 진동으로 감지

Another reason for the sandfish's locomotive adaptation is hunting. The desert is a **barren** place, and the predator doesn't have a high **vantage point** from which to look for prey. Further, spotting prey from ground level is difficult because even a small change in elevation will block the lizard's field of view. This impediment becomes even worse when your prey is tiny insects which are hard to notice **in the first place.** So instead of using sight, the sandfish buries itself in the sand and detects small vibrations above. Being underground **amplifies** the vibrations sent by the movement of the prey because its entire body can sense the vibration. This way, the sandfish can detect even small insects without having to use its eyes at all.

문제

Using the examples from the professor's lecture, explain the two benefits of subsurface locomotion.

References

[참고자료]

샌드피쉬 (sandfish)

Photo by Wilfried Berns, available under the Creative Commons Attribution-Share Alike 2.0 Germany license.

Task 4   Sample Response    TEST 08_R4   4번 문제 모범 답안

In the lecture, the proféssor is expláining the two advántages of subsúrface locomotion, which is swimming through sand undergróund. He is using a lizard called the sandfish as an exámple.	강의에서 교수는 모래 속에서 헤엄치는 지표 밑 이동능력의 두 장점을 설명하고 있습니다. 그는 샌드피쉬라는 도마뱀을 예로 들고 있습니다.
❶ First, sand swimmers are able to contról their body temperature. When the surface temperature of the sand is too high, they hide under the surface to avóid the heat.	❶ 첫째로, 모래 속을 헤엄치는 동물은 체온을 조절할 수 있습니다. 표면 온도가 너무 높으면, 열을 피하려고 지표 밑으로 숨습니다.
❷ Second, hunting for prey becómes a lot easier. Since the sandfish cannót stay in high places, it cannot use vision to look for prey. Instéad, it burrows undergróund and senses even the slightest movements of prey.	❷ 둘째로, 먹잇감 사냥이 훨씬 쉬워집니다. 샌드피쉬는 높은 곳에 있을 수 없어서 시력을 써서 먹잇감을 찾을 수 없습니다. 대신에 모래 밑에 숨어 사냥감의 아주 작은 움직임까지 감지합니다.

Vocabulary

subsurface [sʌbsə́ːrfəs]	a. 지표 밑의		locomotion [lòukəmóuʃən]	n. 이동능력
barren [bǽrən]	a. 불모의		vantage point	phr. 유리한 고지
in the first place	phr. 애당초		amplify [ǽmpləfài]	v. 증폭하다

USHER
iBT TOEFL
FINAL TEST SPEAKING
TEST 09

Independent Tasks

Task 1 - 모범 답안
Question 1   usherin.usher.co.kr > 시험리스트 > Speaking 시험리스트 > Task 1 > #1013

Integrated Tasks

Task 2 - Script / 해석 / 모범 답안
Question 2   usherin.usher.co.kr > 시험리스트 > Speaking 시험리스트 > Task 2 > #2009

Task 3 - Script / 해석 / 모범 답안
Question 3   usherin.usher.co.kr > 시험리스트 > Speaking 시험리스트 > Task 3 > #3009

Task 4 - Script / 해석 / 모범 답안
Question 4   usherin.usher.co.kr > 시험리스트 > Speaking 시험리스트 > Task 4 > #4009

자기평가표

1번 문제 유형은 학생들이 본인에 생각을 주제에 맞춰서 말 해야하는 시험입니다.
본인이 처음부터 끝까지 45초 동안 말해야하다 보니 학생들이 제일 어려워 하는 시험입니다.
하지만, 먼저 외우고 익힌후에 말하는것이 가능할수 있게 하겠습니다.
가장 기본이 되는 뼈대 입니다. 먼저 외우도록 합시다.

> if i were to answer the question, i would say
> there are many reasons why, but here is a couple
> first
> for example,
> second
> for instance
> that's why

다음은 2번 문제 유형입니다.
2번 문제는 리딩에 학교에 계획이 적혀있거나 학교가 변해야하는 방향에 대해서 학생들에 주장이 적혀있습니다.
리딩에서 빠르게 파악해야하는 것은 도대체 누가 무엇을 주장하는가 입니다.
45~50초에 리딩 지문이 나오고 난 다음에 리스닝으로 학생들에 대화가 나오는 문제입니다.
리스닝에서는 학생이 리딩 지문에 대한 본인에 좋고 나쁜지에 대한 의견을 얘기해줄겁니다.
이유 2가지와 예시 2가지를 꼭 말할 수 있어야 합니다.

이에 따라서 2번 스피킹 문제에 뼈대는

> The reading states that university (plans to) / (should)
> the (woman / man) in the conversation thinks it is a good / bad idea.
> He/she provides two reasons to support his / her opinion.
> first,
> Second,
> the woman / man thinks it's a great / horrible idea.

다음은 3번 문제 유형입니다.
3번 문제는 2번 문제 유형과 같이 리딩과 리스닝이 나오는 문제 입니다. 하지만, 이번에는 이전 문제와는 달리 매우 학술적인 내용이 들어 있습니다. 리딩에서는 교과서에 나올만한 주제 한개를 자세하게 다룹니다. 여기서 학생분들은 제목과 이에 대한 정의를 잘 받아적으셔야 합니다. 리스닝에서는 교수님이 리딩에 나온 내용으로 예시를 들어 줍니다.

> The article is about
> which the passage defines as
> The professor provides an example of
> first,
> Second,
> The example clearly illustrates

다음은 4번 문제 유형입니다.
4번 문제는 이전 문제와 달리 리스닝만 나오는 문제 유형입니다. 3번 문제에 나온 리딩 지문이 리스닝으로 변환되었다 라고 생각 하시면 됩니다. 그렇기에 3번 문제에 리스닝 내용보다 리딩 길이 만큼 깁니다.

> In the lecture, professor explains
> first,
> second,
> That's how the professor explain it.

USHER

01: Planned vs Compulsive Shopping
계획적 vs 충동적 쇼핑

Independent Task

QUESTION

Some people prefer to make a plan before shopping. Others prefer to shop compulsively. Which one do you prefer? Use reasons and examples to support your answer.
(어떤 이들은 쇼핑 전에 계획 세우기를 선호합니다. 다른 이들은 충동적으로 쇼핑하기를 선호합니다. 당신은 어떤 것을 선호합니까? 이유와 예를 들어 답하세요.)

브레인 스토밍 (아래에 놓여있는 12간지 내용들을 보고 어떤 것을 사용할 수 있을지 확인해보세요)
첫번째 이유 :
두번째 이유 :

뼈대에 맞춰서 작성을 해봅시다.

_____
_____
_____
_____
_____
_____

아래 이미지는 학생들을 위한 만능 템플릿 12간지 입니다. 학생분들이 제일 먼저 암기해야하는 것이며, 본인 스스로 문장을 단기간 안에 못 만들거 같을 때에 도와주는 친구입니다. 가까이 두고 매일 외우세요.

Academic Courses
…because I think students should concentrate on academic courses.

Academic courses are the most important thing for students because good grades will help them get into good universities and, eventually, get great jobs.

As students get older, a good academic record is the only thing that actually matters.

This may sound a little far-fetched, but it's true, and for this reason, investing time in other activities is a waste of time.

Stay Healthy
It can be a great way to stay healthy. People join a cycling group through the internet. The members use bicycles to commute to work or school.

It is a great outdoor activity because people have a chance to work out while having fun.

Also, it is a great way to meet new people with similar interests. People nowadays do not have much chance to become close to each other.

However, there are numerous unique groups active on the internet, and this would not have been possible without the internet.

Follows your heart
Carpe diem, seize the days, and YOLO all stand for one thing. Do whatever your heart makes you do.

Life is too short to hesitate or do things to please others. It is essential to make yourself happy.

Actions speak louder than words. Whatever I do to make myself happy is better than sitting in a room thinking about it.

So I would just do it even if it means I am biting off something more than I can chew.

Stress
…if it can possibly be a way to relieve stress.

People nowadays are living a busy and hectic life, so they are under great stress, but a lot of them don't even realize they are stressed out.

Stress is known to be a major factor that keeps us from being healthy, and many people are suffering from various problems.

This is more serious than we think, so if it can ever be a way to relieve stress…

Money
…because it's the best way to save money. When it comes to spending money, every penny counts.

A thrifty spending habit is indispensable in our lives because little drops of water make the mighty ocean.

If we don't get used to working on a tight budget, we'll always be short on cash later.

A penny-pinching lifestyle will lead to financial stability, and it will give us peace of mind.

Saving Time
…because it's the best way to save time. There's an old saying, "Time is gold".

This proverb emphasizes the value of time, and this cannot be more true in modern society.

We're living a busy and hectic life, so saving time means we can do a lot more things later.

Many say that life is not fair, but everyone has twenty-four hours a day and seven days a week, so I would save time by…

Social Skills
Nowadays, people have smartphones with them all the time, and that information is no longer limited to elites.

Therefore, rather than learning, having social skills became the be-all and end-all to succeed rather than education.

Also, social skills are more than meet the eyes. To have social skills, one must also be able to read others like a book.

There will be times when one will truly need them.

Environment
because eventually, it can contribute to protecting the environment.

I think it's THE most important task for humanity because we cannot bring it back to life once it's too late.

Saving Earth all starts from seemingly insignificant actions.

Small actions from everyone bring about bigger changes, so I'm willing to participate.

Patience is virtue
Patience is a virtue. Saving time is indeed important, but waiting calmly is needed in this case.

There are times when one must wait patiently for things to go accordingly, and this is when time is the solution.

When going against the clock, they are more susceptible to making mistakes than taking some time.

In the long run, one will be glad that one has waited in this case.

Just because
I love it more than the given choices. Since I have so many great memory about it, It brings so many great reminiscences.

time flies whenever I am doing it, so how can I not choose it?

Also, not only do I love it, but I am also good at it. Everyone has talent, and it is like "a dime a dozen."

This was the inborn talent I had that I always surpassed everyone. Since a bird in the hand is worth two in the bush, I will choose it.

Politeness
It is important to maintain good relationships with other people because we never know what will happen in the future.

Decisions made by other people can affect others, and such decisions are usually based on personal and sentimental reasons.

So, people should not do anything that may offend or disturb others. It is also crucial to have a good reputation and get along well with others.

It Makes sense
It makes sense to choose it when considering many aspects such as time, money, and efficiency.

When people are considering between the given choices, they must consider many aspects economically.

They must choose the most efficient method because there are limits on what they have.

Also, one should think about it realistically and practically because they should not count chickens before they hatch.

So, down to Earth, people should choose it because it is the most economical

QUESTION

Some people prefer to make a plan before shopping. Others prefer to shop compulsively. Which one do you prefer? Use reasons and examples to support your answer.
(어떤 이들은 쇼핑 전에 계획 세우기를 선호합니다. 다른 이들은 충동적으로 쇼핑하기를 선호합니다. 당신은 어떤 것을 선호합니까? 이유와 예를 들어 답하세요.)

money와 saving time을 사용해서 뼈대에 맞춰서 모범답안을 만들어 봅시다.

stress와 follow your heart를 사용해서 뼈대에 맞춰서 모범답안을 만들어 봅시다.

social skills와 patience is a virtue를 사용해서 뼈대에 맞춰서 모범답안을 만들어 봅시다.

just because와 it makes sense를 사용해서 뼈대에 맞춰서 모범답안을 만들어 봅시다.

QUESTION

Some people prefer to make a plan before shopping. Others prefer to shop compulsively. Which one do you prefer? Use reasons and examples to support your answer.
(어떤 이들은 쇼핑 전에 계획 세우기를 선호합니다. 다른 이들은 충동적으로 쇼핑하기를 선호합니다. 당신은 어떤 것을 선호합니까? 이유와 예를 들어 답하세요.)

money와 saving time을 사용해서 뼈대에 맞춰서 모범답안을 만들어 봅시다.

If I were to answer the question, I would say I prefer to make a plan before shopping. There are many reasons why, but here is a couple.

money

First, it can be a way to save money without compulsive shopping. For example, when it comes to spending money, every penny counts. A thrifty spending habit is indispensable in our lives because little drops of water make the mighty ocean.

saving time

Second, planning can be a way to save time because I do not have to just walk around doing anything in the mall. For instance, there is an old saying "time is gold." This proverb emphasizes the value of time, and this cannot be more true in modern society.

That's why I like to shop compulsively

stress와 follow your heart를 사용해서 뼈대에 맞춰서 모범답안을 만들어 봅시다.

If I were to answer the question, I would say I prefer to shop compulsively. There are many reasons why, but here is a couple.

stress

First, shopping compulsively can be a way to relieve stress. For example, people nowadays are living a busy hectic life, so they are under great stress. Therefore, if shopping compulsively can relieve stress, they should do it.

follow your heart

Second, people should do something instead of planning. For instance, life is too short to hesitate. Actions speak louder than words. Doing whatever I do to make myself is happy is better than sitting in a room planning something.

That's why I just want to shop compulsively.

social skills와 patience is a virtue를 사용해서 뼈대에 맞춰서 모범답안을 만들어 봅시다.

If I were to answer the question, I would say I prefer to plan before shopping. There are many reasons why, but here is a couple.

social skills

First, a habit of planning is very important. For example, planning is a great habit to have. It is more than meets the eyes. There will be times when one will be needing them truly.

patience is a virtue

Second, being patience while planning is a virtue. For instance, there are times when one must wait patiently for things to go accordingly. Having a habit of planning will help them be patient in any situation.

That's why I think it is important to plan.

just because와 it makes sense를 사용해서 뼈대에 맞춰서 모범답안을 만들어 봅시다.

If I were to answer the question, I would say it is better to shop compulsively. There are many reasons why, but here is a couple.

just because

First, I love to shop compulsively. For example, I have so much great memory about shopping compulsively, it brings so many great reminiscences. How can I not choose it?

it makes sense

Second, planning takes too much time. For instance, it makes sense to choose planning when considering many aspects such as time and efficiency. People must choose the most efficient method because there are limits on their time.

That's why I think I like to shop compulsively

02. Writing Center 글쓰기 센터

Integrated Task

읽기 지문

Plans to Open the Writing Center

A university official announced plans to open a writing center on campus, stating that the center will work to help increase the writing skills of students through various writing activities. **Aside from helping** potential students, the writing center will also be offering jobs to those skilled enough in writing. Thus, there will be helpers to help the students who come to the center in a **one-on-one manner**. We can only benefit from the writing center, so whoever is in need of help in writing, or those looking for a way to help others and make money at the same time, should come to the writing center after it opens.

대화 스크립트

STEP 01 뼈대를 먼저 작성해 보도록 하겠습니다.

STEP 02 작성하신 뼈대 빈칸에 맞춰서 리딩 지문을 읽고 주요 포인트를 넣어주세요.

STEP 03 하단에 리스닝 노트테이킹을 해주세요. 음원은 학원 홈페이지에서 무료로 다운받으실 수 있습니다. 또한 2009번 문제 번호로 문제를 풀어보실 수 있습니다.

 아래 하단에 리스닝 스크립트를 보고 베꼈어야 하는 부분을 찾아서 적어 보도록 하겠습니다.

대화 스크립트

🎧 뉴토플 - TEST 09_Q2

Now listen to two students discussing the announcement.

M: Did you read the article in the campus newspaper about the writing center?

W: Yeah.

M: What do you think of the idea?

여자의 의견 — 찬성

W: I personally think it's a great idea. My professors are always so busy with other things, so they don't really look at my writing errors in detail.

M: Yeah?

이유 ❶ — 더 개인적이고 세부적으로 봐줌

W: Yeah! I get my paper back and sometimes I catch grammar errors that they hadn't. It's really frustrating as a student, not that I can blame the teachers. But, I think having skilled students helping us individually will really help us increase our skills.

M: Hmm… I guess. Individual attention will allow us to ask whatever questions we have.

W: Yep, and it's a good idea looking at it from both ways.

M: What do you mean?

W: Well, when looking at it from the point of view of students looking for jobs, it's good, too!

M: How so?

W: Mmm… Teaching is learning, right?

M: Right.

이유 ❷ — 일하는 학생들에게도 가르치는 경험이 이득이 됨

W: Well, giving students a chance to teach others will be beneficial for them too. They can increase their own skills and earn extra money while doing it, too! Furthermore, working at such an institution will help them get experience.

M: And this experience will help them how…?

W: The teaching experience from the center may not **be of use** currently, but later on, when they're looking for jobs, it will look good on their **resumes**.

이제 발표에 대해 논의하는 두 학생의 대화를 들어보세요.

남: 캠퍼스 신문에 실린 글쓰기 센터에 대한 기사 읽어봤어?

여: 응…

남: 그거에 대해서 어떻게 생각해?

여: 개인적으로 좋은 아이디어인 것 같아. 교수님들은 다른 일 때문에 항상 바쁘시니까, 내 글쓰기를 세부적으로 보시지는 않거든.

남: 아, 그래?

여: 응! 레포트를 다시 돌려 받으면 교수님들이 못 보신 실수들을 내가 가끔 보거든. 학생으로선 짜증나지, 교수님을 탓하는 건 아니지만. 그래도, 실력 있는 학생들이 일대일로 도와주는 건 우리 실력을 키우는데도 큰 도움을 줄 거야.

남: 흠… 그렇네. 개인적으로 지도해주면 어떤 질문이던 다 물어볼 수 있겠다.

여: 그렇지, 그리고 양쪽 입장에서 봐도 좋은 생각이야.

남: 무슨 말이야?

여: 음, 일자리를 구하는 학생들 입장에서 보면 역시 좋다 이거지!

남: 어떻게?

여: 흠… 가르치는 것은 배우는 것이잖아?

남: 그렇지.

여: 다른 학생들을 가르칠 수 있는 기회를 주는 건 그들에게도 좋은 거지. 그들도 실력을 키울 수 있고 그러면서 돈을 벌 수 있으니까! 그리고, 그런 센터에서 일하는 건 더 많은 경험을 하게 하지.

남: 그럼, 이런 경험은 무슨 도움이 되는데?

여: 이런 센터에서 가르치는 경험이 지금은 **쓸모** 없을지 몰라도 나중에, 그들이 일자리를 구할 때, **이력서**에 쓰면 보기 좋을 거야.

문제 — **The woman expresses her opinion about the college's plan. State her opinion and explain the reasons she gives for holding that opinion.**

여자는 대학의 계획에 대해 자신의 의견을 밝히고 있습니다. 그녀의 의견을 말하고, 그 의견을 고수하는 이유를 설명하세요.

STEP 05 Note-taking

STEP 06 다시한번 모범 답안을 작성해 보도록 하겠습니다

Plans to Open the Writing Center

A university official announced plans to open a writing center on campus, stating that the center will work to help increase the writing skills of students through various writing activities. **Aside from helping** potential students, the writing center will also be offering jobs to those skilled enough in writing. Thus, there will be helpers to help the students who come to the center in a **one-on-one manner**. We can only benefit from the writing center, so whoever is in need of help in writing, or those looking for a way to help others and make money at the same time, should come to the writing center after it opens.

Note-taking	노트테이킹
Reading - a writing center on campus will be opened - in order to improve the students' writing skills - to receive personal teachings from the helpers **Woman** - supporting **Reason ❶** - the writing center will help students more personally - busy professors often miss errors in the papers **Reason ❷** - the helpers will benefit from the program - they will get paid and the experience will benefit them	**지문** - 캠퍼스 글쓰기 센터가 열림 - 학생의 글쓰기 실력향상을 위해 - 도우미의 개인지도를 받을 것임 **여자** - 찬성 **이유 ❶** - 학생들을 개인적으로 도움 - 교수들은 작은 실수를 놓침 **이유 ❷** - 도우미에게도 도움이 됨 - 돈도 받고 경험도 쌓음

Task 2   Sample Response   🎧 뉴토플 - TEST 09_R2   2번 문제 모범 답안

The two students are discussing the college's plan to open a writing center on campus in order to improve the students' writing skills. The woman is supporting the plan for two reasons.

❶ First, the writing center would be able to help students in a more personal way. Professors are usually busy, so they don't have time to read papers carefully enough. They sometimes miss some grammatical errors.

❷ Second, the students working at the center would benefit from the program as well. They would get paid and learn a lot from the teaching experience. The experience would help them in the future. (This is why he is supporting the plan.)

두 학생은 학생들의 글쓰기 실력을 향상시키려고 글쓰기 센터를 열려는 대학 측의 계획에 대해서 의논하고 있다. 여자는 두 가지 이유를 들어 그 계획에 찬성하고 있다.

❶ 첫째, 글쓰기 센터는 학생을 더 개인적으로 도와줄 것이다. 교수들은 보통 바빠서 레포트를 주의 깊게 읽지 않는다. 그들은 가끔 문법적인 실수를 놓치곤 한다.

❷ 다음, 센터에서 일하는 학생들에게도 이롭다. 그들은 돈도 벌고 가르치는 경험에서 많은 것을 배울 것이다. 이 경험은 미래에 도움이 될 것이다. (이것이 그녀가 이 계획이 필요하다고 생각하는 이유이다)

Vocabulary

| aside from ~ing | phr. ~하는 것 이외에 | an one-on-one manner | phr. 일대일 방식 |
| of use | phr. 쓸모있는 (=useful) | resume [rézjuməi] | n. 이력서 |

03. Prenatal Learning 태아기 교육 — Integrated Task

읽기 지문

Prenatal Learning

The ability of children to learn has led to many different methods of teaching and interaction with educational material. One newly identified method of learning is prenatal learning. This term refers to the ability of **embryos** to learn through auditory stimulation during the gestational period. As the brain is at its most **receptive** stage of learning during **gestation**, it has been theorized that embryos can absorb and appreciate far more of their environment if they are exposed to auditory environmental **stimuli**. This can be seen in the both humans and in other animals as well.

대화 스크립트

STEP 01 뼈대를 먼저 작성해 보도록 하겠습니다.

STEP 02 작성하신 뼈대 빈칸에 맞춰서 리딩 지문을 읽고 주요 포인트를 넣어주세요.

STEP 03 하단에 리스닝 노트테이킹을 해주세요. 음원은 학원 홈페이지에서 무료로 다운받으실 수 있습니다. 또한 3009번 문제 번호로 문제를 풀어보실 수 있습니다.

USHER

STEP 04 아래 하단에 리스닝 스크립트를 보고 베꼈어야 하는 부분을 찾아서 적어 보도록 하겠습니다.

대화 스크립트

🎧 뉴토플 - TEST 09_Q3

Now listen to part of a lecture in a biology class.

During the stage of prenatal learning, the brain is most receptive to outside stimuli. For this reason, many gestating or **incubating** mothers interact with their embryos. One great example of this is the sea-dwelling murre of the Northern Atlantic and Pacific oceans.

예시 ❶
바다오리의 생활

세부사항
서식지가 너무 커서 새끼를 못 알아봄

These sea-dwelling birds spend nearly their entire lives at sea, coming ashore only to **mate** and raise their chicks in colonies on the rocky shores of the islands. They form huge colonies of breeding and incubating couples that are often so close as to be touching. Due to this large colony size and the **nondescript** chicks, parents have difficulty locating their chick when returning to the colony. To assist them in finding their chicks later, the incubating mothers utilize prenatal learning.

예시 ❷
어미 소리의 각인

세부사항
어미가 부르면 새끼들이 알아 듣고 반응함

They constantly **chirp** and make noises to their egg from the time it is laid. By doing this, the external sounds **permeate** the eggs and the mothers **imprint** their voices on their chicks, so that they will later recognize them after they hatch. When flying back into the colony, the mother birds call to their chicks. When the chick hears this call, it recognizes it as the voice imprinted on it in the egg and responds by calling back or going to its mother. In this way, the sounds learned in the egg are utilized later in life, and this is a great example of prenatal learning.

이제 생물학 수업의 일부를 들어보세요.

태아기 교육 단계 동안, 뇌는 바깥 자극에 가장 수용적입니다. 그렇기 때문에 **임신중**인 어미들은 태아와 상호작용을 합니다. 좋은 예는 대서양과 태평양 북부의 바다오리입니다.

이 바다오리는 평생을 바다에서 보내고, **짝짓기**나 돌이 많은 섬에 서식지를 꾸려 새끼를 키울 때만 해안가로 올라오곤 합니다. 아주 큰 서식지를 꾸리고 새끼를 품는 바다오리들은 서로 닿을 만큼 가까이 붙어 있습니다. 서식지가 매우 크고 새끼들도 **구분하기 힘들기** 때문에, 부모들은 서식지로 돌아올 때 새끼들을 찾는데 어려움을 겪곤 합니다. 새끼를 나중에 쉽게 찾기 위해, 어미들은 태아기 교육법을 사용합니다.

그들은 알을 낳고 지속적으로 **짹짹거리며** 소리를 냅니다. 이렇게 해서, 외부의 소리가 알 속으로 **침투하여** 어미는 자신의 음성을 새끼에게 **각인시켜서** 알에서 깨어났을 때 어미의 소리를 구분할 수 있도록 합니다. 서식지로 돌아올 때, 어미는 새끼들을 부릅니다. 새끼가 그 소리를 들으면, 그 소리가 알 속에 있을 때 각인되었던 것임을 알고 어미를 부르거나 어미 쪽으로 가면서 반응합니다. 이러한 방법으로 알 속에서 습득한 소리는 나중에 이용되는데, 그것은 태아기 교육의 좋은 예입니다.

문제
Using the example from the professor's lecture, explain what prenatal learning is and how it works.

교수의 강의를 예로 들어, 태아기 교육이 무엇이고 어떻게 작용하는지 설명하세요.

STEP 05
다시한번 음원듣고 노트테이킹 해보도록 하겠습니다.
Note-taking

STEP 06
다시 한번 뼈대와 함께 모범 답안을 작성해 보도록 하겠습니다.

Prenatal Learning

The ability of children to learn has led to many different methods of teaching and interaction with educational material. One newly identified method of learning is prenatal learning. This term refers to the ability of **embryos** to learn through auditory stimulation during the gestational period. As the brain is at its most **receptive** stage of learning during **gestation**, it has been theorized that embryos can absorb and appreciate far more of their environment if they are exposed to auditory environmental **stimuli**. This can be seen in the both humans and in other animals as well.

USHER

References

Photo by USGS

Photo by Beeblebrox, available under the Creative Commons Attribution-Share Alike 3.0 Unported license.

[참고자료]

❶ 바다오리 (murre)
❷ 바닷가 절벽의 바다오리 서식지

Task 3   Sample Response 🎧 뉴토플 - TEST 09_R3   3번 문제 모범 답안

Prenatal learning is the ability of embryos to learn through auditory stimulation before they are born or hatched. The professor is giving an example of certain birds to explain it.

❶ These birds spend most of their time at sea and return to their colony only to mate and raise chicks. There are so many nests in the colony that it is difficult for the birds to recognize their own chicks.

❷ Before the chicks hatch, mothers keep chirping at the eggs. Later, the chicks can recognize the mother's voice and respond back. This way, the mother can find its chicks, and this is a good example of prenatal learning.

태아기 교육은 태아가 태어나거나 알을 깨기 전 청각 자극으로 학습하는 능력을 말한다. 교수는 특정 새를 예로 들어 설명한다.

❶ 이 새들은 생의 대부분을 바다에서 보내고 짝짓기를 할 때나 새끼를 기를 때만 육지로 돌아온다. 서식지에는 아주 많은 둥지가 있기 때문에 새는 자신의 새끼를 알아보는데 어려움을 겪는다.

❷ 새끼가 태어나기 전, 어미는 알에 지속적으로 소리를 낸다. 나중에 새끼는 어미의 소리를 구분하고 반응한다. 이러한 방식으로, 어미는 새끼들을 찾을 수 있고, 이것은 태아기 교육의 좋은 예이다.

Vocabulary

embryo [émbriòu]	n. 태아	gestation [dʒestéiʃən]	n. 임신, 잉태
receptive [riséptiv]	a. 잘 받아들이는	stimuli [stíˈmjəlaiˌ]	n. stimulus의 복수
incubate [ínkjubèit iŋ-]	v. 배양하다	mate [meit]	n. 동료 / v. 교미하다
nondescript [nɑ̀ndiskrípt]	a. 정체를 알 수 없는	chirp [tʃəːrp]	v. 짹짹 울다
permeate [pə́ːrmièit]	v. 배어들다	imprint [ímprint]	v. 각인시키다

04 | Ants 개미 | Integrated Task

STEP 01 4번 뼈대를 먼저 작성해 보도록 하겠습니다.

STEP 02 하단에 리스닝 노트테이킹을 해주세요. 음원은 학원 홈페이지에서 무료로 다운받으실 수 있습니다. 또한 4009번 문제 번호로 문제를 풀어보실 수 있습니다.

STEP 03 뼈대에 맞춰서 모범 답안을 완성해 보겠습니다.

대화 스크립트

뉴토플 - TEST 09_Q4

Listen to part of a lecture in a biology class.

생물학 강의의 일부를 들어보세요.

주제
개미가 먹이를 찾아 모으는 방법

Ants are one of the most complex organisms on Earth. But I'm not talking about their bodily **complexities**; I mean they develop very organized, **hierarchical** communities, with differentiated tasks and cooperative behaviors. I think that the best way to observe ant intelligence is from their food **scavenging** and harvesting strategies.

개미는 지구상에서 가장 복잡한 생물 중 하나입니다. 하지만 전 그 신체적 **복잡함**에 대한 얘기를 하는 것이 아니라, 개미들은 분류된 작업, 협동적인 행동과 함께 굉장히 체계적이고, **계급적** 사회를 구축했다는 겁니다. 개미의 지능에 대해 말하자면 **먹이를 찾아 모으는** 전략에 대해 얘기하는 것이 가장 좋은 방법이라 생각합니다.

예시 ❶
페로몬 분비
세부사항
먹이의 위치를 알리고, 서로 소통한다.

Ants are able to release chemicals called pheromones, to communicate with their own species. So, when a worker ant scavenging for food locates a food source, it releases pheromones on the way back to the colony. Then, other worker ants of the colony follow the scent given off by the pheromone and are led right to the food source. With more workers on the trail, the harvesting speed increases and they **procure** large quantities before being discovered by other species. When their food source is discovered by another species, ants can release a different type of pheromone to confuse the rivals, drive them away, or make them fight among themselves. They also release alarm pheromones, which calls soldier ants to fight off the unwanted.

개미들은 서로 소통을 하기위해 페로몬이란 화학물질을 분비할 수 있습니다. 그래서 일개미 하나가 먹이를 찾으면, 오는 길에 페로몬을 분비합니다. 그 다음, 개미굴에 있었던 다른 일개미들은 페로몬 냄새를 따라 먹이 쪽으로 갈 수 있습니다. 더 많은 일개미가 흔적을 찾아가면 먹이를 모으는 속도가 빨라지고 다른 종이 오기 전까지 많은 양의 먹이를 **획득할** 수 있습니다. 만약 다른 종의 개미가 먹이를 발견하면, 여러 페로몬을 사용하여 적을 혼란시키고, 쫓아내거나 서로 싸우게 만들 수 있습니다. 개미들은 또한 경보용 페로몬을 통해 군인 개미를 불러내 불청객과 싸우게 합니다.

예시 ❷
방해공작
세부사항
상대 개미굴의 입구를 돌로 막아 시간을 번다.

Additionally, ants have another way of preventing food from being stolen by other species. During their **foraging** period, some species of ants surround the entrances of rival colonies and drop small stones down the entrances. This causes the rival species to concentrate on repairing and opening up the entrances of their colony. You see, having many, usable entrances is a higher priority than **obtaining** food. So the rival ant colony completely **halts** the foraging process. This results in two things: first, because there are less rivals on their playing field, the ants are less likely to face battles, reducing their **mortality** rate, and second, because the rival colony does not get a chance to collect food, there is more available for the offensive colony.

또, 개미는 다른 방법으로 다른 종들에게서 먹이를 지켜낼 수 있습니다. 먹이 **채집** 기간에 적대적 관계에 있는 다른 개미굴 입구에 조그마한 돌을 집어 넣습니다. 이는 상대편 개미들이 입구를 수리하는 것에 집중하게 만듭니다. 개미굴에 쓸만한 입구를 되도록 많이 갖고 있는 것은 음식을 **획득하는** 것보다 중요합니다. 그래서, 적대관계에 있는 개미들은 음식을 찾는 것을 완전히 **멈추게** 되죠. 이는 두 결과를 가져 옵니다. 첫째, 경쟁자가 줄어서 싸울 염려가 줄고, **사망률**을 낮출 수 있으며, 둘째, 경쟁자가 음식을 모을 기회가 없어서 공격했었던 개미굴은 더 많은 먹이를 얻을 수 있습니다.

문제

Using the examples from the professor's lecture, explain the two methods ants use to collect food more effectively.

교수의 강의를 예로 들어, 먹이를 더 효율적으로 모으기 위해 개미가 사용하는 두 가지 방법을 설명하세요.

References

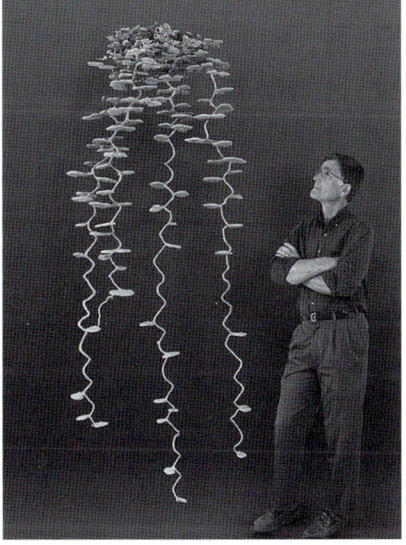

[참고자료]
개미집에 석고 반죽을 부어 모양을 뜬 견본

Photo by shaners becker, available under the Creative Commons Attribution-Share Alike 2.0 Generic license.

Task 4   Sample Response   TEST 09_R4   4번 문제 모범 답안

In the lecture, the proféssor expláins strategies ants use to collect food more efféctively. There are mainly two ways of doing so.

❶ The first way is to use special chemicals to infórm other members of the locátion of food. A different chemical can also be used to confúse other species, make them fight one anóther, or call soldier ants to fight agáinst them.

❷ Anóther way is to block the entrances of their rivals' colony. Since clearing entrances is more impórtant, the rivals will have to stop collecting food. This results in two benefits, one being a lower chance of having battles, and the other being more aváilable food.

강의에서 교수는 개미들이 더 효율적으로 먹이를 모으려고 사용하는 전략을 설명하고 있습니다. 그 방법은 크게 두 가지 입니다.

❶ 첫 번째 방법은 특별한 화학물질로 다른 개미에게 먹이의 위치를 알리는 것입니다. 다른 화학물질은 다른 종을 혼란에 빠트리거나, 서로 싸우게 하고, 군인 개미를 불러 싸우게 하는 데에도 쓰일 수 있습니다.

❷ 또 다른 방법은 상대 개미굴 입구를 막는 것입니다. 입구를 수리하는 것이 음식을 찾는 것보다 중요하기 때문에 경쟁 개미들은 먹이를 찾는 일을 그만 둘 것입니다. 이는 두 가지 이득을 낳는데, 싸울 확률이 낮아진 것과 더 많은 음식입니다.

Vocabulary

complexity [kəmpléksəti]	n. 복잡성		**hierarchical** [hàiərá:rkikəl]	a. 계층제의
scavenge [skǽvindʒ]	v. 썩은 고기를 찾아 다니다		**procure** [proukjúər / prə-]	v. 획득하다
forage [fɔ́:ridʒ / fár-]	v. 먹이를 찾아 다니다		**obtain** [əbtéin]	v. 획득하다
halt [hɔ:lt]	v. 멈추다		**mortality** [mɔ:rtǽləti]	n. 죽을 운명, 사망자 수

USHER
iBT TOEFL
FINAL TEST SPEAKING
TEST 10

Independent Tasks

Task 1 - 모범 답안
Question 1   usherin.usher.co.kr > 시험리스트 > Speaking 시험리스트 > Task 1 > #1005

Integrated Tasks

Task 2 - Script / 해석 / 모범 답안
Question 2   usherin.usher.co.kr > 시험리스트 > Speaking 시험리스트 > Task 2 > #2010

Task 3 - Script / 해석 / 모범 답안
Question 3   usherin.usher.co.kr > 시험리스트 > Speaking 시험리스트 > Task 3 > #3010

Task 4 - Script / 해석 / 모범 답안
Question 4   usherin.usher.co.kr > 시험리스트 > Speaking 시험리스트 > Task 4 > #4010

자기평가표

1번 문제 유형은 학생들이 본인에 생각을 주제에 맞춰서 말 해야하는 시험입니다.
본인이 처음부터 끝까지 45초 동안 말해야하다 보니 학생들이 제일 어려워 하는 시험입니다.
하지만, 먼저 외우고 익힌후에 말하는것이 가능할수 있게 하겠습니다.
가장 기본이 되는 뼈대 입니다. 먼저 외우도록 합시다.

> if i were to answer the question, i would say
> there are many reasons why, but here is a couple
> first
> for example,
> second
> for instance
> that's why

다음은 2번 문제 유형입니다.
2번 문제는 리딩에 학교에 계획이 적혀있거나 학교가 변해야하는 방향에 대해서 학생들에 주장이 적혀있습니다.
리딩에서 빠르게 파악해야하는 것은 도대체 누가 무엇을 주장하는가 입니다.
45~50초에 리딩 지문이 나오고 난 다음에 리스닝으로 학생들에 대화가 나오는 문제입니다.
리스닝에서는 학생이 리딩 지문에 대한 본인에 좋고 나쁜지에 대한 의견을 얘기해줄겁니다.
이유 2가지와 예시 2가지를 꼭 말할 수 있어야 합니다.

이에 따라서 2번 스피킹 문제에 뼈대는

> The reading states that university (plans to) / (should)
> the (woman / man) in the conversation thinks it is a good / bad idea.
> He/she provides two reasons to support his / her opinion.
> first,
> Second,
> the woman / man thinks it's a great / horrible idea.

다음은 3번 문제 유형입니다.
3번 문제는 2번 문제 유형과 같이 리딩과 리스닝이 나오는 문제 입니다. 하지만, 이번에는 이전 문제와는 달리 매우 학술적인 내용이 들어 있습니다. 리딩에서는 교과서에 나올만한 주제 한개를 자세하게 다룹니다. 여기서 학생분들은 제목과 이에 대한 정의를 잘 받아적으셔야 합니다. 리스닝에서는 교수님이 리딩에 나온 내용으로 예시를 들어 줍니다.

> The article is about
> which the passage defines as
> The professor provides an example of
> first,
> Second,
> The example clearly illustrates

다음은 4번 문제 유형입니다.
4번 문제는 이전 문제와 달리 리스닝만 나오는 문제 유형입니다. 3번 문제에 나온 리딩 지문이 리스닝으로 변환되었다 라고 생각하시면 됩니다. 그렇기에 3번 문제에 리스닝 내용보다 리딩 길이 만큼 깁니다.

> In the lecture, professor explains
> first,
> second,
> That's how the professor explain it.

USHER

01 | College Education 대학 교육 | Independent Task

QUESTION

 Do you agree or disagree with the following statement? College education should be available only to those who are good students. Use reasons and examples to support your answer.
(당신은 다음 주장에 찬성하십니까, 반대하십니까? 성적이 좋은 학생들에게만 대학 교육의 기회가 주어져야 한다. 이유와 예를 들어 답하세요.)

 브레인 스토밍 (아래에 놓여있는 12간지 내용들을 보고 어떤 것을 사용할 수 있을지 확인해보세요)
첫번째 이유 :
두번째 이유 :

 뼈대에 맞춰서 작성을 해봅시다.

_____
_____
_____
_____
_____
_____

아래 이미지는 학생들을 위한 만능 템플릿 12간지 입니다. 학생분들이 제일 먼저 암기해야하는 것이며, 본인 스스로 문장을 단기간 안에 못 만들거 같을 때에 도와주는 친구입니다. 가까이 두고 매일 외우세요.

Academic Courses
…because I think students should concentrate on academic courses.

Academic courses are the most important thing for students because good grades will help them get into good universities and, eventually, get great jobs.

As students get older, a good academic record is the only thing that actually matters.

This may sound a little far-fetched, but it's true, and for this reason, investing time in other activities is a waste of time.

Stay Healthy
It can be a great way to stay healthy. People join a cycling group through the internet. The members use bicycles to commute to work or school.

It is a great outdoor activity because people have a chance to work out while having fun.

Also, it is a great way to meet new people with similar interests. People nowadays do not have much chance to become close to each other.

However, there are numerous unique groups active on the internet, and this would not have been possible without the internet.

Follows your heart
Carpe diem, seize the days, and YOLO all stand for one thing. Do whatever your heart makes you do.

Life is too short to hesitate or do things to please others. It is essential to make yourself happy.

Actions speak louder than words. Whatever I do to make myself happy is better than sitting in a room thinking about it.

So I would just do it even if it means I am biting off something more than I can chew.

Stress
…if it can possibly be a way to relieve stress.

People nowadays are living a busy and hectic life, so they are under great stress, but a lot of them don't even realize they are stressed out.

Stress is known to be a major factor that keeps us from being healthy, and many people are suffering from various problems.

This is more serious than we think, so if it can ever be a way to relieve stress…

Money
…because it's the best way to save money. When it comes to spending money, every penny counts.

A thrifty spending habit is indispensable in our lives because little drops of water make the mighty ocean.

If we don't get used to working on a tight budget, we'll always be short on cash later.

A penny-pinching lifestyle will lead to financial stability, and it will give us peace of mind.

Saving Time
…because it's the best way to save time. There's an old saying, "Time is gold."

This proverb emphasizes the value of time, and this cannot be more true in modern society.

We're living a busy and hectic life, so saving time means we can do a lot more things later.

Many say that life is not fair, but everyone has twenty-four hours a day and seven days a week, so I would save time by…

Social Skills
Nowadays, people have smartphones with them all the time, and that information is no longer limited to elites.

Therefore, rather than learning, having social skills became the be-all and end-all to succeed rather than education.

Also, social skills are more than meet the eyes. To have social skills, one must also be able to read others like a book.

There will be times when one will truly need them.

Environment
because eventually, it can contribute to protecting the environment.

I think it's THE most important task for humanity because we cannot bring it back to life once it's too late.

Saving Earth all starts from seemingly insignificant actions.

Small actions from everyone bring about bigger changes, so I'm willing to participate.

Patience is virtue
Patience is a virtue. Saving time is indeed important, but waiting calmly is needed in this case.

There are times when one must wait patiently for things to go accordingly, and this is when time is the solution.

When going against the clock, they are more susceptible to making mistakes than taking some time.

In the long run, one will be glad that one has waited in this case.

Just because
I love it more than the given choices. Since I have so many great memory about it, it brings so many great reminiscences.

time flies whenever I am doing it, so how can I not choose it?

Also, not only do I love it, but I am also good at it. Everyone has talent, and it is like "a dime a dozen."

This was the inborn talent I had that I always surpassed everyone. Since a bird in the hand is worth two in the bush, I will choose it.

Politeness
It is important to maintain good relationships with other people because we never know what will happen in the future.

Decisions made by other people can affect others, and such decisions are usually based on personal and sentimental reasons.

So, people should not do anything that may offend or disturb others. It is also crucial to have a good reputation and get along well with others.

It Makes sense
It makes sense to choose it when considering many aspects such as time, money, and efficiency.

When people are considering between the given choices, they must consider many aspects economically.

They must choose the most efficient method because there are limits on what they have.

Also, one should think about it realistically and practically because they should not count chickens before they hatch.

So, down to Earth, people should choose it because it is the most economical

QUESTION

Do you agree or disagree with the following statement? College education should be available only to those who are good students. Use reasons and examples to support your answer.
(당신은 다음 주장에 찬성하십니까, 반대하십니까? 성적이 좋은 학생들에게만 대학 교육의 기회가 주어져야 한다. 이유와 예를 들어 답하세요.)

academic courses와 it makes sense를 사용해서 뼈대에 맞춰서 모범답안을 만들어 봅시다.

follows your heart와 social skills를 사용해서 뼈대에 맞춰서 모범답안을 만들어 봅시다.

saving time과 saving money를 사용해서 뼈대에 맞춰서 모범답안을 만들어 봅시다.

environment와 politeness를 사용해서 뼈대에 맞춰서 모범답안을 만들어 봅시다.

QUESTION

Do you agree or disagree with the following statement? College education should be available only to those who are good students. Use reasons and examples to support your answer.
(당신은 다음 주장에 찬성하십니까, 반대하십니까? 성적이 좋은 학생들에게만 대학 교육의 기회가 주어져야 한다. 이유와 예를 들어 답하세요.)

academic courses와 it makes sense를 사용해서 뼈대에 맞춰서 모범답안을 만들어 봅시다.

If I were to answer the question, I would say college education should be available only to those who were good students. There are many reasons why, but here is a couple.

academic courses

First, those are the ones who will concentrate on academic courses. For example, academic courses are the most important thing for students because good grades will help them get into a good university, and eventually get great jobs. Therefore, not everyone should go to college.

it makes sense

Second, it makes sense to agree with the topic when considering many aspects such as time spent on college education and money spent on tuition. When considering between the given choices, they must consider aspects economically.

That's why I think college education should be available only to those who were good students.

saving time과 saving money를 사용해서 뼈대에 맞춰서 모범답안을 만들어 봅시다.

If I were to answer the question, I would say I agree. There are many reasons why, but here is a couple.

saving time

First, people who weren't good students should not waste their time. For example, there is an old saying "time is gold." This proverb emphasizes the value of time, and this cannot be more true in modern society.

saving money

Second, they should save tuition fees on something else. For instance. When it comes to spending money every penny counts. A thrifty spending habit is indispensable in our lives because little drops of water make the mighty ocean.

That's why I agree with the statement.

follows your heart와 social skills를 사용해서 뼈대에 맞춰서 모범답안을 만들어 봅시다.

If I were to answer the question, I would say college education should be available only to everyone. There are many reasons why, but here is a couple.

follows your heart

First, it is their choice. For example, life is too short to hesitate or do things to please others. It is important to make oneself happy. so, they should do whatever they want to do.

social skills

Second, they have other good abilities. For instance, rather than learning, having social skills became the be-all and end-all. They might not be good students, but they can have other good qualities such as social skills

That's why I think college education should be available only to everyone.

environment와 politeness를 사용해서 뼈대에 맞춰서 모범답안을 만들어 봅시다.

If I were to answer the question, I would disagree. There are many reasons why, but here is a couple.

environment

First, they should be in a good environment. For example, being in good environments is the most important task for mankind because people cannot undo what they have done once it's too late. Being successful starts from seemingly insignificant actions like going to college.

politeness

Second, they can be good people. For instance, being a good person is important because people never know what's going to happen in the future. They might not have been good students, but they might be good people.

That's why I disagree.

02. Research Writing 논문 쓰기 — Integrated Task

읽기 지문

Research Writing Class

Starting next semester, the university will be opening a research writing class for students. It has come to the attention of many university professors that even many upper class students **are unaware of** how to write a proper research paper. **With the hope of teaching** students how to write a research paper early on in their college lives, the writing class will be offered to all students. Also, a part of the class curriculum will include peer editing. Fixing each others' errors will help students not to make the same mistakes later on. This class is mainly aimed at incoming freshmen, but will be offered to students of all levels.

대화 스크립트

STEP 01 뼈대를 먼저 작성해 보도록 하겠습니다.

STEP 02 작성하신 뼈대 빈칸에 맞춰서 리딩 지문을 읽고 주요 포인트를 넣어주세요.

STEP 03 하단에 리스닝 노트테이킹을 해주세요. 음원은 학원 홈페이지에서 무료로 다운받으실 수 있습니다. 또한 2010번 문제 번호로 문제를 풀어보실 수 있습니다.

 아래 하단에 리스닝 스크립트를 보고 베꼈어야 하는 부분을 찾아서 적어 보도록 하겠습니다.

대화 스크립트

뉴토플 - TEST 10_Q2

Now listen to two students discussing the announcement.

W: Hey, did you read the announcement about the research writing class?

M: Yeah, I think it's brilliant!

W: Really? Why? It's not that difficult to write a research paper, is it?

M: Maybe not for you, but for freshmen, it can be really difficult.

W: Yeah?

M: Yeah, I mean, I remember my freshman year. I didn't know the first thing about writing a research paper, so when the professors assigned research papers **left and right**, I was totally **dumbfounded**. If this class opens, it will help freshmen a lot. If they learn how to write a good research paper in the beginning, they can develop strong writing skills, which will really help them later.

W: Yeah, I struggled with research papers my first year, too.

M: I like the part about peer editing, too. It may not be the main part of the class, but putting it in the announcement means that it'll take up a pretty big part of it, right?

W: Right, but is it actually helpful? I prefer getting direct help from professors.

M: Yeah, but peer editing can be really helpful as well. There are some things that the professors can't catch, but other students can. Also, if we catch each others' mistakes, we can not only learn from each other to not make those mistakes again, but also how to solve these problems together. Two heads are better than one.

남자의 의견 — 찬성

이유 ❶ — 신입생들이 논문을 잘 쓰기는 힘들다

이유 ❷ — 급우간의 첨삭은 서로를 도와줄 것

이제 지문에 대해 논의하는 두 학생의 대화를 들어보세요.

여: 야, 논문 쓰기반에 대한 안내문 읽었어?

남: 응, 완전 좋은 생각인 것 같은데.

여: 정말? 왜? 논문 쓰는 것 별로 어렵지 않잖아?

남: 넌 안 어려워도, 신입생에겐 어려울 수 있지.

여: 그래?

남: 응, 내가 신입생 때 어땠는지 기억 나. 논문을 어떻게 쓰는지 몰라서, 교수님들이 **여기저기서** 논문 숙제를 내주면, 완전 **어찌할 바를 몰랐어**. 만약 이 수업이 시작되면, 신입생들은 큰 도움을 받을 거야. 만약 초기에 논문을 쓰는 법을 잘 배우면, 그들은 탄탄한 글쓰기 실력을 키울 수 있고 이것은 나중에 크게 도움이 될 거야.

여: 아, 나도 1학년 때엔 논문 때문에 힘들어 했지.

남: 급우간의 첨삭 부분도 맘에 들어. 그게 수업의 중점은 아닐지라도, 안내문에 이 말을 쓴다는 건 이게 수업을 꽤 차지한다는 거겠지?

여: 그렇지, 근데 그게 정말 도움이 될까? 난 교수님한테 직접 도움을 받는 게 더 좋은데.

남: 응, 근데 친구들과의 첨삭도 굉장히 도움이 돼. 교수님들이 발견 못하는 게 있는데, 그걸 다른 학생들이 할 수 있거든. 그리고, 만약 학생들이 서로 잘못된 점을 찾으면, 같은 실수를 만들지 않게 서로한테 배울 수 있을 뿐만이 아니라, 그 문제를 같이 해결할 수 있잖아. 머리 두 개가 하나보다 나으니까.

문제 — **The man expresses his opinion about the college's plan. State his opinion and explain the reasons he gives for holding that opinion.**

남자는 대학의 계획에 대해 자신의 의견을 밝히고 있습니다. 그의 의견을 말하고, 그 의견을 고수하는 이유를 설명하세요.

STEP 05 Note-taking

STEP 06 다시한번 모범 답안을 작성해 보도록 하겠습니다

Research Writing Class

Starting next semester, the university will be opening a research writing class for students. It has come to the attention of many university professors that even many upper class students **are unaware of** how to write a proper research paper. **With the hope of teaching** students how to write a research paper early on in their college lives, the writing class will be offered to all students. Also, a part of the class curriculum will include peer editing. Fixing each others' errors will help students not to make the same mistakes later on. This class is mainly aimed at incoming freshmen, but will be offered to students of all levels.

Note-taking	노트테이킹
Reading - introduce research writing class - to help students write better research paper - includes peer editing **Man** - supporting **Reason ❶** - it's difficult for freshmen to write well - lessons from the class will help them later **Reason ❷** - students can learn from peer editing - they learn to solve the problems	**지문** - 논문 쓰기반 개설 - 논문을 더 잘 쓰기 위해 - 급우간의 첨삭 포함 **남자** - 찬성 **이유 ❶** - 신입생은 잘 쓰기 어려움 - 수업에서 배운 게 나중에 도움이 됨 **이유 ❷** - 급우간의 첨삭으로부터 배움 - 문제를 해결하는 법을 배움

Task 2   Sample Response   🎧 뉴토플 - TEST 10_R2

2번 문제 모범 답안

The two students are discussing the college's plan to open a research writing class for students. The man is supporting the plan for two reasons.

❶ First, the class would be a great help for freshmen. It is difficult for freshmen to write good research papers in their first year. The class will help them write better, and lessons from the class will help them later on.

❷ Second, the idea of peer editing would be an efficient way for students to help one another. Professors sometimes miss details, and students can catch and learn from them. They can also learn to solve the problems, so it will be beneficial for everyone. (This is why he is against the plan.)

두 학생은 학생을 위해 논문 쓰기반을 시작하려는 대학 측의 계획에 대해 의논하고 있다. 남자는 두 가지로 그 계획에 찬성하고 있다.

❶ 첫째, 이 수업은 신입생들에게 큰 도움이 될것이다. 1학년 때 신입생이 좋은 논문을 쓰기는 어렵다. 이 수업은 학생들이 더 잘 쓰도록 도와줄 것이고, 이 수업에서 배운 것들은 나중에 도움이 될 것이다.

❷ 다음, 급우간의 첨삭은 학생들이 서로 도움을 주는데 효과적인 방법이다. 교수님들은 가끔 자세한 것을 놓치고, 학생들은 그것을 잡아내고 그로부터 배울 수 있다. 그들은 또한 문제를 해결하는 법도 배울 수 있어서, 이 수업은 모든 사람에게 유익하다. (이것이 그가 이 계획이 필요하다고 생각 하는 이유이다.)

Vocabulary

be unaware of	phr. ~을 모르다	with the hope of	phr. ~한다는 희망을 갖고
left and right	phr. 여기저기, 사방으로	dumbfounded [dʌmfáundid]	a. 어쩔 줄 모르는

03 Choice-Supportive Bias
선택을 지지하는 편견

Integrated Task

읽기 지문

Choice-Supportive Bias

During a decision-making process, people may **encounter** various **conflicts** and **become subject to** hesitation. Once an action has been taken, however, the ways in which we evaluate the outcome of what we did maybe biased in some way. In psychology, the term choice-supportive bias refers to one's **tendency to ascribe** positive **attributes** to a choice that has been made. Not only do people remember their choices as better than they actually were, but also tend to overattribute negative features to options not chosen. The purpose of this phenomenon is to justify their decisions and to lower the possibility of regrets.

대화 스크립트

STEP 01 뼈대를 먼저 작성해 보도록 하겠습니다.

STEP 02 작성하신 뼈대 빈칸에 맞춰서 리딩 지문을 읽고 주요 포인트를 넣어주세요.

STEP 03 하단에 리스닝 노트테이킹을 해주세요. 음원은 학원 홈페이지에서 무료로 다운받으실 수 있습니다. 또한 3010번 문제 번호로 문제를 풀어보실 수 있습니다.

 아래 하단에 리스닝 스크립트를 보고 베꼈어야 하는 부분을 찾아서 적어 보도록 하겠습니다.

대화 스크립트

뉴토플 - TEST 10_Q3

Now listen to part of a lecture in a psychology class.

It's hard to **get by in life** without making any decisions. Sometimes these decisions are followed by regret. But, whether there is regret or not, everyone tends to eventually reason with themselves to conclude that they made the right decision. They start to see only the advantages, and as a result, do not end up regretting their choices. They become blind to the negatives of their decisions, no matter how **blatant** the drawbacks may be.

예시 ❶
주택 구입

세부사항
직장에 가깝지만 너무 작아서 고민

As an example, let me tell you about my friend who was **contemplating** whether or not to buy a certain house. He could not decide right away because it had both advantages and disadvantages, as is the case with most decisions. Its biggest advantage was that it was located close to his job. The downside was that it was too small. He did not know what to do, and weighed the pros and cons repeatedly, but eventually he ended up buying the house.

예시 ❷
몇 년 후

세부사항
직장에 가깝다는 장점만 언급

A few years later, we were talking and catching up on old times when he started talking about his house again. He was telling me how nice and convenient it was because it was so close to his job. He did not, however, mention its small size at all. I knew he had had difficulties stuffing in all his furniture and **housewares** when he moved in, but he honestly didn't seem to care much about the small space he had got because he came to have choice-supportive bias.

문제

Using the example from the professor's lecture, explain what choice-supportive bias is and how it works.

이제 심리학 강의의 일부를 들어보세요.

결정을 내리지 않고 **인생을 사는** 것은 어려운 일입니다. 어떨 땐 이 결정들에 후회가 따르기도 합니다. 그러나, 후회를 하든지 안 하든지, 모든 사람들은 그들이 올바른 결정을 내렸다고 정당화하는 경향이 있습니다. 그들은 장점만 보기 시작하여 결과적으로 그들의 선택에 대해 후회를 하지 않게 됩니다. 그들은 단점이 얼마나 **눈에 띄는지** 간에 그들의 결정의 단점에 대해서는 무감각해집니다.

예로, 집을 살지 말지에 대해서 **심사숙고 하던** 제 친구에 대해서 말씀 드리겠습니다. 대부분의 결정과 같이 이 또한 장점과 단점을 모두 갖고 있기 때문에 그는 바로 결정할 수 없었습니다. 이것의 가장 큰 장점은 그의 직장과 가까운 곳에 있다는 것이었습니다. 단점은 집이 너무 작다는 것이었습니다. 그는 어찌할 지 몰라서 계속해서 장단점을 재다가 결국 집을 구입했습니다.

몇 년 후, 우리가 이야기를 하며 옛 이야기를 할때 그는 그의 집에 대해서 다시 이야기하기 시작했습니다. 그는 집이 직장과 가까워서 얼마나 좋고 편한지에 대해서 이야기 해 주었습니다. 그러나 그는 집이 좁은 점에 대해서는 전혀 언급하지 않았습니다. 저는 그가 이사를 할 때 그의 가구와 **살림살이**를 들여놓는데 있어서 얼마나 힘들었는지 알고 있었지만 그는 선택을 지지하는 편견에 사로잡혀 집이 좁은 것에 대해서는 진심으로 신경 쓰는 것 같지 않았습니다.

교수의 강의를 예로 들어, 선택을 지지하는 편견이 무엇이고 어떻게 작용하는지 설명하세요.

STEP 05
다시한번 음원듣고 노트테이킹 해보도록 하겠습니다.
Note-taking

STEP 06
다시 한번 뼈대와 함께 모범 답안을 작성해 보도록 하겠습니다.

Choice-Supportive Bias

During a decision-making process, people may **encounter** various **conflicts** and **become subject to** hesitation. Once an action has been taken, however, the ways in which we evaluate the outcome of what we did maybe biased in some way. In psychology, the term choice-supportive bias refers to one's **tendency to ascribe** positive **attributes** to a choice that has been made. Not only do people remember their choices as better than they actually were, but also tend to overattribute negative features to options not chosen. The purpose of this phenomenon is to justify their decisions and to lower the possibility of regrets.

References

Daniel Kahneman

[참고자료]

다니엘 카너먼(Daniel Kahneman)
1972년 아모스 트버스키 (Amos Tversky)와 함께 인지적 편향 이론을 발표했다.

선택을 지지하는 편견은 인지적 편향 (Cognitive Bias)의 일종이다.

Task 3　Sample Response　🎧 뉴토플 - TEST 10_R3　　3번 문제 모범 답안

Choice-suppórtive bias is people's tendency to try to stick to the decísions they have made. The proféssor is giving an exámple of her friend to expláin what it is.

❶ One of the proféssor's friends had a dilémma over whether to buy a house. It was very close to his work, but too small for him to live in. At the time, he didn't know what to do.

❷ Later when she met her friend agáin, they talked abóut the friend's house. He mentioned only the advántages, like how convénient and close it was to work. He could not see the disadvántages becáuse of a choice-suppórtive bias.

선택을 지지하는 편견은 그들이 내린 결정을 고수하려는 사람들의 경향입니다. 교수는 이에 대해서 설명하기 위해 그녀의 친구를 예로 듭니다.

❶ 교수의 친구 중 한 명은 집을 구입하는데 있어서 딜레마를 겪고 있었습니다. 집은 그의 직장에서 아주 가까웠지만 그가 살기에 너무 작았습니다. 그 시기에 그는 무엇을 어찌할지 몰랐습니다.

❷ 후에 그녀가 친구를 다시 만났을 때 그들은 친구의 집에 대하여 이야기 하였습니다. 그는 그의 직장과 가까워서 얼마나 편한지와 같은 장점에 대해서만 언급하였습니다. 그는 선택을 지지하는 편견으로 인해 단점을 볼 수 없었습니다.

Vocabulary

encounter [inkáuntər]	v. 부딪히다, 마주치다	conflict [kənflíkt]	n. 갈등
become subject to	phr. ~에 영향받기 쉽다	ascribe [əskráib]	v. ~의 탓으로 돌리다
attribute [ətríbju:t]	v. ~탓으로 하다 / n. 속성	tendency to	phr. ~하는 경향
get by	phr. 통과하다, 빠져나가다	blatant [bléitənt]	a. 떠들썩한, 뻔뻔한, 노골적인
contemplate [kántəmplèit]	v. 심사 숙고하다	housewares [háuswerz]	n. 가재도구

04. Bats 박쥐 — Integrated Task

STEP 01 4번 뼈대를 먼저 작성해 보도록 하겠습니다.

STEP 02 하단에 리스닝 노트테이킹을 해주세요. 음원은 학원 홈페이지에서 무료로 다운받으실 수 있습니다. 또한 4010번 문제 번호로 문제를 풀어보실 수 있습니다.

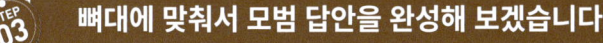

STEP 03 뼈대에 맞춰서 모범 답안을 완성해 보겠습니다.

대화 스크립트

Listen to part of a lecture in a zoology class.

동물학 강의의 일부를 들어보세요.

주제
박쥐가 거꾸로 매달리는 이유

Bats are one of the most unique animals in the world. As you know, they are the only **mammals** that can fly and they always hang upside down. I'm pretty sure that most of you have a fear of bats because you associate them with vampires, thinking that they suck blood. Of course some do, but only two or three types. Most others eat insects or fruit, and they aren't harmful to humans at all. But, that's not what we are going to talk about today. Today, we are going to talk about why bats hang upside down. Have you ever wondered about why they do so? I mean, there must be a reason, right? Well, let's find out now.

박쥐는 세상에서 가장 독특한 동물 중 하나입니다. 아시다시피, 그들은 날 수 있는 유일한 **포유류**이고 항상 거꾸로 매달려 있습니다. 저는 여러분 중 대부분이 박쥐를 흡혈귀와 연관시켜서 피를 뺀다고 생각하기 때문에 무서워한다고 확신합니다. 물론 몇몇은 그렇지만, 두세 종류만 그렇습니다. 대부분의 다른 종들은 벌레나 과일을 먹고, 인간에겐 전혀 해롭지 않습니다. 하지만, 우리가 오늘 토론할 주제는 이것이 아닙니다. 오늘, 우리는 박쥐들이 왜 거꾸로 매달리는지에 대해 얘기하겠습니다. 여러분은 그들이 왜 그러는지 생각 해 본적이 있습니까? 이유가 있지 않겠습니까, 그렇죠? 음, 지금 알아봅시다.

예시 ❶
천적을 피함

세부사항
낮에 잘 수 있고 천적이 닿을 수 없음

The first reason that bats hang upside down is to hide from danger. Hanging upside down hides the bats from predators. During the day, when bats sleep and when their predators are active, bats **huddle up** in a **secluded** spot, such as the roof of a cave, the underside of a bridge, or the inside of a **hollowed-out** tree. By doing so, they look like a part of their hiding place and their enemies can't see or reach them there. This keeps them safe until the night, when they become most active.

박쥐가 거꾸로 매달리는 첫 번째 이유는 위험으로부터 숨기 위해서입니다. 거꾸로 매달리는 것은 박쥐를 천적으로부터 숨겨줍니다. 낮 동안, 박쥐는 자고 천적들이 활개를 칠 때, 박쥐들은 동굴의 천정이나, 다리의 아랫면이나 **속이 빈** 나무 같은 **외딴곳**에서 **몸을 웅크리고** 모여 있습니다. 이렇게 그들은 은신처의 일부처럼 보이고, 천적들은 그들을 보지 못하거나 그들에게 닿을 수 없습니다. 이는 그들이 가장 활동적인 밤이 될 때까지 그들을 지켜줍니다.

예시 ❷
도약하는데 도움

세부사항
양력이 부족하고 다리가 약해서 높은 곳에서 시작해야 함

Another reason for hanging upside down is because it puts them in an **ideal** position for **takeoff**. Unlike birds, bats can't takeoff from the ground because their wings don't produce enough lift to **launch** them from a **dead stop.** Further, their hind legs are so small and underdeveloped that they can't run to build up the necessary takeoff speed. By sleeping upside down in a high location, bats are always ready to drop and takeoff if they need to escape from their predators, or if they spot their prey.

거꾸로 매달리는 또 다른 이유는 그것이 **도약하기**에 가장 **이상적인** 자세이기 때문입니다. 새와 달리, 날개가 **멈춰있는 상태**에서 **날아오르기**에 충분한 양력을 만들지 못하기 때문에 박쥐는 땅에서 도약하지 못합니다. 더 나아가, 그들의 뒷다리는 너무 작고 발달이 안되어있어서 도약할 때 필요한 속도까지 달리지 못합니다. 높은 장소에서 매달려 잠으로써 박쥐들은 천적들로부터 도망가거나 먹이를 찾았을 때 언제든지 떨어져서 날 준비가 되어있는 것입니다.

문제

Using the examples from the professor's lecture, explain why bats hang upside down.

교수의 강의를 예로 들어, 박쥐가 왜 거꾸로 매달리는지에 대해 설명하세요.

References

[참고자료]

황금모자 과일박쥐
(Golden-capped Fruit Bat)

필리핀에 분포되어 있고 몸길이는 30cm가 넘어 박쥐 중에 가장 크다. 멸종위기 동물이다.

Photo by , available under the Creative Commons Attribution ShareAlike 3.0

Task 4 Sample Response 🎧 TEST 10_R4

4번 문제 모범 답안

In the lecture, the professor gives two reasons of why bats always hang upside down.

❶ First, hanging upside down hides the bats from predators. They need to sleep during the day when predators are active, so the bats stay in dark places and hide themsélves until night time.

❷ Second, hanging allows bats to takeoff more easily. Bats cannót fly from the ground due to insufficíent lift. Also, their legs are too weak to build up enóugh speed to fly. Thus, the hanging allóws them to fly from the high locátion, such as running from predators or hunting preys.

강의에서 교수는 왜 박쥐들이 항상 거꾸로 매달리는지에 대해 두 이유를 들고 있습니다.

❶ 첫째, 거꾸로 매달리는 것은 천적으로부터 그들을 숨겨줍니다. 그들은 포식자들이 활발한 낮 동안 자야 해서 어두운 곳에서 밤까지 몸을 숨깁니다.

❷ 둘째, 매달리는 것은 박쥐들이 더 쉽게 날도록 합니다. 박쥐들은 부족한 양력 때문에 땅에서 날아오르지 못합니다. 또, 다리는 나는데 필요한 속도를 만들기에 너무 약합니다. 따라서, 천적으로부터 도망치거나 사냥할 때, 매달리는 것은 높은데서 날 수 있게 해줍니다.

Vocabulary

mammal [mǽməl]	n. 포유류	huddle up	phr. 몸을 웅크리다
secluded [siklúːdid]	a. 한적한, 외딴	hollowed-out	phr. 속을 파낸
ideal [aidíːəl]	a. 이상적인, 가장 알맞은	takeoff [teikɔːf]	n. 출발, 도약, 이륙
launch [lɔːntʃ, láːntʃ]	v. 시작하다, 발사하다	dead stop	phr. 완전히 멈춘 상태

TEST 10 ··· 199

USHER
iBT TOEFL
FINAL TEST SPEAKING
TEST 11

Independent Tasks

Task 1 - 모범 답안
Question 1   usherin.usher.co.kr > 시험리스트 > Speaking 시험리스트 > Task 1 > #1060

Integrated Tasks

Task 2 - Script / 해석 / 모범 답안
Question 2   usherin.usher.co.kr > 시험리스트 > Speaking 시험리스트 > Task 2 > #2011

Task 3 - Script / 해석 / 모범 답안
Question 3   usherin.usher.co.kr > 시험리스트 > Speaking 시험리스트 > Task 3 > #3011

Task 4 - Script / 해석 / 모범 답안
Question 4   usherin.usher.co.kr > 시험리스트 > Speaking 시험리스트 > Task 4 > #4011

자기평가표

1번 문제 유형은 학생들이 본인에 생각을 주제에 맞춰서 말 해야하는 시험입니다.
본인이 처음부터 끝까지 45초 동안 말해야하다 보니 학생들이 제일 어려워 하는 시험입니다.
하지만, 먼저 외우고 익힌후에 말하는것이 가능할수 있게 하겠습니다.
가장 기본이 되는 뼈대 입니다. 먼저 외우도록 합시다.

> if i were to answer the question, i would say
> there are many reasons why, but here is a couple
> first
> for example,
> second
> for instance
> that's why

다음은 2번 문제 유형입니다.
2번 문제는 리딩에 학교에 계획이 적혀있거나 학교가 변해야하는 방향에 대해서 학생들에 주장이 적혀있습니다.
리딩에서 빠르게 파악해야하는 것은 도대체 누가 무엇을 주장하는가 입니다.
45~50초에 리딩 지문이 나오고 난 다음에 리스닝으로 학생들에 대화가 나오는 문제입니다.
리스닝에서는 학생이 리딩 지문에 대한 본인에 좋고 나쁜지에 대한 의견을 얘기해줄겁니다.
이유 2가지와 예시 2가지를 꼭 말할 수 있어야 합니다.

이에 따라서 2번 스피킹 문제에 뼈대는

> The reading states that university (plans to) / (should)
> the (woman / man) in the conversation thinks it is a good / bad idea.
> He/she provides two reasons to support his / her opinion.
> first,
> Second,
> the woman / man thinks it's a great / horrible idea.

다음은 3번 문제 유형입니다.
3번 문제는 2번 문제 유형과 같이 리딩과 리스닝이 나오는 문제 입니다. 하지만, 이번에는 이전 문제와는 달리 매우 학술적인 내용이 들어 있습니다. 리딩에서는 교과서에 나올만한 주제 한개를 자세하게 다룹니다. 여기서 학생분들은 제목과 이에 대한 정의를 잘 받아적으셔야 합니다. 리스닝에서는 교수님이 리딩에 나온 내용으로 예시를 들어 줍니다.

> The article is about
> which the passage defines as
> The professor provides an example of
> first,
> Second,
> The example clearly illustrates

다음은 4번 문제 유형입니다.
4번 문제는 이전 문제와 달리 리스닝만 나오는 문제 유형입니다. 3번 문제에 나온 리딩 지문이 리스닝으로 변환되었다 라고 생각 하시면 됩니다. 그렇기에 3번 문제에 리스닝 내용보다 리딩 길이 만큼 깁니다.

> In the lecture, professor explains
> first,
> second,
> That's how the professor explain it.

USHER

01 — Places to Live 살 곳 — Independent Task

QUESTION

 Some people prefer to live in one place. Others prefer to live in different places. What do you prefer to do? Use reasons and examples to support your answer.
(어떤 이들은 한 곳에서 살기를 선호합니다. 다른 이들은 여러 곳에서 살기를 선호합니다. 당신은 어떻게 하기를 선호합니까? 이유와 예를 들어 답하세요.)

 브레인 스토밍 (아래에 놓여있는 12간지 내용들을 보고 어떤 것을 사용할 수 있을지 확인해보세요)
첫번째 이유 :
두번째 이유 :

 뼈대에 맞춰서 작성을 해봅시다.

_____
_____
_____
_____
_____
_____

아래 이미지는 학생들을 위한 만능 템플릿 12간지 입니다. 학생분들이 제일 먼저 암기해야하는 것이며, 본인 스스로 문장을 단기간 안에 못 만들거 같을 때에 도와주는 친구입니다. 가까이 두고 매일 외우세요.

Academic Courses
…because I think students should concentrate on academic courses.

Academic courses are the most important thing for students because good grades will help them get into good universities and, eventually, get great jobs.

As students get older, a good academic record is the only thing that actually matters.

This may sound a little far-fetched, but it's true, and for this reason, investing time in other activities is a waste of time.

Stay Healthy
It can be a great way to stay healthy. People join a cycling group through the internet. The members use bicycles to commute to work or school.

It is a great outdoor activity because people have a chance to work out while having fun.

Also, it is a great way to meet new people with similar interests. People nowadays do not have much chance to become close to each other.

However, there are numerous unique groups active on the internet, and this would not have been possible without the internet.

Follows your heart
Carpe diem, seize the days, and YOLO all stand for one thing. Do whatever your heart makes you do.

Life is too short to hesitate or do things to please others. It is essential to make yourself happy.

Actions speak louder than words. Whatever I do to make myself happy is better than sitting in a room thinking about it.

So I would just do it even if it means I am biting off something more than I can chew.

Stress
…if it can possibly be a way to relieve stress.

People nowadays are living a busy and hectic life, so they are under great stress, but a lot of them don't even realize they are stressed out.

Stress is known to be a major factor that keeps us from being healthy, and many people are suffering from various problems.

This is more serious than we think, so if it can ever be a way to relieve stress…

Money
…because it's the best way to save money. When it comes to spending money, every penny counts.

A thrifty spending habit is indispensable in our lives because little drops of water make the mighty ocean.

If we don't get used to working on a tight budget, we'll always be short on cash later.

A penny-pinching lifestyle will lead to financial stability, and it will give us peace of mind.

Saving Time
…because it's the best way to save time. There's an old saying, "Time is gold."

This proverb emphasizes the value of time, and this cannot be more true in modern society.

We're living a busy and hectic life, so saving time means we can do a lot more things later.

Many say that life is not fair, but everyone has twenty-four hours a day and seven days a week, so I would save time by…

Social Skills
Nowadays, people have smartphones with them all the time, and that information is no longer limited to elites.

Therefore, rather than learning, having social skills became the be-all and end-all to succeed rather than education.

Also, social skills are more than meet the eyes. To have social skills, one must also be able to read others like a book.

There will be times when one will truly need them.

Environment
because eventually, it can contribute to protecting the environment.

I think it's THE most important task for humanity because we cannot bring it back to life once it's too late.

Saving Earth all starts from seemingly insignificant actions.

Small actions from everyone bring about bigger changes, so I'm willing to participate.

Patience is virtue
Patience is a virtue. Saving time is indeed important, but waiting calmly is needed in this case.

There are times when one must wait patiently for things to go accordingly, and this is when time is the solution.

When going against the clock, they are more susceptible to making mistakes than taking some time.

In the long run, one will be glad that one has waited in this case.

Just because
I love it more than the given choices. Since I have so many great memory about it, It brings so many great reminiscences.

time flies whenever I am doing it, so how can I not choose it?

Also, not only do I love it, but I am also good at it. Everyone has talent, and it is like "a dime a dozen."

This was the inborn talent I had that I always surpassed everyone. Since a bird in the hand is worth two in the bush, I will choose it.

Politeness
It is important to maintain good relationships with other people because we never know what will happen in the future.

Decisions made by other people can affect others, and such decisions are usually based on personal and sentimental reasons.

So, people should not do anything that may offend or disturb others. It is also crucial to have a good reputation and get along well with others.

It Makes sense
It makes sense to choose it when considering many aspects such as time, money, and efficiency.

When people are considering between the given choices, they must consider many aspects economically.

They must choose the most efficient method because there are limits on what they have.

Also, one should think about it realistically and practically because they should not count chickens before they hatch.

So, down to Earth, people should choose it because it is the most economical

QUESTION

Some people prefer to live in one place. Others prefer to live in different places. What do you prefer to do? Use reasons and examples to support your answer.
(어떤 이들은 한 곳에서 살기를 선호합니다. 다른 이들은 여러 곳에서 살기를 선호합니다. 당신은 어떻게 하기를 선호합니까? 이유와 예를 들어 답하세요.)

academic courses와 stress를 사용해서 뼈대에 맞춰서 모범답안을 만들어 봅시다.

___

social skills와 politeness를 사용해서 뼈대에 맞춰서 모범답안을 만들어 봅시다.

___

saving money와 saving time을 사용해서 뼈대에 맞춰서 모범답안을 만들어 봅시다.

___

follows your heart와 just because를 사용해서 뼈대에 맞춰서 모범답안을 만들어 봅시다.

___

QUESTION

Some people prefer to live in one place. Others prefer to live in different places. What do you prefer to do? Use reasons and examples to support your answer.
(어떤 이들은 한 곳에서 살기를 선호합니다. 다른 이들은 여러 곳에서 살기를 선호합니다. 당신은 어떻게 하기를 선호합니까? 이유와 예를 들어 답하세요.)

academic courses와 stress를 사용해서 뼈대에 맞춰서 모범답안을 만들어 봅시다.

If I were to answer the question, I would prefer to live in one place. There are many reasons why, but here is a couple.

academic courses

First, I cannot concentrate on my academic courses if I move around. For example, students should be able to concentrate on academic courses by staying in one place. Academic courses are the most important thing for students because good grades will help them get into good universities and eventually, get great jobs.

stress

Second, moving around is stressful. For instance, Stress is known to be a major factor that keeps us from being healthy, and many people are suffering from various problems. This is more serious than we think, so if it can ever be a way to relieve stress, I do not want to move around. That's why I prefer to stay in one place

social skills와 politeness를 사용해서 뼈대에 맞춰서 모범답안을 만들어 봅시다.

If I were to answer the question, I would prefer to live in different places. There are many reasons why, but here is a couple.

social skills

First, I can develop my social skills by meeting strangers. For instance, having social skills became the be-all and end-all to succeed. Also, social skills are more than meet the eyes. To have social skills, one must also be able to read others like a book.

politeness

Second, I can get help from them by maintaining a good relationship with them. For instance, It is important to maintain good relationships with other people, because we never know what's going to happen in the future. Decisions made by other people can affect others, and such decisions are usually based on personal and sentimental reasons. That's why I would prefer to live in different places.

saving money와 saving time을 사용해서 뼈대에 맞춰서 모범답안을 만들어 봅시다.

If I were to answer the question, I would agree with the former. There are many reasons why, but here is a couple.

saving money

First, people can save money by spending money on moving fees. For example, When it comes to spending money, every penny counts. A thrifty spending habit is indispensable in our lives because little drops of water make the mighty ocean.

saving time

Second, people can save time by not spending time on the roads. For instance, There's an old saying, "Time is gold." This proverb emphasizes the value of time, and this cannot be more true in modern society. That's why I agree with the former

follows your heart와 just because를 사용해서 뼈대에 맞춰서 모범답안을 만들어 봅시다.

If I were to answer the question, I would agree with the latter. There are many reasons why, but here is a couple.

follows your heart

First, people should see the world. For example, Carpe diem, seize the days, and YOLO all stand for one thing. Do whatever your heart makes you do. Life is too short to hesitate or do things to please others. It is important to make yourself happy. People should move around to see the world.

just because

Second, I love moving around. For instance, Since I have so much great memory about it, It brings so many great reminiscences. To make a long story short, time flies whenever I am doing it so how can I not choose it. That's why I think people should move around

Drama Requirement

University's Drama Performance Requirements

The university has made a new requirement for graduation. Students must now attend a minimum of two performances of art or drama. Further, after watching the performances, students will be required to hand in a short paper on them to the humanities department. The university is hoping that this will increase the number of students interested in culture and the arts. Since students nowadays are too busy with schoolwork and other activities, they do not take the time to enjoy art and culture. Making this a graduation requirement will force students to watch such works, and **in turn**, become **well-rounded** people in both academics and cultural life.

 아래 하단에 리스닝 스크립트를 보고 베꼈어야 하는 부분을 찾아서 적어 보도록 하겠습니다.

대화 스크립트

🎧 뉴토플 - TEST 11_Q2

Now listen to two students discussing the announcement.

이제 지문에 대해 논의하는 두 학생의 대화를 들어보세요.

M: Hey, what do you think of the university's new plan?

남: 야, 학교의 계획에 대해 어떻게 생각해?

여자의 의견
반대

W: About watching drama performances as a requirement for graduation? I think it's ridiculous.

여: 연극 보는 걸 졸업 조건으로 만드는 거? 웃기는 처사라 생각해.

M: Really? Why?

남: 정말? 왜?

이유 ❶
공연을 즐길
시간이 없음

W: I mean, we barely have enough time to sleep with all the extra activities we are doing, especially those of us in our last years of college. I just don't understand the university's point in forcing us to go to performances.

여: 특히 우리 같은 졸업반 학생들은, 다른 활동 때문에 잠도 잘 못 자잖아. 도대체 그런 데를 가라고 하는 의도를 이해 못하겠어.

M: Yeah, I guess you're right. We, in our senior years, do get pretty busy preparing for life after college.

남: 응, 네 말이 맞는 것 같다. 졸업반에 있는 우리는 졸업 후의 인생 때문에 바쁘지.

W: Exactly! It's not like we don't want to go enjoy cultural events. Who wouldn't want to relax and catch a drama performance! If we had the spare time to do so, we would go even without the university making us.

여: 그래! 우리가 문화 생활을 즐기기 싫은 것도 아니고. 누군들 쉬면서 공연을 보러 가고 싶지 않겠어! 만약 여가시간이라도 있으면, 학교에서 가지 말라고 해도 갈걸.

M: Yeah.

남: 맞아.

이유 ❷
나중에 학생들의
문화생활에
악영향을 미칠
것임

W: Also, since the university is making us, it might actually have the opposite effect. Like most things, when someone is forced to do something, they **tend to** go the other way.

여: 그리고, 학교에서 시키니까, 오히려 역효과를 낼 것 같아. 대부분 그렇지만 강제로 무엇을 하라고 하면, 반대로 가는 **경향**이 있잖아…

M: Go the other way? What do you mean?

남: 반대로 간다고? 무슨 말이야?

W: I mean, since performances have been made a mandatory part of education, students might just go to them for the grades and not really enjoy it. Then, later, because they had been past assignments, students might not go to cultural events after graduation, having the opposite effect of the university's purpose.

여: 공연이 교육의 의무사항이 됐으니까, 학생들이 그냥 점수 때문에 가고 즐기진 않을 수 있잖아. 그러면 나중에, 옛날에 숙제였던 거니까, 학생들은 졸업 후에도 그런 문화생활을 즐기지 않을 거야. 그건 대학의 의도와는 반대지.

문제

The woman expresses her opinion about the college's plan. State her opinion and explain the reasons she gives for holding that opinion.

여자는 대학의 계획에 대해 자신의 의견을 밝히고 있습니다. 그녀의 의견을 말하고, 그 의견을 고수하는 이유를 설명하세요.

Note-taking

다시한번 모범 답안을 작성해 보도록 하겠습니다

University's Drama Performance Requirements

The university has made a new requirement for graduation. Students must now attend a minimum of two performances of art or drama. Further, after watching the performances, students will be required to hand in a short paper on them to the humanities department. The university is hoping that this will increase the number of students interested in culture and the arts. Since students nowadays are too busy with schoolwork and other activities, they do not take the time to enjoy art and culture. Making this a graduation requirement will force students to watch such works, and **in turn**, become **well-rounded** people in both academics and cultural life.

Note-taking	노트테이킹
Reading - watching drama performances will be a requirement - watch at least 2 performances and submit papers - to increase the number of students interested in culture **Woman** - against **Reason ❶** - students don't have enough time - seniors are busy preparing for graduation **Reason ❷** - students can't enjoy them when forced - it may have negative effects on cultural life later	**지문** - 연극을 보는 게 의무화될 것 - 최소 2개를 보고 감상문을 낼 것 - 더 많은 학생이 문화에 관심을 갖도록 **여자** - 반대 **이유 ❶** - 학생들은 시간이 부족함 - 4학년들은 졸업 준비로 바쁨 **이유 ❷** - 강제적이면 즐길 수 없음 - 나중에 문화생활에 악영향을 미칠 수 있음

Task 2 Sample Response 🎧 뉴토플 - TEST 11_R2   2번 문제 모범 답안

The two students are discussing the college's plan to make the students watch at least two drama performances as a graduation requirement. The woman is against the plan for two reasons.

❶ First, students don't have enough time to attend these performances. It's not that they don't enjoy watching them; they are just too busy to go to theaters.

❷ Second, when students are forced to do something, they do not really enjoy it. This requirement might have a negative effect on the future lives of students. They would go to the performances purely as a school requirement, not for their own entertainment. Thus, after graduation, this might negatively affect their cultural life. (This is why she thinks the plan is unnecessary.)

두 학생은 졸업 조건으로 최소 2개의 연극을 보게 하려는 대학의 계획에 대해 의논하고 있다. 여자는 두 이유를 들어 반대하고 있다.

❶ 첫째, 학생들은 이런 연극을 볼 시간이 없다. 그들은 보기 싫어서 안 보는 것이 아니다; 극장에 가기엔 너무 바쁘다.

❷ 다음, 학생들은 뭔가를 강제로 하면, 그것을 즐길 수 없다. 이 필수조건은 학생들의 미래에 **악영향을 미칠 수 있다**. 그들은 자신의 재미를 위해서가 아닌, 단지 학교 필수조건으로써 공연을 볼 것이다. 그러므로, 졸업 후 이것은 학생들의 문화생활에 악영향을 미칠 수 있다. (이것이 그녀가 이 제안이 필요없다고 생각하는 이유이다)

Vocabulary

in turn	phr. 결과적으로	well-rounded	phr. 다재 다능한
tend to	phr. (~하는) 경향이 있다	have a negative effect on	phr. 악영향을 미치다

03. Specialist Species 특화종 — Integrated Task

읽기 지문

Specialist Species

According to their **tolerability** of habitat, food, and other environment conditions, animals can be **distinguished** into two types: generalist or specialist species. Generalist species are animals which can thrive in many different environmental conditions due to their varied diets. Although they can adapt to **a wider range of** environments, they have more competition with other species. On the other hand, specialist species can only **prosper** in certain habitats due to their limited diets. Although they don't have to compete with others for food or habitat, they aren't able to prosper in many different environments.

대화 스크립트

STEP 01 뼈대를 먼저 작성해 보도록 하겠습니다.

STEP 02 작성하신 뼈대 빈칸에 맞춰서 리딩 지문을 읽고 주요 포인트를 넣어주세요.

STEP 03 하단에 리스닝 노트테이킹을 해주세요. 음원은 학원 홈페이지에서 무료로 다운받으실 수 있습니다. 또한 3011번 문제 번호로 문제를 풀어보실 수 있습니다.

 아래 하단에 리스닝 스크립트를 보고 베꼈어야 하는 부분을 찾아서 적어 보도록 하겠습니다.

대화 스크립트

뉴토플 - TEST 11_Q3

Now listen to part of a lecture in a biology class.

이제 생물학 수업의 일부를 들어보세요.

예시 ❶
코알라의 장점

세부사항
유칼립투스를 두고 경쟁할 필요가 없음

Okay, the most evident example of species that is classified as a specialist is the koala. The koala has a limited diet, almost entirely depending on eucalyptus leaves for food. Eucalyptus leaves contain **large amounts of** oil which act as powerful **disinfectants** that can even be used for cleaning or as a natural **insecticide**. It can be toxic to animals when consumed in large amounts. Koalas are, however, very tolerant of it, which allows them to rely heavily on it. They do not need to fight over food because of this specialization. Because they have a secure and abundant food source, that they do not need to compete with other animals. By staying in the eucalyptus trees, Koalas can eat and sleep without much threat most of the time.

좋아요, 특화종으로 분류된 동물 중 가장 눈에 띄는 예는 코알라입니다. 코알라는 제한된 식성을 가지고 있어서 거의 전적으로 유칼립투스 잎에 의존합니다. 유칼립투스 잎은 청소할 때 자연 **살충제**로 쓰일 정도로 강한 **살균제** 역할을 하는 기름이 **다량** 함유되어 있습니다. 다량으로 섭취하면 동물들에게 독이 될 수 있습니다. 하지만 코알라는 내성이 강하여 그 잎에 의존해 살 수 있습니다. 이러한 특화성 때문에 먹이를 두고 싸울 이유가 없습니다. 다른 동물과 경쟁 안 해도 안전하고 풍부한 먹이가 공급됩니다. 유칼립투스 나무에 머무르며 코알라는 거의 대부분의 시간 동안 위협없이 먹고 자고 할 수 있습니다.

예시 ❷
코알라의 단점

세부사항
유칼립투스가 없으면 살지 못함

There is also a downside to this specialization in koalas. Because there are limited places that have large quantities of eucalyptus trees, they can only **thrive** in a narrow environmental range. As eucalyptus trees are most abundant in Australia, Koalas tend to thrive there. Consequently, once the eucalyptus trees' habitat is destroyed, or disturbed by ecological factors or human developments, they lose their only food source, which could threaten their survival. In fact, Koalas are classified as a threatened species for this reason.

코알라의 이러한 특화성에도 단점은 있습니다. 유칼립투스 나무가 많은 곳은 몇 군데 없기 때문에 좁은 환경 범위에서만 **번창할** 수 있습니다. 유칼립투스 나무는 호주에 가장 많아서, 코알라는 그곳에서 번창하는 경향이 있습니다. 결과적으로 유칼립투스 나무가 환경적인 요소나 인간의 개발로 파괴되거나 훼손된다면 그들이 유일한 식량원을 잃게 되고 생존의 위협을 받을 수 있습니다. 실제로 코알라는 이 이유 때문에 절멸 위기 종으로 분류됐습니다.

문제

Using the example from the professor's lecture, explain what specialist species are and their specialization.

교수의 강의를 예로 들어, 특화종 무엇인지 그리고 그들의 특화에 대해 설명하세요.

STEP 05 다시한번 음원듣고 노트테이킹 해보도록 하겠습니다.
Note-taking

STEP 06 다시 한번 뼈대와 함께 모범 답안을 작성해 보도록 하겠습니다.

Specialist Species

According to their **tolerability** of habitat, food, and other environment conditions, animals can be **distinguished** into two types: generalist or specialist species. Generalist species are animals which can thrive in many different environmental conditions due to their varied diets. Although they can adapt to **a wider range of** environments, they have more competition with other species. On the other hand, specialist species can only **prosper** in certain habitats due to their limited diets. Although they don't have to compete with others for food or habitat, they aren't able to prosper in many different environments.

USHER

References

Photo by Arnaud Gaillard, available under the Creative Commons Attribution-Share Alike 1.0 Generic license.

Photo by TTaylor, available under the Creative Commons Attribution-Share Alike 3.0 Unported, 2.5 Generic license.

[참고자료]

❶ 유칼립투스 잎을 먹고 있는 코알라
❷ 유칼립투스 숲

Task 3 Sample Response — 뉴토플 - TEST 11_R3   3번 문제 모범 답안

Specialist species are types of animals that live within a limited habitat range with a specific type of food. In the lecture, the proféssor gives an exámple of the koala to explain it.

❶ First, specialist species don't need to compéte with other species for food. Koalas spend most of their time in eucalýptus trees. These leaves can be toxic for other animals, but koalas are tolerant of it.

❷ Howéver, this specializátion can also limit the species' ability to survíve in new envíronments. If the number of eucalyptus trees in Austrália decreases, koalas have no places to live; their exístence would be in jéopardy.

특화종은 제한된 범위의 서식지에서 특정 음식만 먹는 동물입니다. 강의에서 교수는 코알라를 예로 들어 설명합니다.

❶ 첫째, 특화종은 다른 동물과 먹이를 두고 경쟁하지 않아도 됩니다. 코알라는 대부분의 시간을 유칼립투스 나무에서 지냅니다. 이 잎들은 다른 동물에겐 독이지만 코알라는 내성이 있습니다.

❷ 하지만 이 특화성은 새 환경에서 살아가는 능력을 제한합니다. 유칼립투스의 수가 줄면 코알라는 살 곳이 없어서 위험에 처하게 됩니다.

Vocabulary

tolerability [tàlərábíləti]	n. 참는 능력
a wide range of	phr. 광범위한
disinfectant [dìsinféktənt]	n. 살균제, 소독제
large amounts of	phr. 다량의
distinguish [distíŋgwiʃ]	v. 구별하다, 돋보이게 하다
prosper [práspər]	v. 번창하다
insecticide [inséktəsàid]	n. 살충제
thrive [θraiv]	v. 번영하다

04. Eco-Travel 생태관광　　　　Integrated Task

STEP 01 4번 뼈대를 먼저 작성해 보도록 하겠습니다.

STEP 02 하단에 리스닝 노트테이킹을 해주세요. 음원은 학원 홈페이지에서 무료로 다운받으실 수 있습니다. 또한 4011번 문제 번호로 문제를 풀어보실 수 있습니다.

STEP 03 뼈대에 맞춰서 모범 답안을 완성해 보겠습니다.

Listen to part of a lecture in an ecology class.

So, all of you have heard of eco-travel before, right? Well, eco-travel is a way of tourism that has started gaining popularity recently. It is generally defined as 'responsible travel to natural areas that **conserves the environment and improves the well-being of local people.**' So more and more people who are interested in saving the environment are starting to 'eco-travel' and **tourism agencies** are releasing various eco-travel packages. Overall, eco-travel **plays an important role** in improving the environment.

One aspect of eco-travel that helps the environment is reducing pollution. People try to do activities that minimize impact on the environment as much as they can during eco-travel. For example, when moving from one area to another, they would do so by walking, hiking, rafting, or riding animals such as horses or elephants instead of, say, riding buses or cars that **emit air pollutants**. They also do beneficial things for the environment as well such as planting trees or preserving the habitats of species. Some people directly provide financial benefits for the local people so that they can conserve their environment. So you can see that those who 'eco-travel' try as much as they can to reduce pollution and improve the nature of the eco-travel sites.

Well, another helpful aspect of eco-travel is **raising awareness** regarding environmental issues. It can educate the public with knowledge of biological and cultural diversity in the areas they visit. This causes the travelers to have more respect for the environment, culture, and people of the areas. So, those who 'eco-travel' know very well about what's good and what's not good for the environment so they can find other ways to protect it. What's more, these people are looking for **various measures** so the future generations can experience the aspects of the environment relatively untouched by human **intervention**.

Using the examples from the professor's lecture, explain how eco-travel helps the environment.

References

Photo by JKDs, available under the Creative Commons Attribution 2.0 Generic license.

[참고자료]

환경보호를 위해 자동차를 이용하지 않고 코끼리로 이동하는 관광객들.

생태관광은 Eco-tourism이라고도 한다.

Task 4 Sample Response 🎧 TEST 11_R4   4번 문제 모범 답안

In the lecture, the professor gives two examples of how eco-travel saves the environment. Eco-travel is traveling to natural areas and improving the quality of the indigenous peoples' lives.

❶ First, the travel improves the environment by reducing pollution. These people usually choose not to use automobiles to travel. They also plant trees and protect the natural habitats. Some even provide financial benefits for the locals.

❷ Next, eco-travel educates people about the natural surrounding world and other cultures, so they know what is good or bad for the environment. People also try to think of the next generation and protect the environment, so that they can enjoy the nature undamaged by humans.

강의에서 교수는 생태관광이 환경을 보호하는 두 가지 예를 들고 있다. 생태관광은 청정지역을 여행하고, 현지인의 삶의 질을 높이는 여행이다.

❶ 첫째, 생태관광은 공해를 줄임으로써 환경을 보호한다. 이 사람들은 보통 자리를 옮길 때 자동차를 타지 않는다. 나무를 심기도 하고, 서식지를 보호하기도 한다. 어떤 이들은 현지인을 위해 재정적 지원도 아끼지 않는다.

❷ 다음으로, 생태관광은 사람들에게 자연의 세계와 다른 문화에 대해 알려줌으로써 무엇이 환경에 좋고 나쁜지 알게 한다. 사람들은 손때가 묻지 않은 자연을 즐길 수 있도록, 다음 세대를 생각하고 환경을 보호한다.

Vocabulary

conserve [kənsə́ːrv]	v. 보존하다	tourism agency	phr. 여행사 (=travel agency)
play a role	phr. 역할을 하다	emit [imít]	v. 방사하다, 내뿜다
air pollutant	phr. 공기오염물질	raise awareness	phr. 경계선을 높이다
various measures	phr. 다양한 수단	intervention [ìntərvénʃən]	n. 개입, 간섭

USHER
iBT TOEFL
FINAL TEST SPEAKING
TEST 12

Independent Tasks

Task 1 - 모범 답안

Question 1   usherin.usher.co.kr > 시험리스트 > Speaking 시험리스트 > Task 1 > #1048

Integrated Tasks

Task 2 - Script / 해석 / 모범 답안

Question 2   usherin.usher.co.kr > 시험리스트 > Speaking 시험리스트 > Task 2 > #2012

Task 3 - Script / 해석 / 모범 답안

Question 3   usherin.usher.co.kr > 시험리스트 > Speaking 시험리스트 > Task 3 > #3012

Task 4 - Script / 해석 / 모범 답안

Question 4   usherin.usher.co.kr > 시험리스트 > Speaking 시험리스트 > Task 4 > #4012

자기평가표

1번 문제 유형은 학생들이 본인에 생각을 주제에 맞춰서 말 해야하는 시험입니다.
본인이 처음부터 끝까지 45초 동안 말해야하다 보니 학생들이 제일 어려워 하는 시험입니다.
하지만, 먼저 외우고 익힌후에 말하는것이 가능할수 있게 하겠습니다.
가장 기본이 되는 뼈대 입니다. 먼저 외우도록 합시다.

> if i were to answer the question, i would say
> there are many reasons why, but here is a couple
> first
> for example,
> second
> for instance
> that's why

다음은 2번 문제 유형입니다.
2번 문제는 리딩에 학교에 계획이 적혀있거나 학교가 변해야하는 방향에 대해서 학생들에 주장이 적혀있습니다.
리딩에서 빠르게 파악해야하는 것은 도대체 누가 무엇을 주장하는가 입니다.
45~50초에 리딩 지문이 나오고 난 다음에 리스닝으로 학생들에 대화가 나오는 문제입니다.
리스닝에서는 학생이 리딩 지문에 대한 본인에 좋고 나쁜지에 대한 의견을 얘기해줄겁니다.
이유 2가지와 예시 2가지를 꼭 말할 수 있어야 합니다.

이에 따라서 2번 스피킹 문제에 뼈대는

> The reading states that university (plans to) / (should)
> the (woman / man) in the conversation thinks it is a good / bad idea.
> He/she provides two reasons to support his / her opinion.
> first,
> Second,
> the woman / man thinks it's a great / horrible idea.

다음은 3번 문제 유형입니다.
3번 문제는 2번 문제 유형과 같이 리딩과 리스닝이 나오는 문제 입니다. 하지만, 이번에는 이전 문제와는 달리 매우 학술적인 내용이 들어 있습니다. 리딩에서는 교과서에 나올만한 주제 한개를 자세하게 다룹니다. 여기서 학생분들은 제목과 이에 대한 정의를 잘 받아적으셔야 합니다. 리스닝에서는 교수님이 리딩에 나온 내용으로 예시를 들어 줍니다.

> The article is about
> which the passage defines as
> The professor provides an example of
> first,
> Second,
> The example clearly illustrates

다음은 4번 문제 유형입니다.
4번 문제는 이전 문제와 달리 리스닝만 나오는 문제 유형입니다. 3번 문제에 나온 리딩 지문이 리스닝으로 변환되었다 라고 생각 하시면 됩니다. 그렇기에 3번 문제에 리스닝 내용보다 리딩 길이 만큼 깁니다.

> In the lecture, professor explains
> first,
> second,
> That's how the professor explain it.

USHER

01 Best Teachers 최고의 선생님 — Independent Task

QUESTION

 Do you agree or disagree with the following statement? Parents are the best teachers for their children. Use reasons and examples to support your answer.
(다음 주장에 동의하십니까 혹은 반대하십니까? 부모님들은 자식들에게 최고의 선생님이다. 이유와 예를 들어 답하세요.)

 브레인 스토밍 (아래에 놓여있는 12간지 내용들을 보고 어떤 것을 사용할 수 있을지 확인해보세요)
첫번째 이유 :
두번째 이유 :

 뼈대에 맞춰서 작성을 해봅시다.

_____
_____
_____
_____
_____
_____

아래 이미지는 학생들을 위한 만능 템플릿 12간지 입니다. 학생분들이 제일 먼저 암기해야하는 것이며, 본인 스스로 문장을 단기간 안에 못 만들거 같을 때에 도와주는 친구입니다. 가까이 두고 매일 외우세요.

Academic Courses
…because I think students should concentrate on academic courses.

Academic courses are the most important thing for students because good grades will help them get into good universities and, eventually, get great jobs.

As students get older, a good academic record is the only thing that actually matters.

This may sound a little far-fetched, but it's true, and for this reason, investing time in other activities is a waste of time.

Stay Healthy
It can be a great way to stay healthy. People join a cycling group through the internet. The members use bicycles to commute to work or school.

It is a great outdoor activity because people have a chance to work out while having fun.

Also, it is a great way to meet new people with similar interests. People nowadays do not have much chance to become close to each other.

However, there are numerous unique groups active on the internet, and this would not have been possible without the internet.

Follows your heart
Carpe diem, seize the days, and YOLO all stand for one thing. Do whatever your heart makes you do.

Life is too short to hesitate or do things to please others. It is essential to make yourself happy.

Actions speak louder than words. Whatever I do to make myself happy is better than sitting in a room thinking about it.

So I would just do it even if it means I am biting off something more than I can chew.

Stress
…if it can possibly be a way to relieve stress.

People nowadays are living a busy and hectic life, so they are under great stress, but a lot of them don't even realize they are stressed out.

Stress is known to be a major factor that keeps us from being healthy, and many people are suffering from various problems.

This is more serious than we think, so if it can ever be a way to relieve stress…

Money
…because it's the best way to save money. When it comes to spending money, every penny counts.

A thrifty spending habit is indispensable in our lives because little drops of water make the mighty ocean.

If we don't get used to working on a tight budget, we'll always be short on cash later.

A penny-pinching lifestyle will lead to financial stability, and it will give us peace of mind.

Saving Time
…because it's the best way to save time. There's an old saying, "Time is gold."

This proverb emphasizes the value of time, and this cannot be more true in modern society.

We're living a busy and hectic life, so saving time means we can do a lot more things later.

Many say that life is not fair, but everyone has twenty-four hours a day and seven days a week, so I would save time by…

Social Skills
Nowadays, people have smartphones with them all the time, and that information is no longer limited to elites.

Therefore, rather than learning, having social skills became the be-all and end-all to succeed rather than education.

Also, social skills are more than meet the eyes. To have social skills, one must also be able to read others like a book.

There will be times when one will truly need them.

Environment
because eventually, it can contribute to protecting the environment.

I think it's THE most important task for humanity because we cannot bring it back to life once it's too late.

Saving Earth all starts from seemingly insignificant actions.

Small actions from everyone bring about bigger changes, so I'm willing to participate.

Patience is virtue
Patience is a virtue. Saving time is indeed important, but waiting calmly is needed in this case.

There are times when one must wait patiently for things to go accordingly, and this is when time is the solution.

When going against the clock, they are more susceptible to making mistakes than taking some time.

In the long run, one will be glad that one has waited in this case.

Just because
I love it more than the given choices. Since I have so many great memory about it, It brings so many great reminiscences.

time flies whenever I am doing it, so how can I not choose it?

Also, not only do I love it, but I am also good at it. Everyone has talent, and it is like "a dime a dozen."

This was the inborn talent I had that I always surpassed everyone. Since a bird in the hand is worth two in the bush, I will choose it.

Politeness
It is important to maintain good relationships with other people because we never know what will happen in the future.

Decisions made by other people can affect others, and such decisions are usually based on personal and sentimental reasons.

So, people should not do anything that may offend or disturb others. It is also crucial to have a good reputation and get along well with others.

It Makes sense
It makes sense to choose it when considering many aspects such as time, money, and efficiency.

When people are considering between the given choices, they must consider many aspects economically.

They must choose the most efficient method because there are limits on what they have.

Also, one should think about it realistically and practically because they should not count chickens before they hatch.

So, down to Earth, people should choose it because it is the most economical

QUESTION

Do you agree or disagree with the following statement? Parents are the best teachers for their children. Use reasons and examples to support your answer.
(다음 주장에 동의하십니까 혹은 반대하십니까? 부모님들은 자식들에게 최고의 선생님이다. 이유와 예를 들어 답하세요.)

stay healthy와 follows your heart를 사용해서 뼈대에 맞춰서 모범답안을 만들어 봅시다.

saving time과 saving money를 사용해서 뼈대에 맞춰서 모범답안을 만들어 봅시다.

environment와 just because를 사용해서 뼈대에 맞춰서 모범답안을 만들어 봅시다.

academic courses와 stress를 사용해서 뼈대에 맞춰서 모범답안을 만들어 봅시다.

QUESTION

Do you agree or disagree with the following statement? Parents are the best teachers for their children. Use reasons and examples to support your answer.
(다음 주장에 동의하십니까 혹은 반대하십니까? 부모님들은 자식들에게 최고의 선생님이다. 이유와 예를 들어 답하세요.)

stay healthy와 follows your heart를 사용해서 뼈대에 맞춰서 모범답안을 만들어 봅시다.

If I were to answer the question, I would say they are the best teachers for children. There are many reasons why, but here is a couple.

stay healthy

First, teaching children can be a great way for parents to bond with their children. For example. Teaching children is a great activity because parents have a chance to bond while children are learning. Children and parents nowadays do not have much chance to become close to each other.

follows your heart

Second, children follow the steps of their parents. For instance, parents care about their children so they will do their best to be good role models. Actions speak louder than words. Whatever parents do to make children happy is better than sitting in a room doing nothing. That's why I think they are the best teachers for children.

environment와 just because를 사용해서 뼈대에 맞춰서 모범답안을 만들어 봅시다.

If I were to answer the question, I would agree with the topic. There are many reasons why, but here is a couple.

environment

First, whatever parents do can contribute to children. For example, children are the most important task for mankind. Raising children starts from seemingly insignificant actions.

just because

Second, children love their parents, so they follow what their parents do. for instance, I have so much great memory about my parents and my parents teaching me in many aspects. To make a long story short, time flies whenever I am with my parents. so how can I not choose it?
That's why I agree with the topic.

saving time과 saving money를 사용해서 뼈대에 맞춰서 모범답안을 만들어 봅시다.

If I were to answer the question, I would say they are not the best teachers for children. There are many reasons why, but here is a couple.

saving time

First, parents cannot enough time on children. For example, parents are living busy and hectic life. So, they should spend their time on something else. There's an old saying, "Time is gold." This proverb emphasizes the value of time, and this cannot be more true in modern society.

saving money

Second, parents should work instead of teaching children. For instance, When it comes to making money, every penny counts. Hard-working habit is indispensable in our lives because little drops of water make the mighty ocean. Working hard will lead to financial stability and it will give us peace of mind.
That's why I think they are not the best teachers for children

academic courses와 stress를 사용해서 뼈대에 맞춰서 모범답안을 만들어 봅시다.

If I were to answer the question, I would disagree with the topic. There are many reasons why, but here is a couple.

academic courses

First, parents do not know what they are learning in school. For example, students should learn from actual teachers to learn on academic courses. Academic courses are the most important thing for students because good grades will help them get into good universities and eventually, get great jobs.

stress

Second, learning from parents is too stressful for a student to learn. For instance, students nowadays are living a busy and hectic life, so they are under great stress, but a lot of them don't even realize they are stressed out. So learning from their parents will only make them even more stressed.
That's why I disagree with the topic.

02. Jazz Concert 재즈 콘서트　　Integrated Task

읽기 지문

Jazz Band Concert

The university has announced the plans of the newly formed jazz band. The jazz band was started just a few months ago and is having their very first concert. The players expressed their hope for an outdoor debut and thus, the university has reserved the lawn by the library for tomorrow night's concert. The music's harmony of **brass** instruments will sound beautifully, so if students are looking for a way to relax and relieve the stress of school life, this will be a perfect opportunity. They hope students enjoy the jazz concert with their fellow students.

대화 스크립트

 뼈대를 먼저 작성해 보도록 하겠습니다.

 작성하신 뼈대 빈칸에 맞춰서 리딩 지문을 읽고 주요 포인트를 넣어주세요.

 하단에 리스닝 노트테이킹을 해주세요. 음원은 학원 홈페이지에서 무료로 다운받으실 수 있습니다. 또한 2012번 문제 번호로 문제를 풀어보실 수 있습니다.

STEP 04 아래 하단에 리스닝 스크립트를 보고 베꼈어야 하는 부분을 찾아서 적어 보도록 하겠습니다.

대화 스크립트
뉴토플 - TEST 12_Q2

Now listen to two students discussing the announcement.

자, 이제 지문에 대해 논의하는 두 학생의 대화를 들어보세요.

W: Hey, are you going to go to the new jazz band's concert?

여: 야, 너 그 재즈 밴드 공연에 가?

남자의 의견
반대

M: I don't think so. I think it's a really bad idea.

남: 안 갈 것 같은데. 너무 안 좋은 생각 같아.

W: Why? It would be great to hear some live jazz.

여: 왜? 라이브 재즈를 들으면 좋을 것 같은데.

이유 ❶
콘서트에 갈 시간이 없음

M: Mm… maybe, but I don't think that many students are going to even go to the concert. I mean, students are pretty busy these days. There are just way too many assignments right now. With all the reports and papers being assigned by professors these days, who has extra time to just sit and listen to music?

남: 음, 근데 많은 학생들이 공연에 갈 것 같지도 않은데. 내 말은, 학생들이 요즘 되게 바쁘잖아. 교수님이 내주시는 레포트나 논문들 때문에 요즘 과제가 너무 많아. 누가 그냥 앉아서 음악 들을 시간이 있겠어?

W: Still, it's going to be an outdoor concert. How romantic, right?

여: 그래도, 야외 공연이잖아. 낭만이지 않아?

M: I guess, but definitely not good for the environment.

남: 응 그런데, 환경에는 안 좋지.

W: What do you mean? **How does** environment **come into the picture?**

여: 무슨 말이야? 이게 환경이랑은 무슨 상관이야?

이유 ❷
잔디를 파괴할 것임

M: Well, since the concert is going to be held on the lawn by the library, there are going to be lots of chairs set up, and possibly **a fair amount of** people attending, right?

남: 음, 공연이 도서관 옆 잔디밭에서 열리니까, 의자들도 많이 설치 될 것이고 아마 **꽤 많은** 사람들이 오겠지?

W: Right…

여: 그렇지…

M: Well, that means a lot of **trampling** on the grass. That is fatal for plants. With so many people stepping on the grass, including the performers, they will be killing a lot of grass. I just don't understand why they want to have an outdoor concert.

남: 음, 그 말은 잔디가 많이 **짓밟힐** 거라는 뜻이지. 그건 식물들한테 치명적이고. 연주자들을 포함해서 많은 사람들이 밟으면, 잔디를 많이 죽일 거야. 왜 야외공연을 하고 싶은지 이해가 안돼.

문제

The man expresses his opinion about the college's plan. State his opinion and explain the reasons he gives for holding that opinion.

남자는 대학의 계획에 대해 자신의 의견을 밝히고 있습니다. 그의 의견을 말하고, 그 의견을 고수하는 이유를 설명하세요.

STEP 05 Note-taking

STEP 06 다시한번 모범 답안을 작성해 보도록 하겠습니다

Jazz Band Concert

The university has announced the plans of the newly formed jazz band. The jazz band was started just a few months ago and is having their very first concert. The players expressed their hope for an outdoor debut and thus, the university has reserved the lawn by the library for tomorrow night's concert. The music's harmony of **brass** instruments will sound beautifully, so if students are looking for a way to relax and relieve the stress of school life, this will be a perfect opportunity. They hope students enjoy the jazz concert with their fellow students.

USHER

Note-taking	노트테이킹
Reading - open an outdoor jazz concert - to help students relax and have fun - will be held in the open lawn by the library **Man** - against **Reason ❶** - students don't have enough time to enjoy the concert - they are loaded with school work **Reason ❷** - the audience and chairs will trample the grass - it will damage the environment	**지문** - 재즈 야외 공연이 열릴 것 - 학생들이 쉬고 즐기는데 도움 - 도서관 옆 잔디밭에서 열림 **남자** - 반대 **이유 ❶** - 콘서트를 즐길 시간이 없음 - 과제가 너무 많음 **이유 ❷** - 관객들과 의자가 잔디를 밟을 것임 - 환경을 파괴함

Task 2 Sample Response 🎧 뉴토플 - TEST 12_R2 | 2번 문제 모범 답안

The two students are discússing the college's plan to open an outdoor jazz concert to help students reláx and have fun. The man is agáinst the plan for two reasons.

❶ First, most students don't have enóugh time to go to the concert and enjóy jazz music as they are pretty busy alréady. They are loaded with reports and papers from class.

❷ Second, becáuse the concert is held in the open lawn, many people are going to sit on chairs. The audience and their chairs would be trampling on the grass, which would kill a lot of it. This would damage the envíronment. (This is why he thinks the plan is unnécessary.)

두 학생은 학생들이 쉬고 즐길 수 있게 야외 재즈 공연을 열려는 대학 측의 계획에 대해서 의논 하고 있다. 남자는 두 가지 이유를 들어 그 계획에 반대하고 있다.

❶ 첫째, 대부분의 학생들은 이미 바쁘기 때문에 공연에 가서 재즈 음악을 즐길 시간이 없다. 그들은 써야 할 학교 레포트나 논문들이 너무 많다.

❷ 다음, 공연은 야외 잔디밭에서 열릴 것이기 때문에, 많은 사람들이 의자에 앉을 것이다. 관객들과 객석들은 잔디를 짓밟을 것이고 잔디를 파괴할 것이다. 이것은 환경을 손상시킬 것이다. (이것이 그가 이 계획이 필요하지 않다고 생각하는 이유이다.)

Vocabulary

brass [bræs, brɑːs]	n. 금관악기		**come into the picture**	phr. 등장하다
a fair amount of	phr. 상당한 양의		**trample** [træmpl]	v. 짓밟다

03. Test Customer 시험용 고객 — Integrated Task

읽기 지문

Test Customer

There are a variety of methods employers can use to evaluate their employees. They could assess them themselves, but the problem with this is that the evaluation could be slightly **biased.** Especially, if their employer was assessing them and the workers were aware of it, they would most likely be on their best behavior, making it hard to evaluate their true work quality. Thus, in order to fairly evaluate the level of service and work attitudes of employees, employers secretly hire outsiders and **disguise** them as customers - test customers to fairly assess employees with no prejudice.

대화 스크립트

STEP 01 뼈대를 먼저 작성해 보도록 하겠습니다.

STEP 02 작성하신 뼈대 빈칸에 맞춰서 리딩 지문을 읽고 주요 포인트를 넣어주세요.

STEP 03 하단에 리스닝 노트테이킹을 해주세요. 음원은 학원 홈페이지에서 무료로 다운받으실 수 있습니다. 또한 3012번 문제 번호로 문제를 풀어보실 수 있습니다.

USHER

아래 하단에 리스닝 스크립트를 보고 베꼈어야 하는 부분을 찾아서 적어 보도록 하겠습니다.

대화 스크립트

뉴토플 - TEST 12_Q3

Now listen to part of a lecture in a marketing class.

Okay, so there was this manager of a really big restaurant, who wanted to know how kind and polite his wait staff was to customers. So, he decided to evaluate them himself by walking around while his employees were serving customers.

예시 ❶
매니저가 직접 평가함

세부사항
직원들이 평소답지 않아 공정한 평가가 어려움

He discovered that this was **of no use** because his employees were aware that they were being watched by their manager so they acted kinder and more polite than they usually were. It's kind of like when you're taking a test and your eye meets your teacher's. What do you do? You **sit up** straighter and act like you're thinking really hard for the answer, right? The employees, in the same way, would **put on an act**, and obviously, this would not be a fair, or correct, evaluation. So, he decided to use a test customer.

예시 ❷
시험용 고객이 평가함

세부사항
자신이 평가되고 있다는 사실을 몰라 정확한 평가가 가능

The manager hired someone to be a customer at his restaurant. The test customer would act like a normal customer - ordering and eating - but **at the same time,** while evaluating the waiter or waitress. He would order food, ask various questions, and then **observe** them. Since he would be able to evaluate the employee without them knowing that they were being evaluated, the employees would act normally. After completing the evaluation, the test customer would then report back to the manager, and the manager would be able to get a true evaluation of his employees.

문제
Using the example from the professor's lecture, explain what test customer is and how it works.

이제 마케팅 수업의 일부를 들어보세요.

자신의 종업원들이 손님들에게 얼마나 친절하고 예의가 바른지를 알고 싶어하는 큰 레스토랑의 매니저가 있었습니다. 그래서, 그는 직원들이 손님을 모시는 동안 돌아다니면서 스스로 직원들을 평가하기로 결정했습니다.

그는 그의 직원들이 매니저에 의해 감시 당하고 있다는 것을 알고 있어서 평소보다 더 친절하고 예의 바르게 행동하기 때문에 이것이 아무 **소용이 없음**을 발견합니다. 이는 여러분이 시험을 보다가 선생님과 눈이 마주칠 때와 같은 경우입니다. 여러분은 어떻게 하죠? **똑바로 앉아서** 답을 열심히 생각하는 것처럼 행동합니다, 그렇죠? 같은 방식으로, 직원들은 **가식적으로 행동할** 것이고, 당연히 이는 공평하거나 정확한 평가가 되지 않을 것입니다. 그래서, 매니저는 시험용 고객을 쓰기로 합니다.

매니저는 그의 레스토랑의 손님이 될 어떤 사람을 고용합니다. 시험용 고객은 종업원들을 평가하는 **동시에** 주문하고 먹으면서 일반 손님처럼 연기를 합니다. 그는 음식을 주문하고, 여러 가지 질문을 하고 그들을 **관찰합니다**. 그는 직원들이 자신들이 평가되고 있다는 것을 모르는 사이에 그들을 평가할 수 있으므로, 직원들은 평소와 똑같이 행동할 것입니다. 평가를 마친 후, 시험용 고객은 매니저에게 보고를 하고, 매니저는 그의 직원들에 대한 정확한 평가를 할 수 있을 것입니다.

교수의 강의를 예로 들어, 시험용 고객이 무엇이고 어떻게 작용하는지 설명하세요.

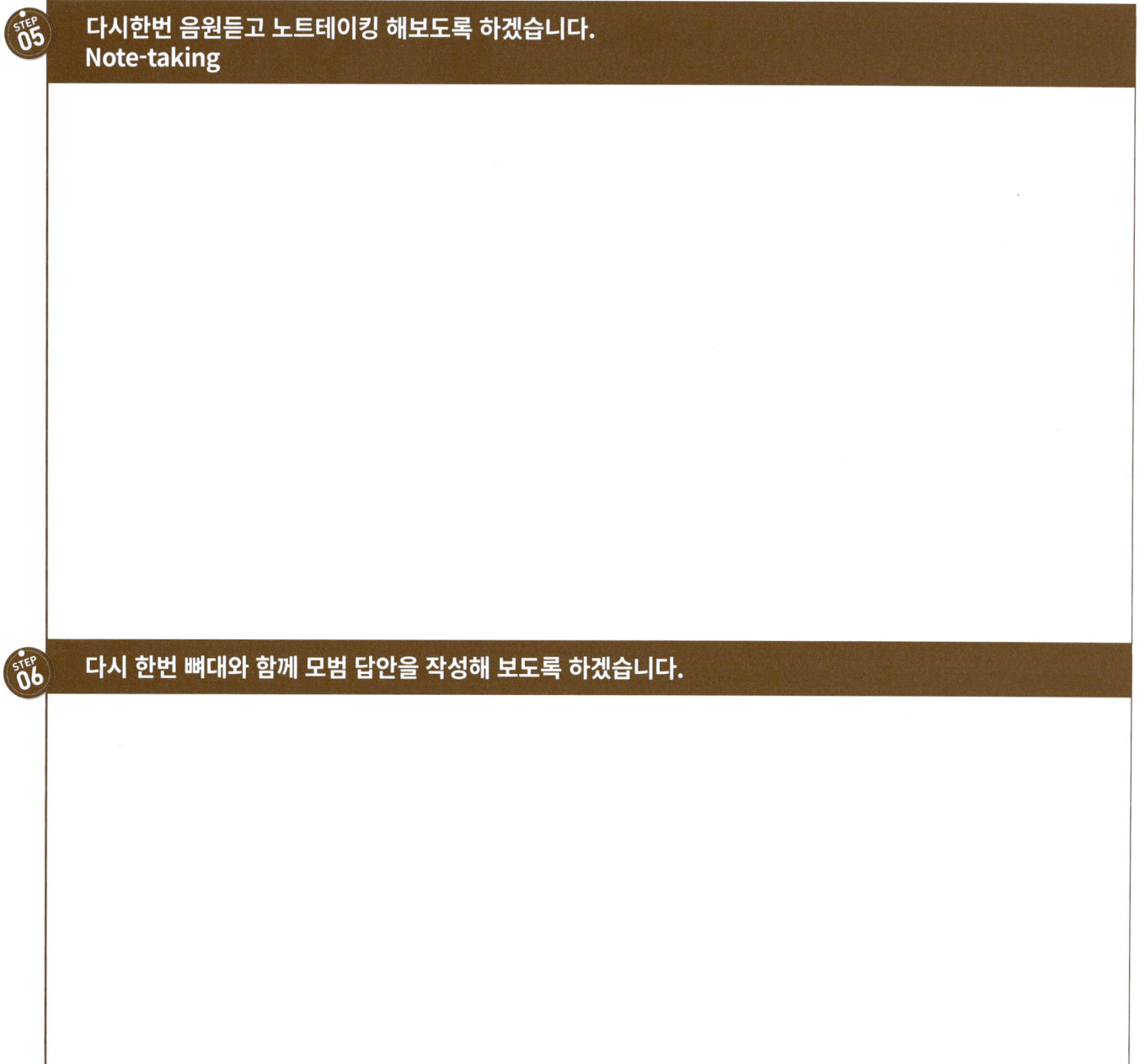

Test Customer

There are a variety of methods employers can use to evaluate their employees. They could assess them themselves, but the problem with this is that the evaluation could be slightly **biased.** Especially, if their employer was assessing them and the workers were aware of it, they would most likely be on their best behavior, making it hard to evaluate their true work quality. Thus, in order to fairly evaluate the level of service and work attitudes of employees, employers secretly hire outsiders and **disguise** them as customers - test customers to fairly assess employees with no prejudice.

References

[참고자료]

Photo by Alan Light, available under the Creative Commons Attribution 2.0 Generic license.

Task 3　Sample Response　🎧 뉴토플 - TEST 12_R3　　3번 문제 모범 답안

Test customers are people who are disguised as customers in order to fairly evaluate employees' performance without prejudice. The professor gives an example of a restaurant manager to explain what it is.

❶ The manager wanted to know how nice his wait staff was to customers. The problem was that the workers acted differently when they saw him nearby, so he had to find another way to evaluate them.

❷ He decided to hire someone to act like a customer. The test customer acted naturally but asked questions and watched the workers carefully. Afterwards, he told the manager how good the employees were.

시험용 고객은 직원들의 성과를 편견 없이 공정하게 평가하기 위해 손님으로 가장한 사람들입니다. 교수는 이를 설명하려고 레스토랑의 매니저를 예로 듭니다.

❶ 매니저는 그의 종업원들이 손님들에게 얼마나 친절한지에 대해 알고 싶어했습니다. 문제는 그가 주변에 있으면 직원들이 다르게 행동하여 그는 그들을 평가할 다른 사람을 찾아야 했습니다.

❷ 그는 손님처럼 행동할 사람을 고용하기로 결정했습니다. 시험용 고객은 자연스럽게 연기하면서 질문을 하고 그들을 주의 깊게 관찰했습니다. 후에 그는 매니저에게 직원들이 얼마나 잘했는지 말해줬습니다.

Vocabulary

biased [báiəst]	a. 편향된	disguise [disgáiz]	v. 변장시키다
of no use	phr. 쓸모없는 (= useless)	sit up	phr. 바로 앉다
at the same time	phr. 동시에 (= simultaneously)	observe [əbzə́ːrv]	v. 관찰하다
put on an act	phr. 가식적으로 행동하다, 연기하다		

04. Intrinsic vs Extrinsic Factors
내재적 vs 외적 요소

Integrated Task

STEP 01
4번 뼈대를 먼저 작성해 보도록 하겠습니다.

STEP 02
하단에 리스닝 노트테이킹을 해주세요. 음원은 학원 홈페이지에서 무료로 다운받으실 수 있습니다. 또한 4012번 문제 번호로 문제를 풀어보실 수 있습니다.

STEP 03
뼈대에 맞춰서 모범 답안을 완성해 보겠습니다.

대화 스크립트

Listen to part of a lecture in a marketing class.

In recent years, marketers have learned many interesting facts about what makes people, or more specifically, consumers, choose a certain product over another. Although there are numerous things people consider before they decide to open their wallets, they are mainly divided into two categories, and we call these categories information cues. So, in other words, when consumers judge certain products, there are two types of information cues: the intrinsic factor and the extrinsic factor.

So, "what is this intrinsic factor?" you may ask. The intrinsic factor **constitutes** the aspects of the product which are used to determine its **perceived** quality and the level of satisfaction the consumer feels after using the product. For example, consumers assume the quality of fruit juice **on the basis of** its color, freshness, and contents. If the consumers approve of the expected quality of the juice, they will purchase it and taste it and go through a second evaluation to **assess** the experienced quality. This evaluation will be used in further purchases depending on how the experienced quality compares to the expected. Well, one thing to remember is that, um, most of the time, the experienced quality matches the expected quality.

The second factor is the extrinsic factor, and this is where most marketers try to lure the consumers. The extrinsic factor deals with the reputation of the product, which is affected by its price and presentation. Additionally, **promotions** and reputation of the brand or recommendation by others act as product-related cues. In the fruit juice example, this would be the packaging. Consumers would buy the fruit juice in fancy bottles because they assume the one in pretty bottles to be of better quality. What's interesting to note is that, um, in this case, there is no definite **correlation** between the expected quality and the experienced quality of a product.

주제
물건을 살 때
고려하는
두 가지 요소

예시 ❶
내재적 요소
(색깔, 신선도,
내용물 등)

세부사항
기대치와 만족도의
관련성이 높음

예시 ❷
외적 요소
(포장, 홍보, 상표
이미지 등)

세부사항
기대치와 만족도가
관련성이 낮음

문제
Using the examples from the professor's lecture, explain the two factors consumers consider when purchasing products.

마케팅 강의의 일부를 들어보세요.

요즘 마케터들은, 사람들, 특히 소비자들이 어떤 점 때문에 물건을 사는지에 대한 여러 흥미로운 사실들을 배워왔습니다. 상품을 선택하는 데에 여러 가지 요소들이 있겠지만, 가장 중요한 것은 두 가지 종류로 나뉘는데, 이를 정보 인식 단서라고 합니다. 그래서, 다시 말하자면, 소비자들이 상품을 판단할 때에는 두 가지 정보인식 단서: 내재적 요소와 외적 요소가 있습니다.

"내재적 요소가 무엇인가요?"라고 물을 수 있습니다. 내재적 요소란, **파악된** 제품의 품질과, 구매 후 만족도를 **포함합니다**. 예를 들어, 소비자들은 과일 주스의 질을 색, 신선도 그리고 내용물을 **기초로** 판단합니다. 만약, 소비자가 생각한 것과 비슷한 품질이라 일단 평가되면, 사서 맛을 보면서, 경험한 품질을 **판단하기** 위해 두 번째 평가를 내립니다. 이 평가는 기대치와 만족도에 따라, 이후의 상품 구입 여부를 결정합니다. 음, 한가지 기억해야 할 것은 대체로 기대치와 만족도가 맞아 떨어진다는 것입니다.

두 번째 요소는 외적 요소이며 마케터는 이를 이용해 소비자를 끌어들이려 합니다. 외적 요소는 상품의 가격과 포장의 영향을 받는 이미지와 관련 있습니다. 추가적으로, 홍보와 상표의 이미지 또는 다른 사람의 추천 등은, 상품과 관련된 정보라고 할 수 있습니다. 과일 음료를 다시 예로 들자면, 이 요소는 포장이 되겠습니다. 소비자들은 화려한 병에 담긴 과일음료를 살 텐데, 이는 소비자들이 좋은 병에 담기면, 그 품질도 좋을 것이라고 생각하기 때문입니다. 여기서 흥미로운 점은, 음, 제품에 대한 기대한 품질과 경험한 품질 사이에 뚜렷한 **연관성**이 없다는 것입니다.

교수의 강의를 예로 들어, 소비자가 제품을 살 때 고려하는 두 요소를 설명하세요.

References

Photo by Sting

[참고자료]

제품의 구입을 결정하는 데는 외적 요소보다 내재적 요소가 더 중요하다.

정보인식 단서 (information cues)
어떤 결정을 내리도록 유도하는 정보

Task 4 Sample Response  TEST 12_R4   4번 문제 모범 답안

In the lecture, the proféssor expláins the two factors consumers look at when they decide to purchase products. There are intrinsic and extrinsic factors.

❶ Intrinsic factors refer to obsérved quality and the level satisfáction afterwards. For exámple, a consúmer would closely examine the color and content of fruit juice befóre the purchase. If he/she is happy with the taste, the consúmer will buy the juice again.

❷ Extrinsic factors refér to other elements such as the reputátion, price and presentátion. Consumers would choose fruit juice in fancy bottles becáuse they assúme it would taste better. In this case, the expérienced quality isn't necessárily related to the expécted quality.

강의에서 교수는 상품을 사기전에 고려하는 두 요소에 대하여 설명하고 있습니다. 내재적 요소와 외적 요소가 있습니다.

❶ 내재적 요소는 보이는 품질과, 구입 후 만족도에 관한 것입니다. 예를 들어, 소비자는 주스를 사기 전에 색과 내용물을 살펴봅니다. 만약, 맛에 만족하면 다시 살 것입니다.

❷ 외적 요소는 상표의 이미지와, 가격, 그리고 포장에 관련 있습니다. 소비자는 더 맛있을 것이라 생각해서, 예쁜 병에 담긴 주스를 선택합니다. 이 경우, 경험한 품질은 기대치와 직접적 연관이 없습니다.

Vocabulary

constitute [kánstətjù:t]	v. 구성하다	perceive [pərsí:v]	v. 지각하다, 이해하다
on the basis of	phr. ~을 기초로 하여	assess [əsés]	v. 평가하다
promotion [prəmóuʃən]	n. 승진, 촉진, 판촉	correlation [kɔ̀:rəléiʃən, kɑ̀r-]	n. 상관 관계

USHER
iBT TOEFL
FINAL TEST SPEAKING
출제 예상문제 리스트

Independent Tasks
Task 1 - Universal

Integrated Tasks
Task 2
Task 3
Task 4

USHER 어셔어학원

Independent Task > Task 1 > 선택 말하기

Speaking about familiar topics - 익숙한 주제에 대해 말하기

- 주어진 문제에 동의 / 반대하거나, 2개의 선택 중 하나를 골라 그 이유를 서술하는 방식입니다.
- 답 → 이유 1 → 이유 2의 순으로 답하는 것이 가장 이상적입니다.

Universal

지난 5년간 출제된 모든 문제들을 빠트리지 않고 모두 분석하였습니다. 그 결과, 대부분의 문제들을 몇개의 비슷한 내용 - 이를 앞으로 만능 답안이라 합시다 - 으로 답할 수 있다는 사실을 발견하였으며, 외워야 할 만능 답안의 수를 최소화하여, 학생들의 수고를 덜었습니다.

※ usherin에 접속하셔서 아래 네자리 번호를 입력하시면 인터넷에서 실전처럼 연습하실 수 있습니다.
(usherin.usher.co.kr > 시험리스트 > Speaking 시험리스트)

Task 1

1001	여름방학 보내기: 공부하기 vs 일하기
1002	노인들이 대학에 가는 것에 대한 당신의 생각은?
1003	동의/반대: 언젠가 모든 신문과 책들은 전자화 될 것이다.
1004	찬성/반대: 당신이 교실에서 배운 것은 중요하다.
1005	동의/반대: 성적이 좋았던 학생들만 대학 교육을 받아야 한다.
1006	동의/반대: 휴대폰은 항상 갖고 다녀야 한다.
1007	동의/반대: 당신 조상의 역사에 대해 배우는 것은 필수이다.
1008	경험있는 선생님 vs 새내기 선생님
1009	예술가에게 더 중요한 것: 타고난 재능 vs 노력
1010	여행하기에 더 좋은 것: 자동차 vs 일반 교통수단
1011	자유시간: 계획대로 보내기 vs 계획없이 보내기
1012	대도시에 있는 대학교 vs 당신 동네에 있는 대학교
1013	계획된 쇼핑 vs 충동적인 쇼핑
1014	동의/반대: 아이들은 부모들에게 골칫거리이다.
1015	장보기: 작은 슈퍼마켓 vs 대형 슈퍼마켓
1016	단체로 일할 때: 단체의 리더 vs 단체의 일원

USHER

Task 1

1017	동의/반대: 아이들의 대학 진학에 부모가 관여해야 한다.
1018	개인 스포츠 vs 팀 스포츠
1019	한꺼번에 몰아서 해결하기 vs 따로따로 해결하기
1020	동의/반대: 옷을 차려입고 멋을 지키는 것은 중요하다.
1021	동의/반대: 요즘 사람들은 과거의 사람들보다 건강하다.
1022	동의/반대: 현재에 집중하는 것보다 미래를 대비하는 게 중요하다.
1023	아이들에게 불량식품과 초코바를 광고하는 것은 금지되어야 한다.
1024	대학에서: 길지만 평이한 과목 vs 짧지만 집중적인 과목
1025	동의/반대: 모든 아이들은 16살이 될 때까지 학교를 다녀야 한다.
1026	해외 유학생: 혼자 지내기 vs 현지 가족과 함께 지내기
1027	아이들을 위해: 견학가기 vs 교실에서 공부하기
1028	친구를 위해: 선물을 구입하기 vs 의미있는 것 만들기
1029	공공장소에서 공부하기 vs 인적이 드문 곳에서 공부하기
1030	복잡한 과제물: 아침 일찍 하기 vs 저녁 늦게 하기
1031	여행 후에 사진과 일지 정리하기 vs 정리하지 않기
1032	동의/반대: 아이들이 직업을 고를 때 부모가 관여해야 한다.
1033	어디가 더 좋은가: 기후 변화가 있는 곳 vs 기후 변화가 없는 곳
1034	미래의 직업 고르기: 대학 입학 전 vs 대학 입학 후
1035	같은 생각을 가진 친구 vs 다른 생각을 가진 친구
1036	대학에서 과목 고르기: 쉬운 과목 vs 어려운 과목
1037	동의/반대: 아이들에게 휴대폰이 필요한가?
1038	음악 들으면서 공부하기 vs 조용히 공부하기
1039	과거의 인물로부터 배우기 vs 현재의 인물로부터 배우기
1040	동의/반대: 아이들이 집안일 할 때 돈을 받아야 한다.
1041	혼자 공부하기 vs 함께 공부하기
1042	집에서 공부하기 vs 도서관에서 공부하기

Task 1

1043	한 곳에서 오래 여행하기 vs 여러 군데서 잠깐씩 여행하기
1044	연봉이 높은 직업 vs 만족도가 높은 직업
1045	동의/반대: 요즘 학생들은 과거보다 열심히 공부해야 한다.
1046	동의/반대: 사람들은 자기 조상의 역사를 배워야 한다.
1047	동의/반대: 학생들은 경쟁이 아닌 재미로 스포츠를 해야 한다.
1048	동의/반대: 부모님이 그 아이들에게 최고의 스승이다.
1049	동의/반대: 부수고 새 건물을 짓기보다 오래된 건물을 보존하는게 낫다.
1050	긴 레포트 쓰기 vs 사람들 앞에서 발표하기
1051	대학 과목: 다양한 과목 듣기 vs 정해진 일부 과목 듣기
1052	돈 빌려서 구입하기 vs 돈 모아서 나중에 구입하기
1053	할아버지 세대의 충고 vs 같은 또래의 충고
1054	동의/반대: 집에서 TV로 스포츠 중계를 보는 것은 시간 낭비다.
1055	동의/반대: 40~50년 전보다 건강에 좋은 음식을 먹기가 쉬워졌다.
1056	동의/반대: 종이로 된 책이 전자책보다 더 낫다.
1057	여러 개의 짧은 과제물 vs 한 두개의 긴 과제물
1058	Do you agree or disagree with the following statement? Students learn more by participating in class discussions. Use reasons and examples to support your answer.
1059	Do you agree or disagree with the following statement? Video and computer games have a bad influence on children. Use reasons and examples to support your answer.
1060	Some people prefer to live in one place. Others prefer to live in different places. What do you prefer to do? Use reasons and examples to support your answer.
1061	Some people prefer to exercise in groups and others prefer to work out alone. Which do you prefer and why? Use specific reasons and examples to support your answer.
1062	Do you think it is better to do many things at the same time or focus and do one thing at a time? Explain your answer and include details and examples to support your explanation.
1063	Do you like to have your birthday party with a lot of people or with a few close friends? Use specific reasons and examples in your explanation.
1064	Some people believe that our personalities change as we grow older. Others think that our personalities stay the same from childhood. Which view do you agree with and why? Use specific reasons and examples in your explanation.
1065	Do you agree or disagree with the following statement? The most important characteristic of a successful school is having teachers with many years of teaching experience.

USHER

1066　Do you agree or disagree with the following statement? Students who submitted their work after the deadline should be graded differently.

1067　Do you agree or disagree with the following statement? Science, art, and history classes should not be held in museums.

1068　Some people say college students should join extracurricular activities in their first year. Others say that they should join after waiting for a semester or two. Which view do you agree with?

1069　Some people say that hard work is the most important for a successful career. Others say that good social skills are more important. Which view do you agree with?

1070　If you are given an assignment, would you prefer to write a long report or give a speech?

1071　동의: 대도시들은 중심가에서의 자가용 승용차의 주차를 금지해야 한다.

1072　동의: 대학교들에게는 학문적 명성이 가장 중요한 요소이다.

1073　동의: 재능은 성공이나 실패를 결정하지 않는다.

1074　선호: 오래된 물건 모으기 or 다 쓰고 나면 버리기

1075　동의: non-fiction을 읽는 것보다 fiction을 읽는 게 학생들에게는 더 즐겁다.

1076　선호: 정보를 직접 모으기 or 선생님들에게 충고를 구하기

1077　선호: 대학 1학년부터 과외활동 참여하기 or 한 두 학기 기다렸다 참여하기

1078　동의: 마감일이 지나서 과제를 제출한 학생들은 다르게 채점돼야 한다.

1079　동의: 대학교 도서관에 있는 책들은 전자책(e-book)으로 대체되어야 한다.

1080　동의: 성공하기 위해서는 대학교에 진학해야 한다.

1081　선호: 미래에도 자전거는 인기가 많을 것이다 or 사라질 것이다.

1082　선호: 멸종위기의 동물을 정부가 보호해야 한다 or 개인이 보호해야 한다.

1083　동의: 과학, 미술, 그리고 역사수업을 박물관에서 하면 안 된다.

1084　동의: 학생들은 자기 친구들과 같은 반에 있을 때 더 잘 배운다.

1085　선호: 도서관은 큰 동네의 공원에 지어야 한다 or 동네 가까이에 지어야 한다.

1086　동의: 초등학교에서는 아이들에게 손 글씨 대신 타이핑을 가르쳐야 한다.

1087　선호: 학교나 직장에서는 멀지만 크고 깨끗한 집 or 가깝지만 작고 오래된 집

1088　선호: 이메일을 써서 연락하기 or 전화기를 써서 연락하기

1089　선호: 성공하려면 열심히 일해야 한다 or 좋은 사회성을 갖고 있어야 한다.

1090　선호: 아침 일찍 수업을 듣는 것 or 오후 늦게 수업을 듣는 것

1091　선호: 재미를 위해 들을 수업으로는 미술이 낫다 or 과학이 낫다.

1092	선호: 직업을 고르는데 더 중요한 요소는 연봉이다 or 만족감이다.
1093	선호: 출장이 잦고 연봉이 높은 직업 or 출장이 적고 연봉이 낮은 직업
1094	동의: 미래에는 로봇이 인간을 대체할 것이다.
1095	선호: 카드게임을 더 좋아하느냐 or 컴퓨터 게임을 더 좋아하느냐
1096	선호: 활동에 혼자 참여하기 or 팀이나 그룹으로 참여하기
1097	선호: 큰 대도시에서 살기 or 조용하고 작은 소도시에서 살기
1098	Do you like to make a plan with friends about social activities in advance or plan it when you attend it?
1099	Do you agree or disagree with the following statement? Current celebrities (like musicians, actors/actresses, and athletes) set a good example as role models to the young people.
1100	Do you agree or disagree that experienced teachers are a deciding factor in the success of a school?
1101	Which would you prefer: doing exercise everyday or only when you are free?
1102	Do you agree or disagree that it is important for young people to learn some domestic skills like cooking, sewing and taking care of children?
1103	Some students choose to enter the university immediately after finishing high school, others prefer taking time off before beginning the university class. Which option do you think is better? Explain why.
1104	There are two invitations. One is from a party with your friends, and the other is from having a dinner party with your parents. Which one would you prefer and why?
1105	"Do you agree or disagree with the following statement? Schools need to encourage students to be more creative and use imagination to be a successful person."
1106	Do you agree or disagree with the following statement: It is more important to maintain relationship with family members than with friends.
1107	Some people get to know a person by the first observation while others prefer to get to know a person by long time observation. Which one do you prefer and explain why.
1108	Do you think it is a good idea for parents to give kids monetary rewards if they have good grades in school? Please include details and examples in your explanation.
1109	Do you agree or disagree the following statement? Older doctors are more knowledgeable than young doctors? Use specific details and examples to explain why.
1110	Do you agree or disagree with the following statement? If you want to succeed in business, being outgoing and friendly is very important.
1111	Do you agree or disagree with the following statement? Students learn more when teachers assign a lot of homework. Use specific details and examples to explain why.
1112	Do you agree or disagree with the following statement? A boss or a manager should not form close friendships with their employees. Use reasons and examples to support your opinion.

USHER

1113. Do you agree or disagree with the following statement? Government should not allow violence and bad language in television programs.

1114. Do you agree or disagree with the following statement? It is easier to be an adult than it is to be a child.

1115. Some people prefer to solve a challenge all by themselves. Others prefer to depend on other people's help. Which do you prefer and why? Include details and examples in your explanation.

1116. When students have questions about an assignment for class, some prefer to ask their professors for help, others would rather ask fellow students. Which do you prefer?

1117. When you are watching movies, do you prefer to discuss with others to enjoy the movie quietly on your own? Explain your reasons with details.

1118. Some people prefer to have their schedules fully and specifically arranged. Some people however, prefer to leave themselves a lot of free time. Which do you prefer and why?

1119. Do you agree or disagree with the following statement? Building zoos helps to protect animals. Please give your answer with specific examples and details.

1120. Do you prefer a big family or a small family? Please give your answer with specific examples and details.

1121. Do you agree or disagree with the statement? Employees should be allowed to listen to music at work.

1122. Some people prefer jobs working with computers or other technology, others like jobs working with no such technology. Which do you think is better and why?

1123. Some people prefer to wash dishes with a dishwasher. Others prefer to wash dishes by hand. Which do you prefer and why?

1124. The university plans to turn a long summer holiday into several short holidays. Do you think it's a good idea?

1125. Do you agree or disagree with the following statement? Some people think the stories of famous people on TV have no relevance to ordinary people.

1126. Some people think in the future students will have classes on the internet, but some think students will still have class in traditional classroom buildings. What is your opinion and why?

1127. Some people prefer to live in a traditional building. Others prefer modern ones. Which one do you prefer and why? Please give specific reasons and examples to support your idea.

1128. Do you agree or disagree with the following statement? People should always wear fashionable clothes. Please use specific reasons and examples to support your answer.

1129. Do you agree or disagree with the following statement? Students should do some part-time jobs before they attend college. Please use specific reasons and examples to support your answer.

1130. Some people like to get advice from parents or grandparents, while some people like to get help from their peers. Which do you prefer and why? Please include specific reasons and examples to support your answer.

1131. Some people prefer to make detailed plans for the future. Others prefer to concentrate on present things and don't make any plans at all. Which way do you prefer? Please use specific reasons to support your answer.

1132. Do you agree or disagree with the following statement? Playing computer games or video games is a waste of teenagers' time. Please use specific reasons and examples to support your answer.

1133	Some students take notes very often during class. Other students do not take notes or rarely take notes. Which do you think is better? Please explain with details.
1134	Which shop do you prefer, large department stores or small boutiques? Please give your answer with specific examples and details.
1135	Which do you prefer? A job in a distant city with a high salary, or a job in your current city with a lower salary.
1136	Do you think the government should spend funding to save the animals on the verge of extinction, or should the money come from private sources? Please give your opinion and explanation using specific examples and details
1137	Some people prefer to sit in the front of a classroom during a lecture; others prefer to sit in the back during a lecture. Which do you think is better? Explain your response in details and examples.
1138	Some people think that students should do part-time jobs. Other people think that students should focus on their studies without doing part-time jobs. What is your opinion and why?
1139	Do you agree or disagree with the statement that parents are the best teachers for children? Give specific reasons and details in your response.
1140	Do you agree or disagree with the following statement? It is a good thing to have classes with your best friend. Use examples and details in your response.
1141	Some people prefer to watch movies in theaters, others prefer to watch movies at home. Which one do you prefer? Explain your answer in detail.
1142	Some people prefer to watch a sports game from the audience seat, others prefer to be in the sports field and compete with others. Which do you prefer to do?
1143	Should universities use their funds in entertaining students or spending on academics?
1144	Should children learn how to draw and paint?
1145	Should students participate in club activities or concentrate on academics?
1146	Do you agree or disagree with the following statement? All children should be required to attend school until the age of 16.
1147	Do you prefer traveling alone or traveling with family or friends?
1148	Grading factors: from classroom discussion or from homework?
1149	Better for students: smaller class or larger class?
1150	Do you agree or disagree with the following statement? Teachers should let students participate in class discussions.
1151	Do you agree or disagree with the following statement? Advertisements have too much influence on people's decisions.
1152	Do you agree or disagree with the following statement? It is not good for your health to eat fast food frequently.
1153	Do you agree or disagree with the following statement? People nowadays are healthier than the people from the past.
1154	Do you prefer prepared food or preparing food yourself?
1155	Which is more important for athletes: physical ability or effort?
1156	On a friend's birthday, do you prefer purchasing a gift or making something meaningful yourself?

1157	While traveling, do you prefer staying in one place for a long time or staying in several places for a short time?
1158	Do you agree or disagree with the following statement? How people dress reflects their personalities.
1159	Is spending time on watching television good or bad?
1160	Do you prefer watching documentaries or entertainment programs?
1161	Do you prefer to travel to new places or to places you've been to before?
1162	Do you agree or disagree with the following statement? Parents should not let children choose jobs (such as an athlete or an artist) which are difficult to become successful.
1163	When discussing an assignment with the professor, which one do you prefer: face to face or in written form?
1164	Which one would you prefer? Go to a college in your hometown or go to a university in a new town?
1165	In order to teach young people about good nutrition and health, your school is planning to require students to take cooking classes in addition to other subjects. Do you think this requirement is a good idea? Why or why not?
1166	Do you agree or disagree with the following statement? College education should be available only to those who were good students. Use reasons and examples to support your answer.
1167	What is your opinion on having a part-time job while attending university? Use reasons and examples to support your answer.
1168	Some students like to take university classes that meet early in the morning. Others prefer classes that start later in the day. Which type of class schedule do you prefer, and why?
1169	Do you agree or disagree with the following statement? The more money people have, the more they should give away to charity.
1170	Some managers tend to check workers' tasks closely or frequently, while others tend to check them rarely or casually. Which is better for the management?
1171	Do you think the boss should supervise his employee when they are working, or give his employee more freedom in work?
1172	Children should listen to or read news at an early age. Do you agree or disagree with such a statement? Give your specific explanation in your response.
1173	Your city is about to build a new factory to provide more job opportunities for citizens; however, the factory might lead to environmental pollution to some extent. Do you agree or disagree with building such a new factory?
1174	Do you agree or disagree that in the future, people will read fewer books than they do today?
1175	Do you agree or disagree with the following statement? Business conferences should meet in person instead of using video calls.
1176	Do you agree or disagree with the following statement? Schools should not allow young students to use calculators during exams. Use reasons and examples to support your answer.
1177	Should students be required to evaluate their professors at the end of the semester?
1178	Do you agree or disagree with the following statement: Universities should require every graduating student to take public speaking courses. Give specific examples and details to support your answer.

1179	Some people think that success is most important in their life. Others think that it is more important to be happy when they fail. Who do you agree with and why?
1180	Do you agree or disagree with the statement? Students should be allowed to take snacks and beverages into classrooms.
1181	Students aged 13-18 are taught different subjects by different teachers while younger students are taught by only one teacher all day long. Some people suggest it would benefit young students to be taught by different teachers. Do you agree with this view? Why or why not?
1182	Some schools decide to cancel winter and summer breaks so that children can stay in school all year round. Do you think this is a good idea or not?
1183	Your friend is moving to a new city, and he's nervous about making new friends. What advice would you give your friend about how to make friends in the new city?
1184	What are the advantages of having cooking classes? Use reasons to support your answer.
1185	More and more people are buying items on the internet and from magazines or catalogs. Other people prefer shopping in a store. Which do you prefer, and why?
1186	Do you prefer eating at home or eating outside?
1187	Some people believe that bicycles will remain popular in the future. Others believe bicycles will disappear in the future. Which view do you agree with? Use reasons to support your answer.

Independent Task > Task 2 > 읽고 듣고 말하기 > 대학 생활

Speaking about campus situations - 캠퍼스 상황에 대해 말하기

읽 기 지 문	강 의
제안 학과에 대한 정보는 웹사이트에 이미 있고 시간 잡기가 힘드니 학생과 상담자가 만날 필요가 없다.	**X 반대** 이유 1. 웹사이트의 정보는 한정되어있으나 상담자는 전문가이다. 이유 2. 여유를 두고 약속 날짜를 잡으면, 스케줄을 맞추는데 문제가 없다.
공지 대학 공유지에서 운동하는 것을 금한다.	**O 찬성** 이유 1. 운동을 하면 잔디가 죽는다. 푸른 잔디 운동장이 보고 싶으므로 축구는 다른 곳에서 하겠다. 이유 2. 운동을 하면 시끄러워서 공부에 집중할 수 없다.
제안 국제학부에서 학생에게 자금을 제공하여 해외로 국제문화 인턴쉽을 보내준다.	**X 반대** 이유 1. 우리 도시에도 외국 사업을 주최하는 기업이 많아 해외로 갈 필요가 없다. 언니도 그런 곳에서 일했다. 이유 2. 국제학부가 그 비용을 대기 위해 다른 자금을 줄여야 한다.
공지 다음 학기부터 영문학과 졸업반은 독립적 연구에 기초하여 최종 학년 논문을 써야 한다.	**O 찬성** 이유 1. 전공을 깊게 공부하는데 효과적일 것이다. 그 동안 짧은 에세이만 썼는데, 취약점을 보완해준다. 이유 2. 졸업 논문을 쓰면 효율적이고 실질적인 언급을 받을 수 있어서 실력이 향상될 것이다.
공지 기말고사 기간에 도서관내 교내 식당의 마감시간이 8시에서 새벽 1시까지 연장된다.	**O 찬성** 이유 1. 집에서 음식을 준비해오지 않아도 된다. 절약한 시간을 시험 공부에 쓸 수 있다. 이유 2. 밤에는 도서관 밖으로 나가야만 했는데, 이제는 친구들과 함께 그룹 스터디를 할 수 있다.
공지 필기를 쉽게 할 수 있고 인터넷으로 좋은 예를 찾을 수 있으므로 노트북을 수업에 가져오게 한다.	**X 반대** 이유 1. 대부분 노트북으로 웹 서핑이나 게임을 하기 때문에 집중력이 떨어진다. 이유 2. 모든 학생이 노트북을 가지고 있는게 아니라서, 그런 학생들은 웹에 접근 할 수 없다.
공지 심리학과에서 학생들의 우수 논문을 모은 잡지를 새로 출간한다.	**O 찬성** 이유 1. 글쓴이들의 미래 경력에 도움을 준다. 대학원에서 좋은 논문을 쓸 수 있다는 것을 미리 입증한다. 이유 2. 신입생들이나 타과 학생들은 잡지의 좋은 글을 읽을 수 있다.
공지 일일이 졸업장을 나눠주기 시간이 걸리고 졸업생들이 너무 많아 불편하니 졸업식을 둘로 나눈다.	**X 반대** 이유 1. 시간이 많이 걸리는 것은 졸업 축하 강연자들이 너무 많기 때문이다. 이유 2. 불편한 이유는 졸업생 수가 많은 것보다 축하객들이 너무 많기 때문이다.

☐	제안 책 읽는데 2주면 충분하고 기다리는 학생들이 많으니 대출 기간을 한 달에서 2주로 줄이자.	X	반대 이유 1. 책을 2주 동안 읽는 것은 가능하지만, 레포트를 쓸 때 참고해야 하므로 2주는 짧다. 이유 2. 책을 기다리는 학생들은 다른 도서관과 연계되는 프로그램을 이용하면 된다.
☐	제안 강의실 건물 주위에 있는 학교 주차장을 없애자.	O	찬성 이유 1. 녹지 같은 쾌적한 공간을 확보할 수 있고, 날씨가 좋으면 밖에서 공부도 할 수 있다. 이유 2. 현재 차가 너무 많으니, 주차장을 없애면 교통 체증이 줄어, 학생들은 더 쉽게 강의실에 올 수 있다.
☐	제안 쓰레기가 많아지고, 건강에 좋지 않은 음식을 팔기 때문에 학교 앞 노점들을 금지해야 한다.	X	반대 이유 1. 쓰레기가 많은 건 쓰레기통이 적어서이다. 쓰레기통을 늘리면 된다. 이유 2. 불량 식품뿐 아니라 신선한 과일이나 주스도 쉽게 사서 수업에 갈 수 있어서 좋다.
☐	제안 비용을 줄일 수 있고 사용하기 쉬우니 전자교재로 교체하자.	X	반대 이유 1. 비용이 오히려 더 든다. 고장나거나 새 버전이 나오면 또 사야하기 때문이다. 이유 2. 스크린, 타자기, 조종기, 버튼이 작아 사용하기 힘들고, 밑줄을 그을 수 없어 불편하다.
☐	공지 댄스 수업을 학점 없는 과정으로 제공하는데 첫 수업은 무료다.	O	찬성 이유 1. 시간을 내서 운동하기는 힘들지만, 댄싱은 일주일에 세 번 수업시간에 할 수 있고 재미있다. 이유 2. 일단 가서 확인해 보자. 첫 수업이 무료라서 손해 볼게 없다.
☐	공지 졸업을 위한 필요 조건으로 두 개의 세미나에 반드시 참여해야 한다는 내용.	X	반대 이유 1. 세미나의 내용에 대해 이미 다 알고 있고 경험이 많아 세미나에 참여할 필요가 없다. 이유 2. 세미나가 열리는 시간에는 다른 스케줄이 있다.
☐	공지 새로 구성된 재즈밴드가 넓은 잔디밭에서 콘서트 열 수 있도록 허락했다.	X	반대 이유 1. 콘서트 음악이 너무 시끄러워서 주변에서 쉴 수가 없다. 이유 2. 관객이 너무 많아서 잔디를 밟고 훌륭한 장소를 파괴하면서 진흙탕을 만들 것이다.
☐	제안 현재 밤 9시에 닫는 음악실을 12시까지 쓸 수 있게 해달라.	O	찬성 이유 1. 9시 이후에 장소가 없어서 기숙사에서 연습하는데, 소리를 낮춰도 시끄러워서 남에게 방해된다. 이유 2. 콘서트 전에 더 많이 연습해야 하는데 이미 예약이 꽉 차서 음악실을 사용할 수 없다.
☐	공지 학생들을 도와주기 위해 글쓰기 센터를 개설한다.	O	찬성 이유 1. 교수들은 바빠서 자세히 안 봐주지만 그곳에선 꼼꼼히 봐줄 수 있다. 이유 2. 지원자들은 그곳에서 용돈을 벌 수 있고 경력도 쌓여서 나중에 취직할 때 좋다.
☐	공지 기숙사에서 컴퓨터 시설을 설치하는 대학교의 계획에 대한 내용	O	찬성 이유 1. 더 쉽고 빠르게 이메일을 체크할 수 있다. 이유 2. 레포트를 쓰는데 훨씬 더 적은 시간이 소요된다.

☐	공지 건강에 좋지 않은 식품을 팔고, 나가서 사먹을 수 있기 때문에 자판기를 내년부터 철거한다.	X	반대 이유 1. 안 좋은 음식 말고, 땅콩이나 쥬스 같은 것으로 대체할 수 있다. 이유 2. 바빠서 학교 밖까지 나갈 수 없고, 밤에는 다들 문을 닫아서 먹을 것이 없다.
☐	제안 글쓰기 센터에 선생님이 부족하니 주말에도 열자.	O	찬성 이유 1. 글쓰기 센터에 선생님이 둘만 있어서 기다리는 시간이 너무 길다. 이유 2. 주말에 열게 되면 학생들이 쓸 수 있게 되니 주중에 붐비지 않을 것이다.
☐	공지 찾아가지 않은 자전거가 많고 없애면 공간 활용을 할 수 있으니 자전거 거치대를 제거하겠다	O	찬성 이유 1. 주인이 없는 것이 많으니 없애도 문제가 안 된다. 잊어버린 것들은 노트를 붙이면 된다. 이유 2. 묶여있는 자전거들 때문에 실제로 자전거 탄 사람들이 이용할 수 없다.
☐	제안 1주일간의 봄방학 같은 가을방학이 필요하다.	O	찬성 이유 1. 첫 해는 힘들기 때문에 신입생들은 중간에 휴식을 갖는 것이 좋다. 이유 2. 시험을 준비하고 숙제를 하기 위해 중간에 방학을 가질 필요가 있다.
☐	제안 더 잘 찾을 수 있고, 직원을 고용하지 않아도 돼서 도서관에서 DVD 빌릴 때 학생이 직접 찾는 게 낫다.	X	반대 이유 1. 컴퓨터 시스템을 통해 직원이 쉽게 검색할 수 있다. 제목, 감독, 주연 배우 중 하나를 입력하면 된다. 이유 2. 직원을 고용하는데 많이 지불하는 것은 아니므로 학교 예산에 큰 차질이 없다.
☐	공지 아침에 학생들이 체육관을 많이 찾아 농구팀이 제대로 훈련할 수 없으니 저녁에 이용하라.	X	반대 이유 1. 저녁에는 아르바이트나 다른 대외활동이 있어서 아침에 체육관을 이용해야 한다. 이유 2. 농구팀의 문제는 몇몇 사람들이 오래 써서 그런 것이니 시간을 제한하거나 기구들을 구분하면 된다.
☐	공지 수업 전에 토론 질문 2개씩 만들어서 교수에게 미리 보내라는 숙제 내용	O	찬성 이유 1. 토론 질문들은 2개 만들면 여러 생각을 하게 되므로 토론이 활성화될 것이다. 이유 2. 기말 과제 주제를 찾는 데 도움이 돼서 기말 시험기간에 서두르지 않아도 된다.
☐	제안 방학 동안 캠퍼스 안에서 운행하는 버스들을 공항까지 운행하도록 하자.	O	찬성 이유 1. 공항까지 가려면 택시를 타야 하는데 너무 비싸다. 돈을 절약할 수 있다. 이유 2. 지금 방학이라 정규 수업이 없어서 학교 버스 일부를 공항까지 운행하는데 문제가 없다.
☐	공지 학교 방송국에서 더 많은 음악을 내보내기로 했다.	X	반대 이유 1. 많은 상업 방송국에서 이미 많은 음악을 내보내고 있다. 이유 2. 더 많은 음악을 내보내면 일반 교양 방송이 줄어든다.
☐	제안 낮게 말하면 방해되지 않으며 긴급 전화를 받을 수 있으니 도서관에서의 휴대폰 사용을 허락해야 한다.	X	반대 이유 1. 아무리 낮게 말해도 상대가 안 들린다고 하면 크게 말해야 하므로 결국 시끄러워 진다. 이유 2. 긴급한 경우에 상대방이 메세지를 남길 것이므로 밖에 나가서 자주 체크하면 된다.
☐	제안 빈 시설을 활용할 수 있고 새로운 운동에 도전해 즐거움을 찾을 수 있으니 체육을 필수 과목으로 해야 한다.	X	반대 이유 1. 시설을 이용하지 않아도 운동할 수 있다. 달리고, 자전거를 타고, 테니스를 치고 있다. 이유 2. 학생들은 새로운 운동보다는 이미 알고 잘하는 운동을 하는 것을 더 좋아한다.

	제안/공지	찬반	이유
☐	제안 중앙광장은 사람들의 통행이 많아져 자전거 사고가 빈번하게 발생하고 있으니 자전거 통행을 금지해야 한다.	X 반대	이유 1. 자전거를 금지해야 할 만큼 자전거 사고가 빈번하게 발생하는 것은 아니다. 이유 2. 강요하면 역효과를 낳을 수 있으니 표지판 설치를 하는 것으로 충분하다.
☐	제안 근처에 사는 학생들끼리 그룹을 만들어서 같이 차를 타고 다니면 경제적, 환경적으로 좋다.	O 찬성	이유 1. 기름값이 덜 들고 차 유지비도 덜 든다. 이유 2. 교통 혼잡을 줄이고 매연 또한 줄어들어 공기가 좋아진다.
☐	제안 소수만 시 낭송 모임에 참석하고, 시 낭송 CD가 도서관에 있으므로 시 낭송 모임이 없어져야 한다.	X 반대	이유 1. 학교가 광고를 안 해서 학생들이 참석하지 않는 것이기에 광고를 하면 많이 참석할 것이다. 이유 2. CD로 시 낭송을 듣는 것보다는 직접 참석해서 보고 들으면 훨씬 좋다.
☐	제안 홀이 혼잡하기 때문에 테이블을 홀 밖에 두자.	X 반대	이유 1. 몇 주 후면 다른 홀의 공사가 끝나기 때문에 그때까지 참으면 된다. 이유 2. 밖에는 학생들이 축구하고 공 던지며 놀기 때문에 소란스러워서 식사하기에 좋지 않다.
☐	제안 학교 기숙사에 부엌을 만들자.	O 찬성	이유 1. 식당 메뉴가 한정되어 있지만, 부엌이 있으면 자기가 원하는 음식을 만들 수 있다. 이유 2. 함께 요리하면 재미있고 서로 배울 수 있어서 좋으며, 혼자 살 때를 대비할 수 있다.
☐	공지 신입생들이 학교 생활에 도움이 되는 세미나 3개를 듣는 게 요구 사항이 될 것이다.	O 찬성	이유 1. 세미나를 들으면 본인이 신입생 때 겪었던 어려움을 겪지 않을 것이다. 이유 2. 세미나를 듣는 신입생들끼리 서로 도움을 주고 받을 수 있다.
☐	제안 자전거 대여 시간을 줄이고, 보증금 대신 학생증을 내고 자전거를 빌리게 하자.	X 반대	이유 1. 학생들이 하루 종일 자전거를 쓸 수도 있다. 나도 친구와 공원에서 하루 종일 탄적이 있다. 이유 2. 학생증을 맡기면 학교 시설을 이용할 때 불편하다. 도서관이나 학생식당에서 필요하다.
☐	공지 봉사활동 지원자를 모집한다.	O 찬성	이유 1. 돈 안들이고 일을 배울 수 있다. 이유 2. 실제적으로 일을 배우고 적용할 기회를 갖는다.

USHER

	읽기지문	강의
☐	**공지** 신입생들에게 1년 동안 무료 개인지도 프로그램을 제공하려 한다.	**O 여자 동의** 이유 1. 신입생은 학교를 잘 몰라서 여러 정보를 얻을 수 있는 프로그램이 필요하다. 이유 2. 맞춤형 정보를 얻을 수 있고, 다른 시각에서 수업이나 교수에 대한 정보를 얻을 수 있다.
☐	**제안** 대학은 청강을 허용해야 한다. 학생들이 관심있는 수업을 들을 수 있고, 과제가 없으므로 교수의 일도 늘지 않는다.	**X 여자 반대** 이유 1. 청강생들은 숙제도 없고, 열심히 안 해서 토론시간의 질이 떨어진다. 이유 2. 교수는 청강생들 때문에 프린트도 더 만들어야 하고, 질문에 답도 해야 해서 부담이 된다.
☐	**공지** 대학교 홈페이지에 있기 때문에 "예술과 연예" 뉴스레터를 없앤다.	**X 남자 반대** 이유 1. 학생들은 아무도 학교 홈페이지를 방문하지 않는다. 이유 2. 뉴스레터는 항상 사방에 널려있는데, 많은 사람들이 이벤트에 대해 알지 못하면 모두에게 손해이다.
☐	**공지** 신입생들이 5개 이상의 과목을 택하지 못하게 하고 4개까지로 제한한다.	**O 남자 동의** 이유 1. 신입생들이 그 시간에 다른 많은 것들을 경험할 수 있다. 이유 2. 아직 새로운 시스템에 적응하지 못한 신입생들이 적응하는 시간을 가질 수 있다.
☐	**공지** 쓰레기가 너무 많아서 청소를 도와줄 자원봉사자를 모집한다.	**X 남자 반대** 이유 1. 애초에 쓰레기가 그렇게 많지 않다. 이유 2. 청소는 전문 인력을 고용해서 해야 한다. 등록금은 그런 곳에 쓰라고 있는 것이다.
☐	**공지** 대학신문에서 언론학 4학년생들에게 인턴쉽 기회를 주고, 학점도 인정해준다.	**O 여자 동의** 이유 1. 전문적인 경험을 쌓을 수 있고, 이력서 쓸 때도 도움이 될 것이다. 이유 2. 마침 마지막 학기에 학점이 하나 남았는데, 학점이 인정되니 수업을 안가도 된다.
☐	**제안** 무작위로 선택된 룸메이트들끼리 잘 안 맞고 갈등도 잦으니까, 룸메이트를 직접 선택하자.	**X 여자 반대** 이유 1. 모르는 사람과의 갈등 해결법을 배울 수 있으니, 멀리 보면 좋은 경험이다. 이유 2. 룸메이트와 안 맞을 사람이면 캠퍼스 밖에서 사는 게 낫다. 싼 맛에 기숙사에서 살고 싶은 사람은 갈등이 있어도 산다.
☐	**제안** 인문학 과목들이 인문학 건물에 있으니 그 곳에 스터디 라운지를 짓자.	**O 남자 동의** 이유 1. 수업 사이에 30분 밖에 없는데, 10분 거리의 도서관까지 가는 건 비효율적이다. 이유 2. 문학시간에 햄릿을 공부하는데, 어려워서 수업이 끝나고 토론하려니, 할 곳이 마땅치 않아 결국 추운 날 밖에 서 있었다.
☐	**제안** 학교 버스의 편수를 늘려 기다리는 시간을 줄이자.	**O 여자 동의** 이유 1. 너무 오랫동안 버스를 기다리다가 지각을 한 적이 많다. 이유 2. 그렇다고 자가용을 갖고 다니자니 기름값이 너무 비싸다.
☐	**제안** Directory book에 사진을 넣고, 홈페이지에도 항상 공개하자.	**O 남자 동의** 이유 1. 이름을 잘못 알아서 다른 곳에 전화한 적 있음. 사진이 있었더라면 그런 일이 없었을 것이다. 이유 2. 방을 치우다가 잃어버렸는데, 홈페이지에 있으면 어디서나 찾아볼 수 있다.
☐	**공지** 토요일에 Clean-up Day가 있다. 캠퍼스 관리의 중요성을 알리고, 음악과 다과가 준비돼 있다.	**O 남자 동의** 이유 1. 지원하지 않아도, 친구들을 보며 배울 수 있다. 자신도 친구가 봉지를 줍는걸 본 후로 쓰레기를 버리지 않는다. 이유 2. 다과가 준비되어 있어, 많은 사람들이 몰려들어 서로 어울릴 수 있다.
☐	**공지** 대학교에서 전자책을 학생들에게 무료로 제공한다.	**O 여자 동의** 이유 1. 안 그래도 전공서적이 너무 비쌌는데, 돈을 아낄 수 있다. 특히 미술사 전공은 컬러사진 때문에 더 많은 돈을 써야 했다. 이유 2. 무거운 책들을 갖고 다녀야 했는데, 더 이상 허리 아프게 다닐 필요가 없다.

☐	공지 내년부터 의대 지원자들은 여름 3개월 동안 온전히 인턴만 할 수 있게 된다.	O 여자 동의 이유 1. 인턴은 좋은 경험이지만 체력적으로 힘든데, 인턴에만 집중할 수 있게 돼서 다행이다. 이유 2. 다른 일정과 겹치지 않아서 좋다.
☐	제안 부엌에 냉장고 수를 늘리고, 부엌을 이용하기 전에 sign-up을 하자.	X 남자 반대 이유 1. 부엌에 냉장고를 여러 개 놓을 자리가 없다. 이유 2. 하루 종일 공부하느라 바빠서 언제 배고파질지 모르는 마당에, 부엌을 언제 쓰겠다고 알리는 건 시간낭비다.
☐	공지 문학수업이 인기가 너무 많아서 저녁 수업도 열고, 인원수도 늘리기로 했다.	X 남자 반대 이유 1. 인원이 늘면 토론할 기회가 줄어들고, 학생들은 많은 것을 배울 수 없다. 이유 2. 많은 학생들이 과외 활동이나 아르바이트를 하기 때문에, 저녁에 수업을 듣는 것은 현실적이지 못하다.
☐	제안 졸업식을 잔디밭 같은 더 큰 곳에서 하자.	X 남자 반대 이유 1. 사람들은 무대 위에 관심이 있을 뿐, 그 주변 공간은 별로 안보기 때문에 넓은 공간은 필요 없음. 이유 2. 이미 충분히 크고, TV로도 방송되니까 걱정할 필요가 없다.
☐	제안 미술행사 참석률을 높이려면 학기 말에서 학기 중으로 바꾸자고 교수가 이메일을 보낸다.	O 여자 동의 이유 1. 직접 가서 사진도 보고 싶고, 사람들도 더 많이 왔으면 좋겠다. 이유 2. 만약 행사 일정이 학기 중으로 바뀐다면 보러 갈 시간 있을 것이다.
☐	제안 도서관의 책상과 의자가 낡았으니, 이왕이면 편한 걸로 바꾸면 학생들이 많이 올 것이다.	X 여자 반대 이유 1. 의자랑 책상을 편한 것으로 바꾸면, 오히려 집중이 안되고 쉽게 피곤해진다. 이유 2. 도서관에 학생들이 안 오는 이유는 콘센트가 모자라서 노트북을 충전할 수가 없기 때문이다.
☐	제안 정치학을 전공하는 학생들이 신문을 읽을 수 있도록 도서관에 newspaper room을 만들자.	O 남자 동의 이유 1. 신문을 읽으면 조사하고 있는 주제나, 세상을 움직이는 큰사건을 이해하는데 도움이 될 것이다. 이유 2. Newspaper room은 앞으로 학생들이 공부하는 데에 여러모로 도움이 될 것이다.
☐	제안 수학 건물에 구내식당을 새로 열고, 콘센트도 많이 만들자.	O 여자 동의 이유 1. 수업 사이에는 학생회관에서 밥을 먹었는데, 이제는 멀리 갈 필요가 없다. 이유 2. 수학 건물이 너무 오래 됐는데, 콘센트가 많아지면 노트북도 충전하고 여러가지를 할 수 있다.
☐	공지 누가 전기를 많이 아끼는지 경연이 펼쳐지고, 이기는 팀에게는 피자파티를 열어줄 것이다.	O 여자 동의 이유 1. 전기를 아끼는데 도움이 될 것이다. 스위치 옆에 "불을 끕시다"라는 메모도 붙였다. 이유 2. 관심이 없는 사람들도 피자파티는 좋아할테니 이 경연에 참여할 것이다.
☐	제안 학생들이 휴식을 취하고, 과제를 할 수 있도록 중간고사 직전에 3일짜리 가을방학을 만들자.	O 남자 동의 이유 1. 대학에서의 생활방식이나 공부법이 고등학교와 다르기 때문에, 1학년이 학교에 적응하는데 큰 도움이 될 것이다. 이유 2. 일주일에 시험이 몇 개씩 있는데, 과제물도 많다며 역사수업을 예로 든다.
☐	공지 책으로 낼 것이니, 각자 한 단원씩 읽고 레포트를 쓰라는 과제를 물리학 교수가 냈다.	X 여자 반대 이유 1. 학생이 자기가 담당한 단원만 열심히 해서 전체의 내용은 알 수 없다. 이유 2. 기말시험 기간에는 학생들이 바쁘기 때문에, 다른 사람들에게 자신이 맡은 단원을 설명해 줄 여유가 없다.
☐	제안 학생들에게 안 좋은 기억만 생기고 주변지역과의 관계도 악화되니, 지역봉사활동을 없애자.	X 여자 반대 이유 1. 학생들은 봉사활동을 좋아해서 이 학교에 들어왔기 때문에, 앞으로도 계속할 것이다. 이유 2. 글쓴이가 개인적으로 안 좋은 경험을 했기 때문에, 문제를 과장한 것이다.

USHER

☐	**제안** 다른 라디오 방송과 비슷한 음악 말고, 잘 알려지지 않은 음악과 함께 설명을 곁들이자.	O	**남자 동의** 이유 1. 지금은 음악이 너무 뻔해서 아무도 대학방송을 듣지 않는데, 더 많은 사람들이 관심을 갖고 듣게 될 것이다. 이유 2. 어차피 대학의 목적은 교육이라서, 아나운서의 설명이 길어져도 문제없다.
☐	**제안** 부엌마다 냉장고를 한 대씩 더 놓고, 부엌을 쓸 일이 있으면 사전에 예약하도록 하자.	X	**남자 반대** 이유 1. 부엌에 공간이 부족하기 때문에, 냉장고를 추가로 놓을 곳이 없다. 이유 2. 학생들이 바쁘기 때문에 언제 식사를 할지 아무도 모른다. 누군가 부엌을 쓰고 있다면 잠시 기다리면 된다.
☐	**제안** 다른 학생들도 배려하고, 룸메이트도 미리 만나볼 겸, 오리엔테이션을 여름에 하자.	X	**여자 반대** 이유 1. 많은 학생들이 여름동안 일하거나 멀리 살아서 오리엔테이션에 오지 못한다. 이유 2. 룸메이트와 연락하는 것이 목적이라면, 이메일 주소만 알면 되지 굳이 미리 만날 필요는 없다.
☐	**공지** 심리학과 학생들이 교수들과 토론도 하고 서로 가까워지도록 새 프로그램을 시작한다.	O	**여자 동의** 이유 1. 교수들은 평소에 바빠서 만나기 힘든데, 격식 없는 대화를 나눌 수 있는 좋은 기회다. 이유 2. 학생들이 서로 알게 될 좋은 기회다. 지금까지는 그런 기회가 없었다.
☐	**공지** 학생들은 졸업 전에 이틀짜리 career workshop을 초여름과 늦여름에 두 번 참여해야 한다.	X	**남자 반대** 이유 1. 이력서를 쓰는 방법이나 면접 보는 방법을 대학교에서 알려줄 필요가 없다. 이유 2. 많은 학생들이 기말고사 직후부터 개강 직전까지 인턴을 하거나 일을 해서 여름에는 참여할 수 없다.
☐	**제안** 과학 전공자는 글 쓸 일이 없고 실험도 오래 하니 글쓰기 수업을 필수과목에서 빼자.	X	**남자 반대** 이유 1. 과학 전공자들도 실험을 설명하고 학계에서 인정받으려면 글을 잘 써야 한다. 이유 2. 과학 전공자들만 바쁜 것도 아니다. 인문계 학생들은 실험은 없지만 자료도 많이 찾고 글도 많이 쓴다.
☐	**공지** 의대 지원자들은 내년부터 여름 3개월 동안 병원에서 환자들을 돌봐야 한다.	O	**여자 동의** 이유 1. 의사가 되는 게 생각보다 힘들다는데, 미리 경험해 볼 수 있어서 도움이 된다. 이유 2. 의대 지원자뿐 아니라, 모든 학생은 학기동안 바쁘기 때문에, 인턴쉽을 여름에 하는 것도 좋은 생각이다.
☐	**공지** 대학 도서관에서 4학년생들의 자료수집을 돕기 위해 사물함을 만든다.	X	**여자 반대** 이유 1. 4학년만 바쁜 게 아니다. 우리도 2학년이지만 할 것도 많고 가방도 무겁다. 이유 2. 책을 사물함에 넣고 다니면 도서관 측에서 찾을 방법이 없다. 아무도 데스크에 안 갈 테니까.
☐	**제안** 교실도 가까우니 학생들이 수업 사이에 쉴 수 있도록 인문학 건물에 라운지를 만들자.	O	**남자 동의** 이유 1. 쉬는 시간이 30분인데, 10분 거리에 있는 도서관에 다녀오는 건 말이 안 된다. 이유 2. 다른 학생들과 셰익스피어의 햄릿에 대해 얘기하는데, 마땅한 곳이 없어 추운 날 밖에서 얘기했다.
☐	**공지** 주중 10시 이후에는 기숙사에서 시끄러운 소리를 내서는 안 된다.	O	**여자 동의** 이유 1. 나는 시끄러워서 도서관에서 공부한다. 소음은 아침수업 때문에 일찍 자는 학생들에게도 방해가 되었다. 이유 2. 친구도 룸메이트가 음악을 크게 틀어서 싸우는데, 관계개선에도 좋을 것이다.

☐	**Shut the gym down** 1) To update locker rooms and shower facilities 2) Students can use an off-campus gym freely	X girl disagrees Reason1 : Unnecessary to shut the whole gym down, just shut the area they are working on, and students can change their clothes and take shower in their dorms because dorms are close to the gym. Reason2 : the off-campus gym is far away from campus, it will take 30 mins to there and another 30 mins back to school, plus students will always feel exhausted after working out, so they may not willing to walk anymore.
☐	**Selling snacks during movie screening** 1) Students will enjoy watching movies more if they can eat some snacks. 2) The club can raise money by selling snacks.	X girl disagrees Reason1 : Eating will be annoying and noisy. Crunching will be a great distraction since it is a small room. Reason2 : It is not financially beneficial for the clubs. That is because only a small number of students will go to watch the movies on campus. They cannot sell much. And this little money is not worth the effort the club needs to take.
☐	**Build a campus garden** 1) Students can relax with flowers and trees 2) There is an empty land behind the scientist buildings which is suitable for being a garden	X The guy disagrees Reason1 : It's cold for most of the time here. The only blooming time for plants is summer break. During the rest of the time when the campus is full, the flowers can't grow, the campus garden is meaningless. Reason2 : The empty land is gonna be used to expand the scientist buildings
☐	**Dining Hall to close during Spring Break** 1) There are not enough students on campus. 2) Students could go to a the restaurant in town to have some food.	X Man disagrees Reason1 : There are some students on campus during the spring break. They have to stay here to study or work. In fact, the school could have another option. To open the dining hall for only an hour or to provide a smaller menu. Reason2 : Going to town for food would be too time-consuming. Students want to make the best use of their time finishing their big assignments or something.
☐	**Create a website for student musicians** The student proposes that the university should create a website for student musicians where they can find people of the same interests and post information about concerts or music-related events.	O The woman agrees Reason1 : She and her friends always practice songs together, and they play rock music. However, they don't happen to know a drummer who could play the drum. But now, with the website, they could find one easily. Reason2 : When she goes to campus concerts, there are few people there. That's because people don't know about those concerts. So now, with the website, more people will come to the concerts.

	Topic	Response
☐	**Open the university gym to the off-campus people** 1) The university can charge them a monthly fee and use the money to upgrade the gym facility. 2) It won't affect the students' life that much.	O The woman agrees Reason1 : Her first reason is that it'd be necessary now for the university to upgrade the facilities because some of them are really old. This way the university doesn't have to charge the students or the faculty. Reason2 : As for the second reason, she mentions that it's a pretty small town anyway, so not a lot of people will use the gym and it won't make too big a difference for students.
☐	**School will add computers in the lobby of dorms** 1) Students can check e-mails or read the news. 2) During a the busy time, every student can only use for 10 minutes	O Woman agrees. Reason 1 : It's convenient. For example, once she forgot to e-mail her professor, but she didn't want to go all the way back to her dorm only for using her computer. So, she used the computer in the lobby to send the e-mail and check the direction. Reason 2: Some students use the computer in the lobby to talk with friends or write papers. It's good to make a rule to control the time of using the computers in the lobby.
☐	**The university decides to add music conceits during the lunchtime.** 1) Good for music students to have chances to perform. 2) Provide food during the intersection	O the woman agrees Reason1 : The university usually has only one concert at the end of the year, so that music students are not able to perform many pieces of music. Adding concerts during the lunchtime would provide them opportunities to perform more pieces of music that they practiced. Reason2 : The music building is far away from other class buildings. Students have to squeeze their time to attend to the concert. So it is great that the university provides food for them for their convenience.
☐	**The university adds a small coffee shop to the lobby.** In the Newsletter a student suggests the university adds a small coffee shop to the lobby of fine art building.	O the woman agrees Reason1 : Students have no place to buy coffee or snacks between classes. Reason2 : Draw attention to the work of fine art students.
☐	**Proposal of selling snack and drinks in the campus bookstore.** 1) It provides students with food and drinks when they are finding books to read. 2) Students may get hungry during class breaks.	X the student disapproval Reason 1 : Students may spill drinks on books and ruin them. Some books are expensive. Reason 2 : There is already a convenience store in campus close to the building where classes are held. Students are unlikely to go to the other side of the campus to buy food from the book store.

☐	**The university should organize bus trips for 1st year students** 1st year students don't have a car. Seniors can be more familiar with the city.	O the woman thinks it is a good idea. Reason 1 : First, the city is far from campus, and no public transportation available. Reason 2 : Second, because there is no bus, she did not know the time and place for music concerts.

Independent Task > Task 3 > 읽고 듣고 말하기 > 대학 강의

Speaking about academic course content - 학교 과목 내용에 대해 말하기

읽 기 지 문	강 의
우림에 적응한 식물들 비가 많이 오는 숲에서 어떻게 적응했는가에 대한 설명이다.	- 항아리 식물은 나무 맨 위에 기생하기 때문에 햇볕 받기가 쉽다. - 잎사귀가 사발모양이라 비가 고이고, 함께 떨어진 곤충들이 썩어서 양분이 된다.
자신감 효과 어떤 일이든 뜻대로 이룰 수 있다고 자신의 능력을 믿는 굳센 마음이 있으면 실제로 해낼 수 있다.	- 줄곧 1등만 하던 교수 아들이 1명만 뽑는 신문사 입사시험에 응시했지만 떨어졌다. - 하지만 좌절하지 않고 자신감을 가지고 열심히 공부해서 실력을 키워서 다른 직장에 합격했다.
편리공생 관계 한쪽만 이익을 얻고, 다른 쪽은 이익이나 불이익을 받지 않는 공생관계이다.	- 콩만한 게와 갯지렁이는 공생관계인데 천적을 피하기 위해 갯지렁이의 관 속에서 산다. - 이 관계에서 콩만한 게만 갯지렁이에게 도움을 받고 갯지렁이는 어떤 도움이나 피해도 받지 않는다.
양쪽 지향성 자녀들이 부모한테 영향을 받고 부모도 자녀에게 영향 받는 것을 말한다.	- 한 아이가 많이 웃고, 부모와 대화를 좋아해서 그 부모도 자주 웃고, 말을 걸었다. - 그래서 그 아이는 더 자주 웃고 더 많은 말을 하므로 서로 반응이 더 좋아진다.
끌림의 보상 이론 좋은 상황에서 친구를 사귀면 좋은 관계를 유지할 수 있고, 안 좋은 상황에서 만나면 그럴 수 없다.	- 교수가 이웃집 파티에 초대 받아 갔는데 흥미와 적성이 너무 비슷한 사람을 만나서 지금도 친구로 지낸다. - 얼마 후 두통을 느낄 때 다른 이웃을 만났는데, 그는 굉장히 친절했지만 별로 친해지지 않았다.
식물 방어 식물이 곤충의 공격을 방어하려고 화학물질을 내뿜는다. 그러면 다른 식물들도 연속으로 화학물질을 내뿜는다.	- 과학자들이 한 나무를 잘라서 건강한지 확인했다. - 그 나무에다 벌레 먹은 것처럼 만들어 놨더니 그 나무에서 화학물질이 나왔다.
이미지 마케팅 이미지를 마케팅에 이용하면, 관련 없는 내용이라도 상품과 연결시킬 수 있고, 브랜드를 쉽게 기억한다.	- 쿠키모양을 곰 모양으로 하고, 상품 포장에 곰을 그리고 TV 광고에도 곰을 이용했다. - 어린이들은 이 쿠키에 친밀감을 갖게 되어 큰 곰을 볼 때마다 이 쿠키를 연상하게 됐고 판매량이 늘었다.
문화 지체 현상 변하는 문화의 일부를 쉽게 받아들이지 못하거나 받아들이기를 거부하여 새로운 생활에 뒤쳐지는 현상이다.	- 예전 사람들은 전화로 말하는 것은 무례하다고 생각해서 일 얘기가 아니면 전화를 하지 않았다. - 하지만 지금은 대부분 전화를 사용하고 있으며 전화로 하는 것을 무례하게 생각하지 않는다.
굴절적응 동물이 원래 가지고 있던 특성이 원래 목적과는 다른 용도로 사용되는 것을 말한다.	- 백로가 물고기를 잡으려고 하는데 햇빛이 물에 반사되어 물 속을 볼 수 없다. - 그래서 날개를 머리 위로 올려 햇빛을 가리고 그림자를 만들어 물 속을 들여다 보고 물고기를 잡는다.

	주제	내용
☐	**최적 섭식 이론** 동물들은 최대의 먹이를 발견하고 먹는데 최소한의 에너지를 사용한다.	- 까마귀는 가장 큰 고둥을 떨어뜨려 깨는데 그 이유는 살이 많기 때문에 사냥 횟수를 줄일 수 있기 때문이다. - 너무 낮게 날면 고둥이 깨지지 않아서 반복해야 하고, 너무 높이 날면 에너지가 낭비된다.
☐	**거짓 신호 보내기** 포식동물이 먹이를 속이기 위해 거짓 신호를 보낼 때 먹이는 진짜 신호인 줄 알고 착각할 수 있다.	- 암컷 나방은 짝짓기 준비가 됐을 때 화학물질을 방출해서 수컷 나방에게 신호를 보낸다. - 거미는 수컷 나방을 잡아먹기 위해 암컷이 내보내는 것과 같은 종류의 화학물질을 내보내 유인하여 잡아먹는다.
☐	**집단 지능** 개미나 벌의 행동은 그 자체로는 별 의미가 없지만, 집단으로 합쳐지면 큰 일을 해낸다.	- 개미들은 가끔 먹이를 찾을 때 장애물에 부딪힌다. - 나뭇가지 사이에 빈 공간이 있을 때, 그들은 서로 몸을 연결해 다리를 만들어 넘어가서 먹이를 구한다.
☐	**인체공학 디자인** 사람이 사용하는 기계나 장치가 너무 큰 힘을 쓰지 않고 사용할 수 있도록 설계하는 것을 말한다.	- 교수가 예전에 텔레마케팅을 하던 시절, 두 손이 자유롭지 않아 불편했고 목이 불편하여 효율이 떨어졌다. - 헤드셋을 사용하니 손이 자유로워서 불편함이 없어졌고, 목도 아프지 않아 더 많은 일을 잘하게 되었다.
☐	**불신의 유예** 문학과 예술에 쓰이는 용어로서, 현실이라면 절대 인정하지 않을 상황을 실제처럼 받아들이는 태도를 말한다.	- 교수의 룸메이트가 연극에서 노인 역을 맡았는데 처음엔 어색했으나 점점 룸메이트가 실존 인물처럼 느껴졌다. - 그 노인과 가족은 가난했고, 그가 병이 들었을 때 교수는 슬픔에 잠겼지만 해피엔딩으로 끝났을 때 안도감을 느꼈다.
☐	**관찰법** 사람들의 행동을 보고 그들의 생각을 파악하여 어떤 형상을 분석하는 방법이다	- 미술관에서 가장 인기 있는 섹션을 알아내려고 사람들과 인터뷰를 했는데 사람들이 솔직한 비판을 꺼려했다. - 그래서 경비원에게 방문객들이 얼마나 오랫동안 머무는지 기록하게 하여 인기를 파악할 수 있었다.
☐	**반박-설득 전략** 기업이 자기 제품의 단점을 우선 인정하고 그 단점이 오히려 장점이 될 수 있다고 설득하는 방식이다.	- 한 광고에서 여자가 단지와 냄비들이 비싸다고 인정하지만, 장기적으로 봤을 때 돈을 절약할 수 있다고 주장한다. - 평생 보증서를 받을 수 있고 제품이 잘못됐을 때 무상으로 교체해주기 때문이다.
☐	**승진 위험** 회사에서 누군가를 승진시킬 때 위험 부담이 있다.	- 어떤 사람이 프로그램 디자인을 너무 잘해서, 회사가 관리직으로 승진시켜주었다. - 그런데 디자인만 잘 했지 관리는 엉망이었지만 회사는 강등시키지도 못하고 그냥 놔둘 수 밖에 없었다.
☐	**수렴진화**	- 돼지와 비슷한 형태의 한 동물은 아프리카에 서식하는데 외피가 딱딱하여 포식동물에게 잡아 먹히기 어렵다. - 두 번째 동물은 호주에 서식하고 사이즈가 더 작은데, 혀에 끈적한 물질이 있어서 벌레를 잡기 쉽다고 한다.
☐	**확대해석** 부정적인 생각을 가지면 잘한 게 있어도 잘못한 것만 생각나서 결국엔 부정적인 결과를 가져온다	- 교수는 아들이 연극하는 걸 가서 봤는데, 겨우 대사 한 줄 까먹었지만 최악이었다면서 괴로워하였다. - 아들은 아무리 칭찬해도 안 듣고 자신감 상실해서 결국 다음 학기엔 연극을 그만두었다.

	광고 효과	- 탄산음료 광고를 보여주고, 며칠 뒤에 그 이름을 물으니 거의 아무도 기억하지 못했다. - 같은 광고 마지막에 "이 음료의 이름이 뭐지?"라고 문구를 넣었더니 더 많은 사람들이 기억했다.
	분산 저장 동물들이 겨울에 식량이 없을 때를 대비해서 한 군데가 아니라 여기저기 비축해 놓는 습성이다.	- 가을에 겉껍질을 벗기고 한 개씩 여기저기 저장하면 나중에 다른 동물이 발견해도 걱정 없다. - 못 찾으면 나중에 그 씨앗들이 발아하여 싹을 틔우는 데에도 도움을 준다.
	심적 회계 사람이 마음 속으로 각 계정을 분류하고 그 계정들을 다르게 인식하고, 처리하고, 평가하는 것이다.	- 교수는 예전에 사무실 월급은 집을 사려고 예금하고 주말 알바 월급은 왠지 여윳돈 같아서 막 썼다. - 주말 알바 월급도 절약해서 예금했다면 더 빨리 집을 살 수 있었을 것이다.
	환경 방해 환경의 영향으로 거기서 자라는 식물의 성장 형태가 방해될 수 있다는 이론이다.	- 블루그라스는 일조량이 적은 곳에서는 천천히 자라고 많은 곳에서는 너무 빨리 자라 다른 식물들을 가렸다. - 소들을 이 지역에 방목했더니 블루그라스 수가 줄어 다른 야생화들이 서식할 수 있게 됐다.
	작동되고 있는 진화 인간의 개입으로 더욱 빠르게 진행되는 진화	- 원래 박하는 숲에서 자라던 야생 풀인데, 미국사람들이 집을 짓자 집 주변의 잔디밭에서 자라기 시작했다. - 약 100년 전, 잔디깎이가 발명되자 박하는 수직으로 자라지 않고 옆으로 자라게 되었다.
	선택을 지지하는 편견 사람들이 어떤 선택을 하고 나서, 그것을 옹호 하려는 경향을 말하는데, 보통 단점보다는 장점만 기억하려 한다.	- 교수의 친구가 알아본 집은 직장에선 가까웠지만 너무 작아서 살지 말지 고민하다 결국은 사게 됐다. - 집을 사고 몇 년 뒤에 만났을 때, 그 친구는 집이 직장에서 가까워 얼마나 좋은 지 모르겠다며 장점만 말했다.
	예상 후회 선택을 하기도 전에 후회를 예상하는 것을 의미하는데, 사람들은 이런 일이 생기지 않도록 노력한다.	- 교수가 공항을 가기 위해 고속도로를 탔는데 너무 막혀서 다른 길로 빠질까 생각했다. - 하지만 다른 길도 여러 사정으로 막힐 수 있다고 생각해 결국 고속도로에 남아 있었다.
	테스트용 고객 직원들의 서비스나 근무 태도를 평가하기 위해 몰래 사람을 고용한 후 고객으로 위장시켜 직원을 평가하는 방법이다.	- 한 음식점 지배인은 직원들의 근무태도를 평가하고 싶었지만, 그들이 자기를 의식해서 제대로 평가할 수 없었다. - 그래서 한 남자를 테스트용 고객으로 고용했고, 그는 주문도 하고 이것저것 물어보며 평가해서 지배인에게 보고했다.
	동화 마케팅 감성 마케팅의 한 종류로, 특정 제품을 갖게 되어 생기는 자부심이나 특권의식을 소비자에게 주는 방법이다.	- 새로운 탄산음료를 출시할 때 멋진 디자인과 비싼 가격으로 명품 이미지를 주면 아무 소비자나 그 음료를 살 수 없다. - 이 음료를 구입한 소비자는 아무나 살 수 없는 음료를 샀다는 자부심과 특권의식을 갖는다.

☐	**절정과 종결 법칙** 사람들은 어떤 경험을 전반적으로 기억하는게 아니라 최고조나 마지막에 일어난 일만 기억한다는 이론이다.	- 교수가 휴가를 가서 처음 며칠은 비만 와서 방에 있었는데, 날씨가 풀려서 돌고래 쇼도 보고 파티에서 동향사람도 만났다. - 친구가 휴가가 어땠냐고 물어보자, 교수는 돌고래 쇼와 파티에서 만난 사람 얘기만 했다.
☐	**기술적 무능** 기업이 크고 복잡해지면, 직원이 자기 분야가 아닌 영역에서 무엇을 어떻게 해야 하는지 모르는 현상이다.	- 휴대폰 회사에서 매뉴얼 담당 직원이 매뉴얼을 포장에 넣는 것을 깜박했다. - 휴대폰을 시험하는 직원은 이를 알았지만 어쩔 줄을 몰라 제품을 그냥 내보냈고 결국 소비자가 불평했다.
☐	**신호 이론** 품질을 보증하기 위해 소비자들에게 객관적이고 공정한 정보를 제공하여 그들이 안심하고 제품을 구입할 수 있게 하는 것이다.	- 교수의 친구가 보석상을 운영하는데 손님들에게 객관적이고 공정한 정보를 제공하려고 감정사를 데려왔다. - 진품임을 확인한 후 소속 감정기관의 표시를 붙임으로써 손님들은 그 보석들을 믿고 구매할 수 있게 됐다.
☐	**대인관계 기술** 아이들의 사회부적응을 해결하기 위해 어른들이 아이들에게 어떻게 행동하는지를 보여줘 대인관계 기술을 가르친다.	- Mary가 Paul의 크레용을 함부로 집었다가 Paul이 화를 냈는데 Mary는 왜 그러는지 이해하지 못했다. - 이를 본 선생님이 남의 것을 만질 때는 먼저 물어봐야 한다고 가르치니 Mary는 크레용 만져도 되냐고 정중하게 물었다.
☐	**교란전시** 천적으로부터 자신을 직접 보호할 수 없는 동물들이 취하는 행동으로, 어미가 알이나 새끼를 보호하기 위해 천적을 둥지로부터 유인한다.	- 물떼새는 여우가 나타났을 때 여우의 주의를 다른 곳으로 돌리기 위해 교란전시를 실행한다. - 날개를 다친 것처럼 흉내 내서 여우를 둥지에서 멀리 떨어진 곳으로 유인한 후에 도망친다.
☐	**광고에서 모델링 기술** 소비자들이 사용하기 어렵다고 느끼는 제품의 사용법을 광고를 통해 보여주는 광고 전략이다.	- 교수의 딸이 아이스크림 만드는 기계를 사달라고 졸랐을 때 처음에는 안된다고 했다. - TV 광고에서 여자 모델이 어떻게 사용하는지 보여주니까 살 마음이 생겨 구입 했다.
☐	**전략적 동맹** 둘 이상의 조직이 특정 사업 활동을 하면서 협력을 맺는 약속이다. 서로 강점을 공유해서 신제품을 만든 후 경쟁우위를 얻는 것이 목적이다.	- 한 프레첼(pretzel) 회사가 초콜릿 회사와 동맹을 맺고 초콜릿 묻힌 프레첼을 개발해서 큰 성공을 거두었다.
☐	**환경 수용 능력** 환경이 지탱할 수 있는 종의 개체 수를 의미 한다. 개체수가 허용 수준 이상으로 증가하면 환경의 저항으로 인해 다시 허용치까지 감소한다.	- 어떤 해에 나방의 먹이가 많아지면 나방의 개체 수는 증가하고, 많은 알들을 낳는다. - 이 알들이 나방으로 자라서 개체수가 너무 많아지면 먹이가 부족해져 나방 수는 다시 적정 수준으로 감소한다.
☐	**분노의 폭발** 처음 화가 났을 때 화를 표출하지 않으면 그 억제된 감정은 나중에 비이성적 방법으로 폭발한다.	- 교수는 자신의 여동생과 있었던 일을 예로 들어 설명한다.

읽기지문	강의
친숙성 선호 이론 (Familiarity Preference Theory) 사람들이 이전에 경험해서 익숙하다고 여기는 것을 선호하는 경향이다.	학생들에게 한 물체는 어두운 실루엣만 오랫동안 보여주고, 다른 물체는 명확하게 잠깐 보여주었다. 그 후, 같은 학생들에게 두 물체를 제대로 보여주고 어떤 것을 선호하느냐고 물었더니, 대부분 첫 번째를 선호했다.
통합 농업 (Integrated Farming) 작물과 가축을 함께 관리하는 방법으로, 가축을 키우면 작물 재배에 이롭다.	바닥이 없는 작은 집에서 닭을 키우면 닭이 토양을 쪼고, 잡초를 먹는다. 이 닭장을 다른 곳으로 옮기고, 거기에 콩 같은 작물을 심으면, 토양이 부드럽고 잡초가 없어 잘 자란다.
계획오류 (Planning fallacy) 실제보다 낙관적으로 계획해 여러 변수들을 과소평가하여 일이 지연되는 현상이다.	교수가 학생시절, 레포트를 10장 써야 하는데, 마감일을 코앞에 앞두고 6장밖에 못 썼다. 급히 도서관에 갔는데 문을 닫아서, 결국 제 시간에 제출하지 못했다. 내용은 칭찬을 받았지만 늦어서 점수가 깎였다.
운반공생 (Phoresy: 편승) 어떤 동물이 다른 곳으로 이동할 때 다른 동물의 몸에 붙어서 이동하는 공생 관계	진드기(mites)는 꽃가루와 꿀을 먹고 산다. 먹이가 떨어지면 다른 꽃으로 옮겨야 하는데, 자유로이 움직이기엔 너무 작다. 벌새(humming birds)도 꽃가루와 꿀을 먹는데, 그 사이 진드기가 벌새에 올라탄다.
고객 가두기 (Customer lock-in) 회사가 제품을 디자인할 때 타회사의 제품과 서로 맞지 않도록 디자인하는 상술	교수가 사진 찍는 취미가 있어서 A사의 35mm카메라를 샀는데, 쓰다가 렌즈가 깨졌다. 마침 B사의 렌즈가 할인 중이었지만 호환이 안 된다는 이유로 더 비싼 A사의 렌즈를 구매할 수 밖에 없었다.
내재주의 (Internalism) 어떤 일에 관한 이유를 자신의 내면에서 찾을 수 있다는 믿음	어떤 자동차 회사의 첫 주 판매량이 너무 저조한 나머지 회사 내부에서 그 이유를 찾은 끝에 사업구조가 엉성하고 효율성이 떨어진다는 결론을 내렸다. 결국 경영방식을 바꿔서 효율성을 높이는데 성공했다.
풍토적 적응 (Climatic adaptation) 기후나 서식지가 바뀜에 따라 생물이 그에 맞춰 적응하는 것	원래 유럽이 원산지였던 제비(sparrow)의 한 종류가 남미로 옮겨가게 되면서 기후에 따라 크기가 달라졌다. 추운 지방으로 간 새들은 체온을 유지하기 위해 커졌고, 반대로 더운 지방으로 간 새들은 작아졌다.
동료 강화 (Peer reinforcement) 사람의 행동을 바꾸기 위해 직접 지적하는 대신 동료를 칭찬하고 이를 보게 하는 것	교수가 초등학교 수업하던 때, Sarah가 노는 시간이 끝나도 나무 블록을 정리하지 않자, 혼내는 대신 정리를 잘한 Paul을 칭찬해줬더니, 이를 본 Sarah도 정리를 잘하게 됐다.
정서표현법칙 (Display rules) 속으로는 감정을 경험하지만 이를 겉으로 나타내기 싫을 때의 지침	교수의 딸은 원래 인형을 좋아하는데, 4살 생일파티 때 인형이 아닌 다른 선물을 받더라도 감사하는 게 중요하다고 했다. 할머니가 옷을 선물해줘서 실망하려던 찰나, 엄마가 예쁘다고 했더니, 고맙다고 할머니를 안아주었다.
소리의 은폐효과 (Masking) 한 가지 소리가 다른 소리를 덮어버리는 현상	범고래(orca)는 초음파로 위치를 파악하고 먹이를 찾는다. 과학자들의 연구에 의하면 선박에서 나오는 소음이 클 경우, 범고래가 먹이를 찾을 수 있는 반경이 20%나 줄어든다.
책임효과 책임이 적게 주어지면 일의 완성도가 높아진다	5살짜리 애들은 크레용을 다 쓰고 나면 칸이 작아 정리하기 힘들어한다. 그래서 엉망이 되기 쉬운데, 이 때 큰 상자를 하나 준비해서 그 안에 크레용을 넣게 하면 잘 치운다.

☐	광고 추적 (Advertisement profiling) 인터넷 상에서 방문자의 정보를 수집하여 광고의 효율성을 높이는 기술	우유광고에 반응을 보이는 방문자들의 정보를 수집해 분석해봤더니, 거의 대부분이 여성 방문자였다. 이 사실을 알게 된 후에, 우유회사들은 여성들을 목표로 한 광고를 제작해 큰 효과를 보았다.
☐	사회적 책임 (Social Responsibility) 회사들이 사회에 끼칠 영향을 고려해 행동하는 것	교수가 사는 곳 주변에 카페에 있는데, 원래 플라스틱 컵을 쓰다가 환경을 생각해서 재활용 컵을 쓰고, 자신의 머그잔을 가지고 오는 사람들한테는 추가할인도 해줬다. 처음에는 조금 비쌌지만 결국 성공했다.
☐	통찰 학습 (Insight learning) 무의미한 반복이 아니라 환경요소에 의미를 두고 통찰에 의해 배우는 과정	바나나가 들어있는 상자를 높이 두고선 침팬지에게 먹으라고 했더니 처음에는 뛰어올라서 먹으려고 하다가 실패했다. 더 생각하다가 결국 다른 상자를 쌓아서 계단을 만들고 그 위로 올라가서 바나나를 먹었다.
☐	자극 감소 특정 자극제를 줄임으로써 집중을 도와주는 것	수업시간에 어느 학생이 창가 쪽에 앉아 창 밖의 모습만 쳐다보고 수업에는 집중하지 않길래, 선생님이 자리를 바꾸라고 하자 그 이후부터는 수업에만 집중하게 되었다.
☐	가용성 오류 (Availability error) 인상적인 일을 경험한 후, 그럴 수 없음에도 그런 일이 또 일어날 수 있다고 믿는 현상	교수가 부인과 섬으로 여행을 갔는데, 다음 날 하루 종일 비가 와서 해변에 나갈 수 없었다. 그 이후로, 교수가 아무리 날씨를 확인해도 부인은 섬으로는 다시는 여행가고 싶어하지 않았다.
☐	중간 기착지 (Stopover habitat) 철새들이 이동하는 중간에 들러 재충전하고 쉴 수 있는 곳	휘파람새(warbler)는 북쪽으로 이동하다가 서남부 지역에서 쉬어가는데, 여기엔 곤충들이 많아 부족한 체력을 보충하기에 더없이 좋고, 수풀이 우거져있어 천적의 공격을 피해 편히 쉬다 갈 수 있다.
☐	자기중심적 세계관 (Egocentric worldview) 아이들이 어릴 때, 남들이 자신과 같은 관점에서 세상을 볼 거라는 생각	연구원이 꼬마를 모델하우스에 집어넣고, 처음엔 함께 빨간 문을 쳐다본다. 다음, 연구원이 모델하우스 뒤에 벽만 보이는 곳으로 가서 "지금 나는 뭐가 보이게?"라고 물으면 꼬마는 벽이라고 하지 않고 빨간 문이라고 대답한다.
☐	욕구불만 내성 (Tolerance frustration) 처음 시도할 때 몇 번을 실패해도 계속 도전하도록 하여 성공할 수 있게 하는 것	교수의 아들이 블록을 쌓다가 무너지니까 울며 도와달라고 했다. 처음에는 곧바로 도와줬는데, 이후 도와주러 가는 시간을 점점 늦춰서 결국에는 아들이 도움을 기다리지 않고 노력해서 혼자 블록 쌓기에 성공함.
☐	대비효과 (Contrast effect) 사람들이 원래 자신이 익숙한 것들과 어떤 것을 비교해서 생각하려는 경향	교수가 학생 때, 방을 구하러 다녔는데 첫 번째 방은 정말 작고 두 번째 방은 넓고 현대적이었다. 생각해보니, 두 번째 방도 크지는 않았는데, 상대적으로 커 보인 것이었다. 결국 후자로 결정했지만, 짐이 안들어갈 정도로 작았다.
☐	확산효과 (Diffusion effect) 그룹을 나누어 실험할 때, 통제집단이 다른 집단의 영향을 받아 실험이 실패하는 현상	어느 회사에서, 운동이 직원의 피로를 풀 수 있는지에 관한 실험을 하고자, 직원들을 둘로 나눴고, 한 쪽에 다른 쪽 직원들에게 말하지 말라 했으나, 몇 주 후, 이것이 지켜지지 않아 실험이 실패했다.
☐	기회주의 식물 (Opportunist) 한 지역의 식물들이 사라지면, 그 틈을 놓치지 않고 그 지역에 번창하는 식물	소들을 초원에 방목하였더니, 왕성한 식욕으로 풀을 다 뜯어먹었고, 다른 풀들이 사라진 틈을 타 특정 종류의 식물이 번창하였다. 하지만 다른 풀들이 다시 자라나자 경쟁에서 밀려 서서히 그 수가 줄어들었다.
☐	업무 분할 (Task partitioning) 멤버들이 일을 나누어 함으로써 효율을 높이는 방법	잎을 자를 때, 개미는 셋으로 나뉜다. 나무에서 잎을 자르는 그룹, 떨어진 잎을 자르는 그룹, 그리고 집까지 옮기는 그룹이다. 이는 아주 효율적인데, 모두 독립적으로 일하며, 일제히 나무를 오르내리지 않아 지치지 않는다.

회복 생태학 (Restoration ecology) 인간이 파괴한 자연을 회복하려면, 그곳에 어떤 필수요소가 있었는지 꼭 알아야 한다.	옛날에 미국 대초원에는 분홍바늘꽃(fireweed)라는 식물이 아주 많았는데, 지나치게 옥수수만 재배하다 보니 거의 사라졌다. 이 식물은 씨앗이 불 속에서도 살아남는 특성이 있어 일부러 불을 냈더니 다시 번성했다.
찾는 이미지 (Search image) 새들의 기억에 이미지의 형태로 남아있는 특정 곤충의 외관상의 특징	북유럽의 어떤 새는 초록색 애벌레를 먹고 사는데, 애벌레들이 알에서 깨어나는 초여름에는, 나뭇잎 색깔과 구분이 어려워 잘 알아보지 못한다. 시간이 지날수록, 애벌레의 더듬이와 주름진 몸통을 보고 쉽게 구분해낸다.
창시자 효과 (The founder effect) 새로 격리된 개체들은 조상 수가 몇 안되기 때문에 유전적 다양성이 떨어지는 현상	오래된 냉장고의 에너지 효율이 떨어져 전기를 아끼기 위해 새로운 냉장고를 샀는데 에어컨(air conditioner)을 사서 켜는 바람에 결국 전기소비는 이전과 비슷해져고 돈도 아끼지 못했다.
정보의 폭포현상 (Information cascade) 사람들이 자신이 아는 것과 다르다는 걸 알면서도 몇몇 사람의 결정을 따르는 현상	교수가 낯선 도시에서 식당 가이드북을 봤는데, 이태리식당은 평이 좋았고, 프랑스식당은 별로였다. 근데 프랑스식당에 사람이 많길래 들어갔더니 역시 별로였다. 이후의 손님들도 사람들이 북적이는 걸 보고 들어오는 듯 했다.
억압해제 효과 (The disinhibiting effect) 남이 나쁜 행동을 하고 벌을 받지 않는 걸 보면, 나도 더 이상 그 행동을 참지 않는다.	교수가 졸업직후에 법률사무소에 취직했는데, 격식있는 분위기라 긴장하며 일했다. 개인적으로 먹으면서 일하는 건 상상도 못했는데, 동료 Jane이 샌드위치를 먹으며 회의에 임하는 걸 보고, 결국 그도 그렇게 됐다.
신념집착 (Belief perseverance) 자기 생각의 토대가 잘못된 것임이 판명된 후에도 처음의 생각에 매달리는 경향	교수가 어렸을 때, 추우면 감기에 걸린다며 어머니께서 옷을 단단히 챙겨주셨는데, 어른이 되니 감기는 바이러스가 일으킨다는 사실을 배웠다. 하지만 교수는 어머니와 같은 말을 하며 자식들이 나갈 때 옷을 챙긴다.
전속시장 (Captive market) 선택의 여지 없이 특정 상품을 사지 않을 수 없는 소비자층	교수가 타려던 비행기편이 취소가 되어 어쩔 수 없이 기다리게 됐는데, 배가 고파서 뭔가를 먹으려니 밖에 나갈 수 없어서 시가보다 2배나 비싼 샌드위치를 사먹어야 했다.
촉진 (Facilitation) 직접 지시하거나 보여주지 않고 간접적 힌트를 통해 목표를 이루게 하는 것	교수가 8살짜리들에게 도서관에서 책 찾는 법을 가르쳐줬는데, 한 소녀가 "이상한 나라의 앨리스"를 찾지 못해 도와달라고 했다. 교수는 직접 찾아주는 대신, 질문을 통해 그 소녀가 직접 책을 찾을 수 있도록 했다.
후방적 틀짓기 (Backward framing) 특정 제품을 이미 경험한 후에도 광고에 따라 소비자의 의견이 변할 수 있다는 이론	지원자들에게 새로운 원두커피를 시식해보라고 했는데, 여기에 연구원들이 소금과 식초를 몰래 타서 맛을 망쳤다. 시식 후에 커피의 훌륭한 맛을 강조하는 내용의 광고를 보여줬는데, 설문지에서 맛있다는 평가를 받았다.
충격 편향 (Impact bias) 우리가 뭔가를 얼마나 강하게 느끼고 그 느낌이 얼마나 갈지를 잘못 예상하는 경향	교수의 딸이 정말 가고 싶어하던 대학이 있었는데, 거기서 떨어지면 인생을 망치게 될 거라고 했다. 결국 떨어졌고, 아예 대학 자체를 가지 않겠다며 집구석을 뒤집어놨지만, 결국 다시 생글거리며 다른 대학으로 진학했다.

☐	**Dormancy** In the really harsh natural environment, some animals will use dormancy to protect themselves from nature. In a word, they will avoid exposure to certain elements in the environment and use slow metabolism to preserve energy.	Professor used an example of the lungfish to demonstrate the term, lungfish lives in the shallow lakes that face the possible consequences of drying up. If the lake dries up, then the lungfish is cooked, so they will explore a certain method to prevent that from happening. So basically what the lungfish do is to dig a hole through the mud at the bottom of the lake, its body will be curled up and berried in the mud, so the covered mud could be a proactive coat for the lungfish that keeps them away from the heat and also keep the moisture inside the body. The lungfish will keep the body still and breathe really slow, the heartbeat is slowing down as well. Usually, the lungfish relies on eating crabs and small fish to survive but since it lives in the shelter, it doesn't need to eat anything at all. They can survive in this shelter for months, or even years until the lake returns.
☐	**Nudge Marketing** To gently push customers toward buying a product by using indirect cue or signal.	A grocery store wants to persuade customers to buy more fresh vegetables. They first put up a big poster to meet their end. However, their customers didn't respond. Then they spare a section in their carts and put it in green color so as to remind customers to eat more vegetables. The customers turned out to fill it up with more vegetables and the grocery store made a bigger profit.
☐	**Consensus bias** People will think that the rest of the world will think and behave like themselves.	Experiment: ask some students if they're willing to go into a crowded but quiet library, and sit down, starting to talk to themselves loudly, could be any topic, silly ones, like maybe talk about ice cream. Some students said they're willing to do so, others refused immediately. Then the next question is "what do you think others will do?" The student who said yes will also think other students will say yes, and students who refused to do so also consider other students will refuse this silly action.
☐	**Stimulates Discrimination** Animals respond to sounds and noises known as stimuli created by the environment, they have developed the capacity to distinguish the stimuli as to whether or not they are dangerous is known as stimulates discrimination.	Professor used an example of a seal, it is an animal threatened by whales. However, only one type of whale will eat seal, the other types eat fish. The whales make rather slightly different noises that can be distinguished by seals. Whether the seal is about to run for its life depends on the noise it hears. The type of whale that eats seal makes a simple anonymous sound with one note, when the seal hears it, it will run away. The other type of whales that prey on fish make a complex sound, when the seal hears it, it will continue eating rather than wasting energy and time on running.
☐	**Create grouping** Group the items in a new way in order to increase the sales	The professor uses a watch as an example to illustrate this concept. He said that in the past, watches are seen as expensive and luxury jewelry, always use gems or expensive metal to make watches and people are willing to pay big money on them. One company started to make watches, they use plastic materials instead of metal, and they made their watches fun and fashion, people will pay less money to get a watch like that and it also changed the way people buy it, instead of just buy one watch a time, people are more tend to buy several watches a time cuz they are cheap.

USHER

☐	**You too fallacy** When you give other people suggestions or advice, they will think it is completely useless and ignore you when the suggestions or advice are not in accordance with theirs, despite the fact that such suggestions or advice may be very useful objectively.	The professor uses his brother's example to illustrate this. His brother recently told the professor that he was lack of energy. The thing is his brother was eating sugary food junk food, in want of vegetables and nutritious food. The professor suggested his brother eat vegetables and keep healthy and balanced diet, which is scientifically proved to be a good way to regain energy. But his brother just regards this suggestion as stupid and silly one and he will never change his eating habits, for he thinks that the professor himself eats junk food also.
☐	**Environment Scenting** Our powerful sense of smell allows us to tell the difference between many kinds of doors these odors are interpreted and processed in a part of the brain that affects our emotions, behavior, and memory. Given this knowledge, market researchers are studying the effects of what is known as environment scenting, this technique attempts to use pleasant fragrance to attract customer sales. The results of these marketing studies indicate that smells can strongly influence consumers both in their willingness to buy a product and in the value they place on a product.	
☐	**Signal redundancy** Animals will send the same message with different types of signals to inform the other animals of the same species.	The professor gives an example in class. A group of deer sometimes graze together and sometimes one of the deer would go off and eat on its own. When this deer sees a predator like a lion approaching, it will raise its tails to inform the rest of the deer to run away from the area. But sometimes the other deer cannot see the signal. So this particular deer will also dump its foot on the ground to make some noise. When other deer hear the noise, they will run away.
☐	**Generalizing** In the lecture, the professor introduces the concept of generalizing which means children are able to realize that a word doesn't only mean a specific object but also other means other objects of the same category as they grow up.	He offers us an example of his own son. When he was much younger, he learned the word 'train', at first his understanding of this word was pretty limited, he thought it only referred to his toy train. But as he grew up, it came to his understanding that the word 'train' not only refers to his toy train but also other real trains in life. That's how the professor uses the example of his son to illustrate the concept of generalizing.
☐	**Concept testing** A marketing technique company use to find out if customers like a new product idea. Two benefits: to gain information; use feedback to improve the product.	A bicycle company introduced a folding bike. Marketing people talk to a group of consumers. Information gathering: consumers like the folding back. New feedback: wants to have an attached lock. And the company adapted the product and the bike sells well.

☐	**Compound Nesting** Two species live together, which are different enough not to compete for food.	Example of Ants in Africa. The bigger ant collects food, and the smaller one eats the leftover scrambles. For the smaller one, it doesn't need to search for food. For the bigger one, the smaller one makes the nest clean by eating the leftover food, which prevents bacteria.
☐	**Priority effect** Animal species, when first settling on a certain territory, makes the territory less habitable for later species. This is esp. prevailing for small and weak species.	For example, there is a type of small ants that net on akasha trees. As the first group of settlers onto the tree, they destroy part of the tree's nectars and render it unable to produce nectars anymore. This is because another type of bigger ants, which feed on this nectar and are more aggressive than smaller ants, will no longer come to this tree for occupation. Through these this small ants survive.
☐	**Facial feedback** We believe that our emotion causes our facial expression. But it is not true. It is our facial expression that determines how we feel.	The professor gives an example of an experiment. He gives out the same math problem to two groups of students. Everything is the same except one. He asks students in Group A to smile in the experiment and asks students in Group B to present frown and other unhappy faces in the experiment. As a result, students in group A say they enjoy the math, while students in group B say they are tortured.
☐	**Compromising effect** Compromising effect means people usually avoid extreme options and choose to make medium choices when they shop. The companies sometimes develop more expensive product with better quality to stimulate people to purchase the existed product.	A coffee maker company produced a kind of coffee maker with low-end quality and another with average quality, and most of the customers choose to buy the cheaper kind. Then the company came up with the third kind of fancy coffee maker with a high quality that is more expensive, and after that, more customers have started shifting to buying the average kind of coffee maker.
☐	**Evolution in action** Animals and plants adapt to new changed environment quickly.	Mint plants used to grow in a grassy field and woods grew tall and faster, later some houses' owners' plant mint plants in the yard. They cut them into short, quickly, all mint plants become short and hardly being cut, instead, they grow side way become flat.
☐	**Priming** The way people interpret something that they see depends on what their experience has previously had. And people can be affected by previous thoughts and experiences.	Two women hold different views about a man writing on his pad on the bus. One woman met her college classmates on the bus and they recalled the memories in their college life. She thought the man who is writing on the bus is a student who is doing his homework. The other woman who is reading a poetry on the bus thinks the man is writing a poem
☐	**Distraction protections** In the world of animals, some animals confront and fight against predators.	A kind of dove always likes to build the nest on the ground. It's easy to hart. When the fox comes, one dove always pretends to be hurt, and cannot fly (luring). So the small dove will survive.

☐	**Social referencing** Babies can gradually understand new environments and learn to respond to them.	Experiment 1. 6-month babies had no response to their mothers' facial expressions. They played new toy dolls immediately regardless of whether their moms smiled or frowned because they are too young to understand and respond to the environment. Experiment 2. 1-year babies had a response to their mothers' facial expressions. They played new toy dolls immediately if their moms smiled or avoided new toy dolls If their moms frowned.
☐	**Assimilation and Accommodation** When children learn new object, if the objects fit in the concept they knew, they will fill it in that category, this is assimilation.	The professor's daughter, Jenny, always watches birds through windows. When she saw a bird she would shout: "bird! bird!" since it has wings and feathers and it can fly. Later, when the professor took Jenny to the zoo and saw ostrich, she did not know it was a bird. The professor asked her: "what is it?" She hesitated to say: "it is a bird".

Independent Task > Task 4 > 듣고 말하기 > 대학 강의

Speaking about academic course content - 학교 과목 내용에 대해 말하기

강 의
☐ **용기 디자인의 중요성** • 소비자의 편의: 전에는 케첩을 유리병에 담아서 불편했지만, 지금은 플라스틱 용기를 짜내면 된다. • 예쁜 디자인: 쿠키 상자를 고급스럽게 장식하면 판매가 증가한다.
☐ **토양의 침식을 막는 방법** • 번갈아 심기: 언덕에서 옥수수와 밀을 번갈아 심으면 그 뿌리가 흙의 유실을 막아준다. • 받침대 설치: 둑(ridge)을 세우면 이것이 댐 역할을 해서 흙의 유실을 막는다.
☐ **동물이 생존을 위해 독을 사용하는 경우** • 공격을 위해: 뱀이 먹이인 쥐를 물면 쥐는 독 때문에 움직이지 못한다. • 방어를 위해: 벌은 새들에게 잡아 먹히지 않기 위해 벌침을 쏜다.
☐ **페로몬을 이용한 곤충의 소통** • 위치를 알릴 때: 벌들은 페로몬을 공기 중에 보내 소통하기 때문에 먼 곳에서도 잘 돌아온다. • 짝짓기 할 때: 나방 암컷이 준비가 되서 페로몬을 분비하면 수컷은 냄새를 맡고 암컷을 찾아간다.
☐ **생존을 위한 곤충들의 흉내** • 대상의 천적처럼: 파리가 벌처럼 위장하면 파리의 천적은 파리를 벌로 오인해 접근을 피한다. • 천적 자신처럼: 나방이 거미처럼 위장하면 거미들은 같은 종족으로 착각해서 나방을 잡아먹지 않는다.
☐ **기업의 가격 책정법** • 저가 정책: 청량음료는 가격에 민감해서, 가격이 떨어지면 수요가 크게 오른다. • 고가 정책: 컴퓨터는 가격을 낮추면 사람들이 품질이 안 좋다고 생각해서 가격을 높게 책정한다.
☐ **철새와 어류의 장거리 이동법** • 소리: 야생오리는 밤에 별을 따라 이동하는데, 어두운 밤에 움직일 수 있는 것은 소리 덕분이다. • 냄새: 연어는 고향으로 돌아갈 때 자기가 태어난 곳의 특유의 물 냄새를 따라간다.
☐ **풍화작용의 원인** • 물의 작용: 밤에 온도가 떨어지면 바위 틈새의 물이 얼면서 바위를 부서지게 한다. • 식물의 작용: 식물이 뿌리를 내리면서 바위 속 깊게 침투하면 틈이 벌어지고 결국 부서진다.
☐ **친환경적 경영 전략의 이점** • 경영비용 절약: 커피숍에 백열 전구 대신에 형광등을 쓰면 전기료 지출이 줄어든다. • 친환경 이미지 구축: 커피숍에서 재활용된 냅킨과 컵을 쓰면 손님들에게 좋은 이미지를 준다.
☐ **소비자에 따른 광고 전략의 종류** • 시각적 신호: 바닷가 휴양지를 운영하는 회사는 밝은 색채와 노을처럼 강렬한 이미지를 강조한다. • 음성 신호: 성우를 이용해 휴양지의 아름답고 깨끗한 바닷물 등 많은 정보를 전달한다.
☐ **잡초의 긍정적인 효과** • 토양 유실을 막음: 비가 많이 올 때 토양과 유기물질이 쓸려가지 않게 잡아준다. • 병충해로부터 보호: 곤충들이 커피 묘목 대신 잡초를 더 좋아해서 피해가 덜하다.

- ☐ **고대 로마제국의 기술력**
  - 콘크리트: 석회석에서 얻은 콘크리트를 이용, 튼튼한 다리들을 건설하여 길을 서로 연결했다.
  - 상수도: 산에서 도시로 담수를 끌어오는 상수도를 지하에 만들어 오염을 막을 수 있었다.

- ☐ **어린 동물들에게 있어서 놀이의 역할**
  - 먹이를 다루는 연습: 어린 제비는 부리로 깃털을 떨어뜨리고 줍는 행동을 반복한다.
  - 도망치는 연습: 어린 원숭이가 나무에서 나무로 옮겨 다니는 것은 팔 근육을 강화시킨다.

- ☐ **진동을 통한 동종간의 소통**
  - 위험을 알릴 때: 쇠파리 애벌레는 천적이 나타나면 어미에게 진동신호를 보낸다.
  - 먹이를 찾았을 때: 뿔매미는 신선한 잎사귀를 발견했을 때 다른 뿔매미들에게 진동신호를 보낸다.

- ☐ **식물들이 살아남는 방법**
  - 잎을 버리는 경우: 단풍나무가 잎을 떨어뜨리지 않으면 겨울에 눈의 무게로 인해 가지가 꺾인다.
  - 열매를 버리는 경우: 아보카도는 일부 열매들을 떨어뜨려 나머지 열매에 충분한 영양분을 공급한다.

- ☐ **쉽게 기억하는 방법**
  - 사전 지식이 있을 때: 콘서트에 갈 때 사전 지식이 있으면 나중에 더 잘 기억할 수 있다.
  - 특이 사항이 있을 때: 학생들이 많으면 교수는 키가 크거나 똑똑한 학생들을 더 잘 기억한다.

- ☐ **알의 부화에 있어 수분의 필요성**
  - 부드러운 알: 개구리는 물가에 알을 낳아서 수분이 바로 알로 흡수된다.
  - 딱딱한 알: 사막의 뱀의 알은 수분을 유지해주는 내부구조 덕에 건조한 곳에도 문제없다.

- ☐ **상품 포장**
  - 새 기술 적용: 전에는 우유를 유리병에 담았으나 잘 깨지고 비싸서 플라스틱으로 바꿨다.
  - 타사와의 경쟁: 전에는 우유를 큰 용기에만 팔았지만, 다른 음료와 경쟁하려고 작게 포장했다.

- ☐ **어류가 물 속에서 다니는 방법**
  - 지느러미: 지느러미가 물을 밀어내는 역할을 하여 움직일 수 있도록 도와준다.
  - 부레: 부레 안의 공기의 양을 조절하면 밀도가 변해 물에 뜨거나 가라앉을 수 있다.

- ☐ **생태관광의 이점**
  - 공해를 줄임: 자동차나 버스를 타는 대신 걷거나 말이나 코끼리를 타고 이동한다.
  - 경각심을 일깨움: 특정 지역이 직면한 환경문제를 알리고 교육시킨다.

- ☐ **상표의 효과가 떨어지는 이유**
  - 상표의 색상에 문제가 있는 경우
  - 상표의 디자인이 구식인 경우

- ☐ **판매전략**
  - 기존 기술력 이용: TV를 만들던 회사는 컴퓨터 모니터를 쉽게 만들어 팔 수 있다.
  - 관련상품 만들기: 스키를 만들던 회사는 재킷이나 장갑 같은 용품을 팔 수 있다.

- ☐ **사람이 자신감을 획득하는 방법**
  - 자기자신의 경험: 수학을 잘 하는 학생은 자신의 좋은 성적에서 자신감을 얻는다.
  - 타인의 성취에 노출: 피아노를 잘 치는 언니를 보며 피아니스트의 꿈을 키운다.

- ☐ **도마뱀이 모래 속으로 다니는 이점**
  - 온도 조절: 모래 밑에 있으면 뜨거운 열을 피할 수 있다.
  - 사냥에 도움: 땅 위에 있는 곤충의 미세한 진동을 느껴 위치를 파악한다.

- ☐ **지렁이가 식물의 성장에 주는 도움**
  - 흙의 변환: 지렁이는 흙을 먹는데 그러면 흙이 고와지고 자연적 비료로 변한다.
  - 통로의 생성: 지렁이는 이동을 위해 굴을 파는데 이것이 공기와 물의 통로가 된다.

- ☐ **북극 동물들의 적응 방법**
  - 추위를 막음: 북극 부엉이는 발에도 털이 나있어서 눈에 직접 닿는 면이 적다.
  - 열 방출을 줄임: 북극 늑대는 몸과 발이 작아서 큰 동물들 보다 열 손실이 적다.

- ☐ **실연(demonstration) 광고의 종류**
  - 곤란한 상황을 연출: 비가 오는 상황을 연출하고 가방을 열었을 때 내용물이 젖지 않았다.
  - 사용전과 후를 비교: 더러운 셔츠를 세탁할 때 세제 사용 전과 후를 비교하여 보여준다.

- ☐ **소비자의 구매 결정에 영향을 미치는 요소**
  - 내재적 요인: 과일 주스가 맛있으면 그 경험 때문에 계속해서 산다.
  - 외적 요인: 과일 주스가 예쁜 병에 담겨 있으면 좋은 주스라 생각하고 산다.

- ☐ **포장 도로가 주변 생물에 끼치는 악영향**
  - 식물에 악영향: 잡초의 씨가 도로를 따라 이동하면 이것이 자라면서 기존 식물들을 죽인다.
  - 동물에 악영향: 차들이 다니면 여우가 먹이를 찾는 구역을 제한하여 굶어 죽게 한다.

- ☐ **새들이 떼지어 먹이를 찾는 이유**
  - 안전성: 홀로 먹이를 찾는 새에 비해 포식동물의 공격을 받을 가능성이 적다.
  - 정보교환: 집단 내에서 정보를 교환할 수 있기 때문에 더 많은 먹이를 먹을 수 있다.

- ☐ **아비새(loon) 깃털의 종류**
  - 겉깃털: 촘촘하게 얽혀 있고 기름막으로 둘러싸여 물이 들어올 수 없다.
  - 솜깃털: 두껍고 부드러워서 열이 빠져나가는 것을 막아준다.

- ☐ **개미떼의 방해 전략**
  - 화학적 전략: 큰 먹이를 찾았을 때 그 위에 화학물질을 뿌리면 다른 개미는 접근하지 못한다.
  - 물리적 전략: 다른 개미집 입구에 돌을 쌓아서 밖으로 나오지 못하게 막는다.

- ☐ **높은 산악지역에 사는 동물들의 특징**
  - 강한 근육: 야생 염소는 가슴과 앞발 근육이 강해서 가파른 곳을 쉽게 오르내린다.
  - 갈라진 굽: 록키 양은 눈과 얼음 위에서도 미끄러지지 않고 머물 수 있다.

- ☐ **도시가 시골보다 기온이 높은 이유**
  - 기계와 자동차들이 발산하는 배기가스와 열로 인해 도시 열섬(urban heat island)이 발생한다.
  - 아스팔트 등의 짙은 색깔이 햇볕을 흡수한 후 그것을 열 에너지로 바꾼다.

- ☐ **세부적인 계획들의 단점**
  - 현실적 문제: 계획이 너무 세세하면 지키기 어렵고 지키지 못하면 짜증을 유발한다.
  - 시간의 문제: 세세한 계획은 우리의 예상보다 시간이 더 오래 걸린다.

- ☐ **암컷 원숭이의 어미 역할 떠넘기기의 장점**
  - 어미 원숭이: 새끼를 위해 먹이를 채집할 시간을 얻는다.
  - 다른 어린 암컷: 어미로서의 기술을 터득하고 준비를 할 수 있다.

- ☐ **나무 태우기(wood fire)의 장점**
  - 둥지: 딱따구리(woodpecker) 같은 새에게 둥지를 제공한다.
  - 좋은 먹이: 사슴 같은 동물에게는 좋은 먹이도 생긴다.

- ☐ **흰개미(termite)가 개미집을 습하게 유지하는 방법**
  - 재료: 진흙과 나무물질이 마르면 침투가 안 되는 장벽이 되어서 수분을 차단한다.
  - 통풍구: 바닥에서 찬 공기가 들어오고 더운 공기는 위로 빠져 온도와 습도를 유지.

강 의

- [ ] **사막에 사는 개구리들의 체내 수분 조절 방법**
  - 피부에 보호막 형성: 기름막이 피부를 둘러싸 수분의 증발을 막는다.
  - 수분을 저장하는 기관: 비가 오면 수분을 흠뻑 섭취해서 보관 후 필요할 때마다 쓴다.

- [ ] **유물이 잘 보존되는 2가지 조건**
  - 메마른 곳: 이집트 사막의 2000년 된 무덤 속에 있는 그림은 여전히 색이 살아있다.
  - 산소가 부족한 곳: 지중해 바닥의 고대 침몰선(submerged ship)은 여전히 잘 보존돼있다.

- [ ] **동물들이 빠른 물살에서 살아남는 방법**
  - 바위에 몸을 붙인다: 파리매(black fly)의 유충(larva)은 큰 바위에 잘 붙어서 살아남는다.
  - 가라앉는다: 둑중개(slimy sculpin)는 다른 물고기와 달리 부레(swim bladder)가 없어서 가라앉는다.

- [ ] **고대문명의 경제구조 변화**
  - 화폐의 사용: 빵 만드는 사람은 코트 만드는 사람이 빵을 원하지 않을 때에도 코트를 살 수 있게 되었다.
  - 경제권의 확장: 로마시대에 중국에서 들어온 비단의 인기가 높았듯, 진귀한 물건을 위해 먼 거리를 누볐다.

- [ ] **새로운 환경에서의 동물의 변화**
  - 지역이 변하면: 유럽이 원산지였던 어떤 새가 남미로 넘어오면서 크기가 달라졌다.
  - 온도가 변하면: 그 새가 추운 곳에서는 크기가 커지고, 따뜻한 곳에서는 크기가 작아졌다.

- [ ] **연대감(bond)에 따른 동물무리(grouping)의 종류**
  - 연대감이 강한 경우: 코끼리는 사회적인 이유로 무리지어 살고, 누군가가 아프면 서로 돌봐준다.
  - 연대감이 없는 경우: 물고기가 떼지어 다니는 이유는 천적으로부터의 보호일 뿐, 서로 알아보지도 못한다.

- [ ] **개미들이 효과적으로 먹이를 얻는 방법**
  - 서로 다른 방향으로 간다: 한번 갔던 방향은 다시 가지 않음으로써 헛수고를 하지 않도록 한다.
  - 노력을 최소화한다: 과일 하나를 분해하려면 50마리가 필요하지만, 들어서 나르면 10마리만 있으면 된다.

- [ ] **철도의 확장이 미국경제에 끼친 영향**
  - 사업의 확장: 지역주민만을 상대로 사업을 하던 시계회사가 다른 지역으로 사업을 확장할 수 있었다.
  - 공장의 이동: 석탄운송이 가능해져, 전기 때문에 판매처 주변에 짓던 공장을 다른 곳에 짓고 상품을 옮긴다.

- [ ] **원숭이들이 물을 얻는 방법**
  - 유칼립투스(eucalyptus) 나뭇잎을 먹으면 수분이 많아 물을 먹지 않아도 된다.
  - 거미원숭이(spider monkey)는 컵처럼 생긴 나뭇잎을 이용해 물을 떠먹는다.

- [ ] **관측대(observatory)는 어디에 지어야 하는가**
  - 도시에서 멀리 짓는다: 도시 주변에는 빛이 많아 밤하늘이 잘 보이지 않는다.
  - 사막에 짓는다: 밤하늘이 잘 보이려면 습도가 낮고 건조해야 한다.

- [ ] **포유류는 새끼를 낳으면 더 용감해진다.**
  - 새끼가 없는 쥐: 미로(maze)에 풀어놨는데, 구석에서 안전함을 느끼자 더 이상 움직이지 않았다.
  - 새끼가 있는 쥐: 미로(maze)에 풀어놨는데, 넓은 공간을 거침없이 쏘다니며 길을 찾아냈다.

- [ ] **고고학자들이 유적지를 찾는 방법**
  - 지형의 특징(feature of land): 뉴질랜드 산꼭대기에 살던 부족은 집을 크게 지어서 평평한 곳을 필요로 했다.
  - 식물의 특징(plant life): 북미 원주민들은 옛날부터 빵나무(breadnut tree)를 필요로 해서 이 나무를 찾으면 된다.

- [ ] **식물이 곤충을 이용하는 보호법**
  - 포도나무는 화학물질로 무당벌레(ladybug)를 끌어들여 병충(pests)을 잡아먹게 한다.
  - 선인장(cactus)은 꿀을 이용해 곤충을 끌어들여 병충(pests)을 잡아먹게 한다.

- [ ] **어미의 적당한 무관심이 필요한 이유**
  - 새끼의 안전: 암사슴은 새끼를 숨겨놓고는, 하루에 한번만 본다. 너무 자주 보면 위치를 들키기 때문이다.
  - 새끼의 먹이: 쥐나 토끼의 젖은 영양가가 아주 높아서, 하루에 한번 조금 먹이는 것만으로도 충분하다.

- [ ] **달팽이(snail)가 덥고 건조한 날씨에서 살아남는 방법**
  - 더우면: 식물이 우거진 그늘에 피해있거나, 시열이 올라오지 않는 나무나 벽에 붙어 있다.
  - 건조하면: 칼슘성분의 물질분비로 달팽이 집을 막고, 덜 먹고, 덜 움직이면 몇 달 동안 물 없이 살 수 있다.

- [ ] **동물들이 열대 우림 캐노피에서 살아남는 방법**
  - 혼자 먹이를 찾는다: 먹이가 여기저기 퍼져있기 때문에 무리로 다니면 먹이가 부족할 수도 있다.
  - 큰 소리를 내 영역표시를 한다: 짖는 원숭이(howler monkey)는 영역을 넘어가면 큰 싸움이 날 수 있다.

- [ ] **이동 직전에 철새들에게 생기는 변화**
  - 신체적 변화: 식욕증가. 많이 먹어서 지방을 축적한다. 이동 중간에 먹이를 먹지 않아도 된다.
  - 행동의 변화: 사회성 증가. 혼자 지내던 새들이 서로 친해지고 집단으로 이동하여 천적을 피한다.

- [ ] **산불이 동물에게 득이 되는 경우**
  - 먹이를 찾기 쉬워진다: 칠면조는 숲의 가장자리에서 기다렸다가 지렁이들이 기어나오면 잡아먹는다.
  - 새끼가 살아남기 쉽다: 산불 이후엔 나무 안에 독소가 사라져 딱정벌레는 그 안에 알을 낳을 수 있다.

- [ ] **치타가 빨리 달리기 위해 적응한 방법**
  - 질긴 발바닥: 잘 단련되어 있어, 거친 자갈밭에서도 빠른 속도로 달릴 수 있다.
  - 강한 다리: 다리의 길이가 길뿐 아니라 강한 근육을 갖고 있다. (특히 뒷다리)

- [ ] **결핍을 이용한 마케팅**
  - 물량의 결핍: 옷 가게에서 자켓이 얼마 남지 않았다고 하면 손님들이 몰린다.
  - 시간의 결핍: 옷 가게에서 이번 주말에만 반값이라고 하면 손님들이 몰린다.

- [ ] **회사가 직원들을 더 생산적으로 만드는 방법**
  - 정기적인 행사: 소풍 같은 행사를 통해 직원들 사이에 좋은 관계를 형성하고 친목을 도모한다.
  - 교육비 지원: 직원들이 각종 자격증을 따거나 학위를 받게 함으로서 전문적인 발전을 하도록 한다.

- [ ] **식물들이 살아남는 적응법**
  - 먹기 불편하게 한다: 어떤 잔디는 가장자리에 날카로운 이산화규소(silica)가 달려있어, 베일 수 있다.
  - 동물을 속인다: 시계꽃(passion vine)은 나비 알 같은 알갱이를 만들어 나비가 다른 곳에 알을 낳게 한다.

- [ ] **인센티브 제도의 단점**
  - 동기부여가 되지 않는다: 전자제품 가게에 손님이 와서 설명을 듣고 난 다음에 남에게서 사면 일하기 싫다.
  - 직원들끼리 경쟁이 붙는다: 경험이 많은 직원들이 새 직원을 가르칠 이유가 없다. 새 직원은 배울게 없다.

- [ ] **회사가 판매부진을 극복하는 방법**
  - 제품에 대해 모를 경우: 장난감 제품이 아이들 산수실력에 도움이 된다면 광고를 통해 이를 알려야 한다.
  - 돈이 충분치 않을 경우: 컴퓨터가 너무 비싸다면 일단 가져가고 1~2년동안 매달 갚아나가도록 도와준다.

- [ ] **철새들이 먼 거리를 날 수 있는 이유**
  - 잘 발달된 혈관 시스템이 산소를 최대한 많이 수용할 수 있도록 해준다.
  - 가슴근육이 잘 발달해 지치지 않고 먼 거리를 갈 수 있게 해준다.

- [ ] **들쥐와 같은 잡식동물이 병에 걸리지 않는 방법**
  - 조금만 먼저 먹는다: 약간만 먹어보고 몸에 이상이 없으면 조금씩 양을 늘려가며 먹는다.
  - 찰흙을 먹는다: 곰팡이의 독성과 찰흙이 결합하면 몸에 퍼지지 않고 몸 밖으로 내보낼 수 있다.

- [ ] **사바나의 건기를 살아남는 방법**
  - 물이 많은 식물을 먹는다: 코끼리는 큰 덩치와 엄니(tusk)를 이용해 물이 많은 나무를 뜯어먹는다.
  - 물이 많은 곳으로 이동한다: 영양(wildebeest)은 건기 동안 북쪽으로 이동해서 살다가 다시 내려온다.

- [ ] **낙타가 체온을 유지하는 방법**
  - 등의 혹이 열을 흡수한다: 등의 혹은 지방덩어리인데, 다른 장기 대신 열을 흡수해서 체온을 유지한다.
  - 서로 가까이 앉는다: 서있을 때보다 에너지를 덜 쓰고, 서로 그늘을 만들어 태양을 피할 수 있다.

- [ ] **포식자가 큰 무리의 먹이를 노리는 방법**
  - 하나만 노린다: 다 똑같아 보이는 무리 속에서도 포식자가 노리기 쉬운 먹잇감이 눈에 띈다.
  - 일단 분산시킨다: 상어는 물고기떼를 노릴 때 일단 분산시키고 나서 하나씩 잡아먹는다.

- [ ] **해양 포유류가 차가운 물에서 체온을 유지하는 방법**
  - 두꺼운 피하지방층(blubber)이 온몸을 감싸 냉기를 차단시켜준다.
  - 크고 둥근 몸이 표면적(surface area)를 줄여 열의 유출을 최소화한다.

- [ ] **같은 그룹의 사람끼리 한정어(restricted codes)로 소통하는 경우**
  - 배경지식이 같은 경우(background knowledge): 의사들끼리는 몇 마디로 소통이 되지만, 환자와는 안 된다.
  - 이해가 공유된 경우(shared understanding): 같은 상황이면 여러 말보다 엄소를 들어올리면 이해하기 쉽다.

- [ ] **여행객으로부터 환경을 보호하는 방법**
  - 취약한 부분을 보강한다: 예민한 곳은 사람들이 다니도록 판자로 만든 오솔길을 따로 만든다.
  - 여행객의 수를 제한한다: 여행 가이드가 소규모 그룹을 이끌게 하고 여행객의 수를 제한한다.

- [ ] **물 속에서 숨쉬지 못하는 동물들의 대처법**
  - 몸의 기능을 느리게 한다: 악어(alligator)는 먹이를 잡기 위해 움직이지 않고 기다린다.
  - 물 속 시간을 최소화: 펠리칸(brown pelican)은 피부에 공기주머니가 있어 깊이 들어가지 않고 빨리 뜬다.

- [ ] **동물들이 자신을 보호하는 적응법**
  - 몸 구조가 적응한다: 괭이상어(bullhead shark)는 천적을 뿌리치기 위해 꼬리에 가시가 돋았다.
  - 행동이 적응한다: 주머니쥐(possum)는 천적인 여우를 속이기 위해 죽은 척을 한다.

강 의

- [ ] **Human grows trees with seeds, which will remain in dormancy for some time before sprouting.**

    · Imitating nature, like weather, temperature.
    예시 1 : Oak trees. Creating a moist environment and a warmer climate, stimulating the growth.

    · Break the hard outer coating.
    예시 2 : Locust trees. Putting the seed in a can and shaking off the hard outer coating, facilitating the sprouting.

- [ ] **In a mass media class, the professor talks about certain techniques in advertising to persuade consumers.**

    · Direct route.
    예시 1 : If a car is really energy-efficient that it runs on electricity or a small amount of gasoline, in an advertisement, they will use facts and statistics to compare themselves with other cars, the consumers can have a pretty good sense on the functions. This is a direct approach or direct route.

    · Indirect route
    예시 2 : If a car is ordinary in functions, has no other obvious advantages, in the advertisement it will be showing a group of people smiling and laughing, driving themselves to the beach, this is a technique that relates the car with happiness. Using associations and connections other than facts and hard evidence, is an indirect route.

- [ ] **Two benefits of dormancy**

    · To sprout over a large area
    예시 1 : A seed is going to sprout in a place but has to compete with other younger plants around it. But if it is in dormancy and a bird coincidentally falls down to grab it and takes it to another place. The seed could then sprout there and do not have to compete for resources.

    · To sprout in the most favorable weather condition
    예시 2 : In the desert, some seeds in dormancy would like to sprout after it rains since after rain it is easy to access to water and could have plenty of resources.

- [ ] **Two advantages of fire for early humans.**

    · The first one is to allow them to make better stone tools.
    예시 1 : For example, they could use fire to heat the stone to a high temperature which could ship the stone to a sharp edge like a sharp blade. So the early humans could hunt more effectively.

    · The second is to improve the early humans' diet.
    예시 2 : For instance, raw potatoes were hard to digest. But if they used fire to heat the potatoes, it would be much easier to digest.

- [ ] **How do consumers reduce risks when purchasing?**

    · Do thorough research.
    예시 1 : If you want to buy a computer, you can search online to see which manufacturer is better and see the reviews of other buyers.

    · Stay loyal to one brand or company.
    예시 2 : If you have bought a car that functioned well and lasted long, you want to stay with this company next time.

- [ ] **Two ways for whales to use sounds to survive in the deep ocean.**

    · Navigate
    예시 1 : Hear the refection from objects so that wholes can get the right direction.

강 의

- obtain food
  예시 2 : Since whole are in the group, one can call other whales if it finds any fish.

☐ **2 ways that advertisers sell products.**

- Publicity
  예시 1 : Newspapers and magazines. A product can be showcased here because it costs less. It's much cheaper than making a commercial. For example, a new game is showcased on a technology magazine. There's no need to pay more to gain more customers in this way.

- Creditability
  예시 2 : Another reason is that newspapers and magazines have creditability. People tend to trust them more and this is a great way to sell.

☐ **Animal's defense mechanism. Some people like group living, this brings benefits as long as risks. For instance, dangerous diseases might spread among the animals and the whole species might distinct. Animals have different defense mechanisms to deal with it.**

- Behavior mechanism
  예시 1 : Ants clean themselves, especially those who go out and search for food, they clean themselves more often than those who live in the colony, because there's a risk that they bring the virus from the outside world to the whole species.
- Bodily mechanism
  예시 2 : Ants give out a substance to remove virus.

☐ **Two solutions where animals have territorial food resources but they don't defend the territory.**

- When the food resources are abundant, and it's unnecessary to drive the others out of their territory.
  예시 1 : For instance, sunbirds eat a kind of nectar, it's so much that the sunbirds don't even bother to defend their own territory.

- When the food resources are too limited.
  예시 2 : For instance, if there are only a few flowers, the birds would rather take the time and look for another resource instead of wasting the time to drive away from the other birds.

☐ **Two types of adaption to cold weather.**

- basking
  예시 1 : Arctic butterfly expose to sunshine in the daytime, spread its wings to absorb heat.

- chemical substances
  예시 2 : Arctic fly can secrete a kind of chemical can prevent being freezing.

☐ **Two adaptions for fixed ocean-bottom organisms used to get food.**

- active approach
  예시 1 : Like the sea anomy, a colorful sea animal with arm-like structure. The arm-like thing is poisonous and will sting the fishes. So when the fish comes around the anomy, it'll sting the fish and pull it over. So that they are actively trying to get the food.

- passive approach
  예시 2 : Like the oyster, stays in the shell and doesn't move at all. Its shell has little openings so that when the seawater that contains food material and nutrient flows through it, those materials will get into the shell from the opening. They will look still the same from the outside but they are actually eating.

강 의

☐ **2 ways that plowing help crops to get more nutrition.**

- Bring the nutrition to the surface.
  예시 1 : Corn, when it rains, the water brings the nutrition down, by plowing it can bring it from bottom to the surface.

- Prevent other plants to absorb the nutrition.
  예시 2 : Corn, weeds, by plowing it can dirt the weeds and the weeds die.

☐ **Spruce trees in north Canada and Russia avoid injuring.**

- Triangle shape when heavy-snow falls down, slide off to the ground instead of break the branch.
- Dark green color needle

☐ **2 ways of adaptation that trees use to protect themselves from a forest fire.**

- cooling the inner part of the tree down
- remove the resources that might cause a fire

usherin.usher.co.kr

속담 120개
(Proverbs)

USHER
어셔어학원

001. 남의 떡이 커보인다.
The grass is greener on the other side (of the fence).

002. 천생연분
Match made in heaven.

003. 원숭이도 나무에서 떨어질 때가 있다.
Even Homer nods.

004. 낮말은 새가 듣고 밤말은 쥐가 듣는다.
Walls have ears.

005. 똥 묻은 개 겨 묻은 개 나무란다.
The pot calls the kettle black.

006. 백문이 불여일견
To see is to believe. (Seeing is believing.)

007. 선무당이 사람잡는다.
A little knowledge is dangerous.

008. 부전자전
A chip off the old block. Like father, like son.

009. 호랑이도 제 말하면 온다.
Talk of the devil.
(and you'll hear the flutter of his wings).

010. 공자 앞에서 문자쓴다.
To teach a fish how to swim.

011. 그림의 떡
Pie in the sky.

012. 쥐구멍에도 볕들 날 있다.
Every dog has his day.

013. 헌 짚신도 짝이 있다.
Every Jack has his Jill.

014. 건강한 신체에 건강한 정신이 깃든다.
A sound mind in a sound body.

015. 천천히 그리고 꾸준히 하면 이긴다.
Slow and steady wins the game.

016. 세월은 사람을 기다리지 않는다.
Time and tide wait for no man.

017. 공수래공수거
Shrouds have no pockets.

018. 수고가 없으면 이득도 없다.
No pain, no gain.

019. 옷이 날개다.
(Fine) clothes make the man.
(Fine feathers make fine birds.)

020. 유유상종
Birds of a feather flock together.

021. 뜻이 있는 곳에 길이 있다.
Where there is a will, there is a way.

022. 서투른 무당이 장구만 나무란다.
A bad workman blames his tools.

023. 사귀는 친구를 보면 그 사람됨을 알 수 있다.
A man is known by the company he keeps.

024. 서당개 삼년이면 풍월을 읊는다.
The sparrow near a school sings the primer.

025. 금강산도 식후경
A loaf of bread is better than the song of many birds.

026. 재주는 곰이 넘고 돈은 되놈이 번다.
One man sows and another man reaps.

027. 용두사미
Starts off with a bang and ends with a whimper.

028. 믿는 도끼에 발등 찍힌다.
Stabbed in the back.

029. 콩 심은 데 콩 나고 팥 심은 데 팥 난다.
As one sows, so shall he reap.

030. 죽마고우
A buddy from my old stomping grounds.

031. 엎친 데 덮친 격이다.
Adding insult to injury.

032. 호미로 막을 것을 가래로 막는다.
A stitch in time saves nine.

033. 소 잃고 외양간 고친다.
Mend the barn after the horse is stolen.

034. 종로에서 뺨 맞고 한강가서 눈 흘긴다.
Go home and kick the dog.

035. 첫술에 배부르랴.
Rome was not built in a day.

036. 시작이 반이다.
Well begun is half done.

037. 소귀에 경 읽기
Talking to the wall.

038. 돌다리도 두들겨 보고 건너라.
Look before you leap.

039. 돼지 목에 진주목걸이
Casting pearls before swine.

040. 개천에서 용났다.
A rags to riches story.

041. 눈엣가시
Pain in the eye.

042. 이미 엎질러진 물이다.
(It's no use) crying over spilt milk.

043. 손뼉도 마주쳐야 소리가 난다.
It takes two to tango.

044. 일석이조
Kill two birds with one stone.

045. 털어서 먼지 안 나는 사람 없다.
Everyone has a skeleton in the closet.

046. 독안에 든 쥐
A rat in a trap.

047. 벼룩의 간을 빼먹는다.
Can't get blood from a turnip.

048. 구관이 명관
You don't know what you've got until you've lost it.

049. 일각이 여삼추
Every minute seems like a thousand.

050. 줍는 사람이 임자다.
Finders keepers, (loser weepers.)

051. 모르는 게 약이다.
Ignorance is bliss.

052. 금상첨화
Icing on the cake.

053. 세 살 버릇 여든까지 간다.
Habit is a second nature.
What's learned in the cradle is carried to the grave.

054. 콩으로 메주를 쑨다고 해도 믿지 않는다.
You've cried wolf too many times.

055. 팥으로 메주를 쑨다 해도 믿는다.
You could sell him the Brooklyn Bridge.

056. 바늘 도둑이 소도둑 된다.
He that will steal a pin will steal an ox.

057. 웃으면 복이 온다.
If you laugh, blessings will come your way.

058. 헌신짝 버리듯 한다.
Thrown away like an old shoe.

059. 호랑이 굴에 들어가야 호랑이를 잡는다.
Nothing ventured, nothing gained.

060. 긁어 부스럼 만든다.
Let sleeping dogs lie.

061. 미꾸라지 한 마리가 온 웅덩이를 흐린다.
One rotten apple spoils the barrel.

062. 누워서 침 뱉기
Cut off your nose to spite your face.

063. 서울에서 김서방 찾기
Searching for a needle in a haystack.

064. 용자만이 미인을 얻을 수 있다.
None but the brave deserves the fair.

065. 제비 한 마리가 왔다고 여름이 온 것은 아니다.(속단은 금물)
One swallow does not make a summer.

066. 낙숫물이 바위를 뚫는다.
Many drops make a shower.

067. 쇠뿔도 단김에 빼라.
Strike while the iron is hot.

068. 집만한 곳이 없다.
There is no place like home.

069. 무소식이 희소식이다.
No news is good news.

070. 연습하면 완벽해진다.
Practice makes perfect.

071. 행동보다 말이 쉽다.
Easier said than done.

072. 안보면 멀어진다.
Out of sight, out of mind.

073. 어려울 때의 친구가 진정한 친구다.
A friend in need is a friend indeed.

074. 천마디의 말보다 한 번 보는 게 더 낫다.
A picture is worth a thousand words.

075. 아무것도 하지 않느니보다는 늦게라도 하는 게 낫다.
Better late than never.

076. 비가 내렸다 하면 억수로 퍼붓는다. (화불단행)
When it rains, it pours.

077. 오늘 할 일을 내일로 미루지 말라.
Never put off till tomorrow what you can do today.

078. 돈주머니 쥔 자가 가정을 지배한다.
Who holds the purse rules the house.

079. 감언이설에 넘어가지 말라.
It is not good to listen to flattery.

080. 아니 땐 굴뚝에 연기 날까
No smoke without fire.

081. 괴로움이 있으면 즐거움도 있다. (괴로움 뒤에는 기쁨이 있다).
     Every cloud has a silver lining.

082. 김칫국부터 마시지 말라.
     Don't count the chickens before they are hatched.

083. 일찍 일어나는 새가 벌레를 잡는다.
     The early bird catches the worm.

084. 서두르면 일을 그르친다.
     Haste makes waste.

085. 급할수록 돌아가라
     More haste, less speed.

086. 서두른 결혼은 두고두고 후회한다.
     Marry in haste, repent at leisure.

087. 돈이 있으면 귀신도 부릴 수 있다.
     Money makes the mare go.

088. 제 버릇 개 못준다.
     A leopard can't change his spots.

089. 물고기는 큰 물에서 놀아야 한다.
     A big fish must swim in deep waters.

090. 물에 빠지면 지푸라기라도 잡는다.
     A drowning man will catch at a straw.
     A drowning man plucks at a straw.

091. 좋은 약은 입에 쓰다.
     A good medicine tastes bitter.

092. 천리 길도 한 걸음부터
     A journey of a thousand miles begins with a single step.
     Step by step one goes a long way.

093. 친구를 보면 그 친구를 알 수 있다.
     A man is known by the company he keeps.

094. 구르는 돌에는 이끼가 끼지 않는다.
     A rolling stone gathers no moss.

095. 제 눈에 안경이다.
     Beauty is in the eye of the beholder.

096. 집이 세상에서 가장 편한 곳이다.
     There's no place like home.

097. 용 꼬리보다 뱀 머리가 낫다.
     Better be the head of a dog than the tail of a lion.

098. 피는 물보다 진하다.
     Blood is thicker than water.

099. 팔이 안으로 굽는다.
     Charity begins at home.

100. 선을 행하고 대가를 바라지 마라.
     Do good and don't look back.

101. 대접받고 싶으면 남에게 대접해라.
     Do unto others as you would have them unto you.

102. 죽은 사람은 말이 없다.
     Dead men tell no tales.

103. 하룻강아지 범 무서운 줄 모른다.
     Fools rush in the where angels fear to tread.

104. 모든 사람에게 일생에 세 번은 기회가 찾아온다.
     Fortune knocks three times at everyone's door.

105. 실패는 성공의 어머니
     Failure is but a stepping stone to success.

106. 욕심은 끝이 없다.
     Greed has no limits.

107. 하늘은 스스로 돕는 자를 돕는다.
     Heaven helps those who help themselves.

108. 송충이는 솔잎을 먹어야 한다.
     He bit off more than he can chew.

109. 한 귀로 듣고 한 귀로 흘린다.
     In one ear and out the other.

110. 누워서 떡 먹기
     It's a piece of cake.

111. 진퇴양난
     Between a rock and a hard place.

112. 양지가 음지 되고 음지가 양지된다.
     Life is full of ups and downs.

113. 티끌 모아 태산이다.
     Little drops of water make the ocean.

114. 백지장도 맞들면 낫다.
     Two heads are better than one.

115. 나무만 보고 숲은 보지 못한다.
     Cannot see the wood for the trees.

116. 오는 말이 고우면 가는 말이 곱다.
     Claw me and I'll claw thee.

117. 빈수레가 요란하다.
     Empty vessels make the most sound.

118. 달도 차면 기운다.
     Every tide has its ebb.

119. 시장이 반찬이다.
     Hunger is the best sauce.

120. 엎어지면 코 닿을 데 있다.
     It is within a stone's throw.

USHER
iBT TOEFL
FINAL TEST
SPEAKING | 문제집

어셔 iBT 토플 파이널 테스트 스피킹 문제집

어셔 어학 연구소

usherin.usher.co.kr

USHER iBT TOEFL
FINAL TEST SPEAKING
TEST 01

Independent Tasks

Question 1   usherin.usher.co.kr > 시험리스트 > Speaking 시험리스트 > Task 1 > #1027

Integrated Tasks

Question 2   usherin.usher.co.kr > 시험리스트 > Speaking 시험리스트 > Task 2 > #2001
Question 3   usherin.usher.co.kr > 시험리스트 > Speaking 시험리스트 > Task 3 > #3001
Question 4   usherin.usher.co.kr > 시험리스트 > Speaking 시험리스트 > Task 4 > #4001

시험이 끝나고

시험 전에 Check !

펜과 메모지가 있음 ○
핸드폰을 껐음 ○
시간을 체크할 시계가 있음 ○
문제를 들을 준비가 됐음 ○
목소리를 녹음할 준비가 됐음 ○
평소에 연습한대로 발음하겠음 ○
단어의 강세에 유의하겠음 ○
시간을 체크해가면서 발표하겠음 ○

Speaking Section Directions

In this section of the test, you will be able to demonstrate your ability to speak about a variety of topics. You will answer four questions by speaking into the mircrophone. Answer each of the questions as completely as possible.

In question 1, you will speak about a familiar topic. Your response will be scored on your ability to speak clearly and coherently about the topic.

In questions 2 and 3, you will first read a short text. The text will go away and you will then listen to a talk on the same topic. You will then be asked a question about what you have read and heard. You will need to combine appropriate information from the text and the talk to provide a complete answer to the question. Your response will be scored on your ability to speak clearly and coherently and on your ability to accurately convey information about what you read and heard.

In question 4, you will listen to part of a lecture. You will then be asked a question about what you heard. Your response will be scored on your ability to speak clearly and coherently and on your ability to accurately convey information about what you heard.

You may take notes while you read and while you listen to the conversations and lectures. You may use your notes to help prepare your response.

Listen carefully to the directions for each question. The directions will not be written on the screen.

For each question you will be given a short time to prepare your response. A clock will show how much preparation time is remaining. When the preparation time is up, you will be told to begin your response. A clock will show how much response time is remaining. A message will appear on the screen when the response time has ended.

Question 1 of 4

Some people say that It is better for children to go on a field trip. Others say that It is better for them to study in classroom. Which view do you agree with? Use reasons and examples to support your answer.

PREPARATION TIME
00: 00: 15

RESPONSE TIME
00: 00: 45

Dance Classes

There will soon be dance classes offered on campus. We are aware of the fact that university students are always busy taking classes and may not have any extra time to find a way to exercise off campus. Therefore, students can now attend all of their classes, and relieve their stress by exercising, and then leave campus feeling refreshed. The dance classes are open to anyone with an open mind ready to learn. Even better, the first class is offered for free so students can get a taste of what the classes will be like. Do not hesitate to try out the class.

Now get ready to answer the question.

The woman expresses her opinion about the college's plan. State her opinion and explain the reasons she gives for holding that opinion.

PREPARATION TIME
00: 00: 30

RESPONSE TIME
00: 00: 60

Reading Time: 50 seconds

Plant Adaptations in Rainforests

A typical rainforest has a warm, humid environment with abundant oxygen-producing tall trees. It has a high yearly rainfall that supports millions of plants, animals, and microorganism species around the world. 70% of the species that are living in rainforest are trees which resemble one another in some ways. Because the tall trees prevent the sunlight from penetrating the bottom layers of the rainforest, there is always a lack of sunlight there. Due to this fact, rainforest plants usually have large leaves and structures to collect the most sunlight and protect them from the excessive amount of water.

Now get ready to answer the question

Using the examples from the professor's lecture, explain how plants in rainforests ensure their survival.

PREPARATION TIME
00: 00: 30

RESPONSE TIME
00: 00: 60

Now get ready to answer the question.

Using the examples from the professor's lecture, explain how some animals can survive in high altitudes.

PREPARATION TIME
00: 00: 20

RESPONSE TIME
00: 00: 60

시험이 끝나고

	Task 1	Task 2	Task 3	Task 4
시간에 맞춰 발표를 끝냈음	O / X	O / X	O / X	O / X
"아닌 경우," 시간이 남아서라면?				
- 할 말이 부족해서				
- 말이 빨라서				
- 도저히 모르겠음 / 기타				
"아닌 경우," 도중에 잘려서라면?				
- 할 말이 부족해서				
- 말이 빨라서				
- 도저히 모르겠음 / 기타				

	Task 1	Task 2	Task 3	Task 4
발표할 내용을 완벽히 정리했음	O / X	O / X	O / X	O / X
"아닌 경우," 문제를 이해하지 못해서라면?				
- 읽기 / 듣기가 안돼서				
- 배경지식이 부족해서				
- 도저히 모르겠음 / 기타				
"아닌 경우," 내용 정리가 덜 끝나서라면?				
- 준비 시간이 부족해서				
- 내용이 뒤죽박죽 되어서				
- 도저히 모르겠음 / 기타				

다음에 문제를 풀 때에는…

반드시 이렇게 해야지!

절대 이러지 말아야지!

USHER iBT TOEFL
FINAL TEST SPEAKING
TEST 02

Independent Tasks

Question 1   usherin.usher.co.kr > 시험리스트 > Speaking 시험리스트 > Task 1 > #1026

Integrated Tasks

Question 2   usherin.usher.co.kr > 시험리스트 > Speaking 시험리스트 > Task 2 > #2002
Question 3   usherin.usher.co.kr > 시험리스트 > Speaking 시험리스트 > Task 3 > #3002
Question 4   usherin.usher.co.kr > 시험리스트 > Speaking 시험리스트 > Task 4 > #4002

시험이 끝나고

시험 전에 Check !

펜과 메모지가 있음 ○
핸드폰을 껐음 ○
시간을 체크할 시계가 있음 ○
문제를 들을 준비가 됐음 ○
목소리를 녹음할 준비가 됐음 ○
평소에 연습한대로 발음하겠음 ○
단어의 강세에 유의하겠음 ○
시간을 체크해가면서 발표하겠음 ○

Speaking Section Directions

In this section of the test, you will be able to demonstrate your ability to speak about a variety of topics. You will answer four questions by speaking into the mircrophone. Answer each of the questions as completely as possible.

In question 1, you will speak about a familiar topic. Your response will be scored on your ability to speak clearly and coherently about the topic.

In questions 2 and 3, you will first read a short text. The text will go away and you will then listen to a talk on the same topic. You will then be asked a question about what you have read and heard. You will need to combine appropriate information from the text and the talk to provide a complete answer to the question. Your response will be scored on your ability to speak clearly and coherently and on your ability to accurately convey information about what you read and heard.

In question 4, you will listen to part of a lecture. You will then be asked a question about what you heard. Your response will be scored on your ability to speak clearly and coherently and on your ability to accurately convey information about what you heard.

You may take notes while you read and while you listen to the conversations and lectures. You may use your notes to help prepare your response.

Listen carefully to the directions for each question. The directions will not be written on the screen.

For each question you will be given a short time to prepare your response. A clock will show how much preparation time is remaining. When the preparation time is up, you will be told to begin your response. A clock will show how much response time is remaining. A message will appear on the screen when the response time has ended.

 뉴토플 - TEST 02_Q1

USHER iBT TOEFL Speaking

Question 1 of 4

When students study abroad, should they stay alone or stay with a family already living there? Use reasons and examples to support your answer.

PREPARATION TIME
00: 00: 15

RESPONSE TIME
00: 00: 45

Reading Time: 50 seconds

Removal of Food Carts

The university plans to ban food carts already on campus. It is hoped that by removing these carts, the vast amount of trash on campus will decrease as well. There has been way too much trash around campus, all of which are assumed to be the remaining wrappers and such of the products on food carts. By banning food carts, the amount of trash has to be reduced since the areas in which foods are sold will be reduced, and thus, people will not be eating all over campus, trashing the place. Furthermore, the foods sold on these carts are not good in regards to the students' health.

Now get ready to answer the question.

The woman expresses her opinion about the college's plan. State her opinion and explain the reasons she gives for holding that opinion.

PREPARATION TIME
00: 00: 30

RESPONSE TIME
00: 00: 60

Exaptation

Animals undergo various changes in their characteristics over time. The idea of adaptation is widely known to people as a process of natural selection that serves to keep or discard a particular trait. Different from adaptation, however, animals undergo exaptation, which refers to a feature of an animal that has evolved to serve a particular function, but subsequently provides another unintended function. This idea was originated in mid-19th century when interest in evolution of animals was immense. It was firstly known as "preadaptation" among the scientists.

Now get ready to answer the question

Using the example from the professor's lecture, explain what exaptation is and how it works.

PREPARATION TIME
00: 00: 30

RESPONSE TIME
00: 00: 60

Now get ready to answer the question.

Using the examples from the professor's lecture, explain what young animals can learn from play.

PREPARATION TIME
00: 00: 20

RESPONSE TIME
00: 00: 60

시험이 끝나고

	Task 1	Task 2	Task 3	Task 4
시간에 맞춰 발표를 끝냈음	O / X	O / X	O / X	O / X
"아닌 경우," 시간이 남아서라면?				
- 할 말이 부족해서				
- 말이 빨라서				
- 도저히 모르겠음 / 기타				
"아닌 경우," 도중에 잘려서라면?				
- 할 말이 부족해서				
- 말이 빨라서				
- 도저히 모르겠음 / 기타				
	Task 1	Task 2	Task 3	Task 4
발표할 내용을 완벽히 정리했음	O / X	O / X	O / X	O / X
"아닌 경우," 문제를 이해하지 못해서라면?				
- 읽기 / 듣기가 안돼서				
- 배경지식이 부족해서				
- 도저히 모르겠음 / 기타				
"아닌 경우," 내용 정리가 덜 끝나서라면?				
- 준비 시간이 부족해서				
- 내용이 뒤죽박죽 되어서				
- 도저히 모르겠음 / 기타				

다음에 문제를 풀 때에는…

반드시 이렇게 해야지!

절대 이러지 말아야지!

# USHER iBT TOEFL
FINAL TEST SPEAKING
TEST 03

Independent Tasks

Question 1   usherin.usher.co.kr > 시험리스트 > Speaking 시험리스트 > Task 1 > #1058

Integrated Tasks

Question 2   usherin.usher.co.kr > 시험리스트 > Speaking 시험리스트 > Task 2 > #2003
Question 3   usherin.usher.co.kr > 시험리스트 > Speaking 시험리스트 > Task 3 > #3003
Question 4   usherin.usher.co.kr > 시험리스트 > Speaking 시험리스트 > Task 4 > #4003

시험이 끝나고

시험 전에 Check !

펜과 메모지가 있음 ○
핸드폰을 껐음 ○
시간을 체크할 시계가 있음 ○
문제를 들을 준비가 됐음 ○
목소리를 녹음할 준비가 됐음 ○
평소에 연습한대로 발음하겠음 ○
단어의 강세에 유의하겠음 ○
시간을 체크해가면서 발표하겠음 ○

USHER
어셔어학원

Speaking Section Directions

In this section of the test, you will be able to demonstrate your ability to speak about a variety of topics. You will answer four questions by speaking into the mircrophone. Answer each of the questions as completely as possible.

In question 1, you will speak about a familiar topic. Your response will be scored on your ability to speak clearly and coherently about the topic.

In questions 2 and 3, you will first read a short text. The text will go away and you will then listen to a talk on the same topic. You will then be asked a question about what you have read and heard. You will need to combine appropriate information from the text and the talk to provide a complete answer to the question. Your response will be scored on your ability to speak clearly and coherently and on your ability to accurately convey information about what you read and heard.

In question 4, you will listen to part of a lecture. You will then be asked a question about what you heard. Your response will be scored on your ability to speak clearly and coherently and on your ability to accurately convey information about what you heard.

You may take notes while you read and while you listen to the conversations and lectures. You may use your notes to help prepare your response.

Listen carefully to the directions for each question. The directions will not be written on the screen.

For each question you will be given a short time to prepare your response. A clock will show how much preparation time is remaining. When the preparation time is up, you will be told to begin your response. A clock will show how much response time is remaining. A message will appear on the screen when the response time has ended.

Question 1 of 4

Do you agree or disagree with the following statement?

Students learn more by participating in class discussions.

Use reasons and examples to support your answer.

PREPARATION TIME
00: 00: 15

RESPONSE TIME
00: 00: 45

Reading Time: 50 seconds

Computer Installations in Dormitories

We are living in the age of computers, and it is hard to imagine living without one. It is a great pleasure to announce that the university has decided to create computer labs in all the dormitories, with help and support from Orange Computers, Inc. As the computer labs will be built in the lobby, it should be easy to access for all students as well. The computers may be used for various purposes, either for academics or for personal entertainment. For those students who do not have personal computers, it would only be fair to install computer labs, which would prove to be helpful and useful.

Now get ready to answer the question.

The woman expresses her opinion about the college's plan. State her opinion and explain the reasons she gives for holding that opinion.

PREPARATION TIME
00: 00: 30

RESPONSE TIME
00: 00: 60

Optimal Foraging

In ecology, all animals must consume a source of energy which in turn is used for all the bodily functions. Therefore, it is essential that animals not waste energy on unnecessary activities. The ecologists developed a theory called optimal foraging which is the idea whereby organisms forage in a fashion that minimizes the amount of energy and time and maximizes the net energy intake. In other words, all animals attempt to take the most calories by using the least amount of energy. It is believed that the animals developed their methods of foraging through a long process of adaptation to the environment.

Now get ready to answer the question

Using the example from the professor's lecture, explain what optimal foraging is and how it works.

PREPARATION TIME
00: 00: 30

RESPONSE TIME
00: 00: 60

Now get ready to answer the question.

Using the examples from the professor's lecture, explain the functions of the two types of feathers.

PREPARATION TIME
00: 00: 20

RESPONSE TIME
00: 00: 60

시험이 끝나고

	Task 1	Task 2	Task 3	Task 4
시간에 맞춰 발표를 끝냈음	O / X	O / X	O / X	O / X
"아닌 경우," 시간이 남아서라면?				
- 할 말이 부족해서				
- 말이 빨라서				
- 도저히 모르겠음 / 기타				
"아닌 경우," 도중에 잘려서라면?				
- 할 말이 부족해서				
- 말이 빨라서				
- 도저히 모르겠음 / 기타				

	Task 1	Task 2	Task 3	Task 4
발표할 내용을 완벽히 정리했음	O / X	O / X	O / X	O / X
"아닌 경우," 문제를 이해하지 못해서라면?				
- 읽기 / 듣기가 안돼서				
- 배경지식이 부족해서				
- 도저히 모르겠음 / 기타				
"아닌 경우," 내용 정리가 덜 끝나서라면?				
- 준비 시간이 부족해서				
- 내용이 뒤죽박죽 되어서				
- 도저히 모르겠음 / 기타				

다음에 문제를 풀 때에는…

반드시 이렇게 해야지!

절대 이러지 말아야지!

USHER iBT TOEFL
FINAL TEST SPEAKING
TEST 04

Independent Tasks

Question 1   usherin.usher.co.kr > 시험리스트 > Speaking 시험리스트 > Task 1 > #1023

Integrated Tasks

Question 2   usherin.usher.co.kr > 시험리스트 > Speaking 시험리스트 > Task 2 > #2004
Question 3   usherin.usher.co.kr > 시험리스트 > Speaking 시험리스트 > Task 3 > #3004
Question 4   usherin.usher.co.kr > 시험리스트 > Speaking 시험리스트 > Task 4 > #4004

시험이 끝나고

시험 전에 Check !

- 펜과 메모지가 있음 ○
- 핸드폰을 껐음 ○
- 시간을 체크할 시계가 있음 ○
- 문제를 들을 준비가 됐음 ○
- 목소리를 녹음할 준비가 됐음 ○
- 평소에 연습한대로 발음하겠음 ○
- 단어의 강세에 유의하겠음 ○
- 시간을 체크해가면서 발표하겠음 ○

Speaking Section Directions

In this section of the test, you will be able to demonstrate your ability to speak about a variety of topics. You will answer four questions by speaking into the mircrophone. Answer each of the questions as completely as possible.

In question 1, you will speak about a familiar topic. Your response will be scored on your ability to speak clearly and coherently about the topic.

In questions 2 and 3, you will first read a short text. The text will go away and you will then listen to a talk on the same topic. You will then be asked a question about what you have read and heard. You will need to combine appropriate information from the text and the talk to provide a complete answer to the question. Your response will be scored on your ability to speak clearly and coherently and on your ability to accurately convey information about what you read and heard.

In question 4, you will listen to part of a lecture. You will then be asked a question about what you heard. Your response will be scored on your ability to speak clearly and coherently and on your ability to accurately convey information about what you heard.

You may take notes while you read and while you listen to the conversations and lectures. You may use your notes to help prepare your response.

Listen carefully to the directions for each question. The directions will not be written on the screen.

For each question you will be given a short time to prepare your response. A clock will show how much preparation time is remaining. When the preparation time is up, you will be told to begin your response. A clock will show how much response time is remaining. A message will appear on the screen when the response time has ended.

 뉴토플 - TEST 04_Q1

USHER iBT TOEFL Speaking

Question 1 of 4

Do you agree or disagree with the following statement?
Advertising junk food or candy bars should be prohibited for children.
Use reasons and examples to support your answer.

PREPARATION TIME
00: 00: 15

RESPONSE TIME
00: 00: 45

Changes to the Check-Out Policy

Currently, the library allows students to keep books for a period of a month when they check them out. However, it has been determined that one month is too long of a period. By reducing the lending period to two weeks, it will allow the books to be read by a large number of people, who might be waiting for the book. Since the library is limited by the number of books they have, by allowing one person to keep a book for a whole month is unfair, as there might be a lot of students in need of it.

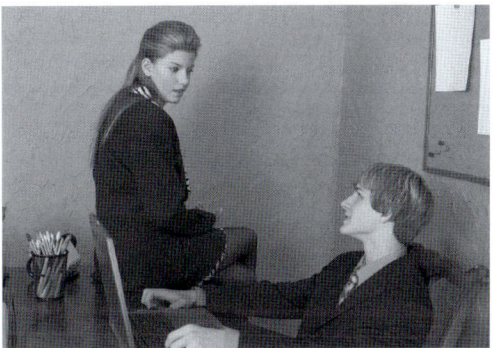

Now get ready to answer the question.

The woman expresses her opinion about the college's plan. State her opinion and explain the reasons she gives for holding that opinion.

Reading Time: 50 seconds

Mental Accounting

Mental accounting refers to the process by which people encode, categorize and evaluate economic outcomes. One example of mental accounting is the so-called behavioral life cycle hypothesis. It assumes that people have a tendency to classify assets into different accounts such as current income, current wealth and future income. In people's minds, the accounts are not interchangeable and their habits of consumption from each account tend to be different. Mental accounting is considered a major psychological problem that people have to overcome, especially when suffering from financial issues.

Now get ready to answer the question

Using the example from the professor's lecture, explain what mental accounting is and how it works.

PREPARATION TIME
00: 00: 30

RESPONSE TIME
00: 00: 60

Now get ready to answer the question.

Using the examples from the professor's lecture, explain how some animals protect themselves from predators.

PREPARATION TIME
00: 00: 20

RESPONSE TIME
00: 00: 60

시험이 끝나고

	Task 1	Task 2	Task 3	Task 4
시간에 맞춰 발표를 끝냈음	O / X	O / X	O / X	O / X
"아닌 경우," 시간이 남아서라면?				
- 할 말이 부족해서				
- 말이 빨라서				
- 도저히 모르겠음 / 기타				
"아닌 경우," 도중에 잘려서라면?				
- 할 말이 부족해서				
- 말이 빨라서				
- 도저히 모르겠음 / 기타				
	Task 1	Task 2	Task 3	Task 4
발표할 내용을 완벽히 정리했음	O / X	O / X	O / X	O / X
"아닌 경우," 문제를 이해하지 못해서라면?				
- 읽기 / 듣기가 안돼서				
- 배경지식이 부족해서				
- 도저히 모르겠음 / 기타				
"아닌 경우," 내용 정리가 덜 끝나서라면?				
- 준비 시간이 부족해서				
- 내용이 뒤죽박죽 되어서				
- 도저히 모르겠음 / 기타				

다음에 문제를 풀 때에는…

반드시 이렇게 해야지!

절대 이러지 말아야지!

USHER iBT TOEFL
FINAL TEST SPEAKING
TEST 05

Independent Tasks

Question 1   usherin.usher.co.kr > 시험리스트 > Speaking 시험리스트 > Task 1 > #1009

Integrated Tasks

Question 2   usherin.usher.co.kr > 시험리스트 > Speaking 시험리스트 > Task 2 > #2005
Question 3   usherin.usher.co.kr > 시험리스트 > Speaking 시험리스트 > Task 3 > #3005
Question 4   usherin.usher.co.kr > 시험리스트 > Speaking 시험리스트 > Task 4 > #4005

시험이 끝나고

시험 전에 Check !

펜과 메모지가 있음 ○
핸드폰을 껐음 ○
시간을 체크할 시계가 있음 ○
문제를 들을 준비가 됐음 ○
목소리를 녹음할 준비가 됐음 ○
평소에 연습한대로 발음하겠음 ○
단어의 강세에 유의하겠음 ○
시간을 체크해가면서 발표하겠음 ○

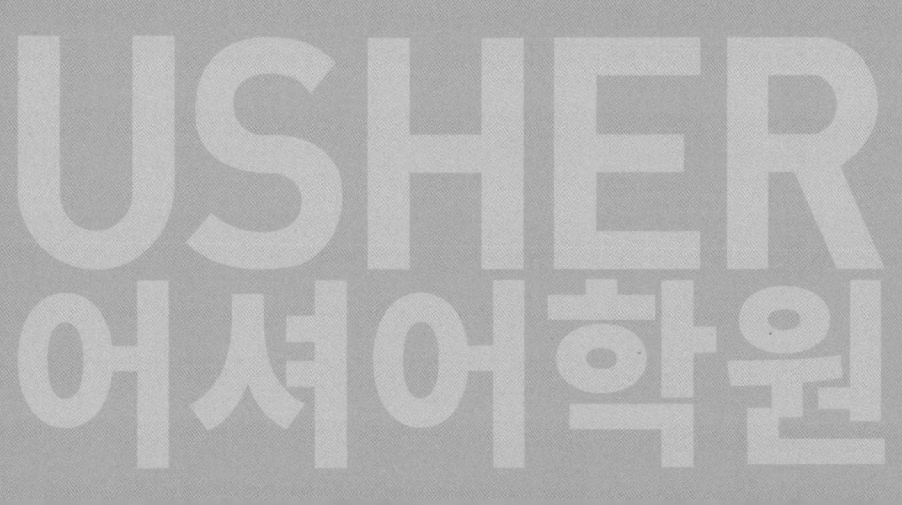

Speaking Section Directions

In this section of the test, you will be able to demonstrate your ability to speak about a variety of topics. You will answer four questions by speaking into the mircrophone. Answer each of the questions as completely as possible.

In question 1, you will speak about a familiar topic. Your response will be scored on your ability to speak clearly and coherently about the topic.

In questions 2 and 3, you will first read a short text. The text will go away and you will then listen to a talk on the same topic. You will then be asked a question about what you have read and heard. You will need to combine appropriate information from the text and the talk to provide a complete answer to the question. Your response will be scored on your ability to speak clearly and coherently and on your ability to accurately convey information about what you read and heard.

In question 4, you will listen to part of a lecture. You will then be asked a question about what you heard. Your response will be scored on your ability to speak clearly and coherently and on your ability to accurately convey information about what you heard.

You may take notes while you read and while you listen to the conversations and lectures. You may use your notes to help prepare your response.

Listen carefully to the directions for each question. The directions will not be written on the screen.

For each question you will be given a short time to prepare your response. A clock will show how much preparation time is remaining. When the preparation time is up, you will be told to begin your response. A clock will show how much response time is remaining. A message will appear on the screen when the response time has ended.

Question 1 of 4

Some people say in-born talent is the most important to become an artist. Others say hard work is more important. Which view do you agree with? Use reasons and examples to support your answer.

PREPARATION TIME
00: 00: 15

RESPONSE TIME
00: 00: 45

Reading Time: 50 seconds

Dormitories to become mandatory for freshmen

A university official has stated that there are plans to make living in the dormitories mandatory for incoming freshmen. Lately, since juniors and seniors are leaning towards the trend of not living in dormitories, for economic reasons, living in the dorms may become a mandatory process that freshmen need to go under. There are some advantages that come with living on campus, including being able to participate in various activities. By living in the dorms, it will become more convenient to take part in school events. Since one's house is nearby, time spent going back and forth from home to school will also be able to be saved.

Now get ready to answer the question.

The woman expresses her opinion about the proposal in the newspaper. State the woman's opinion and explain the reasons she gives for holding that opinion.

PREPARATION TIME
00: 00: 30
RESPONSE TIME
00: 00: 60

Reading Time: 50 seconds

Selling Technique

Selling techniques are the ways in which consumers are motivated to purchase products. These techniques take on many forms, from the modern consultative selling in which salesmen act as expert consultants helping consumers understand a product to the pressurized hard sales approach. While these approaches are based on the sales force, producers' decisions on which products to manufacture also play an important part in the process of selling. By specializing in a certain type of product, producers have the ability to increase their sales through brand recognition and diversification. Both of these make the jobs of their sales people easier.

Now get ready to answer the question

Using the example from the professor's lecture, explain what selling technique is and how it works.

PREPARATION TIME
00: 00: 30

RESPONSE TIME
00: 00: 60

Now get ready to answer the question.

Using the examples from the professor's lecture, explain how animals use cooperation to feed themselves more effectively.

시험이 끝나고

	Task 1	Task 2	Task 3	Task 4
시간에 맞춰 발표를 끝냈음	O / X	O / X	O / X	O / X
"아닌 경우," 시간이 남아서라면?				
- 할 말이 부족해서				
- 말이 빨라서				
- 도저히 모르겠음 / 기타				
"아닌 경우," 도중에 잘려서라면?				
- 할 말이 부족해서				
- 말이 빨라서				
- 도저히 모르겠음 / 기타				

	Task 1	Task 2	Task 3	Task 4
발표할 내용을 완벽히 정리했음	O / X	O / X	O / X	O / X
"아닌 경우," 문제를 이해하지 못해서라면?				
- 읽기 / 듣기가 안돼서				
- 배경지식이 부족해서				
- 도저히 모르겠음 / 기타				
"아닌 경우," 내용 정리가 덜 끝나서라면?				
- 준비 시간이 부족해서				
- 내용이 뒤죽박죽 되어서				
- 도저히 모르겠음 / 기타				

다음에 문제를 풀 때에는…

반드시 이렇게 해야지!

절대 이러지 말아야지!

USHER iBT TOEFL
FINAL TEST SPEAKING
TEST 06

Independent Tasks

Question 1   usherin.usher.co.kr > 시험리스트 > Speaking 시험리스트 > Task 1 > #1024

Integrated Tasks

Question 2   usherin.usher.co.kr > 시험리스트 > Speaking 시험리스트 > Task 2 > #2006
Question 3   usherin.usher.co.kr > 시험리스트 > Speaking 시험리스트 > Task 3 > #3006
Question 4   usherin.usher.co.kr > 시험리스트 > Speaking 시험리스트 > Task 4 > #4006

시험이 끝나고

시험 전에 Check !

펜과 메모지가 있음 ○
핸드폰을 껐음 ○
시간을 체크할 시계가 있음 ○
문제를 들을 준비가 됐음 ○
목소리를 녹음할 준비가 됐음 ○
평소에 연습한대로 발음하겠음 ○
단어의 강세에 유의하겠음 ○
시간을 체크해가면서 발표하겠음 ○

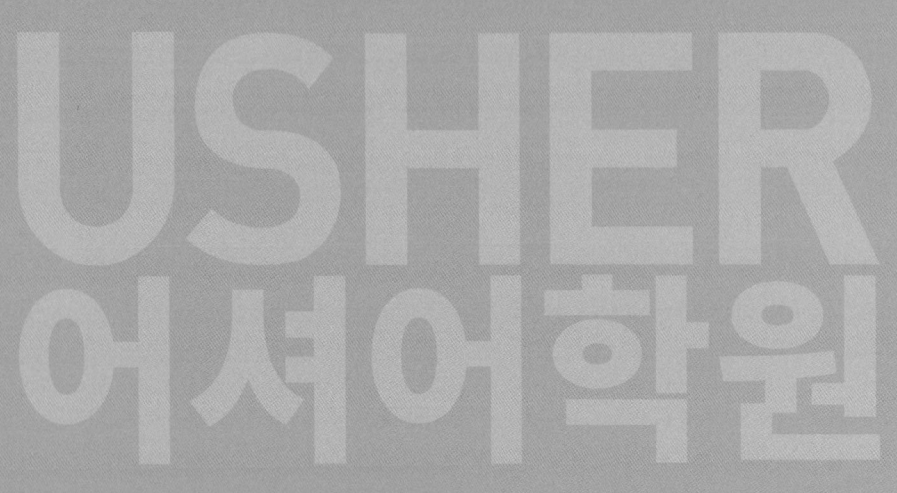

Speaking Section Directions

In this section of the test, you will be able to demonstrate your ability to speak about a variety of topics. You will answer four questions by speaking into the mircrophone. Answer each of the questions as completely as possible.

In question 1, you will speak about a familiar topic. Your response will be scored on your ability to speak clearly and coherently about the topic.

In questions 2 and 3, you will first read a short text. The text will go away and you will then listen to a talk on the same topic. You will then be asked a question about what you have read and heard. You will need to combine appropriate information from the text and the talk to provide a complete answer to the question. Your response will be scored on your ability to speak clearly and coherently and on your ability to accurately convey information about what you read and heard.

In question 4, you will listen to part of a lecture. You will then be asked a question about what you heard. Your response will be scored on your ability to speak clearly and coherently and on your ability to accurately convey information about what you heard.

You may take notes while you read and while you listen to the conversations and lectures. You may use your notes to help prepare your response.

Listen carefully to the directions for each question. The directions will not be written on the screen.

For each question you will be given a short time to prepare your response. A clock will show how much preparation time is remaining. When the preparation time is up, you will be told to begin your response. A clock will show how much response time is remaining. A message will appear on the screen when the response time has ended.

USHER

Question 1 of 4

Some people say it is better to take long but relaxed courses in college. Others say it is better to take short but intensive courses. Which view do you agree with? Use reasons and examples to support your answer.

PREPARATION TIME
00: 00: 15

RESPONSE TIME
00: 00: 45

Reading Time: 50 seconds

Advisory Meetings Should Be Optional

Advisory meetings should not be required by the university, as they are right now. All of the information that the advisors provide to us students can be easily found on the web. Just going to related websites, or even the school website, will give us an organized version of what the advisors will tell us. Thus, meetings are not exactly needed because they don't give us any new information. Also, as it is a meeting between two people, it is difficult to schedule. Students and advisors are both busy, but in order to have an advisory meeting, both the student and the advisor have to be free.

Now get ready to answer the question.

The man expresses his opinion about the proposal in the newspaper. State his opinion and explain the reasons he gives for holding that opinion.

PREPARATION TIME
00: 00: 30

RESPONSE TIME
00: 00: 60

Environmental Disturbance

There are many events which occur in nature that cause harm to not only the environment, but also to the organisms living there. Environmental change can be both natural or anthropogenic, meaning caused by human action. No matter the type however, environment disturbances cause changes that have effects on the plants living there and their ways of growing. Since nature is mostly made up of plants, it is obvious that environmental disturbances would impact them the most. Some of these changes even affect the plants permanently over successive generations and are usually irreversible.

Now get ready to answer the question

Using the example from the professor's lecture, explain what environmental disturbance is and how it works.

PREPARATION TIME
00: 00: 30

RESPONSE TIME
00: 00: 60

Now get ready to answer the question.

Using the examples from the professor's lecture, explain the two methods of sculpting.

PREPARATION TIME
00: 00: 20

RESPONSE TIME
00: 00: 60

시험이 끝나고

	Task 1	Task 2	Task 3	Task 4
시간에 맞춰 발표를 끝냈음	O / X	O / X	O / X	O / X
"아닌 경우," 시간이 남아서라면?				
- 할 말이 부족해서				
- 말이 빨라서				
- 도저히 모르겠음 / 기타				
"아닌 경우," 도중에 잘려서라면?				
- 할 말이 부족해서				
- 말이 빨라서				
- 도저히 모르겠음 / 기타				

	Task 1	Task 2	Task 3	Task 4
발표할 내용을 완벽히 정리했음	O / X	O / X	O / X	O / X
"아닌 경우," 문제를 이해하지 못해서라면?				
- 읽기 / 듣기가 안돼서				
- 배경지식이 부족해서				
- 도저히 모르겠음 / 기타				
"아닌 경우," 내용 정리가 덜 끝나서라면?				
- 준비 시간이 부족해서				
- 내용이 뒤죽박죽 되어서				
- 도저히 모르겠음 / 기타				

다음에 문제를 풀 때에는…

반드시 이렇게 해야지!

절대 이러지 말아야지!

USHER iBT TOEFL
FINAL TEST SPEAKING
TEST 07

Independent Tasks

Question 1 usherin.usher.co.kr > 시험리스트 > Speaking 시험리스트 > Task 1 > #1020

Integrated Tasks

Question 2 usherin.usher.co.kr > 시험리스트 > Speaking 시험리스트 > Task 2 > #2007
Question 3 usherin.usher.co.kr > 시험리스트 > Speaking 시험리스트 > Task 3 > #3007
Question 4 usherin.usher.co.kr > 시험리스트 > Speaking 시험리스트 > Task 4 > #4007

시험이 끝나고

시험 전에 Check !

펜과 메모지가 있음 ○
핸드폰을 껐음 ○
시간을 체크할 시계가 있음 ○
문제를 들을 준비가 됐음 ○
목소리를 녹음할 준비가 됐음 ○
평소에 연습한대로 발음하겠음 ○
단어의 강세에 유의하겠음 ○
시간을 체크해가면서 발표하겠음 ○

Speaking Section Directions

In this section of the test, you will be able to demonstrate your ability to speak about a variety of topics. You will answer four questions by speaking into the mircrophone. Answer each of the questions as completely as possible.

In question 1, you will speak about a familiar topic. Your response will be scored on your ability to speak clearly and coherently about the topic.

In questions 2 and 3, you will first read a short text. The text will go away and you will then listen to a talk on the same topic. You will then be asked a question about what you have read and heard. You will need to combine appropriate information from the text and the talk to provide a complete answer to the question. Your response will be scored on your ability to speak clearly and coherently and on your ability to accurately convey information about what you read and heard.

In question 4, you will listen to part of a lecture. You will then be asked a question about what you heard. Your response will be scored on your ability to speak clearly and coherently and on your ability to accurately convey information about what you heard.

You may take notes while you read and while you listen to the conversations and lectures. You may use your notes to help prepare your response.

Listen carefully to the directions for each question. The directions will not be written on the screen.

For each question you will be given a short time to prepare your response. A clock will show how much preparation time is remaining. When the preparation time is up, you will be told to begin your response. A clock will show how much response time is remaining. A message will appear on the screen when the response time has ended.

Question 1 of 4

Do you agree or disagree with the following statement?

It is important to get dressed up and stay fashionable.

Use reasons and examples to support your answer.

PREPARATION TIME
00: 00: 15

RESPONSE TIME
00: 00: 45

University Should Build a New Parking Lot

The university has a vast area covered with trees near the school library. I think this place would the perfect spot for another parking lot. Since the area is covered by many trees, we would not be affecting the environment too much by using a little space for parking. There are not enough parking spaces on campus in relation to the number of students' cars. There is especially not enough space for cars, by the library, which is frequently used by students. By building a new parking space, students with cars will be able to use the library more conveniently.

Now get ready to answer the question.

The woman expresses her opinion about the proposal in the newspaper. State her opinion and explain the reasons she gives for holding that opinion.

PREPARATION TIME
00: 00: 30

RESPONSE TIME
00: 00: 60

Bait Pricing

Marketing experts use a variety of methods to entice consumers to take note of and purchase specific products or brands. In addition, they often attempt to draw customers into a specific store. One way this can be accomplished is through bait pricing, or a bait-and-switch. This is a tactic through which the consumer is lured to a store through the use of a specific bait product. These products are usually advertised at unrealistically low prices when compared to others in a similar category, thereby attracting more consumers to come in to the store looking for the bait product.

Now get ready to answer the question

Using the example from the professor's lecture, explain what bait pricing is and how it works.

뉴토플 - TEST 07_Q4

Question 4 of 4

Now get ready to answer the question.

Using the examples from the professor's lecture, explain why some animals change the color of their fur.

PREPARATION TIME
00: 00: 20

RESPONSE TIME
00: 00: 60

시험이 끝나고

	Task 1	Task 2	Task 3	Task 4
시간에 맞춰 발표를 끝냈음	O / X	O / X	O / X	O / X
"아닌 경우," 시간이 남아서라면?				
- 할 말이 부족해서				
- 말이 빨라서				
- 도저히 모르겠음 / 기타				
"아닌 경우," 도중에 잘려서라면?				
- 할 말이 부족해서				
- 말이 빨라서				
- 도저히 모르겠음 / 기타				
	Task 1	Task 2	Task 3	Task 4
발표할 내용을 완벽히 정리했음	O / X	O / X	O / X	O / X
"아닌 경우," 문제를 이해하지 못해서라면?				
- 읽기 / 듣기가 안돼서				
- 배경지식이 부족해서				
- 도저히 모르겠음 / 기타				
"아닌 경우," 내용 정리가 덜 끝나서라면?				
- 준비 시간이 부족해서				
- 내용이 뒤죽박죽 되어서				
- 도저히 모르겠음 / 기타				

다음에 문제를 풀 때에는…

반드시 이렇게 해야지!

절대 이러지 말아야지!

USHER iBT TOEFL
FINAL TEST SPEAKING
TEST 08

Independent Tasks

Question 1   usherin.usher.co.kr > 시험리스트 > Speaking 시험리스트 > Task 1 > #1059

Integrated Tasks

Question 2   usherin.usher.co.kr > 시험리스트 > Speaking 시험리스트 > Task 2 > #2008
Question 3   usherin.usher.co.kr > 시험리스트 > Speaking 시험리스트 > Task 3 > #3008
Question 4   usherin.usher.co.kr > 시험리스트 > Speaking 시험리스트 > Task 4 > #4008

시험이 끝나고

시험 전에 Check !

펜과 메모지가 있음 ○
핸드폰을 껐음 ○
시간을 체크할 시계가 있음 ○
문제를 들을 준비가 됐음 ○
목소리를 녹음할 준비가 됐음 ○
평소에 연습한대로 발음하겠음 ○
단어의 강세에 유의하겠음 ○
시간을 체크해가면서 발표하겠음 ○

Speaking Section Directions

In this section of the test, you will be able to demonstrate your ability to speak about a variety of topics. You will answer four questions by speaking into the mircrophone. Answer each of the questions as completely as possible.

In question 1, you will speak about a familiar topic. Your response will be scored on your ability to speak clearly and coherently about the topic.

In questions 2 and 3, you will first read a short text. The text will go away and you will then listen to a talk on the same topic. You will then be asked a question about what you have read and heard. You will need to combine appropriate information from the text and the talk to provide a complete answer to the question. Your response will be scored on your ability to speak clearly and coherently and on your ability to accurately convey information about what you read and heard.

In question 4, you will listen to part of a lecture. You will then be asked a question about what you heard. Your response will be scored on your ability to speak clearly and coherently and on your ability to accurately convey information about what you heard.

You may take notes while you read and while you listen to the conversations and lectures. You may use your notes to help prepare your response.

Listen carefully to the directions for each question. The directions will not be written on the screen.

For each question you will be given a short time to prepare your response. A clock will show how much preparation time is remaining. When the preparation time is up, you will be told to begin your response. A clock will show how much response time is remaining. A message will appear on the screen when the response time has ended.

 뉴토플 - TEST 08_Q1

Question 1 of 4

Do you agree or disagree with the following statement?
Video and computer games have a bad influence on children.
Use reasons and examples to support your answer.

PREPARATION TIME
00: 00: 15

RESPONSE TIME
00: 00: 45

Reading Time: 50 seconds

Internship Programs for Students

The university will be starting an international culture internship as of this year. This idea was thought of a couple years ago, but is finally being put into action this year for the first time. A certain number of students will be picked, after careful consideration, to take part in an internship at businesses in other countries. Furthermore, all expenses will be covered by the international department of our university, so the students picked will not be financially burdened by taking part. We anticipate many students will apply for the positions because this internship will offer lots of hands-on experience, which will look good on their college records.

Now get ready to answer the question.

The woman expresses her opinion about the college's plan. State her opinion and explain the reasons she gives for holding that opinion.

PREPARATION TIME
00: 00: 30
RESPONSE TIME
00: 00: 60

Evolution in Action

Evolution can be defined as a very slow process where life forms go through various changes, and environments, over many generations. It consists of changes that are passed from generation to generation and cannot occur in an individual organism. A narrower form of evolution would be "evolution in action," which is rapid evolution due to human intervention. The term evolution in action is applied when an organism continuously changes its structure or functions to adjust to the environment in order to find a suitable way to survive.

Now get ready to answer the question

Using the example from the professor's lecture, explain what evolution in action is and how it works.

Question 4 of 4

Now get ready to answer the question.

Using the examples from the professor's lecture, explain the two benefits of subsurface locomotion.

PREPARATION TIME
00: 00: 20

RESPONSE TIME
00: 00: 60

시험이 끝나고

	Task 1	Task 2	Task 3	Task 4
시간에 맞춰 발표를 끝냈음	O / X	O / X	O / X	O / X
"아닌 경우," 시간이 남아서라면?				
- 할 말이 부족해서				
- 말이 빨라서				
- 도저히 모르겠음 / 기타				
"아닌 경우," 도중에 잘려서라면?				
- 할 말이 부족해서				
- 말이 빨라서				
- 도저히 모르겠음 / 기타				

	Task 1	Task 2	Task 3	Task 4
발표할 내용을 완벽히 정리했음	O / X	O / X	O / X	O / X
"아닌 경우," 문제를 이해하지 못해서라면?				
- 읽기 / 듣기가 안돼서				
- 배경지식이 부족해서				
- 도저히 모르겠음 / 기타				
"아닌 경우," 내용 정리가 덜 끝나서라면?				
- 준비 시간이 부족해서				
- 내용이 뒤죽박죽 되어서				
- 도저히 모르겠음 / 기타				

다음에 문제를 풀 때에는…

반드시 이렇게 해야지!

절대 이러지 말아야지!

USHER iBT TOEFL
FINAL TEST SPEAKING
TEST 09

Independent Tasks

Question 1   usherin.usher.co.kr > 시험리스트 > Speaking 시험리스트 > Task 1 > #1013

Integrated Tasks

Question 2   usherin.usher.co.kr > 시험리스트 > Speaking 시험리스트 > Task 2 > #2009
Question 3   usherin.usher.co.kr > 시험리스트 > Speaking 시험리스트 > Task 3 > #3009
Question 4   usherin.usher.co.kr > 시험리스트 > Speaking 시험리스트 > Task 4 > #4009

시험이 끝나고

시험 전에 Check !

펜과 메모지가 있음 ○
핸드폰을 껐음 ○
시간을 체크할 시계가 있음 ○
문제를 들을 준비가 됐음 ○
목소리를 녹음할 준비가 됐음 ○
평소에 연습한대로 발음하겠음 ○
단어의 강세에 유의하겠음 ○
시간을 체크해가면서 발표하겠음 ○

Speaking Section Directions

In this section of the test, you will be able to demonstrate your ability to speak about a variety of topics. You will answer four questions by speaking into the mircrophone. Answer each of the questions as completely as possible.

In question 1, you will speak about a familiar topic. Your response will be scored on your ability to speak clearly and coherently about the topic.

In questions 2 and 3, you will first read a short text. The text will go away and you will then listen to a talk on the same topic. You will then be asked a question about what you have read and heard. You will need to combine appropriate information from the text and the talk to provide a complete answer to the question. Your response will be scored on your ability to speak clearly and coherently and on your ability to accurately convey information about what you read and heard.

In question 4, you will listen to part of a lecture. You will then be asked a question about what you heard. Your response will be scored on your ability to speak clearly and coherently and on your ability to accurately convey information about what you heard.

You may take notes while you read and while you listen to the conversations and lectures. You may use your notes to help prepare your response.

Listen carefully to the directions for each question. The directions will not be written on the screen.

For each question you will be given a short time to prepare your response. A clock will show how much preparation time is remaining. When the preparation time is up, you will be told to begin your response. A clock will show how much response time is remaining. A message will appear on the screen when the response time has ended.

Question 1 of 4

Some people prefer to make a plan before shopping. Others prefer to shop compulsively. Which one do you prefer? Use reasons and examples to support your answer.

PREPARATION TIME
00: 00: 15

RESPONSE TIME
00: 00: 45

USHER

Question 2 of 4

Reading Time: 50 seconds

Plans to Open the Writing Center

A university official announced plans to open a writing center on campus, stating that the center will work to help increase the writing skills of students through various writing activities. Aside from helping potential students, the writing center will also be offering jobs to those skilled enough in writing. Thus, there will be helpers to help the students who come to the center in a one-on-one manner. We can only benefit from the writing center, so whoever is in need of help in writing, or those looking for a way to help others and make money at the same time, should come to the writing center after it opens.

Now get ready to answer the question.

The woman expresses her opinion about the college's plan. State her opinion and explain the reasons she gives for holding that opinion.

PREPARATION TIME
00: 00: 30

RESPONSE TIME
00: 00: 60

Reading Time: 50 seconds

Prenatal Learning

The ability of children to learn has led to many different methods of teaching and interaction with educational material. One newly identified method of learning is prenatal learning. This term refers to the ability of embryos to learn through auditory stimulation during the gestational period. As the brain is at its most receptive stage of learning during gestation, it has been theorized that embryos can absorb and appreciate far more of their environment if they are exposed to auditory environmental stimuli. This can be seen in the both humans and in other animals as well.

Now get ready to answer the question

Using the example from the professor's lecture, explain what prenatal learning is and how it works.

PREPARATION TIME
00: 00: 30
RESPONSE TIME
00: 00: 60

Now get ready to answer the question.

Using the examples from the professor's lecture, explain the two methods ants use to collect food more effectively.

PREPARATION TIME
00: 00: 20

RESPONSE TIME
00: 00: 60

시험이 끝나고

		Task 1	Task 2	Task 3	Task 4
시간에 맞춰 발표를 끝냈음		O / X	O / X	O / X	O / X
"아닌 경우,"	시간이 남아서라면?				
	- 할 말이 부족해서				
	- 말이 빨라서				
	- 도저히 모르겠음 / 기타				
"아닌 경우,"	도중에 잘려서라면?				
	- 할 말이 부족해서				
	- 말이 빨라서				
	- 도저히 모르겠음 / 기타				
		Task 1	Task 2	Task 3	Task 4
발표할 내용을 완벽히 정리했음		O / X	O / X	O / X	O / X
"아닌 경우,"	문제를 이해하지 못해서라면?				
	- 읽기 / 듣기가 안돼서				
	- 배경지식이 부족해서				
	- 도저히 모르겠음 / 기타				
"아닌 경우,"	내용 정리가 덜 끝나서라면?				
	- 준비 시간이 부족해서				
	- 내용이 뒤죽박죽 되어서				
	- 도저히 모르겠음 / 기타				

다음에 문제를 풀 때에는…

반드시 이렇게 해야지!

절대 이러지 말아야지!

USHER iBT TOEFL
FINAL TEST SPEAKING
TEST 10

Independent Tasks

Question 1   usherin.usher.co.kr > 시험리스트 > Speaking 시험리스트 > Task 1 > #1005

Integrated Tasks

Question 2   usherin.usher.co.kr > 시험리스트 > Speaking 시험리스트 > Task 2 > #2010
Question 3   usherin.usher.co.kr > 시험리스트 > Speaking 시험리스트 > Task 3 > #3010
Question 4   usherin.usher.co.kr > 시험리스트 > Speaking 시험리스트 > Task 4 > #4010

시험이 끝나고

시험 전에 Check !

- 펜과 메모지가 있음 ○
- 핸드폰을 껐음 ○
- 시간을 체크할 시계가 있음 ○
- 문제를 들을 준비가 됐음 ○
- 목소리를 녹음할 준비가 됐음 ○
- 평소에 연습한대로 발음하겠음 ○
- 단어의 강세에 유의하겠음 ○
- 시간을 체크해가면서 발표하겠음 ○

Speaking Section Directions

In this section of the test, you will be able to demonstrate your ability to speak about a variety of topics. You will answer four questions by speaking into the mircrophone. Answer each of the questions as completely as possible.

In question 1, you will speak about a familiar topic. Your response will be scored on your ability to speak clearly and coherently about the topic.

In questions 2 and 3, you will first read a short text. The text will go away and you will then listen to a talk on the same topic. You will then be asked a question about what you have read and heard. You will need to combine appropriate information from the text and the talk to provide a complete answer to the question. Your response will be scored on your ability to speak clearly and coherently and on your ability to accurately convey information about what you read and heard.

In question 4, you will listen to part of a lecture. You will then be asked a question about what you heard. Your response will be scored on your ability to speak clearly and coherently and on your ability to accurately convey information about what you heard.

You may take notes while you read and while you listen to the conversations and lectures. You may use your notes to help prepare your response.

Listen carefully to the directions for each question. The directions will not be written on the screen.

For each question you will be given a short time to prepare your response. A clock will show how much preparation time is remaining. When the preparation time is up, you will be told to begin your response. A clock will show how much response time is remaining. A message will appear on the screen when the response time has ended.

 뉴토플 - TEST 10_Q1

USHER iBT TOEFL Speaking

Question 1 of 4

Do you agree or disagree with the following statement?

College education should be available only to those who are good students.

Use reasons and examples to support your answer.

PREPARATION TIME
00: 00: 15

RESPONSE TIME
00: 00: 45

Research Writing Class

Starting next semester, the university will be opening a research writing class for students. It has come to the attention of many university professors that even many upper class students are unaware of how to write a proper research paper. With the hope of teaching students how to write a research paper early on in their college lives, the writing class will be offered to all students. Also, a part of the class curriculum will include peer editing. Fixing each others' errors will help students not to make the same mistakes later on. This class is mainly aimed at incoming freshmen, but will be offered to students of all levels.

Now get ready to answer the question.

The man expresses his opinion about the college's plan. State his opinion and explain the reasons he gives for holding that opinion.

PREPARATION TIME
00: 00: 30

RESPONSE TIME
00: 00: 60

Reading Time: 50 seconds

Choice-Supportive Bias

During a decision-making process, people may encounter various conflicts and become subject to hesitation. Once an action has been taken, however, the ways in which we evaluate the outcome of what we did maybe biased in some way. In psychology, the term choice- supportive bias refers to one's tendency to ascribe positive attributes to a choice that has been made. Not only do people remember their choices as better than they actually were, but also tend to overattribute negative features to options not chosen. The purpose of this phenomenon is to justify their decisions and to lower the possibility of regrets.

Now get ready to answer the question

Using the example from the professor's lecture, explain what choice-supportive bias is and how it works.

PREPARATION TIME
00: 00: 30 |//
RESPONSE TIME
00: 00: 60

Now get ready to answer the question.

Using the examples from the professor's lecture, explain why bats hang upside down.

PREPARATION TIME
00: 00: 20

RESPONSE TIME
00: 00: 60

시험이 끝나고

	Task 1	Task 2	Task 3	Task 4
시간에 맞춰 발표를 끝냈음	O / X	O / X	O / X	O / X
"아닌 경우," 시간이 남아서라면?				
- 할 말이 부족해서				
- 말이 빨라서				
- 도저히 모르겠음 / 기타				
"아닌 경우," 도중에 잘려서라면?				
- 할 말이 부족해서				
- 말이 빨라서				
- 도저히 모르겠음 / 기타				
	Task 1	Task 2	Task 3	Task 4
발표할 내용을 완벽히 정리했음	O / X	O / X	O / X	O / X
"아닌 경우," 문제를 이해하지 못해서라면?				
- 읽기 / 듣기가 안돼서				
- 배경지식이 부족해서				
- 도저히 모르겠음 / 기타				
"아닌 경우," 내용 정리가 덜 끝나서라면?				
- 준비 시간이 부족해서				
- 내용이 뒤죽박죽 되어서				
- 도저히 모르겠음 / 기타				

다음에 문제를 풀 때에는…

반드시 이렇게 해야지!

절대 이러지 말아야지!

USHER iBT TOEFL
FINAL TEST SPEAKING
TEST 11

Independent Tasks

Question 1   usherin.usher.co.kr > 시험리스트 > Speaking 시험리스트 > Task 1 > #1060

Integrated Tasks

Question 2   usherin.usher.co.kr > 시험리스트 > Speaking 시험리스트 > Task 2 > #2011
Question 3   usherin.usher.co.kr > 시험리스트 > Speaking 시험리스트 > Task 3 > #3011
Question 4   usherin.usher.co.kr > 시험리스트 > Speaking 시험리스트 > Task 4 > #4011

시험이 끝나고

시험 전에 Check !

펜과 메모지가 있음 ○
핸드폰을 껐음 ○
시간을 체크할 시계가 있음 ○
문제를 들을 준비가 됐음 ○
목소리를 녹음할 준비가 됐음 ○
평소에 연습한대로 발음하겠음 ○
단어의 강세에 유의하겠음 ○
시간을 체크해가면서 발표하겠음 ○

Speaking Section Directions

In this section of the test, you will be able to demonstrate your ability to speak about a variety of topics. You will answer four questions by speaking into the mircrophone. Answer each of the questions as completely as possible.

In question 1, you will speak about a familiar topic. Your response will be scored on your ability to speak clearly and coherently about the topic.

In questions 2 and 3, you will first read a short text. The text will go away and you will then listen to a talk on the same topic. You will then be asked a question about what you have read and heard. You will need to combine appropriate information from the text and the talk to provide a complete answer to the question. Your response will be scored on your ability to speak clearly and coherently and on your ability to accurately convey information about what you read and heard.

In question 4, you will listen to part of a lecture. You will then be asked a question about what you heard. Your response will be scored on your ability to speak clearly and coherently and on your ability to accurately convey information about what you heard.

You may take notes while you read and while you listen to the conversations and lectures. You may use your notes to help prepare your response.

Listen carefully to the directions for each question. The directions will not be written on the screen.

For each question you will be given a short time to prepare your response. A clock will show how much preparation time is remaining. When the preparation time is up, you will be told to begin your response. A clock will show how much response time is remaining. A message will appear on the screen when the response time has ended.

Question 1 of 4

Some people prefer to live in one place. Others prefer to live in different places. What do you prefer to do? Use reasons and examples to support your answer.

PREPARATION TIME
00: 00: 15

RESPONSE TIME
00: 00: 45

University's Drama Performance Requirements

The university has made a new requirement for graduation. Students must now attend a minimum of two performances of art or drama. Further, after watching the performances, students will be required to hand in a short paper on them to the humanities department. The university is hoping that this will increase the number of students interested in culture and the arts. Since students nowadays are too busy with schoolwork and other activities, they do not take the time to enjoy art and culture. Making this a graduation requirement will force students to watch such works, and in turn, become well-rounded people in both academics and cultural life.

Now get ready to answer the question.

The woman expresses her opinion about the college's plan. State her opinion and explain the reasons she gives for holding that opinion.

PREPARATION TIME
00:00:30

RESPONSE TIME
00:00:60

Reading Time: 50 seconds

Specialist Species

According to their tolerability of habitat, food, and other environment conditions, animals can be distinguished into two types: generalist or specialist species. Generalist species are animals which can thrive in many different environmental conditions due to their varied diets. Although they can adapt to a wider range of environments, they have more competition with other species. On the other hand, specialist species can only prosper in certain habitats due to their limited diets. Although they don't have to compete with others for food or habitat, they aren't able to prosper in many different environments.

Now get ready to answer the question

Using the example from the professor's lecture, explain what specialist species are and their specialization.

PREPARATION TIME
00 : 00 : 30
RESPONSE TIME
00 : 00 : 60

Now get ready to answer the question.

Using the examples from the professor's lecture, explain how eco-travel helps the environment.

PREPARATION TIME
00: 00: 20

RESPONSE TIME
00: 00: 60

시험이 끝나고

	Task 1	Task 2	Task 3	Task 4
시간에 맞춰 발표를 끝냈음	O / X	O / X	O / X	O / X
"아닌 경우," 시간이 남아서라면?				
- 할 말이 부족해서				
- 말이 빨라서				
- 도저히 모르겠음 / 기타				
"아닌 경우," 도중에 잘려서라면?				
- 할 말이 부족해서				
- 말이 빨라서				
- 도저히 모르겠음 / 기타				

	Task 1	Task 2	Task 3	Task 4
발표할 내용을 완벽히 정리했음	O / X	O / X	O / X	O / X
"아닌 경우," 문제를 이해하지 못해서라면?				
- 읽기 / 듣기가 안돼서				
- 배경지식이 부족해서				
- 도저히 모르겠음 / 기타				
"아닌 경우," 내용 정리가 덜 끝나서라면?				
- 준비 시간이 부족해서				
- 내용이 뒤죽박죽 되어서				
- 도저히 모르겠음 / 기타				

다음에 문제를 풀 때에는…

반드시 이렇게 해야지!

절대 이러지 말아야지!

USHER iBT TOEFL
FINAL TEST SPEAKING
TEST 12

Independent Tasks

Question 1   usherin.usher.co.kr > 시험리스트 > Speaking 시험리스트 > Task 1 > #1048

Integrated Tasks

Question 2   usherin.usher.co.kr > 시험리스트 > Speaking 시험리스트 > Task 2 > #2012
Question 3   usherin.usher.co.kr > 시험리스트 > Speaking 시험리스트 > Task 3 > #3012
Question 4   usherin.usher.co.kr > 시험리스트 > Speaking 시험리스트 > Task 4 > #4012

시험이 끝나고

시험 전에 Check!

펜과 메모지가 있음 ○
핸드폰을 껐음 ○
시간을 체크할 시계가 있음 ○
문제를 들을 준비가 됐음 ○
목소리를 녹음할 준비가 됐음 ○
평소에 연습한대로 발음하겠음 ○
단어의 강세에 유의하겠음 ○
시간을 체크해가면서 발표하겠음 ○

Speaking Section Directions

In this section of the test, you will be able to demonstrate your ability to speak about a variety of topics. You will answer four questions by speaking into the mircrophone. Answer each of the questions as completely as possible.

In question 1, you will speak about a familiar topic. Your response will be scored on your ability to speak clearly and coherently about the topic.

In questions 2 and 3, you will first read a short text. The text will go away and you will then listen to a talk on the same topic. You will then be asked a question about what you have read and heard. You will need to combine appropriate information from the text and the talk to provide a complete answer to the question. Your response will be scored on your ability to speak clearly and coherently and on your ability to accurately convey information about what you read and heard.

In question 4, you will listen to part of a lecture. You will then be asked a question about what you heard. Your response will be scored on your ability to speak clearly and coherently and on your ability to accurately convey information about what you heard.

You may take notes while you read and while you listen to the conversations and lectures. You may use your notes to help prepare your response.

Listen carefully to the directions for each question. The directions will not be written on the screen.

For each question you will be given a short time to prepare your response. A clock will show how much preparation time is remaining. When the preparation time is up, you will be told to begin your response. A clock will show how much response time is remaining. A message will appear on the screen when the response time has ended.

뉴토플 - TEST 12_Q1

Question 1 of 4

Do you agree or disagree with the following statement?
Parents are the best teachers for their children.
Use reasons and examples to support your answer.

PREPARATION TIME
00: 00: 15

RESPONSE TIME
00: 00: 45

Reading Time: 50 seconds

Jazz Band Concert

The university has announced the plans of the newly formed jazz band. The jazz band was started just a few months ago and is having their very first concert. The players expressed their hope for an outdoor debut and thus, the university has reserved the lawn by the library for tomorrow night's concert. The music's harmony of brass instruments will sound beautifully, so if students are looking for a way to relax and relieve the stress of school life, this will be a perfect opportunity. They hope students enjoy the jazz concert with their fellow students.

Now get ready to answer the question.

The man expresses his opinion about the college's plan. State his opinion and explain the reasons he gives for holding that opinion.

PREPARATION TIME
00: 00: 30

RESPONSE TIME
00: 00: 60

Test Customer

There are a variety of methods employers can use to evaluate their employees. They could assess employees themselves, but the problem with this is that the evaluation could be slightly biased. Especially, if their employer was assessing them and the workers were aware of it, they would most likely be on their best behavior, making it hard to evaluate their true work quality. Thus, in order to fairly evaluate the level of service and work attitudes of employees, employers secretly hire outsiders and disguise them as customers - test customers to fairly assess employees with no prejudice.

Now get ready to answer the question

Using the example from the professor's lecture, explain what test customer is and how it works.

Now get ready to answer the question.

Using the examples from the professor's lecture, explain the two factors consumers consider when purchasing products.

PREPARATION TIME
00: 00: 20

RESPONSE TIME
00: 00: 60

시험이 끝나고

	Task 1	Task 2	Task 3	Task 4
시간에 맞춰 발표를 끝냈음	O / X	O / X	O / X	O / X
"아닌 경우," 시간이 남아서라면?				
- 할 말이 부족해서				
- 말이 빨라서				
- 도저히 모르겠음 / 기타				
"아닌 경우," 도중에 잘려서라면?				
- 할 말이 부족해서				
- 말이 빨라서				
- 도저히 모르겠음 / 기타				

	Task 1	Task 2	Task 3	Task 4
발표할 내용을 완벽히 정리했음	O / X	O / X	O / X	O / X
"아닌 경우," 문제를 이해하지 못해서라면?				
- 읽기 / 듣기가 안돼서				
- 배경지식이 부족해서				
- 도저히 모르겠음 / 기타				
"아닌 경우," 내용 정리가 덜 끝나서라면?				
- 준비 시간이 부족해서				
- 내용이 뒤죽박죽 되어서				
- 도저히 모르겠음 / 기타				

다음에 문제를 풀 때에는…

반드시 이렇게 해야지!

절대 이러지 말아야지!

첨삭권 소개

01 스피킹/라이팅 첨삭이 필요한 이유?

대체로 독학을 할 수 있다고 생각하는 리딩, 리스닝과는 달리 스피킹 라이팅은 독학이 힘듭니다.

이유는? "내가 뭘 틀렸는지 모르니까!!!"
대안은?? 독학이라고 했으니, 과외나, 학원은 빼고, 남는 건 첨삭이나, 그냥 혼자 틀린 걸 계속 보거나….

그런데, 첨삭을 받으러 검색을 해보면 가격이 라이팅 한편당 23000…원…?
한편만 첨삭 받으면 끝날 것 같진 않은 내 실력을 봐서는…
비용 감당 안됨. 어쩌지?

02 학원 다니면 첨삭도 해결되나요?

단과반
(2020.10.05 현재)

학원명		첨삭 횟수	실전 프로그램 사용 여부	수업일수	수업시간	가격(D.C적용가)	
어셔어학원	단과 스피킹	월5회	○	주5일	50분	최저가	160,000
	단과 라이팅	월5회	○	주5일	50분	최저가	160,000
해**어학원	단과 스피킹	월2회	×	주5일	50분		165,000
	단과 라이팅	월2회	×	주5일	50분		165,000
영**어학원	단과 스피킹 (2020.06 이후 단과 수업 진행×)	폐강	○				
	단과 라이팅 (2020.06 이후 단과 수업 진행×)	폐강	○				

03 학원까지 다니고 싶진 않은데 스피킹/라이팅 첨삭만 받을 순 없나요?

라이팅 첨삭
30회권은 어셔수강생에게만 제공됩니다
(2020.10.05 현재)

1회권	어셔	1회 첨삭권 25,000원	최저가 1회당 25,000원
	해**	1회권 없음	1회권 없음
	영**	1회 첨삭(1일 소요)권 28,000원	1회당(1일 소요)권 28,000원
5회권	어셔	5회 첨삭권 75,000원	최저가 1회당 15,000원
	해**	5회 첨삭권 120,000원	1회당 24,000원
	영**	5회 첨삭(1일 소요)권 119,000원	1회당(1일소요)권 23,800원
10회권	어셔	10회 첨삭권 100,000원	최저가 1회당 10,000원
	해**	10회권 없음	10회권 없음
	영**	10회권 없음	10회권 없음
30회권 어셔수강생 한정	어셔	30회 첨삭권 220,000원	최저가 1회당 7,330원 *어셔수강생 한정
	해**	30회권 없음	30회권 없음
	영**	30회권 없음	30회권 없음

스피팅 첨삭
(2020.10.05 현재)

1회권	어셔	1회 첨삭권 15,000원	최저가 1회당 15,000원
	해**	1회권 없음	1회권 없음
	영**	1회 첨삭(1일 소요)권 16,000원	1회당(1일 소요)권 16,000원
5회권	어셔	5회 첨삭권 56,000원	최저가 1회당 11,200원
	해**	5회 첨삭권 139,000원	1회당 27,800원
	영**	5회 첨삭(1일 소요)권 68,000원	1회당(1일소요)권 13,600원
10회권	어셔	10회 첨삭권 80,000원	최저가 1회당 8,000원
	해**	10회권 없음	10회권 없음
	영**	10회권 없음	10회권 없음
30회권 어셔수강생 한정	어셔	30회 첨삭권 144,000원	최저가 1회당 4,800원(1회당) *어셔수강생 한정
	해**	30회권 없음	30회권 없음
	영**	30회권 없음	30회권 없음

04 첨삭 구성은 어떻게 되나요?

스피킹 첨삭   **라이팅 첨삭**

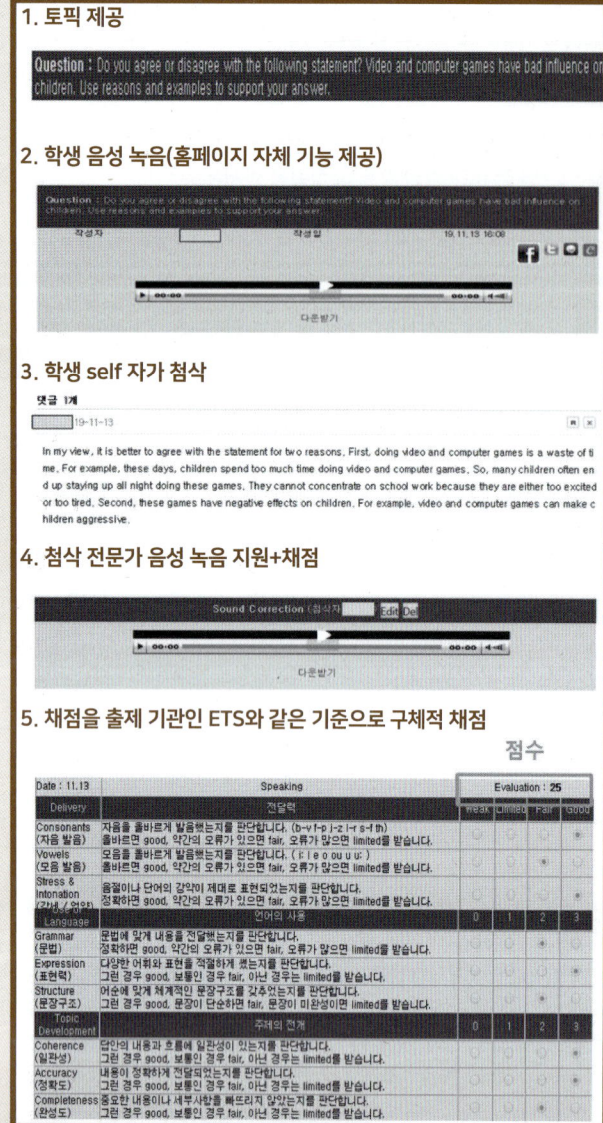

05 첨삭 신청하기

라이팅 첨삭권

30회권은 어셔수강생에게만 제공됩니다

1회 첨삭권	5회 첨삭권	10회 첨삭권	30회 첨삭권
사용기간 15일	사용기간 30일	사용기간 60일	사용기간 90일
25,000원	~~110,000원~~ → 75,000원	~~220,000원~~ → 100,000원	~~660,000원~~ → 220,000원

스피킹 첨삭권

30회권은 어셔수강생에게만 제공됩니다

1회 첨삭권	5회 첨삭권	10회 첨삭권	30회 첨삭권
사용기간 15일	사용기간 30일	사용기간 60일	사용기간 90일
15,000원	~~80,000원~~ → 56,000원	~~160,000원~~ → 160,000원	~~480,000원~~ → 144,000원

방학 중(미국,한국 방학기간(5월말~8월말, 12월초~2월말)에는 너무 많은 학생들의 문의가 있으므로, 학원측에 24시간 이내 처리 가능한지 문의 후 신청 바랍니다. 근무일 기준-주말은 미포함입니다

강의대상

1. 책으로 토플을 공부해왔지만 컴퓨터로 실전 대비가 필요한 학생
2. 단기간 실전과 같은 형식의 문제풀이를 통한 실전감각이 필요한 학생
3. 토플 공부를 제대로 해본 적은 없지만 급하게 제출할 점수가 필요한 학생
4. 영어 실력이 어느정도 있고 실전 연습을 통해 빠르게 점수를 만들고 싶은 학생

강의목표

종이로 공부하고 시험보는 것이 아닌,
컴퓨터로 보는 실제 시험 환경에서,
시험당일 시험보는 스케줄대로 시험을 보고
시험 당일엔 확인할 수 없는 답안들을 확인하는
Reading과 Listening 수업을 듣고,
점수만 주는 Speaking & Writing 시험이 아닌,
점수와, 점수의 근거와, 점수를 올리기 위한 첨삭까지
모든 걸 포함하는 풀 케어 서비스

모의토플 — 별도 구매 가능

시장 최저가로 준비된 시험가격

~~50,000원~~
50% 추가 할인가
25,000원

가격소개

*시중에 나와있는 3사를 비교한 표입니다.

시장구성	USHER	D사	H사
구성	Half and Full (new 토플 반영)	Half and Full (new 토플 반영)	자체시험 (4가지 영역중 하나선택)
가격	27,000원/50,000원	27,000원/52,000원	66,000원
응시날짜	언제든지 응시가능	언제든지 응시가능	매주 토요일
첨삭	있음	없음	있음

등록하기

25% off — 3일 등록
~~600,000원~~
450,000원
하루 15만원

50% off — 5일 등록
~~1,000,000원~~
500,000원
하루 10만원

50% off — 7일 등록
~~1,400,000원~~
700,000원
하루 10만원

가격구성

모의토플 + 첨삭 + 수업

06 모의토플

시장 최저가로 준비된 시험가격

~~50,000원~~
50% 추가 할인가
25,000원

가격소개

*시중에 나와있는 3사를 비교한 표입니다.

시장구성	USHER	D사	H사
구성	Half and Full (new 토플 반영)	Half and Full (new 토플 반영)	자체시험 (4가지 영역중 하나선택)
가격	27,000원/50,000원	27,000원/52,000원	66,000원
응시날짜	언제든지 응시가능	언제든지 응시가능	매주 토요일
첨삭	있음	없음	있음

07 스피킹 첨삭
시장 최저가 첨삭 가격!!!

스피킹 1일 4문제
~~60,000원~~

50% 추가 할인가
30,000원

+

01 스피킹 첨삭
2020. 10. 05 기준

1회권	어셔	1회 첨삭권 15,000원	**최저가**	1회당 15,000원
	해**	1회권 없음		1회권 없음
	영**	1회 첨삭(1일소요)권 16,000원		1회당(1일소요)권 16,000원
5회권	어셔	5회 첨삭권 56,000원	**최저가**	1회당 11,200원
	해**	5회 첨삭권 139,000원		1회당 27,800원
	영**	5회 첨삭(1일소요)권 68,000원		1회당(1일소요)권 13,600원
10회권	어셔	10회 첨삭권 80,000원	**최저가**	1회당 8,000원
	해**	10회권 없음		10회권 없음
	영**	10회권 없음		10회권 없음
10회권 *어셔 수강생 한정	어셔	30회 첨삭권 144,000원	**최저가**	1회당 4,800원 *어셔수강생 한정
	해**	30회권 없음		30회권 없음
	영**	30회권 없음		30회권 없음

08 라이팅 첨삭
시장 최저가 첨삭 가격!!!

라이팅 1일 2문제
~~50,000원~~

50% 추가 할인가
25,000원

+

02 라이팅 첨삭
2020. 10. 05 기준

1회권	어셔	1회 첨삭권 25,000원	**최저가**	1회당 25,000원
	해**	1회권 없음		1회권 없음
	영**	1회 첨삭(1일소요)권 28,000원		1회당(1일소요)권 28,000원
5회권	어셔	5회 첨삭권 75,000원	**최저가**	1회당 15,000원
	해**	5회 첨삭권 120,000원		1회당 24,000원
	영**	5회 첨삭(1일소요)권 119,000원		1회당(1일소요)권 23,000원
10회권	어셔	10회 첨삭권 100,000원	**최저가**	1회당 10,000원
	해**	10회권 없음		10회권 없음
	영**	10회권 없음		10회권 없음
10회권 *어셔 수강생 한정	어셔	30회 첨삭권 220,000원	**최저가**	1회당 7,330원 *어셔수강생 한정
	해**	30회권 없음		30회권 없음
	영**	30회권 없음		30회권 없음

09 수업
국내 유일 수업!

수업 1일 4시간
~~40,000원~~

50% 추가 할인가
20,000원

국내유일
비교대상이 없음

usherin.usher.co.kr

usherin.usher.co.kr